HITLER'S
ART THIEF

HITLER'S ART THIEF

Hildebrand Gurlitt,
the Nazis,
and the Looting
of Europe's Treasures

SUSAN RONALD

ST. MARTIN'S PRESS ⟪M⟫ NEW YORK

Henri Matisse's *Woman Seated by the Open Window,* second photo insert section, last page, © Succession H. Matisse/DACS 2015.

www.stmartins.com

Designed by Meryl Sussman Levavi

The Library of Congress Cataloging-in-Publication Data is available upon request.

ISBN 978-1-250-06109-6 (hardcover)
ISBN 978-1-4668-6682-9 (e-book)

Our books may be purchased in bulk for promotional, educational, or business use. Please contact your local bookseller or the Macmillan Corporate and Premium Sales Department at (800) 221-7945, extension 5442, or by e-mail at MacmillanSpecialMarkets@macmillan.com.

First Edition: September 2015

1 3 5 7 9 10 8 6 4 2

For Alexander Hoyt, Gunther Hoyt

and

my husband, Doug

. . . who would have thought . . .

CONTENTS

Acknowledgments   ix

On Names and Acronyms   xiii

Prologue   1

PART I • THE UNMAKING OF THE MAN

1. New York, May 1944   9

2. At the Beginning—Germany, 1907   14

3. From The Hague to Vienna   24

4. Cause and Effect   33

5. War   42

6. Gurlitt's Struggle   54

7. Peace   71

8. Aftermath   82

9. Weimar Trembles   91

PART II • ART AND POLITICS

10. Rebels with a Cause   103

11. Hopes and Dreams   115

12. From New York to Zwickau   119

13. The Mysterious Mr. Kirchbach 125

14. The Root of Evil 133

15. Chameleons and Crickets 142

16. The First Stolen Lives 153

PART III · WORLD WAR AND WILDERNESS

17. Chambers of Horrors 165

18. The Four Horsemen 174

19. Tradecraft 183

20. The Treasure Houses 190

21. The Posse Years 202

22. Swallowing the Treasure 212

23. Viau 225

24. King Raffke 231

25. Quick, the Allies Are Coming! 246

26. Surrendered . . . or Captured? 253

PART IV · THE STOLEN LIVES

27. House Arrest 265

28. Under the Microscope 280

29. Düsseldorf 295

30. Aftermath and Munich 302

31. The Lion Tamer 308

32. Feeding Frenzy 314

Glossary 321

Notes 325

Selected Bibliography 359

Index 369

ACKNOWLEDGMENTS

I COULD HAVE NEVER WRITTEN THIS BOOK WITHOUT THE INSPIRED support of my dedicatees. My editor, Charles Spicer, and the entire St. Martin's team have been incredible in allowing me to create the book I was compelled to write. To my assistant and researcher, Mara Weiner-Macario, thank you for your tireless efforts in pulling down thousands of documents—a page at a time—from Fold3.com and analyzing all those transcripts in Spanish.

The generosity of a number of people also made this book possible. In alphabetical order, they are Ambassador Ido Aharoni, Julie Goodman Aharoni, Richard Aronowitz-Mercer, Alexander Balerdi, Stephanie Barron, Aurore Blaise, Rolf von Bleichert, Amanda Borschel-Dan, Greg Bradsher, Evelien Campfens, Virginia Cardwell-Moore, Michael Carlisle, Gerald Dütsch, Harry Ettlinger, Maureen Finkelstein, Helen Fry, Christian Fuhrmeister, Patricia Gillet, Dominic Gray, Johannes Hauslauer, Stefan Holzinger, Mieke Hopp, Polly Hutchison, Dotti Irving, Stephan Klingen, Ronald S. Lauder, Monique Leblois-Pechon, Matthias Leniert, Johanne Lisewski, Anton Löffelmeier, Chris Marinello, August Matteis, Richard G. Mitchell, Elisabeth Nowak-Thaller, Ralf Peters, Dirk Petrat, Jonathan Petropoulos, Hubert Portz, Julian Radcliffe, Ruth Redmond-Cooper, Julia Rickmeyer, Peter Robinson, Lena Schwaudecker, Jonathan Searle, Robin and Suzie Sheppard, Delphie Stockwell, Markus Stoetzel, Michael Stoetzel,

Katrin Stoll, Karen Taieb, David Toren, Mel Urbach, Anne Webber, and Lois White.

I am especially grateful to lawyers Chris Marinello, Markus Stoetzel, and Mel Urbach for sharing their knowledge of the fraught area of restitution with me. Jonathan Petropoulos has also been unstinting in sharing two unpublished articles for this book and helping me to understand the tortuous relationship he had with that plausible liar who worked at times with Gurlitt, Bruno Lohse. To Stephan Holzinger, my gratitude for sharing his knowledge base at such a busy time, and letting Cornelius know that I was writing the type of book he had hoped would one day be published (although perhaps he would be less happy with the result). For all of those who wished to remain entirely anonymous, I thank you, too. As always, the staff at all the following libraries and archives have been invaluable: the London Library, the National Archives (Kew, London), Archives Nationales de France, the National Archives (College Park, MD), the Getty Research Library (Los Angeles, CA), the New York Historical Society, the Dresden City Archives, and the Bundesarchiv at Koblenz and Berlin, the National Art Library at the V&A (London), King's College Cambridge, the Bodleian Library Oxford, the British Library, and the Courtauld Institute of Art. Photographs from Germany are included courtesy of the photographic archives of bpk, dpa, SLUB-Dresden, and Stadtarchiv Düsseldorf. In England, the Press Association and Vantage News Agency kindly provided photographs of Hildebrand and Cornelius. The Getty in Los Angeles provided photos of two of Gurlitt's looted works of art. All artworks have been separately licensed (providing royalties to the artists and heirs) through DACS in the UK.

For those of you who helped me on my 26,000-mile-plus trek in the past year, I can hardly express my gratitude for sustenance, free beds, and your support. Marjorie Bliss, Maureen Burgess, Laurette Dieujuste, Sue Froud, James and Philippa Lewis, Rick and Sue Parker, Charlotte and Steve Sass, Barbi and Larry Weinberg, and Jan and Phil Zakowski, you *truly* helped to make this book possible. Most importantly, my husband, Doug, deserves his extra due: not only did he put up with a wife who read *Mein Kampf* cover to cover and had recurring nightmares, but he also accompanied me on my travels, understood when I was silent and reflective, and helped me work through conundrums—all while completing his own book on youth and war propaganda. You're my hero.

For you, the reader, I hope that you have learned a great deal about life in Germany during the First World War and afterward; and in doing so, that you have come to understand the pressures that made three generations of Gurlitts what they were. I am pleased that Cornelius finally broke the mold and can only hope that his wishes will be respected. I implore Germany and the Bern Kunstmuseum to return the art to the heirs as he wished—urgently.

I hope you enjoy reading and learning about Hildebrand Gurlitt, the Nazis, and a billion dollars in looted art. Any errors are, of course, my own.

—SUSAN RONALD
Oxford
December 2014

ON NAMES AND ACRONYMS

OBVIOUSLY, TIMES CHANGE. SO DO NAMES. FOR THOSE WHO LIVED through what we now call World War I, it was known as the Great War. There was no World War II at the time, and so I refer to that first war as the Great War in the book. Similarly, a number of countries changed their names in the period covered. I refer to each of those countries by the name that was current at the time of the events described, save for Great Britain, which I retain throughout. Great Britain, officially called the United Kingdom of Great Britain and Northern Ireland today, comprised the countries of Ireland, Wales, Scotland, and England until the Irish Free State was established, in August 1922. In December 1937, the Irish Free State became Ireland, or Eire in Gaelic. Ireland, where appropriate, is referred to separately. Other examples include the empire of Austria-Hungary, so known until it was carved up into Austria, Hungary, Czechoslovakia (now of course changed again to the Czech Republic and Slovakia), Slovenia, and Croatia; the German Empire under Kaiser Wilhelm II; and Palestine (as a British protectorate), which is now Israel, the West Bank, and Gaza. As these countries adopt their new official names, the text changes to reflect the new national identity. Similarly, as republics or governments change within countries, such as the Weimar Republic in Germany between the world wars, I refer to these governments individually. I feel this will help the reader understand the dislocation felt by all those populations involved.

There are a number of foreign words in this book, mostly German and

French. Words for Nazi organizations like *Reichskulturkammer* (the Reich Chamber of Culture) are abbreviated after the first use into the more acceptable English form—RKK in this example. Some words—from the German, in particular—do not have an exact English translation, so I've taken the most commonly used terminology. Where appropriate, I translate the name of the organization into English. A list of these words is provided in the glossary at the end of the book. The final administrative point is that all translations from French are my own, as I am fluent in French (having lived in France for nearly six years). For German, which I can read but speak far less well than French, I have worked in conjunction with a professional mother-tongue German translator through Trans-Solutions in Oxfordshire who also verified my translations into English for accuracy.

PROLOGUE

THE GURLITT SAGA BEGAN FOR ME IN 1998 ON ONE OF THOSE heavily laden, bone-chilling winter days that curse Europe from late October to April. Back then, I was an investment banker specializing almost exclusively in the restoration of historic buildings and landscapes and their conversion to alternative use. To my knowledge, I was the only such independent beast in the licensed "banking community," which made me as rare as a golden unicorn to some (or a proverbial dragon to others) and gave me a very minor "rock star" status. I recognized that I was able to see and know things and places most people could never glimpse. That said, I'd grown curmudgeonly and badly needed a change. I had no inkling that this would become one of the most significant days in my working life.

It was just another day trip to Zurich, like so many dozens of other day trips I'd made in previous years. Having a Swiss institutional shareholder in my company, Zurich, Geneva, and Lausanne were familiar stomping grounds in the pursuit of bona fide investors. Snow threatened, and before the storm broke I was anxious to meet my prospective investor with his bank manager and swiftly take back proof of his ability to invest millions in the project I was currently working on.

My destination was one of the richest city blocks in the world—Bahnhofstrasse, home to the world's premier banks and, more important, their moneyed clients from across the globe. Swiss bank-secrecy laws

attracted the superrich and ultranotorious alike—especially back then.[1]
Today, things are marginally different.

∽

The meeting with the prospective investor and his personal bank manager
went well, and as a final step for the day, it was necessary to go to the bank's
vault to verify the share certificates, certificates of deposit, jewels, and art.
I was a thorough kicker of tires.

For those readers who have never seen one, there is something quite
incredible about a Swiss bank vault. This enormous vault room held row
after row of tightly-packed, numbered sliding storage walls, each with
dozens of fabulous artworks hanging on them and hidden from prying eyes
when they were closed. As we walked down the wide aisle in the center with
the closed walls to either side of us, I thought how each in its own way
was a Pandora's box. In some cases, the vault is akin to a small, hushed city.
In others, it is like wading through the treasure-houses of yore. The larger
ones do not resemble what we see in films or television. Nor do they look
like an Aladdin's cave, even though they are just as rich in wealth and laden
with threads of golden untold stories to rival those Scheherazade wove.

This particular vault was of the small-hushed-city ilk. The only sound
to be heard was the bank manager's heels clicking against the stone floor—
but even this were muted by the soundproofing. I couldn't help thinking
it was a great place for a murder at closing time—stuff the body between
two rows of sliding walls and it would only be detected by the rank smell
of decomposition days, if not weeks, later . . . unless, of course, some hapless
art owner wanted to visit his treasured trove where the body was hidden.

As we made our way, I noticed that a sliding wall was slightly ajar. I
saw the fringes of what I believed was a nineteenth-century landscape
painting and the letters "RLITT" labeled beneath the frame. Rlitt? Gurlitt?
Could that be a painting by Louis Gurlitt, the nineteenth-century landscape painter? I wondered aloud without realizing it. The bank manager
swiveled round suddenly and glowered at me, pushing the wall shut. "No.
That's the twentieth-century Nazi art dealer," he huffed.

I was never a good poker player. I was stunned and hid it poorly. The
manager immediately realized his blunder and tried to recover himself by
blustering. I shouldn't have been peeking at private property. It was against

Swiss law. I was being brought into the vault at the behest of a valued client (meaning the investor) and represented a highly respected institution. I apologized, but both of us knew that the damage was done. Nonetheless, we continued in a distinctly tense atmosphere to view the assets of the potential investor.

Despite returning to professional dignity, I knew instinctively that there was more to this story. I'd never heard of a twentieth-century Nazi art dealer whose name ended in "RLITT." Surely it couldn't be the landscape painter Louis Gurlitt. If my memory was right, he hadn't lived into the twentieth century, but I couldn't be sure. My art-history studies were part of a life I'd been forced to give up by a demonic father* who believed that all artists were "freaks"—or at least that's what he told me when he burned my art portfolio on my conditional acceptance for a bachelor of fine arts program. Yet that was the past—another country.

As we left the vault, I thought back to other such visits. A day in a Geneva vault virtually smacked me between the eyes—and how that potential investor gloated about how he had saved all the art and artifacts from Egyptian Jews who feared they would be killed if Rommel's Afrika Korps overran Egypt. Stupidly, I asked why the art was still there, given that Rommel failed. He simply smiled, sphinxlike, in reply. So, this is what an art looter looked like. . . .

&

At lunch, the bank manager overplayed his hand once again, trying to ply me with wine. I declined. I could see from his expression that he thought I was a "recovering alcoholic," so why disabuse him? I was used to bankers underestimating me. So, he continued on his set course regardless, apologizing for his outburst in the vault, pouring himself drink after drink after drink. He should never have exploded like that at me, he said. After all, it wasn't my fault that the sliding wall wasn't closed properly. Obviously the prospective investor chewed him out royally. The bank manager's groveling became so overwhelming that I couldn't help but feel sorry for him. It's not often a Swiss bank manager makes such a faux pas.

So, I was mischievous and played on his sudden change of heart helped

---

* Not to be confused with my much loved stepfather.

along by his nervous drinking. I popped the searching question, mustering my best innocent voice, and asked if there was a twentieth-century art dealer called Gurlitt. Was there ever! the bank manager exclaimed. He wasn't just any art dealer—he was Hitler's art dealer. Hildebrand Gurlitt was his name.

∞

Within the year, as if to hog-tie me forever to the Gurlitt story, I unexpectedly inherited two looted artworks from the Nazi era and immediately handed them over to the Art Loss Register in London to locate the rightful owners to return them. As the paintings were from Hungary, I volunteered to go there twice on missions for the British Council and met with the Hungarian culture minister, who informed me that there was no looted art in Hungary. I agreed. All the looted art from Hungary had been taken elsewhere. He was not amused.

For the past fourteen years, I have searched independently from the Art Loss Register for the heirs to the paintings I inherited—without success so far. I've been in touch with Yad Vashem, the Jerusalem Holocaust museum, for help, too. Meanwhile, I inherited a third looted Hungarian painting. I prided myself on my research capabilities, but I was at a loss for how to find an heir when even the best experts failed.

This is my connection with the incredible and—despite huge media coverage—untold story of an illustrious family, the times in which they lived, and the loss of many a moral compass. Cornelius Gurlitt knew about the book before his death and was pleased that someone was taking the time to write the whole story about why things were the way they were. Context is everything in history, and Hildebrand Gurlitt was born at a most critical time in Germany's national development.

To better understand the rise of Nazism in this cradle of European culture and Gurlitt's evolving role as "Hitler's art dealer," I dig back into the origins of both. This book examines the lives of three generations of Gurlitts, focusing on Hildebrand—a well-educated, upper-middle-class boy from an illustrious family set within his period. German Expressionism and the avant-garde, which the Gurlitts loved, was more than mere art. Collecting it meant dedication to a new cultural ideal that often became a "spiritual narcotic," a commitment to a new *Sachlichkeit*—or fresh objectivity—often carrying with it "political expressionism," to use Hannah Arendt's words. This engendered a new *Weltanschauung*, or worldview, enabling the Gurlitts and others to cope with Germany's ever-changing international status. It is the golden thread running through the book and is behind the question *How could such a man become a heartless art thief who stole lives?*

∞

I want to impress on the reader that it is a gross misapprehension to believe that looted art is somehow a lesser crime of the Nazi era. Attached to each artwork is at least one human tragedy and death. Art is intended to unite people of disparate backgrounds in a combined cultural heritage that transcends national boundaries. It takes many forms, as literature, music, fine art, film, and more. It connects our souls. The wholesale theft of art from museums, private individuals, libraries, and archives was highly calculated and well organized by the criminal regime of the Third Reich.

Many Jews, Christians, atheists, and political opponents lost their lives because of their collections. Those who somehow survived never recovered the bulk of their possessions—be they artworks, real estate, stocks, jewels, cash, or gold—giving rise to new laws, restitution departments at auction houses, and an entire insurance industry. Some artworks now reside as ill-gotten gains in museums across the world—perhaps in a museum in your hometown or where you live. Much lingers beneath Bahnhofstrasse in Zurich and elsewhere in Switzerland. Those who salvaged some of their heirlooms or riches remained deeply scarred, afraid, and guilty that they'd somehow survived. Few returned to Germany, some returned to France. They often passed on this guilt and shame to their children. The looting of art deprived these families of a crucial link to their personal histories: memories that remain dear beyond the value of the paintings—often mental pictures of the last time the dispossessed saw their loved ones alive.

Hildebrand Gurlitt was one significant cog in this criminal machinery of state. He brings the scale of the criminality down to a level that most of us can comprehend. As Hitler's art thief, he stole the lives of his victims, as well as the lives of his wife and children. His crime, like the crimes of thousands of others, went unpunished, as it was judged best that the order givers alone should be tried for crimes against humanity. No one was put on trial for art theft in Germany. Most Nazi-approved museum directors continued as before. Gurlitt's boundless zeal and secret hoard of ill-gotten artworks—which were kept without remorse—are his true crimes.

One of the most chilling, and true, remarks Adolf Eichmann made was "A hundred deaths are a catastrophe. The death of millions is a statistic." I hope I have made it possible for you to see the catastrophe that befell Gurlitt's generation as well as the human cost among the thousands upon thousands of artworks that passed through Hildebrand Gurlitt's hands. Had Germany been treated differently after the first Great War, perhaps we would still not be living out the repercussions of the second.

PART I

THE UNMAKING
OF THE MAN

If we say that we have no sin,
We deceive ourselves, and there's
no truth in us.

—CHRISTOPHER MARLOWE,
The Tragical History of Doctor
Faustus, scene 1, line 45

I

៚

NEW YORK, MAY 1944

THE *NEW YORK TIMES* HEADLINES ON THE WAR IN EUROPE FOR
May 1944 revealed "Wounded Dubious on Gains in Italy—Still a Long Way
to Anzio," followed by "Germans Face Destruction in Italy—Whole Army
May Suffer Fate of Stalingrad and Africa by *Fight and Die*." Domestic
headlines ranged from "Aid for War Victims—Jewish Group Will Provide
300,000 Packages This Year" and "Smith, A Pint Please—Appeal Made to
420,000 of That Name to Give Blood" to "No Rise in Sugar Rations" and
"Television Tests Asked for After the War."[1]

The arts—whether on stage, at the movies, in books, or in museums—
gave a welcome escape into another world. The 1944 Oscar winner *Cas-
ablanca*, starring Humphrey Bogart and Ingrid Bergman, still played in
the movie houses, along with *For Whom the Bell Tolls*, based on Ernest
Hemingway's book. Music, too, did its bit to soothe ravaged souls. The
Andrews Sisters, big-band leaders Benny Goodman and Tommy Dorsey,
and singing comedians Bob Hope and Bing Crosby made scores of films.
La Bohème played at the Central Theatre, alternating with *Aida*, *Faust*,
and *La Traviata*. Duke Ellington held his live performances at Carnegie
Hall and also played live with his orchestra at the Brill Building's Hurri-
cane Club on Forty-Ninth Street and Broadway. It was Ellington's swing-
ing big-band draw—more than the naked lady strategically covered with a
palm frond on its menu—that attracted its fully integrated audiences. In
books, fiction reigned supreme. *A Tree Grows in Brooklyn*, by Betty Smith,

topped the *New York Times* best sellers' fiction list. Evelyn Waugh's saga *Brideshead Revisited* was crowned "first" of the worldwide English best sellers.

New York's Museum of Modern Art (MoMA) opened its exhibit of twenty-five-year-old W. Eugene Smith's photographs taken during the previous eight months in the Pacific theater of war. The Metropolitan Museum of Art (the Met) countered with a reopening of its picture galleries, having previously removed its priceless collection to safety. Americans remained generally unaware that they were targeted by art dealers and museum directors to help finance the Nazi war effort for years; and that "trading with the enemy" was the bread and butter of the American and British visual-arts market. Had they known at the time, the more outraged might have called for lynching the culprits, while law-abiding citizens would have cried out for trials based on high treason. Neither happened—then or later—and the art dealers for Hitler already suspected as much.

⁂

On a beautiful and sizzling May 29 morning, a few weeks before the D-day landings in 1944, a large shipment of 391 artworks was off-loaded at Manhattan's West Side docks. As usual, an agent from the Hudson Shipping Company signed off on the consignment and waited for his customs clearance. It wasn't the first shipment consigned to the New York gallery named after the German art dealer Karl Buchholz. In fact, the Buchholz Gallery was one of the Hudson Shipping Company's good clients since 1937. Its manager, Curt Valentin, was—so the agent claimed—the darling of the art world, a suave and sophisticated man of impeccable taste who'd somehow managed to save the modern art that Hitler wanted to destroy.

All of the artists on the manifest were expressionists—such as Ernst Barlach, Max Beckmann, Emil Nolde, Käthe Kollwitz, Gerhard Marcks, Otto Dix, Marc Chagall, Paul Klee, Oskar Kokoschka, and August Macke, to name names. There was even a bronze called *Galloping Horse* by Edgar Degas.[2] Why this particular shipment attracted such attention is lost to posterity. Perhaps it was the sheer scope of the consignment or maybe because customs officials were alert to the fact that every artist was labeled "degenerate" by the Nazis that rang alarm bells. Possibly, the decision to investigate the shipment came from the countless briefings by Washington's Office of Alien Property, designed to confiscate *any* enemy property that would benefit America's foes.

More than likely, no one was more shocked than the luckless agent of the Hudson Shipping Company when he was told that the US government would be seizing the art shipment under the Trading with the Enemy Act. The expediter, Karl Buchholz, was an enemy alien. Valentin, too, had been a German. The Hudson Shipping Company had done nothing wrong, but if they allowed this "outrage" to go ahead, they'd probably lose a valued client. Chances are, threats or promises of cash under the table were made. Why or how such blandishments were refused is also lost in time, as are the names of the officers involved in the sequestration of the 391 artworks under Vesting Order 3711, signed by the Office of Alien Property's trusted second-in-command, James E. Markham.

Under the Trading with the Enemy Act, the custodian for alien property could—if the shipper *or* recipient qualified as an enemy alien, as both Buchholz and Valentin did—hold, use, administer, liquidate, sell, or otherwise deal with the property in question in the interest, and for the benefit, of the United States through the issuance of a "vesting order."[3] Naturally, the stateless Valentin, who had "fled" Germany in 1937 and avoided courting any unwanted government scrutiny successfully until then, was most anxious to have the artworks released. Things would, however, take a turn from bad to worse.

∽

The Port of New York Authority thought, rightly, that there should be an official inquiry by the Federal Bureau of Investigation and contacted the field office on Lexington Avenue between Sixty-eighth and Sixty-ninth Streets.[4] J. Edgar Hoover, the FBI's battle-hardened director, had made staunch efforts against Nazi fifth columnists and saboteurs, and the New York field office was primed and already working on counterintelligence and counterespionage investigations. The link between foreign-exchange transactions, art, and armaments hadn't gone unnoticed by Hoover.

The hunt for enemy aliens attempting to sell loot taken from Nazi victims figured high in the FBI's priorities.[5] Consequently, it was the value,

origin, and destination of the shipment that determined the FBI's need to
ferret out the truth. Yet whether the FBI discovered what that truth was is
anyone's guess. In its infinite wisdom, the FBI destroyed the Karl Buchholz and Curt Valentin file relating to the shipment toward the end of the
twentieth century—without storing the information on microfilm or com-
pact disc.[6]

✍

Earlier that same May, the putative seller of some of the Käthe Kollwitz
artworks in the consignment, Dr. Hildebrand Gurlitt, dictated his own
authorization to the director of Hitler's Führermuseum for unfettered travel
to France, Belgium, and the Netherlands. His purpose was to import artworks to Germany. The authorization made it clear that Gurlitt's use of the
German railway system in these countries must receive top priority—even
before troop movements.[7]

By the time the shipment was vested by the Office of Alien Property
in New York, Gurlitt was safely ensconced in his suite at the Grand Hotel
on rue Scribe in Paris. In fact, he received a telegram there a few days
prior to the vesting order from the director of the Führermuseum, who
headed the "Sonderauftrag Linz," requesting that Hitler's thieving art
dealer Gurlitt thank Walter Weber for the photo of the still-life painting
from the school of Vallayer, but that it was of no interest to the museum
at Linz.[8] Gurlitt remained in Paris at the Grand Hotel during the D-day
landings, leaving the city a mere six days before its liberation, on August
25, 1944.

How did the art dealer Hildebrand Gurlitt engineer such a position of
power, where he could write his own travel authorization *and* use the
railways to ship artwork when the Germans expected D-day at any moment? A second question, seemingly less interesting to some, is why no one
ever made the link between Hildebrand Gurlitt and the shipment.

Even more damning is that on June 7, 1944, the day after D-day, Hildebrand Gurlitt was sent another telegram by Hitler's museum commission, Sonderauftrag Linz: "Acquiring Goya portrait from Edzard in case
not yet packed in transport STOP And Guardi Ruins by the Sea from
Dr. Lohse STOP Bring the pictures with you to Dresden or have them

delivered through the Embassy STOP Regret deferred payment not possible."[9]

∞

Another seventy years would pass before the tie between the seized shipment and the pivotal relationship between Hitler's art thieves Karl Buchholz, Curt Valentin, and Hildebrand Gurlitt would be made.

2

〜

AT THE BEGINNING—GERMANY, 1907

This world is but a canvas to our imagination.

—HENRY DAVID THOREAU

WHAT CHILD COULD HAVE IMAGINED THAT CIVILIZATION WAS ON the brink of its bloodiest and first world war in 1907? Or that the saber-rattling Kaiser Wilhelm II was at loggerheads with his own family, Edward VII of Great Britain, and Czar Nicholas II of Russia, enviously desiring to tear down their empires? Or that something called Bolshevism was harnessing its bad boy Joseph Stalin to rob a bank in the remote Georgian capital of Tiflis? That President Teddy Roosevelt was moved to call the second Hague Convention with the help of the determined peace campaigner and Nobel Peace Prize winner Baroness Bertha von Suttner naturally fell outside any child's scope.[1] Even milestones for youth like the first Montessori school opening its doors in Rome that year and Robert Baden-Powell's first Boy Scout camp on Brownsea Island in England would have gone unremarked. These international and life-changing matters never touched an affluent German boy's life. Yet the world of 1907 would change eleven-year-old Hildebrand Gurlitt—who would become notorious internationally as Adolf Hitler's art dealer in 2013—for good and ill.

In the dying glow of summer, on September 15, Hildebrand would celebrate his twelfth birthday and enroll at long last at the *Realgymna-sium*** with his elder brother, Wilibald, nicknamed Ebb. This would be his last summer of innocence, the last summer where nothing would be expected of him. Like Wilibald, he'd be obliged to declare his major course of study from day one.

Hildebrand's elder sister, Cornelia, called Eitl by the family, opted for fine art, like their grandfather. Wilibald chose music. Although it was uncommon for women to wish to work, it was hardly shocking given the cry for women's rights that raged around the world. Besides, their mother Marie believed that a strong interest of one's own, other than what went on in the nursery, made a woman more interesting to her husband. Such an interest would also inspire a future husband from a good family to ac-cept Cornelia, who seemed, more often than not, melancholic.

The arts also afforded refined opportunities and enrichment for all women of quality. On Hildebrand's paternal grandfather's side, wasn't their great-aunt the famous novelist Fanny Lewald? Their father, Corne-lius, agreed. It was no leap of faith for his temperamental daughter to con-tinue in the tradition, albeit in the fine arts. The male line of the Gurlitt family boasted several generations of successful writers, artists, and musi-cians swelling their ranks—all of whom promoted the Gurlitts to one of the premier cultural families in that most cultured city of Dresden.

∽

Hildebrand looked forward to that summer, free from definitive decisions about his future. It was a miserably wet and cool spring, and hopes of turn-ing his face to the warmth of the sun soon faded in the unseasonably chilly and damp summer. As the weeks inched by, inevitably the choice of his future career path loomed menacingly. The academic life, undertaken by his father and his uncles Wilhelm and Ludwig, was portrayed as appeal-ing in family conversations. The idea of "going into trade" in business or the law, as had uncles Otto and Johannes or even poor dead Uncle Fritz, was never mentioned. As the youngest, Hildebrand instinctively knew it was

---

* This was the local secondary or high school. Hildebrand Gurlitt was born in 1895 and died in 1956.

frowned upon. The Gurlitt family was made for intellectual and artistic prowess, not grubbing about in trade.

Though the promise of warmth in that summer of 1907 was elusive, Hildebrand enjoyed his days in the company of Cornelia, aged sixteen, whom he adored, and their fifteen-year-old—much taller, most musical, and steadfast—brother, Wilibald. The relationship with Cornelia was strong and would haunt him in the years ahead. Often, she would draw him while they chatted about anything and everything. Hildebrand, whom they affectionately called Putz, confided his hopes and fears to her.

Normally, summer meant that he'd see quite a bit of his father, too, since Cornelius Gurlitt kept to the Technical University's calendar as its art and architecture historian. The elder Gurlitt extolled the beauty of Dresden's baroque architecture, though his international reputation as a baroque expert was still developing.

Hildebrand's mother, born Marie Gerlach, hailed from a family of high Saxony administrative officials, among whom numbered Hildebrand's maternal grandfather as a *Justizrat*, or judicial councillor, to the *Land*, or province, of Saxony. Honors, awards, and high praise were at the heart of Marie's upbringing, and it was only fit and proper that she expect more of the same for her husband. Though Cornelius became a *Hofrat*, or privy councillor in 1897, Marie was groomed to act as a true "Madame Privy Councillor."[2] In her world, women never married beneath themselves.

While his parents' airs and graces might, at times, seem annoying to an eleven-year-old boy, the family's position was a matter of extreme pride. They were at the heart of Wilhelmine Germany and Pan-Germanism, proud of their country's vast cultural heritage.* Perhaps part of Hildebrand's annoyance with Cornelius was that he saw his father reflected in himself. The quiet voice, the preference for strict privacy, the desire for an anonymous yet fruitful life—this mirror of his father—was already developed in him. Through his mother, there came a contrary voice. Her adherence to ceremony, her love of pomp and circumstance, was both comforting and maddening. Hadn't Goethe once said, "In the general throng, many a fool receives decorations and titles"? Hildebrand could be forgiven for wonder-

---

* The German Empire was only thirty-seven years old at the time.

ing what other accolades could or should be heaped upon his father, or, indeed, the rest of the Gurlitt family.

Whatever irritations or slights Hildebrand may have felt that summer, or in the ensuing years, he was cosseted in a golden existence in the magical royal city of Dresden. Despite his angst, feigned or real, there was every expectation that this solid cultural reality would endure his entire life.

The elegant dressed-stone family home, at 26 Kaitzer Strasse, in the A-24 district of Dresden, lulled Hildebrand into this false sense of security. The house itself was set in its own grand and private park, behind low sandstone walls with gunmetal railings so passersby could peek in, yet never enter uninvited. It was a grand home that some understandably mistook for a museum, close to Dresden's *Hauptbahnhof*, or main railway station, and within walking distance of the baroque park of the Grosser Garten. Hildebrand could stroll among the garden's serene beauty, which overlooked the River Elbe, secure in the knowledge that his father was instrumental in awakening the world to the splendor of Dresden's baroque architecture. He could even visit a bust of the paterfamilias, now in his fifty-seventh year, which was erected in the garden precincts to commemorate Cornelius's achievements.[3]

Dresden was the only home the boy had known. Cornelius moved his family to the Kaitzer Strasse residence when Hildebrand was only a year old. While they had always been a bourgeois middle-class family of artistic inclination, Cornelius came into money only after the death of Hildebrand's grandfather, the highly successful and admired nineteenth-century landscape painter Louis Gurlitt.[4]

Hildebrand had no memories of the pretty little house at 4 Franklin Strasse, a mere few streets away from the main railway station. It was purchased initially to travel easily to see Uncle Fritz at the sanatorium. His childhood memories were replete with visits to and from the great and the good of Dresden, including the city's artists, writers, and musicians. Gentility, literature, architecture, music, and fine arts were at the heart of Hildebrand's universe. Still, the private, gilded world in which he lived would be shaken in the summer of 1907 by two disappointments and one outing with his mother.

While he never wrote about his disappointments, these emerged over time. Though not unusual for any adolescent boy or girl, in Hildebrand's case they stemmed from a sense of neglect at this crucial time in his life. Hildebrand learned in June that his father was planning his second trip to the Ottoman Empire for an article on the empire's art and architecture. The trip would take much of the summer holidays, and would exclude Hildebrand, Cornelia, Wilibald, and their mother. After all, Cornelius argued, the Ottoman Empire was no place to bring white, fair-haired women and children of quality.[5] If they had voiced their protests, Cornelius would have reminded them that between his duties at the university and those as high councillor of Saxony it was self-evident that summer was the only appropriate moment when he could undertake any meaningful research into foreign art and architecture.

It was in the hubbub of Cornelius's preparations that the second disappointment emerged—once again in the form of the longest of the Gurlitt family sagas, the litigation and family row surrounding the operations of the Fritz Gurlitt Gallery in Berlin. Cornelius feverishly applied himself that June to transferring the ownership of his dead brother's Berlin art gallery to Fritz's eldest son, Wolfgang. It had been a fourteen-year-long litany that the Gurlitt family sought to keep hidden from wagging tongues, since it involved the two stigmas of adultery and insanity.

∽

Cornelius was the third son born to the nineteenth-century landscape painter Heinrich Louis Theodor Gurlitt, known as Louis, and his third wife, Elisabeth—or Else—née Lewald.[6] Else was Jewish, and assimilation into the Christian community was not only common among German Jews of the time, but desirable. In the heyday of Bismarck and German nationalism, anti-Semitism was openly discussed, including among historians like Heinrich von Treitschke, who remarked in 1879, *"Die Juden sind unser Unglück"*—the Jews are our misfortune.[7]

Whereas in previous generations Jewish boys were taught to read and write Hebrew before learning German, in the nationalist fervor of the second half of the nineteenth century learning Hebrew became secondary or was ignored altogether. In many immigrant Jewish families, Jewish observance had broken down in favor of the Jewish-German phenomenon called the *Haskalah*, or Enlightenment. Those who had not given up Judaism altogether developed a bespoke form of Jewishness that echoed the longing for a prosperous, single German nation. Being Jewish had been honed into a fine art of adaptation, perhaps akin to a musical transition, in the fervent hope of escaping the restrictions of Jewish life imposed from outside as well as from within. For the Lewalds, this meant a flight into the intellectual and artistic sphere, sloughing off their Jewish identity for the universally accepted world of the arts.

As elsewhere in Europe, Jews in Germany had been excluded from the mainstream: denied, then given, then denied again their civil rights. It was only after Bismarck's unifying of Germany's disparate fiefdoms, principalities, and regions in 1870 that Jews were at long last allowed citizenship.[8] Those who still practiced their religion recognized the precariousness of their situation. Increasingly, they tweaked their religious observance, as inspired by the philosopher Moses Mendelssohn. In his Reform movement of the Jewish faith, Jews no longer needed to set themselves apart from Christians by their mode of dress, their diet, or their daily routine. Yet marrying into Christian families and converting to Christianity remained viable options for many Jews to prove that they were "good Germans," too.

In fact, Else Gurlitt's older sister, Fanny Lewald, had converted to Christianity at the age of only seventeen.[9] Else herself, Hildebrand later claimed, converted to the Lutheran faith.[10] In these circumstances, it is little wonder that all of Louis and Else's children were brought up in the religion of their father, utterly devoid of Jewish tradition. There would be six sons and one daughter born to the couple.

With the passage of time, Cornelius cultivated a privileged place among his brothers as the family peacemaker. Judging by his letters, he felt closest to the oldest brother, Wilhelm.[11] Six years Cornelius's senior, Wilhelm was a professor of archaeology at the University of Graz in Austria-Hungary. Relations between Cornelius and the second-oldest brother, Otto, were strained in later life, though this could be expected between a brother who was a banker and one who chose higher education and public service.

Yet there are strong hints in the family correspondence that Otto also resented Cornelius's favoring of the next-youngest brother, Friedrich. Fritz, as the family called him, was the fourth son, and indeed, very close to Cornelius. Fritz seemed to show some vulnerable character traits from an early age, though whether this was merely the older brothers protecting him from bullying or a true weakness is difficult to say.[12]

Ludwig, the fifth son, had entered teaching with the zeal of a reformist, and again was not as close to Cornelius, clearly resenting the older brother's management of Fritz's affairs.[13] The economist Johannes, or Hans, was the sixth son, and was separated from his brothers by their only sister, Else. Whenever there were disagreements within the Gurlitt tribe, Wilhelm always called upon Cornelius to negotiate the peace, as he held the position of "leadership . . . to constantly build our sense of family and our togetherness."[14]

∽

Thus cast into the role, it fell to Cornelius to sort out the hornets' nest created by his brother Fritz. Having married the tempting Annarella, daughter of the Swiss sculptor Heinrich Maximilian Imhof, Fritz set up his own Berlin art gallery and shop in 1880, in part with Annarella's dowry. Three years later, he created the first-ever Impressionist art exhibit in Germany with the assistance of his good friends Carl and Felice Bernstein, who were Russian Jewish émigrés from Odessa.

The Bernsteins were remarkable in that they learned about Impressionism during their long sojourn in Paris from their cousin, the connoisseur and Parisian art critic Charles Ephrussi, and the noted art dealer Paul Durand-Ruel.[15] Fritz became the gallery owner of choice for French Impressionists in Germany, while also cultivating a fruitful relationship representing the Düsseldorf school of German Romantic painters, such as Arnold Böcklin, Anselm Feuerbach, and Max Liebermann. Fritz soon became a favorite of the director of Berlin's Königliche National-Galerie, Hugo von Tschudi.[16]

Yet despite this auspicious beginning and four children born to Annarella in rapid succession, by 1890 the once-amiable Fritz began to fall out with people, including Böcklin. Annarella alerted Fritz's family that matters were spiraling out of control, and that the business was now run by Fritz's assistant, Willi Waldecker. Soon everyone acknowledged that Fritz was showing the distressing signs of severe mental imbalance. At last, in 1892, at Cornelius's behest, Fritz was moved to Thornberg, near Leipzig, where he could receive the best treatment available at the renowned sanatorium nearby, initially as an outpatient.

As the year progressed, and hopes for Fritz's recovery faded, Cornelius became aware of Annarella's overt "friendliness" with Waldecker. He wrote to his brother Wilhelm that "we had long ago realized that Annarella looked around for new men—and that riding pillion behind her in the gallery was that Waldecker fellow."[17] When Fritz faded away gently at nine o'clock at night on March 9, 1893—sooner than Cornelius expected—the most almighty family furor began.

The telegram arrived at two in the morning bearing the sad news, awakening Cornelius's household. The following morning, Cornelius and Marie went to tell his parents, who were naturally overcome with grief. "At the end of the day, she [Mama] felt that it was fortunate that Fritz had not lived longer with such an infirmity. She was quiet, cried, and lay down to sleep after dinner."[18]

Yet in no time the rupture with Annarella poisoned the air. Before Fritz was buried, Cornelius wrote with considerable vehemence to Wilhelm:

> Yesterday I learned that there had been a promise of marriage since mid-December between the two [Annarella and Waldecker]. I discussed this with Ludwig and [our sister] Else; and it was agreed that we should say nothing about the matter, so long as Fritz had not been buried. But the evening before the funeral, I could not bring myself to allow Annarella and Waldecker to sit at my table without explaining themselves. I asked her how the matter stood between them, and they conceded that they wished to marry. I called her a whore and asked her to leave my house . . . . It was then that she admitted "love" for him [Waldecker]. . . . Annarella only denied any infidelity in the truest sense of the word.[19]

Despite promises from Annarella, the saga continued. Bankruptcy loomed, while Waldecker tried to milk the business dry. The ignominy of Fritz's madness coupled with Annarella's infidelity brought about the fourteen-year-long chronicle of bitterness, hatred, and legal wrangling to protect Fritz's good name, the gallery, and his children's birthright. In that period, Cornelius placed himself in the role of absent father, constantly fighting on behalf of Fritz's four children and looking after their well-being. It was only in the summer of 1907, after Fritz's eldest son, Wolfgang, came of age, that Cornelius wrested the gallery from the clutches of Waldecker and Annarella.[20]

∽

Any adolescent boy would have been crushed by the attention given to his cousin Wolfgang at this critical time in his life. Unlike today, however, a child's feelings were rarely taken into consideration in such family matters. Perhaps it was Cornelius's concentration on snatching back his nephew Wolfgang's inheritance that motivated Marie into action that summer. Or perhaps it was simply her desire to open her young son's eyes to the world of art. More probably, with artist friends like Ernst Ludwig Kirchner, Karl Schmidt-Rottluff, and Erich Heckel—the founders of Die Brücke, or the Bridge, the Expressionist art movement in Dresden—frequenting their home, Marie thought the time was ripe to expose young Hildebrand to the wonders of their art.

Later, Hildebrand wrote, "I will never forget the moment when I and my mother, 'Madame royal Saxon privy councillor,' saw the first exhibition of The Bridge in a baroque lamp shop, on a desolate street in Dresden . . . these barbaric, passionately powerful colors, this rawness, encased in the poorest of wooden frames—aimed to hit the middle classes like a slap in the face. And that is indeed what it did. I, the young schoolboy, was also startled, but 'Madame privy councillor' said that we should buy a sample of these interesting works, and she took home one of the most astonishing woodcuts."[21] This was rebellion in a form both he and his parents could applaud. From that moment on, Hildebrand proclaimed his love for modern art.

Hildebrand also recalled his father's reaction to the woodcuts and quoted Cornelius verbatim: "It may very well be that this art will become as important to your life as the struggle over Hans Thoma, Arnold Böcklin and Max Liebermann was to mine."[22] They were all represented by Fritz Gurlitt.

∽

In the visual arts, Germans were confident of their superiority, and with good reason. The Munich-based Blue Rider group—Der Blaue Reiter—

hosted such greats of modernism as Russian-born Wassily Kandinsky, the Jewish German Franz Marc, and the Swiss German Paul Klee. Led by Kandinsky, their countercultural antidote to Wilhelminism and anti-bourgeois sentiment set the tone for a community of three thousand artists that attracted even the unknown artist Adolf Hitler to Munich in May 1913. Ignoring the endeavors of the Blue Rider movement, Hitler enthused about Munich, "I was attracted by this wonderful marriage of primordial power and fine artistic mood, this single line from the Hofbräuhaus to the Odeon, from the Oktoberfest to the Pinakothek . . . if even then I achieved the happiness of a truly inward contentment, it can be attributed only to the magic which the miraculous residence of the Wittelsbachs exerts on every man who is blessed."[23]

The Berlin Secession, founded in 1899 and led by Max Beckmann, Lovis Corinth, and Max Liebermann, was complemented by the Bridge in 1905 and five years later by the New Secession, both originally based in Dresden. The Bridge included artists like Ernst Ludwig Kirchner, Max Pechstein, and Emil Nolde. Yet even in their striving to new modernist heights, their desire to break away from the constraints of traditional society sounded a declaration of war.

The 1906 manifesto of the Bridge, which derived its name from Nietzsche's theory that man is the bridge leading to an elevated state for humanity, stated, "Putting our faith in a new generation of creators and art lovers, we call upon youth to unite. We who possess the future shall create for ourselves a physical and spiritual freedom opposed to the values of the comfortably established older generation. Anyone who honestly and directly reproduces the creative force that is within him is one of us."[24]

Mirroring the changes in Germany, 1907 became a pioneering year for Western civilization in its quest to humanize the evil of war. All eyes turned to The Hague and the second convention to promote peace. Failure there, so peace activists like Andrew Carnegie claimed, would herald disaster for the twentieth century.

3

FROM THE HAGUE TO VIENNA

Peace is not merely the absence of war.

—Jawaharlal Nehru

THE YEAR 1907 WAS A CURIOUS TURNING POINT FOR HILDEBRAND
Gurlitt's future, too, in part thanks to the successes of the energetic peace
campaigner Baroness Bertha von Suttner and the equally remote tribu-
lations of Adolf Hitler. The baroness was devoted to peace, Hitler to hatred
and war. Both lived in Vienna that year. Both would change the course of
cultural thought in the twentieth century.

Rising up against the tidal wave of isms and aggression, Baroness von
Suttner represented the Vienna that Hitler loathed. She was an internationalist, and her city was multilingual and multinational. Vienna abounded
with men and women of regal bearing who were proud of their Magyar,
Czech, Slovak, Moldavian, and Austrian descent, and who adored the two-
thousand-year-old metropolis for its diversity. Hers was a Vienna of assured
values and relentless hospitality, a bastion of civilization, where its finely
chiseled stone buildings stood as signposts of timeless customs and good
taste, refusing to argue with its new modernist architecture and grand,
glittering avenues.[1] It was a Vienna that would remain as foreign to Adolf
Hitler as Bertha von Suttner's uncompromising quest for world peace.

Her Vienna mirrored the macrocosm of the treasured Habsburg

monarchy and palaces. Morning newspapers did not sully their front pages with the military or the political or even the commercial, preferring instead to lead with the repertoire of the imperial Burgtheater or other artistic delights. This magnificent building was where Mozart's *Marriage of Figaro* was first performed; where Chopin, Brahms, Liszt, and Rubinstein gave concerts to standing ovations; and where fanaticism for the arts touched people from all walks of life, uniting them despite their diversity.

Though he lived in Dresden, Vienna was a realm that Cornelius Gurlitt readily comprehended. The Gurlitts were leaders in architecture, music, and the arts in the cities where they lived—Dresden, Leipzig, Berlin, and Graz in Austria. Cornelius already enjoyed an international reputation for his defense of baroque architecture. To Bertha and Cornelius, just as to many art historians and artists, true art linked people across national borders and any social milieu.

As a young impoverished aristocratic woman, the baroness was briefly Alfred Nobel's secretary in Paris, before succumbing to her heartache as an elder Juliet for her youthful Romeo, the future Baron von Suttner. Nevertheless, Nobel and Bertha continued to correspond actively, and his ideas for European peace became firmly impressed on her psyche. They would remain fast friends throughout his lifetime, and eventually she would take up his gauntlet for disarmament.

In 1905, she'd been awarded the Nobel Peace Prize—only the second woman after radium discoverer Marie Curie to receive *any* Nobel Prize.[2] Ever the optimist, Nobel decided to institute the prize at the baroness's prompting, and wrote to her from his Paris home that "one hears in the distance its hollow rumble already . . . I should like to dispose of my fortune to found a prize to be awarded every five years" to the person who contributed most effectively to the peace of Europe. Nobel thought that surely after six awards, the prize for peace could terminate "for if in thirty years society cannot be reformed we shall inevitably lapse into barbarism."[3]

When President Teddy Roosevelt convened the second Hague Convention that year, Baroness Suttner worked energetically on the task ahead with the American philanthropist Andrew Carnegie, pressing for a League of Nations to be formed, believing that the man to establish it was Kaiser Wilhelm. For Carnegie, the kaiser was "the man responsible for war on earth."[4] Though he'd made his money in steel, Carnegie had sold his business years earlier to devote himself entirely to philanthropy.*

Unusually for an American diplomat, Carnegie also understood British concerns that the kaiser was hell-bent on breaking the dominance of the British Navy and the empire. Everyone knew that the kaiser, as the nephew of the British king Edward VII and first cousin of Czar Nicholas II of Russia, envied their empires. Roosevelt, for his part, believed that the German Empire was "alert, military and industrial, . . . [and] despises . . . the whole Hague idea."[5]

While disarmament was on the agenda, it was never ratified. Still, an agreement of sorts was reached and ratified by all forty-six nations in attendance. Significantly, definitions and protocols about pacific settlements of international disputes, conventions regarding the opening of hostilities, what constituted an army and belligerents, the conversion of the merchant navy to warships, the treatment of prisoners of war and those reporting on the war, those providing relief to the wounded and prisoners of war, and the treatment of noncombatants were agreed upon.

Though disappointing to the pacifists, the agreement signed on October 18, 1907, provided for a number of safeguards for civilization in the event of war. Article 25 strictly prohibited the attack or bombardment by whatever means of towns, villages, dwellings, or buildings which were undefended. Sieges and bombardments, according to article 27, must take all necessary steps to spare, as far as possible, buildings dedicated to religion, art, science, charitable purposes, historic monuments, hospitals, and places where the sick and wounded are collected, providing that they are not being used simultaneously for military purposes. A peculiar anomaly in article 27 made it the duty of the besieged to indicate the presence of such buildings or places beforehand to the enemy by distinctive and visible signs.[6] This article would touch Hildebrand's life in the war that erupted seven years later.

While the Hague Conference of 1907 apparently made no difference to the gathering tempest, buried deep within the protocol finally agreed

---

* The devastating outcome of the Homestead Strike at Carnegie's steelworks in Pennsylvania haunted him to the end of his days. When J. P. Morgan offered to buy Carnegie Steel for millions, he jumped at the chance.

by all the participants was an annex, "Regulations Respecting the Laws and Customs of War on Land," in section III of which, "Military Authority over the Territory of the Hostile State," is the following:

> Art 46. Family honour and rights, the lives of persons, and private property, as well as religious convictions and practice, must be respected.
>
> Private property cannot be confiscated.

These articles would soon meet their first great challenge in the conflagration that lay ahead.

⁂

For the artist manqué Adolf Hitler, 1907 was the ultimate determining factor leading toward his loathsome future. This was the year that he moved with his mother, Klara, and half sister, Paula, to Urfahr, a suburb of Linz, Austria, nestled in a picturesque Danube valley. Despite Klara's best efforts, the forty-eight-year-old widow long ago learned that she had precious little control over her bombastic son. When Adolf left secondary school in 1905, he had not procured the customary high-school diploma, thereby excluding himself from higher education. To compound her worries, he'd refused to settle down and earn a living—something that she would have welcomed on her monthly pension of 140 kronen and the proceeds of the house she'd sold at nearby Leonding.[7] Described by his teachers as "notoriously cantankerous, willful, arrogant and bad-tempered . . . moreover . . . lazy . . ." this youthful Hitler was recognizable, already angrily defying the world from his teens.[8]

Like so many things, school proved a challenge Hitler was unwilling to tackle. In fact, his performance was so poor that he was sent to a boarding school at Steyr to force him to improve his grades. There his mediocrity abounded, punctuated with outbursts of vile temper. Hitler employed every excuse to explain away his lackluster grades, ranging from illness to his tyrannical father (who had already died), to his artistic temperament fueled by his unbridled ambition to achieve greatness (without toil). His teachers were accused of political prejudice, and they often received a tongue-lashing from the teenage Hitler for their narrow-mindedness against his strongly held social views.

If Klara believed that the move to the city of Linz would improve her tempestuous son's prospects, her hopes were soon shattered. Hitler made no effort to socialize—either with his former classmates or other young men and women his age. His social inadequacy compounded his mother's worries, for he had become a young man who could be described only as an irascible, bone-idle daydreamer. Still, Klara, like many mothers, soldiered on.

During his purposeless days, Hitler often wandered alone along the Danube or up the 1,329-foot-high Freiberg Hill* to take in the panoramic views. In the shadow of the building known as Franz Joseph's outlook, he'd sit on his favorite bench to sketch or read. Naturally, the sketches were a wild and sweeping redesign of Linz to his personal liking, including new bridges and, of course, his own temple to the arts.

His evenings were habitually spent at the theater, particularly if a Wagner opera was slated for a performance. While standing in the gallery one evening, Hitler met a local upholsterer's son, August Kubizek, whose passion was music. Like Hitler, Kubizek was prone to be moody, blaming his artistic temperament for his sullen behavior. Their love of music became their instant bond. As they walked back home that evening, they enthused about the music they'd heard and found they had much in common.[9] In short order, Kubizek became Hitler's only friend. Later, in his book *Adolf Hitler: Mein Jugendfreund*, Kubizek would describe Hitler as "a thread that ran throughout my life."[10]

This young Hitler, a "pale and skinny but well-dressed boy standing next to him in the gallery," dominated all their conversations with his own didactic views on the arts. Yet Kubizek did not recall that Hitler was political in any conversations at this stage of their lives. What did strike him, however, was Hitler's mesmerizing, icy blue, wide-staring eyes.[11]

‎⁂

Despite this new and promising friendship, Klara gazed on helplessly as her nineteen-year-old son became increasingly obsessed, lost in pipe dreams

---

* This is a late Neolithic settlement thought to be the original settlement for the town and is one of two mountains dominating the city and the Danube.

of becoming an architect, or a recognized artistic genius. Klara, of course, knew better. She'd sent Adolf to Vienna to stay with relatives for a few weeks the previous year, hoping he'd find some sensible direction, since she knew full well that without a high-school diploma he could not attend university. Hitler returned home from his Viennese sojourn ablaze with the splendor of the city's art galleries, the opera, and its sublime buildings. As his sketchbook swelled with hundreds of sketches and watercolors, his enthusiasm to redesign a "new" Linz spanning both sides of the Danube became a magnificent obsession that would last until his final days of World War II in his Berlin bunker.[12]

Whether Klara was able to make her son understand that his options were limited is not recorded. However, sometime early in 1907 young Hitler made another journey to Vienna, presumably to find out about enrolling in the Academy of Fine Arts.[13] Hitler applied himself to the process with an unknown vigor. He even hatched a plan with his friend Kubizek for them to share a room. Kubizek would attend the music conservatory and Hitler the fine-arts academy. While Klara remained anxious and reticent, she finally agreed to let her son go.

Hitler left for Vienna early that September to prepare for his entry exams. He stayed at 29 Stumpergasse in the dingy single-story home of a Polish Jewish landlady off the Mariahilferstrasse, Vienna's main shopping street at the time.[14] While Hitler nervously waited, he imbibed the city's prosperity, its theaters and art galleries. He saw that high-society Vienna moved at the pace of a "cavalry camel." Its men, with their black frock coats and flowing tails, their high, stiff collars—called "patricides"—and chimney-pot hats, were strange to him. Wasp-waisted women doing violence to their figures with whalebone corsets and incongruous, billowing bell-like skirts that covered their toes were bizarre to Hitler, too.[15] Both became figures of ridicule to the budding despot.

Hitler later wrote, ". . . preoccupied by the abundance of my impressions in the architectural field, oppressed by the hardship of my own lot . . . in the first few weeks my eyes and my senses were not equal to the flood of values and ideas. Not until calm gradually returned and the agitated picture began to clear, did I look around me more carefully in my new world."[16] Hitler did not see what author Stefan Zweig referred to as the "archangels of progress," the triumphs of human intellect in experimentation in the arts, or modern technological inventions or indeed the pioneering spirit of its proponents.

When Hitler regained focus, he suddenly concentrated on Vienna's nearly two hundred thousand Jews, who dominated, so he believed, a city of some two million souls. Like the dreary burghers who abhorred change, Hitler ranted to his friend Kubizek that the art and designs of Klimt, Schiele, and the other Viennese Secessionists of the *Jugendstil*, or "young style," were pornographic and degenerate.[17] In music, he fulminated that the turbulent composer and conductor Gustav Mahler was nothing but an ill-mannered, untalented Jew, with a reputation for disrupting the performances of his competitors to boot.

Frankly, the art and music world had gone mad, Hitler raged at whoever would listen. There was the new trend for atonal composition in modern music that made him wince in pain. The only beacon on the horizon was that the Viennese audiences agreed with him, hissing and brawling openly when confronted with the shock of atonal modernism. Ingrained in the old traditions of staid Vienna, Hitler saw foreign influences of polyglot Austria-Hungary—and Hitler loathed anything that smacked of the cosmopolitan or foreign, anything that rebelled against his beloved *völkisch*, or folk, ways.[18] Indeed, the cacophony of languages of the Austro-Hungarian Empire revolted him. The thought that Czech, Romanian, Magyar, or Slavic dialects corrupted his beloved German language, as they often did in cosmopolitan Vienna, was a discordant anathema.

Still, Hitler's greatest contempt was reserved for the assault on architecture by the Secessionists. Their "home," designed by Joseph Maria Olbrich and built some nine years earlier, was initially nicknamed the "Mahdi's Tomb." Then some witty Viennese journalist dubbed it the "Assyrian Comfort Station," while others called it a cross between a glasshouse and blast furnace. By the time Hitler saw the building, crowned with its gilded openwork sphere of laurel leaves and berries, it had become known as "the golden cabbage."[19] The façade of the building was adorned with the words of the Jewish feuilletonist and art critic Ludwig Hevesi: *Der Zeit ihre Kunst, der Kunst ihre Freiheit*—"To every age its art, to art its freedom."[20] For the newly alert Hitler, it embodied all that was wrong with Vienna, the changing European avant-garde art scene, and the relationship between art and design.

Naturally, Hitler's entry-exam results for the Academy of Fine Arts were catastrophic. While he scraped through the first part of the examination in September, he failed the drawing test in October. His art was banal, devoid of human form and originality. The academy's classification list states simply:

> The following took the test with insufficient results or were not ad-
> mitted . . .
> Adolf Hitler, [place of birth] Braunau a.Inn, 20 April 1889.
> German. Catholic. Father, civil servant. 4 classes in *Realschule*. Few
> heads. Test drawing unsatisfactory.[21]

Hitler thundered with anger. The examiners were nothing but a lot of fossilized bureaucrats devoid of understanding his exceptional talents. The academy ought to be blown up! How could the academy be so myopic? How could they accept the golden designs of this Gustav Klimt and his *Portrait of Adele Bauer-Bloch*, painted in oils, silver, and gold on canvas that very year, when they denied him his natural calling? Why did the Viennese flock to *see* modernist paintings and not appreciate *his* classicism? Of course, Hitler ignored the recommendation that he reapply for architecture the following term. He would have needed a high-school diploma to attend.[22]

Instead of returning home to Linz, the infuriated and frustrated Hitler remained in Vienna, begrudging every Magyar, Slav, Czech, Marxist, Freemason, homosexual, and Jew their place in a society where he had none. The main exception to Hitler's unrelenting tirade against the city was Vienna's *Bürgermeister*, or mayor, Karl Lueger, dubbed *Der schöne Karl* (handsome Karl) because of his good looks. Lueger adored a good crowd to rouse and was famous for bending their energies to his will. He was also a noted anti-Semite who refused to have Jews, Pan-Germans, or Social Democrats in his administration. A devout Catholic, Lueger swayed public opinion against the Jews in particular, dubbing Budapest "Judapest"— mocking the Hungarian city for its thriving Jewish community. It is little wonder that Lueger became the strategic and tactical catalyst for Hitler's formative political career.

Hitler reasoned that in order to save Austria from itself, the country needed to cease to be a state of multiple nationalities.[23] "In this period," Hitler wrote, "my eyes were opened to two menaces of which I had previously scarcely known the names, and whose terrible importance for the existence of the German people I certainly did not understand: Marxism and Jewry."[24] Hitler the artist manqué, ultranationalist, and racist was already brewing, bubbling over with rancor.

Unexpectedly, shortly before Christmas 1907, Klara Hitler succumbed to cancer, freeing her son to become the sociopath and tyrant who straddled two decades of the twentieth century as its dark force, capable of any evil. Klara's deathbed regret, however, was that she would never see her long-held dream of her beloved son, Adolf, earning a living and at long last gaining his place in society.

Thankfully for her, she never did.

4

CAUSE AND EFFECT

... the Monarchs of Europe have paid no attention to what
I have to say. Soon, with my great navy to endorse my
words, they will be more respectful.
—KAISER WILHELM II to the king of Italy

THE YOUNG LIVES OF HILDEBRAND GURLITT AND ADOLF HITLER,
like the lives of millions, were about to change forever. Communism, Marxism, and socialism vied with age-old empires to wrest away power. Women
wanted the vote.* Conquered nations and downtrodden people clamored
for greater freedom. Ideology and threats had already been transformed
into deeds by the beginning of the century—a century irretrievably
marred by isms and two world wars of unimaginable dislocation and
bloodshed.

Every nation suffered from an embarrassment of riches in new beliefs
that divided regions, cities, places of worship or work, homes, and families.
The age of the ism had arrived vengefully, and colored everything red—
if not in blood, then in the red mist of hotly held convictions. Locking

---

* Men who did not fulfill skilled-labor requirements or who were not deemed countryside working
class had been denied the vote in Great Britain until the Third Reform Act of 1884. Universal male
suffrage was only granted at the same time as votes for women in 1918. In the German Empire
universal male suffrage was granted in 1871. In the United States, universal suffrage was achieved
state by state, and was only accepted nationwide in 1920.

political and social horns in the farthest reaches of the world were imperi-
alism, republicanism, socialism, Marxism, Bolshevism, communism, capitalism, liberalism, libertarianism, fascism, Pan-Germanism, Pan-Slavism,
Pan-Italianism,* trade unionism, nihilism, atheism, anarchism, terrorism,
pacifism, feminism, and anti-Semitism. Some were ideologies, others isms
of blame. The isms of faith—Catholicism, Protestantism, Islamism, Judaism, Buddhism, and other established religions—were subsumed increasingly into the maelstrom of other religious, political, and social isms. Faced
with this onslaught of new ideas, the silent mainstream in society embraced
traditionalism and conservatism, believing that if they spurned anything
new, their world would not be disrupted.

This ignored the threat of Pan-Germanism in the hands of Kaiser
Wilhelm II. From the German-speaking perspective, Kaiser Wilhelm was
fighting the good fight against French and Russian aggression. In less than
ten years, Pan-Germanists and their Alldeutscher Verband, or Pan-
German League, had grown from a radical, unoriginal, hateful right-wing
splinter group to a mainstream political association supported by the
national press throughout Austria-Hungary and Germany. The kaiser chose
to ignore the implied threat the Alldeutscher Verband represented to his
neighbors with their vow to unite all German-speaking peoples, since it
ultimately suited his own expansionist plans. No one wanted to unite
Germans behind the ailing Austro-Hungarian Empire.

∽

Hildebrand Gurlitt attended his secondary school specializing in fine art
amid these quarrelsome and exciting times. At home on Kaitzer Strasse,
"Pan-Germanism" was a word that was pronounced proudly. His father was
among the intelligentsia who adopted Pan-Germanism wholeheartedly,
like many university lecturers. It was intended to unite all German-
speaking peoples under the auspices of a German superstate, and Cornelius
Gurlitt, like Hitler, believed that only the kaiser was worthy of promoting
the German cause.[1]

The Austro-Hungarian Empire had long been hobbled by dissent

---

* *Italia Irredenta* was the territory in Europe inhabited by Italian-speaking people not included in
the Kingdom of Italy. It lay in the main within Austria-Hungary's political boundaries.

among its multiethnic population. Worse still, its German-speaking bourgeoisie, dreaming of a strong Pan-Germanic nation that sprawled across the middle of Europe, were shocked by its ancient emperor, Franz Joseph, who wanted self-government for his Slavic citizens. Similar to German aspirations, the Slavs visualized a Pan-Slavic world stretching from the Mediterranean to the Baltic Sea in Eastern Europe.

Interestingly, the conflicting Pan-German/Pan-Slavic movements had been revived after the unification of Germany in 1870. It was just one of the serious upheavals in thought that led to the war of 1914–1918. Empire building was at the heart of that war, with Germany coming late to the party.

Many Americans were astonished when the United States, too, became a late entry into the empire sweepstakes. After all, republics did not have colonies. Yet when President McKinley was assassinated, in 1901, the new president, Theodore Roosevelt, rode roughshod over Panama. He even bullied the kaiser out of Venezuela. Yet by 1905, Roosevelt uncharacteristically brokered peace between Japan and Russia—in his first adventure into the realm of international peace.[2] Under Roosevelt, the United States waltzed onto an already overcrowded empire stage.

⁊

A European war that would engulf the world's empires was breathed in hushed tones at posh salons and gentlemen's clubs. In 1898 Empress Elisabeth of Austria-Hungary, like McKinley in 1901, was assassinated. The Spanish prime minister Canovas, President Carnot of France, and the king of Italy were assassinated early in the new century, too. The first attempted Russian revolution in 1905 was savagely put down, and the czar's earlier concessions to the Duma (Russia's parliament) were quashed. Nicholas felt personally vulnerable to his cousin Wilhelm's increasingly patronizing and belligerent attitude, his long letters haranguing the young czar to make "more speeches and more parades, more speeches more parades" in an effort to win over the Russian people, whom "the curse of God" had "stricken forever."[3]

For over fifteen years, Kaiser Wilhelm lusted after a navy and empire to rival that of Great Britain and had even sacked the maker of the German Empire, Otto von Bismarck, over their disagreement about unnecessary expansionist policies and Germany's seizure of Alsace and Lorraine from France in 1871.

Notwithstanding Bismarck's vast contribution to the German ideal of greatness, Wilhelm's view was one shared by many Germans, including the Gurlitts. The kaiser's brand of German nationalism was best summed up by the militaristic Prussian general Friedrich von Bernhardi, who claimed that Germany's "legitimate aims" were to "secure to the German nationality and the German people throughout the globe that high esteem which is due them . . . and has hitherto been withheld from them."[4] From Vienna, Hitler, too, heartily concurred.

In France, the humiliating recollection of the Imperial German Army marching down the Champs-Élysées in 1871 after the loss of Alsace-Lorraine was as vivid and suffocating as if it were yesterday. Then Bismarck made war "pay" by demanding an indemnity of 5 billion francs from a defeated France—the first time that the cost of waging war was firmly and officially placed on the shoulders of the defeated.[5]

Still, Bismarck had the foresight to appreciate that the French desire for revenge would lead to alliances hostile to the German Empire, and that these coalitions could ultimately unleash renewed hostilities. The kaiser, however, continued on regardless, concluding alliances with Austria-Hungary in a Dual Alliance (1879), which became the Triple Alliance with Italy in 1882.[6] A truncated France responded, albeit slowly, and sealed the Franco-Russian Alliance in 1894 with the czar.

Aside from the kaiser's envy of his cousins' empires, "living space" further drove German aggression. Fear of *Einkreisung*, or encirclement, resulting from the Franco-Russian alliance was a factor. The Entente Cordiale signed in a series of agreements in 1904 between the French and British positively fed their alarm.

Germany must strike at its enemies before encirclement ripped it apart, the kaiser urged. Cornelius Gurlitt and Adolf Hitler staunchly supported him. Yet the only way to successfully attack France, with its massive fortifications in the east, was to invade via Belgium. When Field Marshal Goltz profoundly espoused that "we have won our position through the sharpness of our sword, not through the sharpness of our mind," the last qualms about the invasion of Belgium, whose neutrality had been guaranteed by the British since 1839, were erased.

The oily and self-important foreign minister Count Bernhard von Bülow, who would scribble the kaiser's latest wishes on his shirt cuffs, sermonized freely on Belgian acquiescence.[7] It was simple common sense that the Belgians wouldn't resist, he claimed, rubbing his hands together in full triumphalist zeal. Unfortunately for Bülow's pride, the kaiser had other ideas, and offered the notoriously greedy Belgian king, Leopold, two million pounds sterling to secure Belgian neutrality.[8] Leopold was so aghast that he left his meeting with the kaiser wearing his ceremonial helmet backward.

France, on the other hand, was mindful of the kaiser's hostile intent. After the invidious defeat in 1871, and the declaration of the German Empire in the Hall of Mirrors at Versailles, France had walled herself in by virtue of two fortified entrenched lines: Belfort-Epinal and Toul-Verdun, guarding the eastern front, and Maubeuge-Valenciennes-Lille, watching over the western half of the Belgian frontier. "France will have but one thought," Victor Hugo wrote, "to reconstitute her forces, gather her energy, nourish her sacred anger, raise her young generation to form an army of the whole people . . . then one day she will be irresistible. Then she will take back Alsace-Lorraine."[9]

Fear of the powerful Teutonic empires at the heart of Europe continued to engender new alliances. Serbia sought reassurances from Russia while Austria-Hungary, threatened by anti-Habsburg propaganda emanating from Serbia, wanted to push its way with its *Drang nach Osten*—or drive to the East—bolstered by German arms. Of course, this conflicted sharply with czarist Russia's "historic mission" of acquiring Constantinople and the Bosporus Strait, as well as its time-honored protection of the Slavic peoples. London had tired of voicing its alarm that the German demand for its "place in the sun" was against Britain's interests. It was time to increase pressure on the kaiser to rethink his policies.

∾

Meanwhile, in Vienna, Hitler learned his future despotic craft by watching the Austrian Social Democrats, Georg von Schönerer's Pan-German nationalists, and Vienna's own Karl Lueger and his Christian Social Party. Not surprisingly, it would be from the Social Democrats that he would discover the power of mass demonstrations and propaganda.

"I gazed on the interminable ranks, four abreast, of Viennese workmen parading at a mass demonstration," Hitler wrote in *Mein Kampf*. "I stood dumbfounded for almost two hours, watching this enormous human dragon which slowly uncoiled itself before me."[10] Georg von Schönerer and his Pan-Germans—the antisocialist, anti-Semitic, anti-Habsburg organ seeking to unite through hatred—taught Hitler his greatest lessons. "The art of leadership consists of consolidating the attention of the people against a single adversary and taking care that nothing will split up this attention. . . . The leader of genius must have the ability to make different opponents appear as if they belonged to one category."[11]

Again, Vienna's mayor, Karl Lueger, was the only person to succeed in Hitler's eyes in creating a mass movement—despite the glaring fact that Lueger's anti-Semitism was based on religious and economic arguments, not on race like Hitler's. In a remark that Hermann Göring would later echo, Lueger proclaimed, "I decide who is a Jew." Still, it was Lueger's rejection of German supremacy over the Habsburg state, with its multiethnic origins, that most perplexed young Hitler. Later, he'd write that the Austrian "leaders recognized the value of propaganda on a large scale and they were veritable virtuosos in working up the spiritual instincts of the broad masses of their electorate."[12]

Like Hitler's, Cornelius Gurlitt's ideal of a Pan-German state administered by Germany resounded throughout the movement. In Germany, chauvinism was at its height, with the most influential militaristic Prussian Junkers leading the way in building the Alldeutscher Verband, the Flottenverein (Naval League), and the Wehrverein (Defense League)—"gigantic organizations, extending over the whole empire, which were preparing her in accordance with a definite program for the 'inevitable' war for world supremacy."[13] An estimated two million people were members of these various associations in Europe, with another two million believed to be "overseas" members by 1913. The avowed purpose of these bodies was to deepen national pride and impel all Germans to recognize their responsibilities as a major world power abroad. For the Pan-Germanist, the state was absolved of any question of morals. All means justified the desired result.

To meet their aims, education needed to be controlled by a national policy. All tendencies to oppose nationalism must be suppressed, and all nationalistic and patriotic policies encouraged. To spread German influence and responsibility abroad, immigration to German colonies was actively encouraged. German financial special interests were furthered by energetic politics that led to practical results. It was the Pan-Germanists who coined the now well-worn terms "realpolitik," "*Weltpolitik*," "Anglo-Saxon Menace," "Slavic Peril," and "big business."[14]

ℐ

The purifying salt of Pan-Germanism and saber rattling of militarism were only two weapons in the kaiser's arsenal for German domination of Europe. As Hildebrand Gurlitt would learn, German culture remained overshadowed internationally by the French, the British, and even the Italians, despite its own great musicians, artists, and literary figures. In the hands of Wilhelm II, it would become a lofty shield behind which all German-speaking peoples could rally. Hugo von Tschudi, once director of the Berlin Königliche National-Galerie, was exiled to the Bavarian State Collections by the kaiser, simply because he favored French modern art, including Picasso. Tschudi would not recover from offending the kaiser's sense of German superiority.

Hitler, too, learned the political significance of culture and art from the kaiser. Art, that calm refuge whose cultural message was intended to connect all peoples, irrespective of their ethnic diversity, nationality, or social standing, was becoming a divisive political tool.

The arts, too, in exploring their own boundaries, were not immune from discord or the new isms. Impressionism, Postimpressionism, Cubism, Futurism, Expressionism, Fauvism, Progressivism, avant-gardism, and more dominated fine art, literature, and music, dividing thought and engendering argument. Each had its champions and its detractors.

Technology, too, bore down on the arts. Advances in photography and film challenged the artist to seek new worlds, new expressions, and new ideas to differentiate their craft from the photograph so they could continue to make a fresh impact on a rapidly changing cultural landscape. In music, the challenge was met at times with a trend toward the dissonant; or, conversely from traditionalists, a rejuvenated fluid melodiousness, redolent of rolling countryside that had remained unchanged for centuries. In literature, experimental philosophies and concepts abounded.

Industrialization had led to progress and advances beyond the comprehension of Hildebrand Gurlitt's father's and grandfather's generations. Great tools and inventions unchained human energies, bringing the world into the machine age with extraordinary inventions like electricity, the automobile, and the internal-combustion engine. Productivity had increased fivefold in fifteen years. Improvements in hygiene slowed the death rate. Medicine was at long last a burgeoning science capable of cures. The result was an increase of one hundred million people in Europe alone—as much as the entire European population had been in 1650.[15]

In the United States, the large corporations that belonged to the men who built America—Vanderbilt, Morgan, Rockefeller, and Carnegie—soared to new profits. The value of Carnegie's steel company grew from $6 million in 1896 to an astounding $40 million only four years later. Aluminum and other light alloys were developed, while the chemical industry created new processes and materials.

The "American system" of utilizing interchangeable parts became standard practice in all industrialized nations. Like steel, dynamite changed the face of the world, making possible mammoth excavations and epic construction projects like the Panama Canal and the Simplon Railway Tunnel through the Alps. In the thirty years from the initial marketing of dynamite, in 1867, the manufacture grew from eleven tons to 66,500 tons.[16]

Yet nowhere was progress as cutting-edge as in the armaments industry. Dynamite's success was turned toward military uses. Smokeless gunpowder, patented by dynamite inventor Alfred Nobel, made firing at the enemy from hidden locations a reality. The small-bore rifle, with improved trajectory and accuracy for shooting farther, came on the market, allowing warfare to take place from a distance. Automatic recoil for field guns, too, contributed to the streamlining and mechanization of warfare. Land and naval mines, torpedoes, and the future promise of the submarine gave military commanders reason to rejoice.

Each side could now kill the other without ever having to come close to the enemy. Even the czar recognized that it was impossible for Russia to catch up with technological advances, lamenting to his mother in a letter,

"Many strange things happen in this world. One reads about them and shrugs one's shoulders."[17]

∽

With colonies in North and South America, the Pacific, the entire Indian subcontinent, Africa and the Caribbean, Britain's empire was the gold standard of its day. The British colonial secretary Joseph Chamberlain spoke of "manifest destiny" as the key to empire and Britain's right to defend itself against any and all newcomers. Yet, by then, the crippling arms race had changed the complexion of imperial defense.

The German Empire under Kaiser Wilhelm II set the pace in armaments production with an increase of 79 percent, closely followed by czarist Russia with 75 percent. Britain, by far the largest of the imperial nations, increased its armaments and armed services by 47 percent, and France by 43 percent. The result was that by 1914 the German and Russian empires were the dominant land powers in Europe, with the British Royal Navy feeling the severe threat posed by imperial Germany.[18]

Naturally, arms required men to use them, and the Germans became the first to use conscription. The German Navy League, a special-interest group headed by Admiral Tirpitz for German expansionism, had the necessary backing of the Ruhr industrialists and armaments manufacturers, and held a cherished link directly to the Naval Bureau in Berlin. Soon, all continental Europe followed the German example. Conscription was used in propaganda to show how life as a man-at-arms could improve health and extend life. It also had the added benefit of making the armed forces accept poor pay, regimentation, and absolute obedience.[19]

With all these reserves of firepower and men, wars *needed* to be fought to prove sovereignty over colonies and superiority against rival empires on land and sea. The kaiser had been working since the turn of the century to award Germany its just place as a leader among nations. As early as 1906, Count Alfred von Schlieffen, a German staff general, had finalized his plan for the conquest of France: it should take a mere six weeks and seven-eighths of Germany's 1.5 million men under arms to defeat the French.

Yet the kaiser would need to swat away cousin Nicky's Russia, too; protect Austria-Hungary's interests; and break Britain's hundred-year stranglehold on international diplomacy at the point of a gun.

5

WAR

> If your own father came across with those from the other
> side you wouldn't hesitate to hurl a hand-grenade straight
> at him!
>
> —Erich Maria Remarque, *All Quiet on the Western Front*

Just before the guns of August 1914 were fired, Hildebrand
spent those last halcyon days of July visiting Cornelia in Paris. He graduated with good grades from the *Realgymnasium* in Dresden, and was due
to enroll at University of Frankfurt for the following September as an art
student.[1] At eighteen, he had grown a mustache and stood with impeccable posture. Though not tall, and seemingly rather thin, he was handsome, with deep-set brown eyes, brown hair, and an intelligent gaze.
Cornelius and Marie Gurlitt had every reason to be proud of their two
sons: Hildebrand's older brother Wilibald graduated that same June from
Leipzig University with his degree in music.

Cornelia was another matter altogether. In fact, the family was obliged
to turn away from the accomplishments of the sons to focus instead on
her. The task ahead was simply how to extricate Cornelia from Paris with
the minimum of fuss, for rumor had it that she had tottered off the rails
and become involved with a married man. As Hildebrand was always seen
as the "little one" by Cornelia, everyone thought that a visit from him would

be welcomed, where one from Wilibald might be seen as a threat to their sister's newfound freedom. From Hildebrand's perspective, his mission had the added benefit of letting him survey the active Paris art scene for himself.

Clearly, Cornelia had a rebellious streak and a dark side that concerned the family. Still, she had blossomed into a beautiful young woman. Her heart-shaped face and fine features belied the turmoil that brewed within. Deeply inspired by the works of the Bridge in Dresden, she'd decided to abandon her studies in 1909 against her parents' wishes. Despite her father's rather forceful suggestions that she become an academic, Cornelia—as obstinate as a mule refusing to be led—insisted that she had no intention of teaching art. Instead, she rather hoped to become an expressionist artist in her own right.[2] Here was a woman determined to live her life as she saw fit, a most modern woman even by today's standards, who would brook no opposition.

Like many artists, Cornelia felt her schooling did not prepare her for life as a painter. Armed with her firm resolve, she enrolled in Hans Nadler's art school in Gröden in 1910, where she met her lifelong friend Lotte Wahle.* From Gröden, she continued her studies at Hittfeld, near Hamburg, and struck up what may have been something more than a platonic friendship with dashing Rolf Donandt, son of the mayor.

By 1913, Cornelia was in Paris, seemingly living her dream among her fellow artists, while sharing the bed of the married Moravian-born, Austrian expressionist painter Anton Kolig. Her lover attracted the interest of Gustav Klimt in 1911, and it was Klimt who arranged for Kolig's travel scholarship to Paris.[3] Remembered today for his nudes of both sexes, Kolig would later paint *The Lament*—a large oil of a reclining male nude in the foreground with a small male and female nude couple kneeling and facing each other in the background. It was dedicated to Cornelia by a banner with her name written clearly painted beneath the reclining man. "I don't know how you lived and negotiated through those times of my affair with Cornelia," Kolig wrote his wife afterward. "In all events I came home

---

* Johanne Charlotte Wahle (1884–1952), expressionist artist and later partner of artist Conrad Felixmüller.

late to avoid seeing the pain I had inflicted on you . . . but how could I interfere with destiny?"[4]

What, if any, scenes erupted between Cornelia and Hildebrand when he was in Paris is anyone's guess. Yet a clue to her frame of mind has been left behind in the form of a small portrait. Cornelia painted her brother on paper purchased from an artists' dealer in Montparnasse, and in the image he appears almost Mephistophelian, with devilishly peaked eyebrows and a sinister smile. Nevertheless, whatever the personal dramas facing brother and sister, a far greater calamity loomed ahead.[5]

∽

At precisely the same time as the Gurlitt siblings were embroiled in their discussions, the world around them was disintegrating apace. On Sunday, June 28, 1914, at 10:45 a.m. in Sarajevo, Archduke Franz Ferdinand and his wife, Sophie, were assassinated, releasing the final brake on tensions between Austria-Hungary and the Kingdom of Serbia. Their assassin, Gavrilo Princip, aged only nineteen, was a member of the revolutionary organization Young Bosnia, which had been encouraged into action by the secret military society known unofficially as the Black Hand.

Although Franz Ferdinand's relationship with his uncle the emperor was characterized by "raging thunder and lightning," this final assassination in the twisted thread of assassinations stretching back some seventeen years was enough to create the irretrievable crisis that would lead to war. Franz Ferdinand was not particularly well liked, and was frequently described as *not* harboring an anatomical region called a heart. Still, Austria-Hungary demanded satisfaction like an aging duelist of the eighteenth century and planned to enfold Serbia into its midst just as it had done with Bosnia and Herzegovina in 1908. Russia, though severely weakened by the arms race, was obliged to stand shoulder to shoulder with Serbia as the world's foremost Slav power.[6]

"Within an hour or two of the tragedy becoming known, Budapest had changed to a city of mourning," English governess Beatrice Kelsey wrote in her diary that fateful day. "All entertainment was canceled and black streamers and flags at half-mast appeared on public buildings. The few people in the streets moved quietly and spoke in hushed voices."[7]

Wilhelmine Germany was prepared to embrace the moment. On July

5, the kaiser publicly pledged his "faithful support" to Emperor Franz Joseph should Austria-Hungary's punitive action against Serbia roll out Russian guns. Thereafter, the headlong plunge into war was assured. Austria-Hungary delivered its ultimatum to Serbia on July 23 and rejected the Serbian response that came three days later. Yet, in a margin note on a copy of the Austrian ultimatum, Kaiser Wilhelm remarked that the conciliatory message from the Serbs "dissipates every reason for war."[8] All that remained was a last-ditch attempt to keep Britain neutral.

∽

In Winston Churchill, the British prime minister Henry Herbert Asquith had a First Lord of the Admiralty with a real nose for battle. Churchill alone had a clear vision of the action that Britain should take. Consulting with the First Sea Lord, Prince Louis of Battenberg,* on that "very beautiful day" of July 26, Churchill gave the order that the fleet should *not* disperse after it completed its unrelated test mobilization maneuvers. He was determined "that the diplomatic situation should not get ahead of the naval situation and that the Grand Fleet would be in its War Station before Germany could know whether or not we should be in the war *and therefore if possible before we had decided ourselves.*"[9]

Equally significant, Churchill persuaded the prime minister to authorize the War Office and Admiralty to send a "warning telegram" to Germany to initiate an official precautionary period. This measure "invented by a genius . . . permitted certain measures to be taken on the *ipse dixit* of the Secretary of War without reference to the Cabinet . . . when time was the only thing that mattered."[10] The device was tailor-made for Asquith's deeply divided cabinet of "Little Englanders" and battle-hardened warhorses.

The German declaration of *Kriegesgefahr* (danger of war) followed on July 30. At noon the following day, the German ultimatum to Russia expired without response. The German ambassador to Russia was instructed to declare war on the country by five o'clock that afternoon. Yet

---

* He, like the rest of the royal family, would be compelled to change his name during the course of the war to something less "Germanic." Battenberg became Mountbatten, and King George V would head the House of Windsor, formerly the Royal House of Saxe-Coburg and Gotha.

the kaiser, who had been building a war economy with a fleet to rival Britain's, suddenly became "sick as a Tom-cat" at the prospect of a general all-
out war.* Wilhelm II wanted the laurels of winning a war without its
battles—the pleasure of saber rattling without drawing blood. Now that
war had nearly arrived, so did the bluster against the British in the margi-
nalia of his telegrams: "Aha! The common cheat" and "Rot!" and "Mr Grey
is a false dog"† and even "The rascal is crazy or an idiot!"[11] The kaiser suspected the British of duplicity.

Owing to Foreign Secretary Edward Grey's habitual avoidance of
straight talk, his written communiqué to the German ambassador in
London, Prince Lichnowsky, was misunderstood. The most earnest of
Anglophiles, Lichnowsky had, more than most, a willingness to believe that
the British wished to avert war. He erroneously signaled that the British
wanted peace.[12]

Nonetheless, militarily, it was too late. Mobilization had begun and
could not be altered. German troops were advancing toward Luxembourg.
A telegram wafting the prospect of peace at the British was drafted,
guaranteeing that troops would not cross the border before August 3 at 7:00
p.m.

In France, French general Joseph Joffre was incandescent with rage.
Recall the soldiers from their harvest furloughs; deploy more troops at
the frontiers; assure the cooperation of the British, he fulminated. Still,
the cabinet—the tenth in five years—was slow to react. War broke out on
Monday, August 3, on the western front.

∽

The European war, however, remained remote to most Americans. The
liberal internationalist president Woodrow Wilson was just old enough to
recall the devastation caused by America's Civil War, and like many, saw
the death of thousands of young men as a fruitless abomination. Worse still,
he felt powerless to stop a European war, believing that the arrogance of
the Europeans was hardwired into them. For Wilson, it was this arrogance

---

* Naturally, armies and navies cost money. The kaiser's navy created a national debt that had
  doubled in the previous ten years.
† Sir Edward Grey (1862–1933) was the British foreign secretary.

that led to the unremitting quest for power between nations and wars in Europe. Militarism was, in his opinion, a danger to democracy. If war came, it ought to have nothing to do with America.

As in Europe, many Americans went about their daily business, oblivious of the dangers that lay only days ahead. Nellie Bly, William Randolph Hearst's *New York World* former star reporter, boarded the RMS *Oceanic* and set sail from New York on August 1, bound for Vienna via Southampton and Le Havre. Her mission had little to do with journalism, and everything to do with saving herself from bankruptcy.[13]

Oskar Bondy, whose heirs would later become victims of Hildebrand's thieving cousin Wolfgang, was Nellie's good friend. Bondy was a Jewish Viennese businessman who had made his fortune in the sugar trade and had already agreed to pay off Bly's $10,000 mortgage on her 15 West Thirty-seventh Street home. Meanwhile, Nellie tried to recover from being swindled by the manager of the steel-barrel company she'd inherited from her husband.[14] Her intention was to meet Bondy in Vienna and agree on further financing for her Iron Clad Company, then return to New York within the month. That Austria had declared war on Serbia, and Germany was poised to invade Luxembourg four days before her departure, hadn't figured remotely in her calculations. War, obviously, did not hold the same fear for her as bankruptcy.

When it was rumored aboard ship that the Germans would attack and steal the $4 million in gold in the cargo hold, "I hope they do" was Nellie's reply. "It will be a fine experience."[15]

☙

With the declaration of war against Serbia, Cornelia's lover Anton Kolig knew he had to return to Austria-Hungary at once. Whether it was his determination to leave Paris first or Hildebrand's pleading with Cornelia that ended their affair, we shall never know. Nonetheless, by July 29 Kolig and his wife were on a train to Vienna, while Hildebrand and Cornelia made their way back across a beleaguered Belgium to Cologne, and on to Dresden. The Gurlitt siblings were potentially in the gravest danger, as German troops were already advancing on the Belgian border. On Tuesday, August 4, 1914, Britain declared war on Germany. The final diplomatic panic of five days to avert war probably saved Cornelia and Hildebrand from disaster. They had arrived back safely in Dresden. The question was, as a good Pan-Germanist would Hildebrand enlist?

∽

Each European city greeted the war with its own brand of euphoria. "Overpowered by stormy enthusiasm," Hitler wrote, "I fell down on my knees and thanked Heaven from an overflowing heart for granting me the good fortune to live at this time."[16] In Berlin, a special edition of the newspaper carried the headline "The Blessing of Arms." According to the editorial, "It is a joy to be alive. . . . The sword which has been forced into our hand will not be sheathed until our aims are won." Others who were left of center persuasion, however, were depressed, fearing huge losses of German and international workers.[17]

One hour after the German invasion of Belgium, the Belgian royal family rode through Brussels. Houses lining the streets were decorated with garlands of flowers and Belgian flags. People flocked outdoors to cheer. Strangers greeted one another as old friends. The people cried "Down with the Germans! Death to the assassins! *Vive la Belgique indépendante!*" The Austrian ambassador watched the royal procession from the parliament's windows, wiping the tears from his eyes.[18]

The scene in Paris varied only in the color of the uniforms saluted. French soldiers in their full-dress red trousers and dark blue tunics chanted as they marched: *"c'est l'Alsace et la Lorraine, c'est l'Alsace qu'il nous faut, oh, oh, oh, OH!"* At 6:15 p.m., Myron Herrick, the American ambassador in Paris, telephoned Premier Viviani to tell him, in a cracking voice, that he had just received a request to hoist the American flag over the German embassy. He would accept the charge, but must refuse to raise the flag.[19]

In London, the mood was more somber. Britain was a nation that was deeply divided by class, often visibly discerned by the type of hat you wore to determine your social status. Those who wore cloth caps or bonnets were likely to be living in ramshackle terrace houses or dark brick tenements if they lived in towns or cities, laboring down coal mines or in deafening factories. The lucky ones lived in farmworkers' accommodations on country estates, working for masters who sported boaters, bowlers, or toppers. As in France and Germany, the British working classes were clamoring for better wages and living standards. After all, most working-class men lived only to the age of forty-nine, women to the age of fifty-three. Many were malnourished, had rickets, or had lungs that rattled loudly with tuberculosis.[20]

The cabinet was no less divided. Two ministers—Lord Morley and John Burns—had resigned, while that dominant Welsh force of nature David Lloyd George havered. Margot Asquith, the prime minister's wife, recalled watching the mantel clock in the Cabinet Room at 10 Downing Street until 11:00 p.m. on August 3. Deeply troubled, she left shortly after midnight and mounted the stairs. The last image she saw was a smiling Winston Churchill bounding toward the double doors of the Cabinet Room.[21]

When the kaiser heard that Britain had declared war, he moaned disingenuously, "If only someone had told me beforehand that England would take up arms against us!"[22] The greatest pity of it all was that both sides firmly believed, and told their people, that the soldiers would all be home for Christmas.

∽

Within days, although too late to see the first Great Retreat of the Allies from Mons on August 23, 1914, and the invasion of France, Wilibald Gurlitt was attached as an officer to the List Company of the Hundredth Regiment of the Twenty-Third Reserve Division, Twelfth (Royal Saxon) Reserve Corps of the Fourth Army.[23] Hildebrand had enrolled at University of Frankfurt as planned, but during the first semester was assessed and conscripted into the army in Dresden. By 1915, he joined his brother, but in the Seventh Company of the same Hundredth Regiment, as a fresh-faced lieutenant.[24]

On the eastern front, in early September, the Russian army had been defeated at Tannenberg near East Prussia by Field Marshal Paul von Hindenburg and General Erich Ludendorff's Eighth Army.[25] Within the week, the massacre of Russia's First Army occurred in East Prussia at the Masurian Lakes.* Over 170,000 Russians were killed, wounded, missing, or prisoners of war out of a total Russian contingent of 490,000 men.

September was a terrible month for Cornelia, too. She had heard that her special friend Rolf Donandt had fallen at the Battle of the Marne on

---

* Today situated in Poland.

the first day. Most likely realizing the enormity of the losses Germany might sustain during the war, and how she could possibly lose both of her brothers, Cornelia felt she, too, should enter the fray. Again to some parental dismay, Cornelia volunteered for training as a Red Cross nurse, before being posted to the bloodiest theater of the war, the eastern front at Vilna.*

By October, Germany had persuaded the decaying Ottoman Empire to enter as an ally in the hope of depriving Russia of its longed-for warm-water port. Meanwhile Germany planned to invade India.[26] Though no longer the scourge of Europe, the Ottoman Empire was a gigantic region spanning the entire Middle East, including vast swaths of Saudi Arabia to the Caucasus Mountains of Russia and ancient Mesopotamia and into what is today modern Iraq.

By the third month of the war, the trench had become every soldier's home or stinking, muddy cold coffin. Those who still believed that they would be home for Christmas knew instinctively that this was a war of attrition. When the First Battle of Artois began, on December 17, 1914, Cornelia wrote to Wilibald, not knowing where he was or how he and Hildebrand were coping. Naturally, soldiers' letters were censored, for fear that they might reveal some crucial information about the combat or reinforcements. She had no way of knowing that her brothers were at Artois the day she wrote. The letter showed a much calmer Cornelia, dedicated to her fourteen-or-fifteen-hour days, perhaps with only three hours off between shifts. She claimed she painted when possible. She feared that her letter would not reach Wilibald before Christmas, but immediately stated, without emotion, that she would be missing Christmas Eve herself, and that this Christmas sharply contrasted with the past. Then she thought of those who were in trenches, "wet and hungry and tired and so brave and pleased to be simply alive," and begged Wilibald to take care of himself in this "hostile land" and have the "best, most German Christmas celebration ever, and perhaps with lights and music."[27]

The last thing she wrote was "I have had a very personal letter from our Putz [Hildebrand] wondering why men, like him, like his comrades and his superiors, have to come out for the first time [into battle] and find

---

* Vilnius, Lithuania, today.

the best way instinctively and with ease to apply themselves to their vo-
cations. I am only sad that you are not with him."[28]

∽

That same month, the stranded Nellie Bly's articles from the Austrian front
appeared in the *New York World*. The return to her old job was down to
her former boss and Hearst's right-hand man, Arthur Brisbane. While
Brisbane wanted to be helpful, having a reliable eyewitness account of the
carnage was irresistible. After all, both he and Hearst learned during the
Spanish-American War that war sells newspapers, and despite the president's reticence to become involved, Americans of European origin were
mightily interested in the outcome.[29]

Bly was lucky with her Viennese connections. Her benefactor Oskar
Bondy introduced her into Austrian high society, and soon the US ambassador to Austria, Frederic C. Penfield, found himself vouching for Bly to
Ritter Oskar von Montlong, press department chief of the Austro-Hungarian
Foreign Ministry.[30] Writing from the front near the fortress town of
Przemyśl at the Polish-Czech border, Bly portrayed a penned-in garrison
of 150,000 Austrian soldiers whose deprivation and misery were beyond
imagining. The constant cannonading, horses bleeding to death among
the human corpses, assailed her senses. The stench of death and utter
filth at the front line rocked her back. "I write for the sake of humanity," Bly
stated.[31]

∽

New Year's Day 1915 came and went without any sign of the fighting
abating. Nineteen fourteen had seen Mons, the First Battle of the Marne,
the First Battle of Ypres, the British entering Basra, and high-seas battles
as far afield as the Falkland Islands. The news pages of the London papers
reflected a troubled nation at home and abroad. News from the home front
was dominated by strikes, news from abroad by death and destruction. On
January 19, the first zeppelin attack hit Great Yarmouth and King's Lynn
in Norfolk, killing five civilians. It was the first airborne attack on British
soil.

The Gurlitt family had worrying news, too. Cholera had broken out in
the Hundredth Regiment, and two soldiers were already dead. Worse was

still to come. Wilibald had been wounded, and according to the first notice was on the island fortress of Château d'Oléron, off the coast of France in the Atlantic. Their distress was soon relieved, when a "correction" to the earlier telegram came through in the lists of February 15 that Wilibald was mistakenly reported as a prisoner. Yet until he was finally sent home, over a month later, they understandably fretted about which report to believe. For his parents, the waiting seemed nearly intolerable. Though Wilibald had obviously been through hell, Cornelius and Marie were relieved that he had been only "lightly" wounded in the leg.[32]

✐

Still, the war pulverized millions of fighting men. President Woodrow Wilson remained adamant that the United States must maintain its policy of neutrality; he had sought the personal assurances of the kaiser that Germany would halt the use of unrestricted warfare against neutral shipping. The kaiser was happy to comply. It came as a shock, therefore, to the president when the Cunard liner *Lusitania*, bound for Liverpool, was sunk on May 7.

On September 25, Hildebrand Gurlitt took part against the "great allied offensive" at the Second Battle of Champagne, ten days after his twentieth birthday. The offensive was quickly bogged down in the face of a determined and better-equipped enemy. According to the German general Erich von Falkenhayn, there were undiminished and furious bombardments in Champagne on the twenty-fourth and in Flanders on September 25. The "great allied offensive" produced no definitive advance, and the credit, according to Falkenhayn, belonged to the German soldiers. "It must not be forgotten that the German soldier on the Western Front is entitled to most of the credit for the fact that the reinforcements from the East came up in time. His marvelous resistance in the pitifully shattered positions . . . Not content with that, he attacked with magnificent self-sacrifice the enemy masses surging over and around him."[33]

Less than a month later, on October 15, 1915, Nurse Edith Cavell was executed by a firing squad in Brussels for having aided the escape of stranded British soldiers. Under the strict letter of military law, the Germans felt justified in ordering her execution. They were unprepared, however, for the outcry and revulsion that followed. Franz von Rintelen, a

German prisoner of war at Donington Hall in England, then used as a prison camp, wrote, "The news of the, shall I call it, grotesque, [*sic*] execution of Nurse Cavell seemed most revolting . . . [German] officers openly expressed themselves that they would have flatly refused, had they been called upon, to order a firing squad to shoot a woman; others, like myself were grieved as well on the gross miscalculation of the British spirit."[34]

Nurse Cavell could well have been the patriotic Cornelia Gurlitt.

6

GURLITT'S STRUGGLE

> There is nothing in the world more shameful than establishing one's self on lies and fables.
>
> —Johann Wolfgang von Goethe

MANY WHO FOUGHT IN THE GREAT WAR WERE SCARRED, NOT ONLY by their injuries, but also by the emotional and mental trials they were made to endure. The sight of such wholesale slaughter to gain a few feet of land, to be bogged down in a congealed aspic of blood and guts and mud without any idea of when or how their ordeal would end, twisted many minds and made it impossible for even time to heal their wounds.

Adolf Hitler was the exception. A fanatical believer in the Pan-German ideal, he would never waver from his absolute faith in German superiority. He was already twisted with lethal racial hatred and a warped worldview. The Great War was simply the making of him and the beginning of his struggle. He proclaimed during a speech in 1934 that the Great War created a "stupendous impression . . . upon me . . . the greatest of all experiences."[1] It also kindled his appreciation of politics—although initially as a Communist, according to a fellow dispatch rider, Hans Mend.[2] The interest was naturally short-lived, as Hitler was seeking to create a new political reality to reflect his personal convictions.

Hitler volunteered and enrolled in the First Company of the Sixteenth Bavarian Reserve Infantry Regiment, known as the List Regiment. His comrades included Rudolf Hess; regimental clerk Sergeant-Major Max Amann (later the Nazi Party's* and Hitler's business manager); and fellow dispatch rider and "wholesome son of the soil" Hans Mend—who would write a best-selling book entitled *Adolf Hitler im Felde 1914–1918*. Published in 1931, it caused some considerable embarrassment.† Their battalion adjutant was Lieutenant Gutmann, a Jewish typewriter manufacturer from Nuremberg, who recommended Hitler for his Iron Cross second class at Christmas 1914.[3]

Hans Mend claimed that Hitler "never had anything to do with guns." He was "a runner based behind the lines at regimental headquarters. Every two or three days he would have to deliver a message; the rest of the time he spent 'in back,' painting, talking politics, and having altercations." Mend claimed that Hitler was soon known as "crazy Adolf" and claimed that the future despot "struck me as a psychopath from the start . . . often flew into a rage when contradicted, throwing himself on the ground and frothing at the mouth."[4]

Yet Hitler was awarded an Iron Cross first class, on August 4, 1918—a highly unusual distinction for a mere corporal. While the official history of the List Regiment is silent on Hitler's military exploits, it was claimed that he single-handedly captured fifteen (others claimed ten or twelve) French soldiers. Or was it Englishmen?[5] Their nationality seemed immaterial to the honor, just like his reasons for refusing promotion.

∽

Hildebrand Gurlitt provided an unusual insight into his wartime struggle.[6] By February 1916 at Verdun, the war of attrition had firmly set in and German impatience was laid bare. Operation *Gericht*—or Judgment—was set in motion against the French on what was to become aptly known as *Mort-Homme* (Dead Man's) Ridge. Hildebrand's regiment moved on from the Second Battle of Champagne to Verdun—the longest battle of the Great War. The Battle of Verdun lasted over ten months, costing the lives of more than a million men. Only the attempted push at the Battle of the Somme

---

* The Nazi Party was known as the NSDAP, or National Socialist German Workers' Party.
† Mend would also write a statement to the Abwehr called the *Mend-Protokoll*, accusing Hitler of homosexuality.

by the British and Commonwealth soldiers gave some relief from starvation and death to the French.

Then February 1916 brought salvation. Unsurprisingly, given the conditions at Verdun and Gurlitt's obvious reluctance to fight, he seemed to be suffering from some sort of psychological breakdown or shell shock, and was sent home to rest. In a letter to Wilibald dated May 14, 1916, Hildebrand is quite chatty. Still based at his parents' home some three months later, he writes cockily, "I am faring much better, the war, which so far has cost me little time (I was spared ¾ of a year of school and the year of service) and has not torn me away from work."[7]

Hildebrand's arrogance becomes more tempered when he is trying to excuse himself to his brother for not writing. "Apart from a certain laziness" becomes a familiar refrain in all his letters; Hildebrand blames his silence on the gulf of "experiences that lie between us." Then, confusedly, he explains this away with "at least essentially you have not changed as any change would separate us even more, but as long as I can remember you have always been reliable, unchangeable. But for me it's different."

Hildebrand had changed. He "had to go through a time of self-discovery, conscription, first term at university and war" and grew "from a pupil who had to be afraid of every teacher, to becoming a lieutenant."[8] Consumed with a desire to be close to his siblings again, he tries to speak to Wilibald through music: "Every sound, every piece of music reminds me of you and I am not forgetting that your Bach Organ Sonatas imparted a first understanding of music to me."

Speaking of his sister, he says, "Things are more difficult for Eitl. She expects more from others than I who can tolerate anything from anybody. And you also know that her assuredness and independence have made her confessor for all the miserable torments of the soul of the other nurses and the young volunteer war carers." Still, Hildebrand fears that "she is now alone again in the endless space known only to her."

Turning to his future, he says, "I want to seek my salvation in art history and initially as a museum administrator. I am trying to gain a lot of knowledge about paintings and buildings in my spare time. Unfortunately one can and may not make any plans. . . . I have no greater wish than to be together with my two siblings."[9]

It would be years before any of Hildebrand's wishes would come true.

Returning briefly to his regiment at Verdun, he was overwhelmed by the inhumanity and destruction surrounding him and sustained "another light wound." This time, it was to a finger on his writing hand, and he was home, yet again, for the summer. "My finger has almost healed and I am able to write." It was August 1916 when he wrote to Wilibald, "I am almost feeling ashamed, when I am sitting at home at my desk and think of my two siblings. . . . It might sound incredible to you, but everything will still be here, when you both return."[10]

The letter invites the question: Was his injury self-inflicted? Given the horrors of Verdun and the length of time that Hildebrand was home, it is probable; otherwise more than his finger would have been wounded. Still, he would never return to full combat duty. Instead, he was seconded to a heritage-conservation unit in Belgium as one of Germany's Monuments Men, charged with safeguarding art in the occupied territories, just behind the front line. While hardly assuring his personal safety, as protecting art was a perilous business, it was a vast improvement on trench warfare.

∽

How did he get so lucky? In the years leading up to the war, his father had been working with the leading force in conservation heritage in Germany, Paul Clemen, professor of art history at University of Bonn. Clemen was the German chief of Art Preservation and Monuments, actively working in Belgium with a specialist colony of German art historians and artists to preserve architecture and artifacts from destruction. It was on Clemen's model—described in his groundbreaking work of 1919, *Kunstschutz im Krieg* (*Art Preservation During War*)—that the heroic World War II Monuments Men were conceived. Until very recently, Germans from the Great War were worshiped with the same veneration as their later Allied colleagues.[11]

"The German Monuments Men [of the Great War] were no art looters like Denon,"* wrote a German historian in 1957, "but were men who found themselves first on the scene with the purpose of protecting art, and whose

---

* Napoleon's art historian, Jean Dominique Vivant Denon, joined him on his Egyptian campaign. In 1802 he was made Baron Denon, director of the Musée Centrale des Arts (the modern Louvre), working tirelessly to requisition artworks throughout Napoleon's empire in the grand looting campaigns.

integrity is beyond doubt, as they never thought about self-enrichment, not for their museums nor their universities, not even for the State."[12]

Indeed, Clemen and Cornelius Gurlitt both worked in Belgium without remuneration. Young architects received five marks as a per diem, often advanced by Clemen personally.[13] During the carnage on the western front, these men of the arts—artists, art-history students, art dealers, writers, archivists, librarians—all formed a hyperactive colony cataloguing *everything* in public collections in the occupied territories of France and Belgium while "protecting monuments." With some reason, they also returned to Germany everything that was deemed to have been stolen from the German principalities during the Napoleonic Wars, a century earlier. It was an example that stood Hildebrand in good stead for the future.

Yet Clemen, Cornelius, and others who documented the efforts of the Great War's German Monuments Men omitted such salient facts as the theft of church bells and intentional destruction of the library at Louvain— that ancient and great seat of Catholic learning since the days of King Philip II of Spain (1527–1598). The historic library had been purposefully targeted as an act of vandalism and immolation in August 1914 in reprisal for Belgian sharpshooters resisting the first onslaught of German troops.[14]

Clemen and Gurlitt knew about that act of barbarity and others, too. Nevertheless, the intended propaganda uses to which the kaiser wanted to put their "preservation" program meant that they looked the other way. Both were devoted Pan-Germanists. Both knew that art was the bedrock of any culture. Both believed that German culture surpassed all others combined.[15] Ergo, no criticism of their work on the western front was considered appropriate.

Nonetheless, reproach *was* leveled at these "altruistic" art saviors by the French. When in 1870–71 the German soldier looted by *gourmandise*, in 1914–18 "the professors of art—historians, museum curators, national librarians—the intelligentsia of Germany—looted with a single-mindedness settled between them before the war began."[16] There was little pillaging by the lowly private in the Great War. Few wall clocks or jewels went missing in an unexplained fashion. Instead, this more understandable and opportunistic crime was replaced by a military system and order that led directly to spoliation. Hitler, too, took note.

In Saint-Quentin, located in the occupied province of Aisne, in France, works of art "safeguarded" by a German soldier were restored to the town only in 1998. The museum at Douai located the painting *La Fille du Pecheur* (*The Fisherman's Daughter*), missing since the Great War, at a Swiss auction in 2000.[17] In what becomes a repetitive act of reinstatement, most artworks were restored to these occupied towns by the vigilance of those searching for them—*not* by the actions of those who claimed to have safeguarded them.

✑

In Belgium, unlike France, the image of the officer-looter was far more prevalent—with the Ghent Altarpiece* standing as the most outrageous example of state-sponsored spoliation. Originally painted by the van Eyck brothers in the early fifteenth century, the altarpiece is deemed to be one of the most important works of art ever created.

First stolen by Napoleon's army in 1812, it was restored to the Ghent cathedral after the Battle of Waterloo. Two of the painting's wings (not including Adam and Eve) were pawned by the diocese that same year to raise funds for repairs to the historic fabric of the building; but when the cathedral failed to redeem the panels four years later, they were sold to an English collector. Eventually, he offered them to the king of Prussia. When it was exhibited in the Gemäldegalerie in Berlin nearly a century later, the kaiser decided unilaterally that the rest of the altarpiece should be reunited with its two wings.

✑

Clemen set up shop in Brussels and swiftly assembled a colony of military and nonmilitary art experts. A monthly scholarly journal, entitled *Der Belfried* (*The Belfry*), became the propaganda tool and the primary instrument of Germany's *Flamenpolitik* (Flemish cultural politics). Between 1915 and 1917, Cornelius Gurlitt published several articles in *Der Belfried* specifically addressing the significance of Walloon art† and Cistercian monasteries. Together with Clemen, he also wrote *The Cistercian Mon-*

---

* Also known as *The Adoration of the Lamb*, it was looted again in World War II and found in the Altaussee salt mine.

† From the French-speaking regions of Belgium.

asteries in Belgium. A Commission from the Kaiser's German General Government in Belgium.[18]

Always leading the way, and seemingly omnipresent, Clemen was soon joined by scores of archaeologists, like Gerhard Bersu; architects and art historians, including Cornelius Gurlitt and Wilhelm Hausenstein; and museum curators, such as Edwin Hensler (also from Dresden), Wilhelm Köhler from Weimar, August Griesbach, and Carl Epstein. While the great art-history professor Heinrich Wölfflin was "too busy" to join his former students in Brussels and The Hague, he profited nevertheless from their intimate knowledge, publishing his textbook on art history.

Hildebrand, a mere art student and junior officer, would have been allotted duties not dissimilar to those of the junior Monuments Men of World War II: rescuing art from bombed-out buildings or precarious places, assisting in assessing which buildings should be marked as off-limits, and cataloguing the artifacts on the orders of his commanders.

He would have been among those whom Clemen approved to give talks on Flemish versus French (Walloon) visual arts to Belgians—so it was claimed—to demonstrate the Germans' philanthropic purpose. Oblivious of the Belgian viewpoint, Griesbach wrote after one such talk, "Brussels seems perfectly calm and quiet, and even towns which have suffered greatly like Louvain, their ruins seem far less terrifying than before. Besides, the more you get used to them, the more I believe these objects could well serve a future tourism industry."[19]

The administrative head of this group of art connoisseurs was the art dealer Alfred Flechtheim, who was in many ways the most knowledgeable of them all, and the least likely to succumb to petty academic jealousies. More significantly, Flechtheim's knowledge across artistic schools, his international reputation, his affable manner, his understanding of the world art markets, his ability to train art connoisseurs and dealers alike, and his impeccable taste made him a natural for the position.[20] Flechtheim would become one of Gurlitt's first victims in the 1930s.

Hildebrand would have met Flechtheim several times during the course of his Belgian sojourn. As a junior officer and an art student, he should have equally stood in awe of such an acknowledged expert. Gurlitt's thirst for knowledge about art, his time at the art colony in Brussels—and particularly at Flechtheim's knee—would prove to be an extremely useful learning experience in the next war.

∽

Belgium was also a home away from home for German artists. They proliferated among the Red Cross: Erich Heckel, Ernst Morwitz, Max Claus, Otto Herbig, Curt Glaser, and the renowned Max Beckmann to name some. Women art dealers, too, like Grete Ring (who later emigrated to England), and Paula Deetjens, the official photographer for the Folkwang Museum in Hagen, headed up the list of female notables working directly under Clemen. Their task was to catalogue and comment on *everything*.

As incredible as it may seem, their stated purpose was to mark out acquisitions for Germany after the war was won. The word "acquisition" was to be interpreted as a prelude to annexation by Germany. Karl Ernst Osthaus, founder of the Folkwang Museum, published a reply to his *Flamenpolitik* colleague Henry van de Velde in an open letter in the *Frankfurter Zeitung* that it was senseless to hide Germany's annexation aims in Belgium; that Walloon or French culture was not a pale copy of German culture, as van de Velde pretended; and that *Flamenpolitik*'s sole purpose was to legitimize the perception at home, in Belgium, and abroad. The permanent annexation of Belgium was considered nothing more than reuniting "Germans of blood."[21]

Flamenpolitik segregated all art and architecture in Belgium as either French Walloon or Flemish—a first step in indoctrinating the Belgians to the notion that the Flemish were German by culture. The Flemish art of Breughel, van Eyck, Bouts, Bosch, Ensor, Rubens, and others was deemed superior to the Walloon equivalent.

According to Cornelius Gurlitt, "failing to find a veritable school of art they [Walloons] exiled themselves abroad." Whether by "genetic disposition" or by "intellectual flexibility" or their "penchant for novelty" or "openness to the Renaissance," the Walloon artist "certainly distinguished himself from the Flemish artist, but he fears to insist on making the important ethnic differences between himself and the French, which also separates him from the Fleming . . . and this is due to his fear of reviving and supporting his German origins."[22] Cornelius's remarks are among the first to classify Flemish art and architecture as essentially German in origin, and base the difference on race and nationality.

This dismemberment of French Walloon from Flemish art ignored history. It discarded local influences; the shared Burgundian origins with Lorraine; the fusion of what was "Latin" or "Germanic"; the origins of modern Belgium as a Spanish Habsburg colony at war against its overlord Spain for nearly a century before its independence; and international influences beyond France or Germany. To be German and be part of German culture was to be superior in the occupier's eyes; to have other origins made the Belgians, and their art, inferior.

⁂

At a stroke, fine art, as the most visible form of culture at the time, became the foundation and silent battleground for propaganda on both the western and eastern fronts. In the War Press Office, art historians and art critics were drafted to head up operations. The colony of art historians in occupied Belgium and France fed information back to Berlin, to men like Hermann Voss, assistant curator at the Leipzig Museum prior to the war, for his onward dissemination to the army and the public. On the eastern front, art critic Paul Fechter, feuilleton editor of the *Deutschen Allgemeinen Zeitung*, headed up the War Press Office in Vilna.[23]

These Monuments Men, with the combined efforts of the War Press Office, headquartered in Berlin, were a reflection of the golden thread running through Wilhelmine Germany, proving that Germany merited its place at the head of the table of great nations. Yet Pan-Germanism would not allow any other culture or race its own merits. By the time Hildebrand had been seconded to the German art unit in Brussels, the first hint of ingrained German anti-Semitism was already under way: the *Judenzählung*, or census of Jews in the military. Jews like Flechtheim were good enough to fight, but were never *real* Germans.

The *Judenzählung* took place in the wake of the 1916 article by the Nazi philosopher Bruno Bauch entitled "On the Concept of the Nation," in his journal *Kantstudien*. Jews were called *fremdvölkisch*—an alien people who would find it difficult to love a German homeland as much as true Germans. He understood why earlier generations had barred Jews from owning land and other property. When the inevitable furor erupted among

German philosophers, both Jewish and non-Jewish, Bauch resigned his editorship and position in the Kant Society, balking at the idea that he was somehow anti-Semitic.[24]

❦

The Gurlitt sons were not part of the *Judenzählung* despite having a Jewish grandmother. In fact, Hildebrand was entirely oblivious of the problematic issue of "Jewish blood" coursing through his veins and continued blithely cataloguing Belgian art and architecture as a true son of German soil.

Hildebrand wrote breezily to Wilibald on September 17, 1917, shortly after his twenty-first birthday, "After short, accidental and aimless expeditions as the war brings . . . I've arrived at the impression that I have seen much: Paintings—(Memling, Rembrandt, Breughel, all German, modern French, Expressionists) Architecture—(in Belgium, Bamberg, Würzburg, Cologne) and many cities where I have lived for a while (Posen, Augsburg, Würzburg, Brussels, Sedan)."[25] Of course, his letters were censored by the military, so any further detail would have been struck out with a thick black marker even if it was included.

A year earlier, in the summer of 1916, Cornelia wrote that Hildebrand was "often very depressed and sad" and helped himself out of his misery by writing in "mighty phrases."[26] Had he suffered a psychological relapse? His September 1917 letter to Wilibald shows signs of both, claiming, "I'm shoring myself up against the 'big one,' that epidemic of war diseases: going mad. I hope so far that certainly intellectually I've been able to maintain my alertness; not only in the field of battle and also now more and more elsewhere."

His way of compensating was to isolate himself "with an ever greater loneliness." In Dresden, "in discussions with our parents, Hanns,* Eitl or Gertrud that evidence of another life exists for me to lead, and that my sense of foreboding . . . is nonsense, and that I can think of my art and construct a life around it, yet this was nothing but an absurdity."[27]

Reading voraciously, Hildebrand carried the works of Goethe, Hölderin, Balzac, Dostoyevsky, and the poet Rilke with him. "You will now ask what have you made from all those books, those experiences, those people and

---

* Hanns was Hildebrand's Jewish friend. Gertrud was Wilibald's future wife.

I could not even with the threat of torture answer you," he wrote. "I have not been lazy, truly not. . . . I have always searched, throughout this dreary situation, and with my inquisitive eyes have considered, that I have used each free minute in search of an answer. . . . I have not really been lazy, honestly." He continues in much the same vein for another half page, imploring his brother to believe again and again that he has not been lazy.

Then suddenly, he bursts out with, "The ever precarious future calls us the 'Prey of the Moment,' a cannibalistic term, so ravenous, isn't that so?" In ever-increasing tiny circles, he reasons through the "dreariness" and "laziness," trying to "think of a way of how we can live [in peace] with mankind, how we must yet live, not in discord. It is reflecting on this that one has the greatest fear—about how one should then live."

The repetition and half sentences show clearly a young man in distress. He meanders through his mind, contradicting himself, repeating thoughts in different ways, before finally bursting forth with, "Here I am reading Nietzsche narrowly. It is your fault that I am reading him with a strange mistrust. . . . It is on yours and Eitl's conscience that I never experience this [joy of discovery], as I know your opinion on everything, which basically is foreign to me. . . . I don't give a damn. . . . You'd say, 'How have you fallen so low?' Curse them, I say to all the older siblings!!"[28]

This is hardly a letter from a young man at ease with life or his situation. Nietzsche naturally troubles him most, because he finds a kinship with the philosopher whom both his brother and sister had rejected. It was once said that "only a conscious National Socialist [Nazi] can completely understand Nietzsche." To compound Hildebrand's confusion, his other great writer of the moment, Tolstoy, had thought that Nietzsche was absurd.

∽

Nietzsche, however, was highly relevant to the times. He had arrived at the idea of "crisis through art history" as taught by his colleague and great friend Jakob Burckhardt. While attending Burckhardt's lectures "On the Study of History" at the University of Basel, describing the historical powers of state, culture, and religion, Nietzsche latched on to what Burckhardt described as "the theory of storms." This characterization of history as a theatrical work of competing and conflicting powers, alternately suppressed then released, claimed that "the suppressed power can either lose or enhance its resilience in the process. . . . Either it is suppressed, whereupon the ruling power, if it is a wise one, will find some remedy . . . A crisis in the whole state of things is produced. . . . The historical process is suddenly accelerated in terrifying fashion. Developments which otherwise take centuries seem to flit by like phantoms."[29]

Both Burckhardt and Nietzsche were dabbling in the dark metaphysics of a heroic Schopenhauerian philosophy. Both believed that "the crisis itself is an expedient of nature, like a fever, and the fanaticisms are signs that there still exist for men things they prize more than life and property."[30] This is what troubled Hildebrand: *Would the drive to make all of Europe bow to Germany's will overshadow his entire life?*

In the fervor of France's defeat in 1871, Nietzsche wrote, "For an unconscionably long time powerful forces from the outside have compelled the German spirit, which had vegetated in barbaric formlessness. . . . But at long last the German spirit may stand before the other nations, free of the leading strings of Romanized culture."[31]

Early Nietzsche writings were influenced by an earlier philosopher and political activist, Johann Gottlieb Fichte. The first to expand on the need for Germany to act and react as one nation in his *Addresses to the German Nation* in 1807—a critical year in the battle against Napoleon—Fichte became the model for many art historians serving over a century later in the Great War. Indeed, the Fichte Society of 1914 was founded amid patriotic fervor. It saw itself as a "comprehensive, folkish, educational community which in all its institutions aims at educating the German into being German."[32]

൙

Hildebrand soon suffered another breakdown. In October 1917 he wrote that he was in Mannheim at a sanatorium "due to my nerves and some personal matters, which are too boring to write about, and shall remain in Königsbrück for a while or go to Eitl, where I have been offered a job with the press."[33]

How had Hildebrand been rescued again and given the opportunity of sitting out the rest of the war in one of the best jobs in the East behind the front line? Had his father prevailed on Clemen to keep Hildebrand away from snipers in Sedan? Hardly. Cornelia was still stationed as a nurse in

Vilna on the eastern front. It was she who arranged for Hildebrand to receive the personal stamp of approval from the press office art critic and boss, Paul Fechter.

Earlier that year, Cornelia wrote that she was unable to "go to Mannheim," presumably to see Hildebrand, as their mother was ill. Hildebrand was at the sanatorium for some eight months before he wrote his own letter.[34] She saw it as her duty to somehow rescue her little brother, and through a combination of desperation and delight, Cornelia ultimately secured Hildebrand a position as a writer of dispatches from the eastern front. The family had no suspicion that she was Fechter's mistress.

By the time that the first American boots hit European soil in April 1917, prompted by the final piece of news that Germany had been coercing Mexico into declaring war on the United States,* Wilibald received a letter from his sister that made her love for Fechter clear. "I love my life here—it's such a beautiful life compared to earlier," Cornelia enthused. "At the heart of it all is a journalist . . . who has also studied philosophy, and is also very learned and with a different understanding, which I believe was also my own whenever I spoke of art. Perhaps this lovely man will later convey his knowledge to me which I so easily and in such a childlike way worship."[35]

⁂

With the weight of battle lifted from his shoulders, Hildebrand seemed cheerier. Though there is no mention of the United States's entry into the war, it is clear that he is accepting his—and Germany's—fate more phlegmatically. "Do you actually know what my new plans for the future are?" he asked Wilibald. Replying to his own question, he wrote of settling "in some city with modern life and major industry, in Bremen or Essen etc.; and there try to influence work via a small museum." There, he believed, art could be used as an "enticement" for everything spiritual.

Why did he want to go to a city with major industry? "I hope to encounter the fewest obstacles and find the greatest demand due to well-

---

* The desire of England and France to bring the United States into the war resulted in a long-running campaign involving propaganda, espionage, and desperation, giving America its well-deserved isolationist badge. It forms one of the most interesting and significant chapters of the war of 1914–18, which sadly cannot be done justice here.

respected art institutions. Of course, these are all castles in the air."
Reverting to his nervy state, he continued, "Above all I want to continue
my PhD in art history and then see what might happen. Of course I have
no idea where I will study, but I just wanted to talk to you about it."[36]

That October, Vladimir Lenin and his Bolsheviks seized power in the
Second Russian Revolution,* sealing the end of hostilities with Russia.
The cease-fire came into effect only on December 15, 1917. Hildebrand's
Christmas letter to Wilibald, dated December 2, showed that he, however,
did not believe in the peace. His mental state remained fragile. Gone were
his notions of Pan-Germanism and the greatness of the German arts. He
comes across as mentally exhausted, fragile, and as though he hardly knows
where to turn. The Christmas letter is forlorn: "It is snowing outside and it
is the Advent season and [I] could almost try to have hope again. But what
for? For peace? I do not think that any message of peace will reach mankind
in the near future; sure it is possible that they get fed up with shooting for
a while, but so long as people do not learn to understand that [it is] not
enemies or states etc . . . [or] the war, but that everyone is guilty, and because
everyone has led the wrong life, there will be no peace."

He likens the war to "an earthquake, which is a necessity of nature,"
fearing that the fighting "will never end." He attempts to find reason in the
madness of war with a bizarre logic: "It seems to me that the cause for this
war is that religion, science and art had reached a certain height and heyday beforehand, but had become increasingly abstract and detached from
daily life. Mankind came into being and lost, and science, religion, etc.
became the focal point."

He blames art, science, and religion for the "terrible aberrations . . .
(because the murder of hundreds of thousands must be an aberration) if
so many ideas believed in by mankind had not rendered all real life in-
sane?" Then he rambles on about how they "should try [to lead] as far as
possible a correct, (if you want) good life . . . Live in the way you want
others to live. Only it is important and only through this we can do something against the war."

---

* The first revolution occurred in March 1917. Czar Nicholas II was forced to abdicate on March 15
and the moderate socialist Aleksandr Kerensky seized power. Romania had also demanded an
armistice with Germany at the same time.

Hildebrand thought that when people lived the wrong sort of life, it caused wars. "I do believe, that only by proving that until now we have led the wrong kind of life (<u>because the war came</u>) and that [in believing] there is a real life with more love we will get closer to peace." His final thoughts turn to the Christmas season, and he brutally admits, "All this is tormenting me dreadfully, because again and again I see the whole hopelessness with ideas in facing the war and the world as a whole. They have failed miserably in this war. What else is Christendom if not a mockery, what is philosophy if nothing other than gibberish, all the world talks about it [Christendom] while killing each other."[37]

Hildebrand was reading Tolstoy at the time, which may account for some of his wrestling with notions of peace and solemnity. Yet at the end of January he admitted that his plans for the future were unsettled. He was preoccupied with life in Vilna—and chasing after women. The life of a civil servant without much to do was boring, but he claimed he saw things better through Cornelia's eyes. Still, he remained deeply troubled and "lived only for the moment"—a common complaint of all those who survived the war.

January came and went with his enclosing an excerpt from Tolstoy's *On Life* to Wilibald. It is a dark passage on the misinterpretation of love, given to his brother "so you can see what is really occupying me. Everything else is incidental and I do not force myself toward these ideas, because I am afraid of them."

Wilibald was shortly due to marry Gertrud Darmstäedter. Was this some sort of coded message? Or is Hildebrand afraid of love or of Tolstoy's view of love? The salient passage reads, "the biggest evil in the world develops from the much praised love for a woman, children, friend, not to mention love for science, art, the Fatherland, which is nothing but a temporary preference of certain conditions of the animal life to others."[38]

Laziness and mental instability, however, remained his main preoccupations: "You can say that I am lazy, at least lately. But I am almost glad about that, because in Königsbrück and especially in Berggiesshübel . . . I suffered from terrible anxieties due to my fear of time. Every minute seemed precious and lost to me, if it was not used to achieve something—yet I did not know what this something was."

Still, his tone remains dark. "I no longer have the energy to want to reach my goal against all the obstacles of the current life. . . . My museum plans have thus become small and ugly. Please don't call me feeble, remember that every few months I have started again in a different place with completely different prospects. . . . Perhaps it is good that I am now staying here for a longer time."[39]

His frame of mind hadn't improved three months later: "I myself am facing this incredible muddle, these cruel, incomprehensible conditions helplessly and am working with some ideas that seem . . . perfectly clear to me. The only thing I want to do (apart from some fantastically impossible plans) . . . is to avoid that my life will become dull and common. . . . Laziness and envy and hatred are infectious, they spread."[40]

⁂

Hildebrand's April 1918 letter foresees an end to the war, where Germany has lost. With the Russian and Romanian peace, the defeat of Bulgaria and the imminent defeat of Turkey, he understood that Germany would be entering a new era—one in which Pan-Germanism was dead and which would require some significant adjustment in his own, his family's, and his country's view of themselves.

As spring turned into summer, Hildebrand's predictions became a reality. The complexion of the war was changing rapidly. Naturally he was at a loss to explain the meaning of it all; how to end it quickly; how to minimize its impact on their futures; and most of all, how to prepare for this "new era." In August, a calmer Hildebrand wrote about canoeing, taking long walks in the rolling countryside, his bourgeois life in lodgings built on the ruins of a fourteenth-century Lithuanian castle, and the piano in his living room.[41]

August, however, also brought a flurry of military activity. Hildebrand's press unit was to be disbanded and reorganized. "You have no idea what that means and how we have to be careful not to be landed in a dreadful job," he wrote Wilibald. "All this is causing us disquiet and takes away the pleasure of writing."

Then another lucky break came. In September, he was transferred to the Art Unit of the Military Government of Lithuania, giving courses to the local population on German art, and reminding soldiers of the beauty of Germany. He apologized to Wilibald for his long silences, but still feared, he claimed, his brother's disapproval. "In the fall of '17 when I was at Berggiesshübel for the first time," Hildebrand recalled, "I had time to think, see it all together, and that my personal experiences in a very strange way reinforced my helplessness. Then came Tolstoy . . . that <u>uncompromising</u> thinker who consistently reminds one of Christ, *What you want, also affects others*. So I isolated myself as far away as possible from everyone except the loud confessions of my thoughts."[42]

Then . . . nothing. Not one letter from September until after the end of the war in November. What had he to confess? Had he suffered a mental collapse yet again? His military record remains as silent on these final months as does his family correspondence.

For Hildebrand Gurlitt, as for many Germans who believed in the great Pan-German ideal, defeat seemed unconscionable. Still, he set himself apart from millions of Germans by peering through the fog of war to see that Germany had truly lost.

∽

Despite his uncanny foresight, his moral compass was distorted by the conflagration, twisting Hildebrand's mind and preventing him from searching for, much less finding, "true north" again. The notion of confession haunted him, though he was a Lutheran. What had he done that affected others? This was a question that he would twist to answer his own ends in the next war. There is a strong sense that he hadn't read his Shakespeare. He was ignorant of Polonius's instruction to his son, Laertes, in *Hamlet*, "To thine own self be true." Perhaps this, as with Hamlet, had caused Hildebrand's Great War madness.

Hildebrand Gurlitt would never live the "good sort of life" again. The war had taught him to adapt morality to his own ends if he wished to survive . . . and survive he would.

7

⊙ШШ℧

PEACE

During the night my hatred increased, hatred for the originators of this dastardly crime.

—ADOLF HITLER, *Mein Kampf*

VERDUN. PASSCHENDAELE. CAMBRAI. BEERSHEBA. ALL SIGNIFICANT battles of 1917. Yet none could claim an absolute triumph to end the war. The cease-fires in December on the eastern front were lauded as German victories over Russia and Romania. In fact, they were victories of Bolshevism. More significantly, the December defeat of the Ottoman Empire in Palestine by British troops liberating Jerusalem ended 673 years of Turkish rule.

An unprecedented opportunity to resolve "the Jewish question" already troubling Germany and other parts of Europe was suddenly presented. Foreign Secretary Arthur Balfour* seized the day and with America's blessing (so long as it was kept secret) made public the Balfour Declaration in the form of a letter to Lord Rothschild on November 2, 1917. The letter stated that the British government favored "the establishment in Palestine of a national home for the Jewish people" on the clear understanding that there was no disadvantage to "the civil and religious rights of existing non-Jewish communities in Palestine, or the rights and political status enjoyed by Jews in any other country."[1]

---

* Balfour (1848–1930) was prime minister from 1902 to 1905.

Then, in January 1918, riots rocked Vienna and Budapest. The people were starving and cried out for an end to the butchery and long years of privation. Soon Paris, too, exploded in social unrest. Unions pressed for better living conditions and greater security. Though most foodstuffs still reached the city despite the lack of horses in the fields and Paris had full employment, the majority were anxious to right the wrongs of 1871. The political cartoon "Let's hope they hold out!" "Who?" "The civilians!" best characterized their impatience.[2] Still, the war continued.

Despite the Treaty of Brest-Litovsk and the Treaty of Bucharest taking Russia* and Romania out of the war in March 1918, the Great War thundered on regardless. The war seemed remorseless, relentless, endless. Yet the long-awaited US Army sailed over the horizon at last, much like some mythical Fifth Cavalry, with its tanks, well-rested soldiers, and battle-hardened General Pershing.† Engaging in the Second Battle of the Marne, the revitalized Allies ended the German spring offensive, with irretrievable losses for the Germans. Only five days after the significant German victory on the western front on September 22, the Allies stormed the German Hindenburg Line.

The next day, General Erich Ludendorff, who was the real leader of the German High Command, insisted with Field Marshal Hindenburg that Germany must seek an immediate cease-fire.‡ Hindenburg did not mince his words—an armistice "at once" was required "to stop the fighting," as the army could not wait even "forty-eight hours."[3] When the announcement of the reversal of Germany's fortunes came, it stunned the nation. "Now the spark leaped across to the people at home. There was panic in Berlin," wrote Germany's chancellor.[4]

By September 30 all Palestine had fallen to the British, and the Ottoman Empire was in final meltdown. That same day, Bulgaria signed an

---

* Called the USSR—Union of Soviet Socialist Republics or Soviet Union—from October 1917.

† The United States had severed diplomatic relations with Germany on February 3, 1917. Officially it was as a result of unrestricted naval warfare, but concerns of fifth columnists and Germany inciting Mexico to declare war on America figured highly, too. The Senate voted to declare war on Germany and its allies on April 4, 1917. Congress ratified it on April 6, 1917. See Boghardt, *The Zimmerman Telegram*, Annapolis, MD, The Naval Institute.

‡ It is most likely the root cause of the myth of the "stab in the back." Some argued, "How can an army have a huge victory then six days later want an immediate cease-fire?"

armistice with the Allies. Germany and the remaining Central Powers were near exhaustion, losing ground daily. Ludendorff and Hindenburg had acted in a cowardly fashion, not telling the civilian government just how bad things were until it was too late. General Freiherr von Schoenaich wrote in the *Frankfurter Zeitung* that he'd "come to the irresistible conclusion that we owe our ruin to the supremacy of our military authorities over civilian authorities. . . . In fact, German militarism simply committed suicide."[5]

∽

Thirteen days later, on a hill south of Wervick in western Flanders, the English tried to burst through the German line with cannonades of shell fire and mustard gas. One of the wounded was Adolf Hitler. He was blinded by the gas attack, and no one was sure if he would ever regain his sight. His voice was also affected. He could only speak in a whisper.

While in the hospital, he'd heard of the German sailors' mutiny* but felt that this was the "product of the imagination of individual scoundrels." By November, even Hitler admitted the navy was in disarray. "And then one day, suddenly and unexpectedly, the calamity descended. Sailors arrived in trucks and proclaimed the revolution; a few Jewish youths were the 'leaders' in this struggle for the 'freedom, beauty, and dignity' of our national existence. None of them had been at the front."[6]

When the sailors at the main Kiel naval base mutinied on October 28, 1918, a revolution seemed inevitable. The cost of the war—the wasted matériel, talents, lives—had maimed the survivors' minds. The despair was incalculable. Yet Germany rightly feared that worse might come. Its calls for a "peace of understanding" met with President Wilson's response for the abolition of the Hohenzollern militarist empire and indeed the abolition of all royal dynasties in Germany.[7]

A week later, the popular, diminutive Jewish writer Kurt Eisner—a familiar fatherly figure in Munich who sported a pince-nez and long gray beard—tramped through the streets to the parliament building at the head

---

* The Jade Mutiny took place on October 29, when the German navy refused to engage the British Fleet.

of a few hundred men and proclaimed a socialist republic. Eisner entreated other German *Länder* to follow his lead.

Seeing Germany threatening to break down into its old principalities and fiefdoms once again, Chancellor Max von Baden called for Kaiser Wilhelm's abdication on November 8. Berlin's workers had taken to the streets, Field Marshal Hindenburg and General Ludendorff had resigned for their failure to win the war, and were replaced by General Wilhelm Groener, who supported Baden. An armistice was in the offing, so long as the kaiser agreed to go. That night the emperor fled to Holland.* At midnight, the Social Democrat leader Friedrich Ebert was appointed chancellor and declared the birth of the Weimar Republic.

"I must confess that I myself feel shocked and surprised at the universal rejoicing manifested at the abdication of the kaiser," the English-born Evelyn, Princess Blücher wrote in Berlin. "They could not be more jubilant if they had won the war. . . . He may deserve his fate, but it seems very hard and cruel to throw stones at him at such a moment, when he must be enduring untold anguish and sorrow." It was the aristocracy who felt Germany's loss most severely: "The grief at the breakdown of their country, more than at the personal fall of the kaiser, is quite heartrending to see. . . . I have seen some of our friends, strong men, sit down and sob at the news, while others seem to shrink to half their size and were struck dumb with pain."[8]

That same day, General Erich Ludendorff skulked across the Baltic Sea to Sweden disguised in a false beard and blue-tinted spectacles. From the safety of his hideaway, he wrote to his wife, "If ever I come to power again there will be no pardon. Then with an easy conscience I would have Ebert, Scheidemann and Co. hanged, and watch them dangle."[9] It was an easy threat from the same cowardly military leader who had suckered Germany into a disgraceful peace.

On November 10, a pastor visited the hospital where Hitler was recovering. When the pastor urged the wounded men to accept "the magnanimity of our previous enemies," Hitler felt compelled to leave the room. Groping his way back to the dormitory, Hitler wrote: "[I] threw myself on my bunk, and dug my burning head into my blanket and

---

* Kaiser Wilhelm eventually found exile in Denmark.

pillow. . . . The more I tried to achieve clarity on the monstrous event in this hour, the more the shame of indignation and disgrace burned my brow."[10]

∾

Though Hildebrand Gurlitt, Adolf Hitler, and Hjalmar Schacht were still unknown to one another then, the investment banker Schacht would play a particularly significant role in the transition of the newborn Weimar Republic of November 1918 to the Third Reich of 1933. At the time of the kaiser's abdication, this former executive at Dresdner Bank had already become politically active through the Klub von 1914, whose members were young businessmen, all democratically minded and increasingly concerned about the power vacuum created by the kaiser's abdication.[11]

They were right to worry. That November, a large group of Socialist and Communist soldiers had risen up as the Spartacus League,* named after the Greek slave who rebelled against the Romans. This prompted Schacht and other members of the Klub von 1914 to form the Deutsche Demokratische Partei (DDP), or German Democratic Party. It was intended to provide a centrist political movement in response to the excesses of both Left and Right, which the DDP believed the Zentrum Party did not fill.† Their aim was to give Germany conservative, yet enlightened, solutions to the troubled times ahead. Essentially a monarchist, Schacht also insisted that their platform should read "We rely on a republican structure" rather than beginning with the simple statement "We are republicans."[12]

Schacht and the DDP sensed the need to present an alternative to the poisonous rhetoric of both Left and Right. The armistice was signed at 5:10 a.m. on November 11 by French general Foch, supreme commander of the Allied Forces, and the German High Command, led by Matthias Erzberger. Like some legendary thieves in the night, huddled in Foch's private dining car on a railway siding in the forest at Compiègne in France, they had— with the benefit of twenty-twenty hindsight—made a declaration of war to come in twenty years' time. The perceived stabilizing influences of the royal

---

* *Spartakusbund* in German.
† The Zentrum Party was a lay Catholic political party. In English it is often called the Catholic Center Party.

houses of Hohenzollern, Habsburg, Romanov, and Ottoman—incongruous
to most Americans—were no more.

∽

Life was moving at a breakneck pace. "I think there is not much point in
writing as the time passes too quickly and the letters are going too slowly,"
Hildebrand wrote to Wilibald at the end of November. "What is right today
is already wrong tomorrow."[13] He was expressing the fears of all Germans,
and their exasperation with the pandemonium that reigned. November was
so anarchic that everyone feared what the next day might bring. Bands of
paramilitary groups, known as Freikorps, ranged everywhere. Hostilities
erupted with the suddenness of an earthquake, only to subside and flare
up again hundreds of miles away in seemingly unrelated incidents.

From the moment the armistice came into effect, and throughout the
brutality of the months to come, President Wilson led the way in setting
down the nonnegotiable points for any treaty. His Fourteen Points, first
mooted in the summer of 1917, were at the heart of the mass European
abdications. In his January 8, 1918, address to the assembled houses of
Congress, Wilson laid them out precisely.[14] As long as Friedrich Ebert
remained the provisional head of the Weimar government, the Allies would
not agree to sign anything. Elections were demanded, but the timing was
wrong from Weimar's viewpoint. The Allies, led by Wilson, chose to ignore
any impact such elections might have on Germany. Consequently, the
upheaval and uncertainty lasted.

January 1919 brought no relief from the "terror"—as it was called at
the time.* One of the key players actively working toward making Germany a socialist republic was the left-wing philosopher Rosa Luxemburg,
nicknamed "Red Rosa," who had been freed from prison in Breslau on the
same November evening that the kaiser fled to Holland. Together, she and
her Spartacus League cofounder, Karl Liebknecht, began the *Red Flag*
newspaper, which demanded amnesty for all political prisoners and the
abolition of capital punishment.

---

* Germans used the word "terror"; today we would most likely term this "political violence"—
namely, organized and unorganized violence, or the threat of it, that is motivated by political
ends.

Hildebrand Gurlitt not only feared a "long-lasting war" but also a coup by the Left. "I think that now the two most important things are unity and the national assembly and above all a government that has courage, i.e. to have Liebknecht and Rosa hanged." He asked his brother, "Who will you vote for in the national assembly? . . . The party we belong to doesn't yet exist, because we cannot see ourselves as part of the nobility, the big landowners or the big capitalists."[15] Schacht's DDP was so new and so far away from Vilna that Hildebrand had most likely not heard of it.

While contemplating this political and social noxious cauldron, albeit from the relative security of his barracks in Vilna, Hildebrand announced that he consulted with their father, and thought it was perhaps best for him to abandon his studies in art to concentrate instead on politics and economics in the hope of discovering if these disciplines have an influence on the spiritual development of nations. "It seems especially important to me to determine how indifferent the individual can be toward political matters while our state as a whole . . . [is] breaking up."[16]

Again, Hildebrand possessed an uncommon farsightedness at a time when most Germans were still smarting from defeat and the cacophony of political voices crying out to join their causes. Rosa Luxemburg and Karl Liebknecht attached themselves to the ill-fated German Revolution in January 1919—also called the Spartacist Uprising—with the more militant Liebknecht persuading Luxemburg to help him occupy the editorial offices of the liberal press in Berlin. The result was catastrophic for both. The fledgling Weimar leader, Friedrich Ebert, felt compelled to restore order quickly, and called upon the paramilitary right-wing Freikorps to use whatever methods it must.[17]

∞

On January 15, the first of the Freikorps political murders were committed. Luxemburg and Liebknecht were captured by the Volunteer Division of Horse Guards and brought to divisional headquarters at the Eden Hotel. There they were separately interrogated by Captain Waldemar Pabst. That evening, Liebknecht was the first to be led out from the back of the hotel, and was clubbed with the butt of a rifle by one of the guards, who had "strict orders from the officers" to do so, before he was bundled into the back of a car.[18] At a desolate spot along the Charlottenburg Highway, the car carrying Liebknecht stopped to let him out. He staggered forward a few steps and was shot in the back while "trying to escape."

While Liebknecht was taken to his place of execution, Luxemburg appeared at the rear of the hotel, guarded by officers. Again the same guard swung his rifle, this time knocking out Luxemburg. She was dragged into the second awaiting automobile. One of her guards, Lieutenant Vogel, emptied his revolver into her bleeding head at point-blank range. Her body was then hurled into the Landwehr Canal. She was found some four months later, bloated and barely recognizable. The mother of German communism—who had worked with Vladimir Lenin in 1907 at the Russian Social Democrats' Fifth Party Day in London—had been unable to conquer militarism with her words. Her followers believed that her death and that of Liebknecht were declarations of all-out war.

Armed outrages in reaction to their murders multiplied; wildcat strikes and atrocities became a common feature of life throughout Germany in the following months. Kurt Eisner, that well-beloved local hero of Munich, was murdered on February 21—shot in the back by the monarchist-federalist Anton Graf von Arco auf Valley. Freikorps units of right-wing paramilitary groups were called upon by Ebert to invade other "council republics" like Bremen, Hamburg, and Thuringia. Atrocities against the Left continued until May 2, 1919, when the last vestige of the left-wing resistance, the Munich Soviet Republic, which had replaced Eisner's free state of Bavaria, fell.

∽

On January 19, the first Weimar election took place in this toxic atmosphere, only four days after the Luxemburg and Liebknecht assassinations. The duly-elected National Assembly met in Weimar on February 6. Controlled by the Socialists, the Zentrum, and the Democrat parties, the independently minded Social Democrat Philipp Scheidemann became the assembly's first chancellor. Friedrich Ebert was selected as Weimar's first president.[19]

Naturally, life went on. Toward the end of January 1919, Hildebrand paid a brief visit home to his parents in Dresden. He was disturbed by what he saw. "The terrible burden that has fallen on Germany is doubly strong at home," he wrote, "because it has hit Father so completely unexpectedly."[20] At sixty-nine, the Pan-Germanist Cornelius was disillusioned and broken by Germany's defeat. A miasma of bewildered mourning hung over the Kaitzer Strasse home. Unlike many Germans, Cornelius refused to accept "that it was hopeless . . . that the <u>whole</u> world did not want our victory." Hildebrand wrote to Wilibald, "that they had already been lied to for years, been given false hope and been made drunk [by the idea of victory]."[21]

Hildebrand also stressed that Germany must drive any thoughts of revenge from its heart and throw its total intellectual weight into the problems that lay ahead. He seemed revitalized at the prospect of having his personal freedom once again, yet still found the need to apologize to Wilibald for his "lingering" in Vilna. Essentially, Hildebrand claimed, there were three reasons for his delay in coming home. He found that he could be more useful in the East than he'd been anywhere for a good long while. Secondly, it wasn't as bad as the press made out; and thirdly, he didn't want to be caught up in the "big rush" home. After all, he might be mistaken for a revolutionary and summarily hanged.[22] Unsaid are other possibilities. Perhaps there was also a woman of whom he was especially fond? Perhaps he also didn't feel quite strong enough mentally to make the journey and see a devastated Germany? Maybe he even feared what he'd find back home, or any aspersions of "laziness" that might be cast at him. Any or all of these are perfectly good reasons for him to have stayed behind in Vilna.

That Hildebrand, a young man of twenty-three who had just been through unimaginable horrors, should feel any need to excuse himself to Wilibald—especially as his thinking seems to be unclouded once more— is again a clear demonstration of his unrelenting need for what can be only seen as his critical older brother's tightfisted approval. The constant allusions to Hildebrand's "laziness" and Wilibald's superiority of conscience and spirit helped to make the younger brother lack an inner confidence, all while projecting an air of bravura to the outside world.

∽

Elsewhere, the world watched in dismay as Germany tore itself apart. The unrest and cruel political violence hardened the Allied positions. Scheidemann's cabinet resigned on June 20, calling the proposed Versailles Treaty a disgrace and refusing to sign. Ebert quickly formed a new cabinet with Gustav Bauer as chancellor; Bauer pragmatically agreed that Germany had no other viable choice, calling it the *Diktat* of Versailles. No negotiation was allowed. In fact, Germany had no voice whatsoever in the outcome. The Allies used the civil unrest since the armistice as proof that the country was barely able to govern itself and that Germans still possessed an unquenchable bloodlust.

When Germany reluctantly signed the treaty, on June 28, 1919, in Versailles's Hall of Mirrors, Wilson's Fourteen Points had crystallized into 440 clauses punishing Germany. For Germans, the most difficult of these clauses was an acknowledgment of Germany's sole war guilt, or *Alleinschulde*, for having begun the war and causing *all* the loss and damage to its enemies. While the treaty was masterminded in many respects by France, the United States and Britain were willing participants in the dismantling not only of the German empire but also of German self-respect and pride. The United States might be accused of a lack of international foresight, if not greed. However, this was its first "allied" entry as a belligerent on the world stage. Britain and France could be accused of greed and revenge respectively. Still, despite his personal reservations, it was John Foster Dulles, as a member of Bernard Baruch's Reparations Committee and Economic Council, who drafted the infamous clauses containing offending economic sanctions that eventually would bankrupt Germany.[23]

Some of the main points of the treaty included forbidding the unification of the new Austrian republic with Germany; the return of Alsace-Lorraine to France; the fifteen years' grant of Germany's Saar-region coalfields to France; the demilitarization of the Rhineland by Germany and the occupation by the Allied forces—which were primarily French— to ensure compliance; the restructuring of all of Germany's colonies as either French or British mandates; the forming of the Covenant of the League of Nations, specifically excluding Germany; the making of the port of Danzig a Free City under League of Nations control; the restriction of the German army to 100,000 men, six battleships, and no submarines; the interdiction of any German air force; the creation of the "Polish Corridor" from rich farmland in the former West Prussia and Posen, separating East Prussia from the rest of Germany; and, of course, the crippling war reparations of 132 billion gold marks.[24]

New countries were formed: Poland, Latvia, Lithuania, and Estonia. The Austro-Hungarian Empire was broken up into Czechoslovakia, Hungary, Yugoslavia, and Austria. Italian-speaking Tyrol was given to Italy.

Over the next year, more treaties would continue to dismantle the European empires, until national boundaries were barely recognizable. The Treaty of Versailles would strangle the very breath from the Weimar Republic, even before it was born. It would resuscitate the Right, and give strength to the Freikorps, who were naturally exempt from the treaty's restrictions and who were constant reminders of the myth of the "stab in the back." The Freikorps would become a blunt instrument also begetting the Third Reich. Yet first, Weimar would be born—after a tumultuous gestation—and give the world its cultural legend.

In the dark recesses of Adolf Hitler's mind, the date of the founding of the Weimar Republic—the ninth of November—would live on in a humiliating cloak of dishonor. The date would be seared into his memory as a day of national calamity. It would become a day he would transform into *his* day and *his* victory.

8

AFTERMATH

> Don't you feel that the time will come again when people
> will yearn for intellectual and spiritual values . . . ?
>
> —JOSEPH GOEBBELS, 1918

IN THE CHAOS OF 1919, HILDEBRAND'S PIPE DREAM OF A CHANGE
to politics and economics was set aside when he returned to Frankfurt
and art-history studies. Precisely what prompted his latest change of heart
is unclear. Still, it is easy to imagine that his father had much to do with
his ultimate decision. When any child who has been through traumatic
experiences speaks to a broken and loved parent, there is an irresistible
force that makes following in the parent's footsteps compelling. For a young
man like Hildebrand, it offered him a level of security and comfort that he
had thought was lost forever.

He was made for better things. He could have written the words of his
exact middle-class contemporary, the diarist, writer, and philosopher Ernst
Jünger:

> *Surely this day that God has given*
> *Was meant for better uses than to kill.*

Jünger was a boy of nineteen when he wrote that. It was before he'd
become consumed by ruthlessness and bloodlust, killer of twenty men and

proud wearer of the medal commonly called the Blue Max. Two years later, when he commanded a Storm Battalion, Jünger's transformation into a killing machine was complete. "The turmoil of our feelings was called forth by rage, alcohol and thirst for blood. . . . The overpowering desire to kill gave me wings."[1]

What made Jünger go down a different path from Gurlitt? Like many who joined the Freikorps in the aftermath of the Great War, Jünger had been an active member in one of the labyrinthine arms of the German Youth Movement. Despite the disparate aims of these groups, which have been lumped together by history as a single youth movement, the best example remains the *Wandervögel* (literally, "the wandering birds"), to which Jünger belonged.

It stressed physical fitness and shaking off the false shackles of society through outdoor activities like rambling and hiking. The familiar image of the blond, Nordic, suntanned, and healthy young men in his *Lederhosen* (leather shorts) singing songs around the campfire, feeling the mystic forces deep within the forest, listening to their own perceived *völkisch* souls, harked back to Nietzsche and the poet Stefan George.[2]

Looking forward, many of those who were part of the *Wandervögel* would not only join the ranks of the Freikorps but also become stalwarts of Hitler's Brownshirts—storm troopers in the Sturmabteilung (SA). These were the hard core of men who truly *believed* in the "stab in the back" (*Dolchstoss*) that brought about Versailles.

Conversely, Hildebrand, like many young men who had tried unsuccessfully to make sense of the war, fell into the category of those who suffered from an intellectual if not ideological unrest. He was unconcerned with physical fitness, though he loved the countryside. He was twenty-three, yet, owing to the war, was stalled at the dreaming and planning stages of his life—and disgruntled that he was not yet living it. His mood swings were rapid, verbally violent, alternating frequently between depression and attempts to hide his deep-seated resentment that the past four years had robbed him of his life for a lie.[3]

Nevertheless, in May of 1919 the portrait Hildebrand paints of his parents has an overarching temperate tone: "The parents are getting old and it has been hard for father that they [the university] want him to retire suddenly, his eyes bother him when he's working and they are hurting. . . .

Still, he is working on his university book and is as busy as ever. Mother is doing better than before; she now has less to do and on the whole has become relaxed about a lot of things."[4]

∽

Cornelia hadn't been in touch with Hildebrand since January, though she'd written to her father that she was painting again and was pleased with her work.[5] Apparently she had decided to follow her lover Paul Fechter back to Berlin. The thought of separation from Fechter was evidently too great for Cornelia to bear, no matter the consequences. Fechter was, after all, married and had children. Given his position of some prominence as an art critic for a major newspaper, there was no possibility of their being together without creating a scandal. In an age where mistresses' and unwed mothers' acceptance in society was virtually unknown, Cornelia was heading toward an impasse. Even worse, Fechter worked at the same newspaper as her father's friend the art aficionado Georg Voss.[6]

Cornelia's dilemma was not yet comparable to that of her good friend Lotte Wahle, who had given birth to a son by her artist lover Conrad Felixmüller the previous December.[7] Unexpectedly, according to the family letters, Cornelia decided to move temporarily into the Berlin home of their older cousin Wolfgang, now aged thirty. Interestingly, Wolfgang was still running his father's gallery and art publishing house on Potsdamer Strasse 113—with his own peculiar touch of larceny, unknown to Cornelius.[8]

Soon the situation imploded. Cornelia let her brothers know that she was unhappy in Berlin; that she hungered once more for the happier days in Vilna among her comrades of the nursing corps. Then, without any reason, her innate sense for high dramatics returned with a vengeance, when she wrote to her brothers, "you are all in league as my enemies!"[9]

The catalyst for this outburst was Cornelia's avowal to her father sometime between February and May that she was pregnant. Cornelius, still smarting from the defeat of Germany and the lies he'd believed, was as supportive as he could be, but inevitably his letter reflected his own pain. Had her words to him, "You have taught us to be silent about whatever is happening in the heart," been indelibly etched in his mind? Had he understood that she was talking about herself? Had he been unable to cope when he asked her to consider others, if only briefly? Cornelia replied, "What we were painting, thinking, feeling [before the war] was anarchism in which we believed deeply and religiously—but when we see it in its political guise then we hate it, too."[10]

When Hildebrand heard of Cornelia's tantrum, he immediately dashed off his own missive to Wilibald. "I don't think that you can do a lot for her . . . and I do not believe that she will come to you, because she is too ashamed. I often asked her previously to come here, away from mad Berlin, but she does not respond."[11]

Somehow Cornelia held on for three months longer. Perhaps she hoped that Fechter would leave his wife and children for her, or maybe she thought she could raise the child at her parents' home, much as Lotte Wahle had been obliged to do with her son. Did her brothers insist that she give the child up for adoption? Or worse still, that she attempt a dangerous and illegal abortion? Whatever was going through her mind, Cornelia was finally consumed by her despair and committed suicide on August 5, 1919.

∽

She named Hildebrand as her executor. He was given the grim task of putting together her artwork, letters, and personal belongings and shipping them back to Dresden. Among the letters were some from Paul Fechter, which were returned to him with silent dignity.[12] The only surviving comment from Fechter about Cornelia concerned her artistic output, which he described as possessing a "strong and crushing, ingenious ability, making her one of those rising artists of the expressionist generation." Her art, he felt, was best placed in the East, where she "drew more and more of the beggarly side of Vilna with her quill pen or lithographs . . . she was influenced by Chagall's work—so personal and individual, that a new and other world stands before one. A harsher world than Chagall's . . . abrasively drawn."[13] Fechter otherwise publicly ignored the tragedy for which he stood partly responsible.

With Cornelia's suicide having come so close on the heels of the war, the January German Revolution, and the humiliation at Versailles, it is impossible to judge the family's overwhelming sense of loss, or how it further affected their lives in the years to come. Marie and Cornelius Gurlitt remained inconsolable throughout the rest of the summer and autumn, and as the evenings drew in, they both fell silent, keeping their thoughts private.[14]

Hildebrand seemed to blot it out, concentrating on his studies—that is, until his November 1, 1919 letter congratulating Wilibald on his successes. "I have not really dared to tackle Eitl's pictures, letters etc. I cannot do it yet. I first have to be freer and have a greater distance. Have to able to forget her death and be able to remember just her and not her dying."[15]

Yet actions speak louder than words. Hildebrand began to take a great interest in the artist Käthe Kollwitz, whose later works bore an uncanny resemblance to Cornelia's style. Kollwitz documented the lives of the downtrodden in society, portraying searing accounts of the horrors of war through everyday occurrences such as a mother cradling her dead child or a starving mother holding out her hand with her emaciated children clinging to her skirts. Grieving parents, widows, unwitting volunteers for the army, anger and angst flowed from her pallete, pen, and pencil after the Great War, urging the German people to look back at what had happened, to stop it from happening again.[16]

∽

In September 1919, Hildebrand was in Munich, making the rounds of its art galleries prior to the beginning of the university term in October.[17] Adolf Hitler, too, had returned to the city. Shortly before the May liberation from the communists, he claimed that he fended off "three scoundrels" with his "leveled carbine" just as they were about to arrest him.[18]

The "liberation" of Munich from the clutches of the Left was a bloody affair. City health officials were in a quandary as to how to handle the vast quantity of rotting corpses cluttering its streets and parks. Outbreaks of disease were feared until the Freikorps came up with what would later become a familiar Nazi solution: they dug shallow trenches and lobbed the decaying corpses into a mass unmarked grave.[19] Not only were there skirmishes and summary executions, but there was also summary justice, in people's courts—run by the Freikorps—where anyone who dared to speak out was convicted and herded into makeshift prisons. Munich, in the autumn of 1919, was ruled by the Freikorps despite the putative reinstatement of a civilian government under its minister-president, Adolf Hoffmann.[20] Hildebrand would have witnessed the brutality firsthand.

Trained during a weeklong course by the commander of "the von Möhl Command," Hitler became one of the paid nationalist agitators within the army to counter militants from the Left.[21] His first assignment was to go to a meeting of the German Workers' Party and report back as to what its leader, Gottfried Feder, said.

Hitler obeyed, and made his way to the down-at-heel Alte Rosenbad tavern in the Herrenstrasse. There, an awestruck Hitler received his first lesson in loan capital and the movements on the international stock exchange. Feder's speech established the speculative and economic character of the stock markets and loan capital with ruthless brutality, making the quest for interest on money abundantly clear to Hitler. "His arguments were so sound in all fundamental questions that their critics from the start questioned the theoretical correctness . . . what in the eyes of others was a weakness . . . in my eyes constituted their strength," Hitler interpreted.[22]

What Feder really said was that capital speculated through the world's stock exchanges was at the root of Germany's economic woes. The need to make capital pay dividends or interest was evil. In a move that would be appreciated today, Feder had even founded an organization called the German Fighting League for the Breaking of Interest Slavery. Hitler saw a simple message that would speak volumes to the masses and the "essential premises for the foundation of a new party" and "sensed a powerful slogan for this coming struggle."[23]

Anton Drexler, a nearsighted and unimpressive-looking locksmith, made the initial offer to Hitler to join, based on his impassioned riposte to a man Hitler called "the professor"—who was critical of Feder's economics and thought that Bavaria should break away from the rest of Germany.* The party's chairman, the journalist Karl Harrer of the *Müncher-Augsburger Abendzeitung*, thought Hitler could make a useful contribution, if for no other purpose than to rabble-rouse. The party secretary, Michael Lotter, a locomotive engineer and good friend of Drexler's, agreed.

Despite some initial reticence, Hitler became the seventh member of the committee of the German Workers' Party.[24] He knew his regiment's former clerk, Rudolf Hess, from the war. Fellow bohemian and drunk

---

* This was a popular notion and reinforced by the Bavarian hatred for all things Prussian. It is a concept that gains ground throughout the early 1920s.

Dietrich Eckart, twenty-one years Hitler's senior, was a clever journalist and a poor dramatist. He was thought by many to be the spiritual father of national socialism. Feder was of course the economist of the group. Yet the real powerhouse of the party was Captain Ernst Röhm, an adjutant to Freikorps commander Ritter von Epp, commander of the infantry stationed in Bavaria.[25]

Röhm was a ruthless soldier, who had grafted his way up to his exalted position from a working-class background. Like Hitler, he viewed the Weimar government as "November criminals" and remained vehemently opposed to it. With the bridge of his nose shot away, his scarred face, and his pig-eyed gaze, meeting Röhm was an unforgettable event. His stocky build and bull neck made him a man not to cross at any price. It was Röhm's task to build the party's membership by bringing ex-servicemen and Freikorps volunteers to their meetings. In Hitler he recognized a budding talent for trouble and a gift for soliloquy. Röhm would be the catalyst for Hitler's rise to power.

～

Of course, Hildebrand Gurlitt was utterly unaware of Adolf Hitler or his little-known German Workers' Party, or how Hitler would change his life and the lives of others. While Eckart was regaling his beer-hall friends in Schwabing, Hildebrand traveled back to Dresden, where he was coerced by his father into studying baroque sculpture. This was a "new plan" by Cornelius, Hildebrand wrote to Wilibald on October 15 with an almost audible sigh. As the days drew on, he feared there would be "cold and darkness" ahead—but claimed he remained "hopeful and cheerful."[26]

Still, self-doubt and stress began to take their toll. He did not return to Frankfurt at the beginning of term in October, remaining ensconced at his parents' home in Dresden. Wilibald evidently berated him again for being lazy by his failure to write, and also for what he saw as his younger brother's overpowering urge to be fed, clothed, and cosseted rather than face the world.

Hildebrand replied that he was annoyed at his father "tearing open any letter without being mindful of the addressee" and that he'd been to see their regimental clerk, who advised him that Wilibald should put in for an army pension, given that he'd been shot in the leg in September 1914. Hildebrand wrote apologetically two weeks later that "the burden of memories and distant future dreams are a bit of a strong burden for me. . . . I fill my day with work and living with our parents."[27]

At the end of November, Hildebrand was more honest with himself and his brother, but still mitigated his dark thoughts with contrary statements. "Our parents only see worry in me, and sometimes I plug into that. I'm so afraid in this house . . . but the sun is still shining."[28] Somehow, he needed to find the courage to take control again. His Christmas letter to Wilibald shows the potency of his mental and emotional struggles—many of which were common to the entire "lost" generation who fought in the Great War:

Five years ago I was in the field and stood guard in the first ditch on Christmas Eve and was nearly shot. And then we were relieved and it was very somber in the narrow trenches.

Four years ago I was at home and Eitl was in the field.

Three years ago I was with Hanns . . . in France. I was with the company of soldiers. I had a little cottage . . . and I took the morning off with my car, and had a fun and wild ride on the hard frozen road. Then there was a company feast in a large stable. The men [sang]. There were lights, and it was warm and happy. . . .

Two years ago I was at Eitl in Antokol in her little room. There was a lot of snow and everything was quiet.

A year ago I was in Vilna during the revolution. The electricity company went on strike, the shops and taverns were closed, and I was one of only a few administrative officers there. . . . I was there with a Jewish lad. . . . On Christmas Eve there was a big masked ball—Poles, Germans, Russians, Jews, all celebrated together. . . . The town was dead and dark on Christmas Eve. We stood at the window and saw the lights burning in the tree of a rich man's home. We were invited to eat at some kind strangers'.

Today I am at home.

What will next year bring? Maybe we can be together all the time. Perhaps one way is for me to find myself, and our parents no longer worry for me.[29]

∽

Despite his melancholia, Hildebrand was back at university by January 2, 1920. His letter to his parents is nearly breathless with enthusiasm about the philosophy of art—not to be confused, his professor advised, with aesthetics. "Kandinsky is all aesthetics—all color and ornament." His professor Ernst Troeltsch was an influential figure in German Protestant thought before the war, espousing the thesis that "disenchantment with the world" posed a threat to Christianity. Troeltsch's philosophy of religion and how it touched on art fascinated Hildebrand. Earlier in the day, he continued writing in his letter, Wiesbach's lecture on rococo art described the Louvre and the *hôtels particuliers* (private mansions) in Paris. Hildebrand finished the tour of his lecture circuit with the comment that "the son of Gurlitt" just gave a superior smile.[30]

Hildebrand also mentioned a friend of his called David, a trained bookbinder, whom he accompanied to the unemployment office. His aunt Else had met David, and thought he was "very nice." Despite the fact that he was "healthy, fresh and willing" and did everything he was told with a friendly manner, David could not find work. He was only nineteen. "No one thinks he's a Jew," Gurlitt wrote, "he has gray eyes and brown hair, and is even very pretty. . . . Although a Jew, he is a decent sort."[31]

Hildebrand Gurlitt was using the commonly accepted language of the day regarding Jews, especially in Berlin. The *Ostwanderer*, or eastern migrants, had flocked to the city as a direct result of the failed Freikorps adventure to recapture the Baltic states before the Treaty of Versailles was signed, in June 1919. He had no inkling that soon his Jewish grandmother would be his own undoing.

9

WEIMAR TREMBLES

The newspapers report only ugly things, sometimes it gets
me terribly sad that everything has degenerated so much
that today I am very uneasy about all "the awfulness."
—MARIE GURLITT, April 3, 1920

THE FREIKORPS DECIDED UNILATERALLY TO RECAPTURE THE
Eastern territories—which Germany believed it had defeated—before the
Versailles *Diktat* was signed. "This is perhaps what had given the Teutonic
Knights," the Freikorps chronicler Ernst von Salomon speculated, "that
restless seeking which ever drove them, again and again, from their solid
castles to new and dangerous adventures."[1]

The Freikorps's very success in retaking Riga in May 1919 at the head
of a makeshift and mostly German volunteer Latvian army simultaneously
tolled the death knell of its ultimate defeat.[2] Abandoned by Germany, and
forced to return home by British artillery and Latvian patriots, the Freikorps men turned freebooter. Finding their powerlessness unbearable, they
cut a swath like barbaric hordes of legend through everything in their path,
reducing entire peaceful villages to ash. They returned to the Fatherland
having burned their hopes and dreams as well as the "laws and values of the
civilized world . . . swaggering, drunken, laden with plunder."[3]

What the Weimar government hadn't fully appreciated was that the
Freikorps commanders would seek to keep their men together to mount a

coup. By the time they were ordered back into Germany, more than one government overthrow had been simmering. In seemingly unrelated circumstances, "labor associations" suddenly sprouted like field mushrooms throughout Germany, spreading west and south through Brandenburg, Saxony, Bavaria, Franconia, and Württemberg toward the French and Swiss borders. In East Prussia and the former Pomerania—just across the border from the territory they had been forced to leave—the former Freikorps members stood in readiness. As men dedicated to fighting, they remained above all else committed to battle, and would join in any effort to overthrow the republic.

⁀⁀

Hildebrand's letters remained so self-absorbed that he made no mention of the rocky political and military state of Germany. While in Berlin in February 1920, a mere month after returning to his studies, he became ill. His landlady wrote to his parents that someone must come at once to help nurse him, since he was too weak to take care of himself. Marie spent the better part of that month sitting by her son's bedside, worrying, until finally she could breathe a sigh as he slowly returned to health.[4] The nature of Hildebrand's illness was not disclosed. Still, given that the illness came a mere month after he returned to his art-history studies, it was possible that he had been haunted once again by his demons—particularly as Cornelius asked Wilibald to have a talk with his younger brother, since "he needs it badly!"[5]

Unknown to the Gurlitts and much of the German population, a putsch was scheduled for that March in Berlin. It was true that Germany had no real history of democracy and there was a great deal of antipathy for its unstable Weimar liberal governments.* However, it was the very existence of the Reichswehr (National Defense Force)—a veritable "state within a state"—and a criminal justice system that thrived as a corrupt extension of the Reichswehr that were at the heart of its problems.[6] Weimar had been unable to wrest control of civil order without its army.

⁀⁀

---

* Sixteen governments in fifteen years. There were seven in the first five years. The Reichswehr was the "official" army.

Economically, Germany teetered on the verge of ruin. At the beginning of the war, the German mark was valued at 4.19 to the dollar. By March of 1920, it was 83.89 to the dollar. With the key steel and coal industries working to only a quarter of their prewar capacity, the government hadn't faced up to the causes of its economic problems. Inflation, which dogged all postwar countries, was rampant in Germany. Though it was not yet at the level of hyperinflation, the German people were suffering privation nonetheless.

Yet the finance minister, Matthias Erzberger, continued to order the printing of increasingly valueless money, ignoring the gap between domestic and international pricing. Returning to the gold standard was unthinkable. Like Germany's military commanders in the final days of the war, Erzberger had run out of ideas.

It came as no surprise to some that on January 26, 1920, Erzberger was shot by a young ex-Freikorps volunteer who had been one of the demobilized freebooters. His assailant's sentence was a mere eighteen months in prison. He served only four.[7] Clearly, the courts approved such acts of violence.

While inflation gripped the country, support for Ebert's already shaky government lessened. Support from the barons, Germany's large landowners, and industry was rapidly cooling. Communist and Socialist enclaves in local government ranged from Saxony to Westphalia. The Gurlitt family's letters show that there were two Germanys living inharmoniously side by side.

Hildebrand's religious philosophy professor, Ernst Troeltsch, had written in the *Spektator* only nine months earlier that Germany was a nation in mourning. "Among the people, the effect was of a visible unity in pain, fury and offended honor," the article began. "One heard once again accusations against a government that had allowed itself to be fooled by [President] Wilson's phrases about peace. . . . The whole legend was once more spreading abroad that only the defeatists at home, the Jews and the Social Democrats had broken the backbone of our proud army. . . . If we had not been so sentimental the most glorious victory could have been ours."[8]

Many people forget that revolutions and insurrections take money. Those who had money, and had previously backed the Weimar Republic, needed to make the strength of their displeasure felt. General Hans von Seeckt—the genius commander of the Reichswehr nicknamed "the Sphinx with the Monocle"—would become their uncompromising mouthpiece. When asked by President Ebert if the Reichswehr would back his government, Seeckt replied enigmatically, "The army, Mr. President, stands behind me."[9] So did the money.

❧

The men of the Ehrhardt Brigade, thought to have disbanded as an outlawed Freikorps unit, began to march from their camp to Berlin before dawn on the morning of March 12, 1920. The large right-facing swastikas painted on their helmets were said to shine in the moonlight. Their boredom of a month in barracks was forgotten, their banners fluttered in the breeze of an early spring, and they sang their "Ehrhardt Lied" as they walked in step to battle. Their route to Berlin was well trodden, and they knew that their leisurely march would end just in time for the ultimatum to the government to expire. Captain Hermann Ehrhardt, a former submarine commander, had promised the government that he would refrain from seizing power until then. He prided himself on being a man of his word.[10]

The men waited in Berlin's Tiergarten, where they sat, smoked, drank from steaming mugs of coffee while Berliners cheerfully greeted them. The Reichswehr night shift called out "good morning and good luck" as they wended their way home. Shortly after, two civilians in mufti approached: Wolfgang Kapp—known to the men as the *Generallandschaftsdirektor* (of a governmental region administrative director)—and the ubiquitous General Erich Ludendorff. They claimed to have just "happened by." Ludendorff saluted the brigade of illegal freebooters, complimenting them on their military bearing, and wished them "Godspeed."[11]

At 7:00 a.m. sharp, the freebooters marched through the Brandenburg Gate and down the Wilhelmstrasse. By noon, all the empty government buildings were occupied and the putsch's administrative leader, Wolfgang Kapp, was working at his desk. The safety catches on their Mausers had never been touched. Shockingly, however, there was an "absolute vacuum of moral support . . . within the first few hours of their capture of the city."[12]

❧

One of the putsch's key men was Captain Pabst, last seen masterminding the brutal murders of the Communists Rosa Luxemburg and Karl Liebknecht. It was Pabst's reactionary political club Nationale Vereinigung to which, among others, the Prussian functionary Wolfgang Kapp, Generals Ludendorff and Lüttwitz, Colonel Bauer (the former section chief of the German Supreme Command), and the wealthy industrialist Hugo Stinnes all belonged. As spiritual guide to the putsch, Pabst was unsuited for the role he was assigned as coordinator of other Freikorps units on a national level. He had forgotten the maxim "Whatever happens in Berlin is not representative for the rest of Germany."

As if to drive that point home, on the evening of March 16, only three days into the putsch, a military aircraft landed at Tempelhof airstrip in Berlin. Two men disembarked. They were met by their contact, whose duty was to take them to meet the new "Chancellor" Kapp. Discovering that the Kapp putsch was already reeling, they decided to return at once to Munich. The elder man was Dietrich Eckart of the German Peoples Workers' Party—the younger one, Adolf Hitler. Their purpose was to discuss events in Bavaria, and see if there was some way they might work together.

Two days later, it was all over. While armed skirmishes took place in the streets of Berlin, Kapp, Lüttwitz, Pabst, and the other rebels fled. Potsdamer Platz and Budapester Strasse were reportedly raked by automatic gunfire. On March 18, the *Manchester Guardian* remarked, "We are living now in Berlin without light, gas or water. The new Government is caught like a rat in a trap."[13] Actually, the big rats of the new government had all fled to safety and exile, leaving history to condemn the conspirators as men who "knew damned little about complicated [political] matters."[14]

The judiciary, that "blackest page in the life of the German Republic," allowed 704 people charged with high treason to walk away from their trials without a sentence. Only Berlin's police commissioner received a sentence, of five years' "honorary confinement" at home.[15]

⸎

On April 1, the German Workers' Party was renamed the National Socialist German Workers' Party—the Nationalsozialistische Deutsche Arbeiterpartei, or NSDAP. Soon, it would be known internationally as "Nazi." Adolf Hitler became its leader, resigning from the army to devote himself full-time to the party. Despite a libelous pamphlet claiming otherwise, Hitler never drew a salary from the party as such, but did accept a "speaker's fee" when asked to talk to other like-minded organizations. After all, Hitler's fledgling party of some 3,600 members did not have the wherewithal to support its chief. Nevertheless, its wealthy cohorts, like Dietrich Eckart, Hermann Göring, and Ernst Hanfstaengl, nicknamed "Putzi" by friends like Hitler, undoubtedly did.[16]

Writing from Dresden a few days after Hitler's success, Cornelius told Wilibald that he was worried by Communist riots that swept Frankfurt in the aftermath of the failed putsch. The unrest and rising costs were most unsettling, and he doubted his ability to visit Wilibald in Freiburg anytime soon. After all, the cost of second-class rail travel between Berlin and Dresden stood at sixty-two marks. With "the ticket to Freiburg at 207 marks, the journey for mother and me alone to you would cost 824 marks; and what with bells and whistles perhaps as much as 1,200 marks. . . . In any case, we need to see how the situation turns out, and think of our financial reserves."[17]

Cornelius also remarked that Hildebrand was still in Berlin. "He's now working for the Curator of Brandenburg, Dr. Georg Voss. Adolphe Goldschmidt, the Berlin art historian, proposed Putz for the job—which makes me very happy. Putz is full of good hope."[18] Understandably, Cornelius feared for his son's well-being—both mental and physical—in difficult circumstances.

"I am starting over and looking around for a friend who has a solid footing and doesn't suffer as I do, with so much doubt and discord in his heart," Hildebrand wrote his parents in July. Desiring to reassure his family, he continued, "I have come through a serpentine of all sorts of anxieties and all sorts of possible destinies, and when I look around, I see around me wild, hateful fanatics (both left and right)." He repeats this thought several times before continuing, "I feel so rich. . . . I realize that when I was in the field [of battle] I saw everything as beautiful. . . . I want to keep trying, despite everything, to live and not just so half-heartedly with my head hung low, but rather now, if quieter and less adventurous although steady, yet without resignation."[19]

Had he truly scaled down his ambitions? As Hildebrand changed mood rapidly, it is difficult to properly evaluate the steadfastness of his resolve to lead a quiet life—particularly from the hubbub of Berlin. As if to prove the point, only three days after reassuring his parents, he berated his father for a letter Cornelius wrote to Georg Voss, Hildebrand's Berlin mentor, who was responsible for his university work experience. Hildebrand was outraged that he was expected to thank Voss—the curator of all Brandenburg—for his unpaid work placement.

"I am somewhat shocked by this letter because I do not understand . . . that he is doing so much good for me. I work a lot for him," Hildebrand argued with barely disguised rage, "and he only pays me in kind. . . . I do not think my work in any way inferior. . . . After all, not everyone lives as sparingly as I did on our field trip. . . . I'd be very glad to earn something . . . without wanting to complain, I live worse than the other workers. . . . But I do not feel miserable or depressed by it."

Hildebrand can't seem to stop himself. His tirade branches out to his father's parsimoniousness. "I knew nothing of what was ahead of me. . . . A wise man would have taken flight, but I was blind, understood everything wrong and have done yet again, a little too late, and I thank you again for your most intense distrust. . . . I wanted to live cheap and not to live for my pleasure [hence my move to Tegel], my preference is to live in Wilmersdorf or Nollendorfplatz or near the Arts and Crafts library."[20]

It is a letter worthy of an eighteen-year-old, not a supposedly mature twenty-four-year-old who had fought in the war. Hildebrand had no inclination to understand the difficulties and the financial burden that putting him through university had become for his parents, much less the need for him to find part-time work to help out. His defensiveness is myopic, arrogant, and graceless.

∞

Cornelius, however, was right to worry. In the year that followed, creeping inflation had gone from a gentle trot to a gallop, then a run before finally stampeding into the stratosphere. By year end 1921, the exchange rate had doubled again, to over 160 marks to the dollar. Nazi Party membership stood at over six thousand people.

Only the most inventive in their financial dealings could survive as inflation became a constant companion. That summer, Cornelius wrote to Wilibald, "An American literary company, The American [Encyclopedia] of the Arts, has asked me to work for them at the rate of 1,000 words for twenty dollars. The dollar is currently at seventy-two marks to one dollar, so he offers 1,440 marks for 1,000 words. That translates in the 320 words approximately it had taken me to write this letter at 460 [sic] marks. If the whole thing is not a farce, I'll ask for early payment of the entire bill!"[21]

By Easter 1922, matters reached crisis proportions. At a conference in Genoa, the Western Allies presented their bill for reparations—$32 billion—which mounted daily owing to inflation when converted from marks. Something needed to be done, quickly.

While still reeling from the dire news, a German delegation traveled a few dozen miles away to the Italian resort of Rapallo, where a secret treaty with the USSR was hastily signed. The treaty canceled all reparations between the signatories and instituted a favored-nation trade status that would help to stabilize both economies well into the 1930s. The irascible French prime minister, Raymond Poincaré, the former wartime general, fulminated when the treaty's terms were revealed. The Germans were cozying up to the "Red Peril"—ergo, the Communists would win out over the Right and seize Germany. Poincaré declared the treaty an open act of renewed hostilities. Paris began to seriously discuss invading the Ruhr.[22] The result was that the mark now stood at 284.19 to the dollar.

✍

The left-wing backlash hit at the heart of industry. Right-wing financier Hugo Stinnes was busy handling the Ruhr Red Army, or Rote Soldaten-bund, occupation of his factories and mines in the Ruhr, as were the steel and ammunitions kings Gustav Krupp and August Thyssen. The cigarette-manufacturing giant Philipp Reemtsma and his Hamburg-based factory fared better than Krupp or Thyssen. Others, like Kurt Kirchbach, grew phenomenally wealthy by manufacturing original equipment and brake systems for tanks, jeeps, and automobiles when world markets were closed to Germany in 1914. Each businessman was perpetually concerned about the state of near civil meltdown and the inexorable devaluation of the mark.

That July, the mark hit 670 marks to the dollar. Inflation firmly gripped the minds of all Germans. That's when the "carpetbaggers" arrived. The ability to change foreign currency into marks, put it to work in acquiring assets or goods or even services in Germany at bargain-basement prices, meant that foreigners tended to get rich quick at the expense of Germans.

Those who took advantage of the crumbling mark were called *Raffkes* (profiteers) in Berlin. Reminiscent of the Northern carpetbaggers infesting the South after the American Civil War, they descended on Germany in greedy hordes, buying factories, businesses, houses, and land with inflated foreign exchange. German industrialists with easy access to foreign funds frequently joined in, making a killing.[23] Rumors of tourists swindled by the Germans were rife, thanks in part to the virulent anti-German views of Lord Northcliffe, then proprietor of the *Times* in London.

Still the rocky Weimar government did not dare to stop printing money. The uncertainty of tomorrow soon grew into fear of the value of the mark later today. Cornelius was forced to sell the gold watch given to him by his father. Commodities became more valuable than paper money: a pound of sugar or few pounds of fruit or vegetables were a more certain form of exchange. Bartering became rife among those who earned a salary. Though wages attempted to keep pace with inflation, often employees or their union leaders were at a loss to calculate just how much they would need to ask for as a pay raise.

By the end of July, the German government demanded a moratorium on cash payments of their reparations until they could stabilize the mark. Poincaré warned that if any moratorium was granted, it would need to be against "productive guarantees," which would include the surrender of majority shares in Germany's chemical and mining companies as well as its vast state-owned forests.

☙

Two weeks later, the exchange rate was 1,134 marks to the dollar. The government's ill-fated economic policy meant that Germany could no longer afford to import food. Meanwhile, its population became millionaires in marks, paupers in other currencies. German agriculture had not recovered. Anything that needed to be imported was too extortionate to buy. Nitrates used in agriculture prior to the war had been diverted into armaments manufacture, leaving the land depleted of nutrients.

Poincaré, however, had a plan. By Christmas 1922, Germany was officially declared in default of its reparations payments. It took 7,589 marks to make one US dollar.[24] Industrialists had long before bought commodities of greater worth than a pound of sugar or several pounds of vegetables: antiques, gold, silver, platinum, jewelry—in particular diamonds, the most concentrated form of wealth—and fine art. These all had international markets and would continue to accrue in value, even in bad times. The Krupp and Thyssen families already possessed superb fine art collections, but would buy only from those who *needed* to sell. Germany's cigarette king Reemtsma, too, began adding to his collection.

Industrialist Kurt Kirchbach began collecting, too, his immediate hobby being signature photographs, which would become a valuable chronicle of their times.

Hildebrand Gurlitt became his personal art advisor.

PART II

ART AND POLITICS

༄

All the human culture, all the results of art, science and technology that we see before us today,
are almost exclusively the creative
product of the Aryan.

—ADOLF HITLER, *Mein Kampf*

10

❦

REBELS WITH A CAUSE

Men of letters are not the creators of new epochs; it is the
fighters, those who truly shape and lead peoples, who make
history.

—ADOLF HITLER, MUNICH, July 1937

THE FOUNDATION STONES FOR THE SECOND WORLD WAR WERE LAID
long before France and Belgium occupied the Ruhr on January 11, 1923.
The pretext for the occupation was that Germany failed to deliver 140,000
telegraph poles on schedule—a "production guarantee" in lieu of money
for its reparations payments. Seeckt, that Sphinx with the Monocle, declared that the "road from Dortmund to Berlin is not very long, but it
passes through streams of blood."[1]

Belgium? the Germans questioned one another, jaws dropping. Then
another blow to national pride was wielded on its eastern flank: Lithuania
reconquered the border city of Memel. The feeble Weimar government
turned to its outlawed Freikorps—redubbed the Black Reichswehr, or
Arbeitskommandos—to protect Germany, while urging the people of the
occupied territories to engage in passive resistance.

The actions of the French, Belgians, and Lithuanians against Germany
were keenly felt by the Gurlitts. A month later, Cornelius wrote that he
suffered "badly but hoped for the awakening of the German 'Michaels' . . .
as it was in 1914."[2] The German Michaels, according to Lutheran tradition

in the Book of Daniel, was the great prince who stood up for the children of his people. It was Michael who led God's armies against Satan's forces in the Book of Revelation.

In the same letter, Cornelius also revealed that he was awarded an honorary doctorate from Halle University, which disappointed him. Leipzig's magnetic professor of art history and archaeology, Wilhelm Pinder, had blocked the honor, in Cornelius's opinion, from his alma mater at Leipzig owing to his alleged lack of scholarship.

Unusually, when Hildebrand wrote his annual birthday letter to Wilibald that February, he made no reference to the cost of living or any hardship (the mark stood at 27,000 to the dollar) other than mentioning that he'd been freelancing for unspecified newspapers. Instead, his letter is full of a wonderful visit to the same culpable art historian Professor Pinder, made at Wilibald's behest, concerning Pinder's important work on the rhythmic structures in Romanesque interiors in Normandy. Hildebrand, naturally, did not discuss his father's accusations with Pinder. He seemed happy in the superficial world of female students—"very, very pretty girls"— who worshiped the professor. Even better, Pinder treated him with the courtesy he felt was his due. In fact, Hildebrand wrote that the visit was a "tonic," probably as much for the very pretty girls who "liked his eyes" as for Pinder's flattery. He, of course, does not mention Pinder's dogged anti-Semitism.[3]

Had Hildebrand met Pinder's most distinguished doctoral student at the same time? Nikolaus Pevsner—later known as Sir Nikolaus, the architectural historian who founded Pelican's *History of Art* and the *Buildings of England* series—would unwittingly stand in Hildebrand's way before the year was out. Or did he meet another, more lackluster student at Pinder's home, Erhard Goepel, with whom Hildebrand would later pillage France, the Netherlands, and Belgium? He does not say.

∞

Two months later, Hildebrand was living in Dresden again, probably thanks to a lack of ready cash. As far back as August 1922, he had begged Wilibald for money, and needed to find an external source of funding for the printing of his doctorate on the cathedral at Oppenheim.[4]

Everywhere, there was only one subject *everyone* else discussed: the increasingly worthless mark. The biggest losers were those who agreed on contracts for work—like artists—and delivered their commissions for a fraction of their original value a few weeks later. George Grosz, a prominent caricaturist and artist of the Dada and New Objectivity art movements, depicted Berlin life in the 1920s. He recalled those days when he ate nothing but "turnip coffee and mussel pudding" until he was befriended by a Berlin chef who'd hoarded food and become a black market *Raffke*. Fortunately for Grosz, he was also an admirer.[5]

By the spring of 1923, checks and credit accounts were no longer accepted. People demanded to be paid in movable valuables—food or cigarettes, usually, for everyday exchanges, and jewelry, rare books, or fine art for more expensive purchases—like automobiles—or for trades outside Germany to acquire foreign currency. For men and women who hadn't anything else, their bodies simply would have to do. Weimar became synonymous with a struggle for survival amid despair and humiliation.

"We were handed champagne, that is: Lemonade with a little alcohol in it," the Russian writer Ilya Ehrenburg wrote of a visit to a respectable bourgeois apartment with his friends in Berlin. "Then the two daughters of the house entered, in an unclothed state, and began to dance. The mother looked hopefully at the foreign guests: Perhaps her daughters would please them and [they] would pay well, in dollars, of course. 'This is what we call life,' the mother shrugged and sighed."[6]

The unparalleled rise in prostitution, nudity, and free expression was curtailed by a government clampdown on all cabarets and shows—as much to stop the outward expression of the decline of German morality as to avoid accusations of a clandestine world steeped in depraved luxury that hid Germany's ability to pay its war reparations.

Yet, despite any financial woes, Hildebrand fell in love. He'd met Helene Hanke, a Mary Wigman modern dancer,* and occasionally played music to watch her dance. It gave him "huge joyous amazement" that was "strangely alien" as it emphasized her controlled physicality.[7] Intriguingly, the Mary Wigman dancers were at the heart of this spirited group of expressionists

---

* Mary Wigman founded an expressionist dance school in Dresden and was considered one of the foremost iconic figures of the Weimar culture. Dresden artist Ernst Ludwig Kirchner portrayed her "Witch Dance" in 1926.

seeking new horizons; but with the suppression of cabarets and shows, Helene Hanke's dreams of dancing professionally perhaps needed sudden rethinking.

∽

Cornelia and Hildebrand Gurlitt had been part of the German Expressionist movement since its inception before the war. Visual artists, musicians, and film and literary figures were united by the expression of their art, despite wildly divergent political views. The members of Novembergruppe, founded in November 1918, are a prime example. The painter Emil Nolde was a racist mystic, who would later be shocked by his exclusion from Hitler's unbridled power in the arts. Walter Gropius, founder of Bauhaus a year later, was entirely apolitical. Others, like the Marxist poet, playwright, and theater director Bertolt Brecht and his favorite composer, Kurt Weill, a Jew, soon joined the Novembergruppe. "The future of art," they proclaimed, "and the seriousness of the hour forces us revolutionaries of the spirit [Expressionists, Cubists, Futurists] toward unity and close cooperation."[8] The Cubists, by and large referring to Picasso and Braque, were the French Expressionists, where the Futurists denoted the Italian movement. Others, like symbolist Norwegian painter Edvard Munch, were heavily influenced by German expressionism and adopted as Teutonic artists. The visual-art market became modern and truly international since the Impressionists. The Expressionists sought to take it a stage further.

With the abolition of censorship from the earliest days of Weimar, expressionism took on an entirely new dimension. In January 1919, the Bauhaus art institute opened its doors in the city of Weimar. Its style, noted for its clean lines and lack of ornamentation, became an international sensation that united design with functionality and beauty. Bauhaus became the most enduring of Weimar's cultural symbols and probably the most universally acclaimed.

The mélange of arts and crafts and design flourished in the visual art of painters like Gustav Klimt, in Picasso's innovation in stage design with Diaghilev's Ballets Russes, in the work of Bauhaus painters like the Swiss-born Paul Klee, the American Lyonel Feininger, and the Russian Wassily Kandinsky. Each invented his own idiomatic form of expression. Despite stylistic differences, they shared an unrelenting passion for groundbreaking work.

This passion gave all their endeavors an individualistic worldview, a distinctive *Weltanschauung*, which carried a forceful message. Be it Otto Dix's social and cultural commentary on pimps and prostitutes, George Grosz's emboldened take on industrialists and war profiteers, or Käthe Kollwitz's mourning mothers, starving children, or farewell to Karl Liebknecht, each of their works gave the world their cultural and social view of Germany in these tumultuous times.

In other media, that *Weltanschauung* was equally potent. The newest of the visual arts and fledgling ubiquitous propaganda tool—film—used allegory as a safety valve. One of the first of myriad arguments between creator/writer and director occurred with the filming and release of another celebrated Expressionist work, *The Cabinet of Dr. Caligari*. Producer Erich Pommer had assigned Robert Wiene to direct this allegory of the insanity and cruelty that seemed to pervade postwar Germany, distorting the writers' intent to show the madness of war. To the writers' eternal consternation, Wiene's *Caligari* was an unparalleled success.[9]

Other groundbreaking films followed. Fritz Lang—once dubbed the Master of Darkness—released *Dr. Mabuse, the Gambler*, an elaborate and stylized tale of crime and insanity that ran for over four hours. In 1923, Bertolt Brecht wrote his first screenplay, too, for the short slapstick film entitled *The Mysteries of the Barbershop*.

From Cornelia and Hildebrand Gurlitt to Brecht and beyond, they all belonged to this expressionist, rebellious, artistic group whose creativity was born from the times in which they lived. Expressionists were a powerful antidote to the powerlessness of Weimar. As the founders of a modern German culture that tried to make sense of life as it had become, they were antithesis of Hitler's Nazi vision of the arts.

While the cultural and political revolutions continued, Hildebrand made a life for himself at long last. At half past one on Saturday, August 23, 1923, he married Helene in a sad little ceremony at the Church of Zion in Dresden. There was a small organ prelude, then the ceremony conducted by Pastor Schulze. "Strength is needed at this terrible time, every bill, every errand comes as a terrible shock, and it is so exhausting that you actually wish for nothing and make do," Marie wrote to Wilibald. "It won't be like your wedding—[just] two sets of parents eating with them here and then they're off. No bridal carriage or decorated altar space or sumptuous feast."[10]

Describing them as good, simple people, Marie seemed to like Helene's parents. She also reflected that Cornelius found it difficult, as if Cornelia's ghost haunted the shadows. Hildebrand, too, had felt her absence, like a dull, aching pain. That Wilibald and his wife were kept away by the cost of the "heavy times in which we live" made it nearly unbearable for Marie.[11]

✧

August was punctuated by more unrest in the Ruhr: food riots in French-occupied Wiesbaden closed grocers' and butchers' shops. Unbelievably, the French turned back all food shipments from the Reich to the Occupied Zone. The mark continued its slide and was now worth 353,412 to the dollar. Chancellor Gustav Stresemann was reshuffled to the post of finance minister in Ebert's cabinet, and immediately announced his battle plan to address hyperinflation: an emergency decree making it illegal to trade the mark outside Germany. By August 20, a loaf of bread cost 200,000 marks and one gold mark was equal to a million paper marks.[12] The Allies, like jackals sensing a kill, moved in.

The agreed loss of Upper Silesia as part of Germany's new border with Poland coupled with the French/Belgian occupation meant that Germany lost over 80 percent of its coal, steel, and pig-iron production. In being deprived of these critical resources, the country was starved of any way to resume its reparations payments.

Hyperinflation reignited the flame of German pride—and the supposed anger of the country's wealthy industrialists. Germany's businessmen and manufacturers turned to profiteering in increasing numbers, taking advantage of their foreign-exchange capabilities and employing their entrepreneurial acumen. They argued, with some plausibility, that they stepped in for the greater good of Germany, trying to keep their businesses afloat and their workers employed. Yet that didn't make their actions moral or right. What they needed was someone who could voice their *Weltanschauung* successfully. Hyperinflation touched every single person living in Germany in a common catastrophe. It destroyed all faith in property and money.[13]

Bewildered, fiscally and mentally damaged by hyperinflation, Germans were unsure if they could breathe more easily during 1924. During that same year, elections were held. Despite its having been made illegal, the

Nazi Party and its allies won thirty-two seats in the Reichstag.[14] Still, their election did nothing to relieve the issue of the French occupation in the Rhineland, which remained a festering sore.*

Amid the political and economic chaos, Hildebrand and his bride Helene settled down to married life in a tiny rented flat. Battered by Germany's economic hardships, they were forced to base themselves in Dresden, taking midday meals with his parents to economize. Yet Hildebrand's mental state changed miraculously. A grim determination to succeed supplanted his endless doubts and fears.

Was it Helene's strong influence or the realization that he must make his own way in the world? Or perhaps it was the responsibility of marriage? Whatever the cause, from 1924 making money became his singular priority. Helene took in dance students to make ends meet while Hildebrand wrote freelance articles related to art and architecture for several newspapers. Yet no permanent jobs were forthcoming as a museum director, as he hoped—or as his father expected. During this period, Hildebrand helped Cornelius edit his next book, *Art Since 1800*, while Marie wrote proudly to family that Hildebrand was "invaluable in writing about modern art."[15]

Despite turning seventy-four and having a second eye operation, Cornelius remained mentally alert and active. He had no choice. Although they lived in a huge home, it had neither central heating nor electricity. The plaster was crumbling, and essential restoration needed to be undertaken. Cornelius continued as a guest lecturer at the Dresden Technical University and was reelected chairman of the German Association of Architects. His seminal work on the baroque architecture and times of August the Strong of Saxony was published in 1924 by Sibyllen-Verlag, sealing Cornelius's international reputation in the field of the German baroque.[16]

∽

There were other rebel and terrible voices which began to make themselves heard in that decisive year of 1923. Hermann Göring had joined the NSDAP

---

* The French would remain in the Rhineland until the end of 1930, and would maintain control of the much smaller Saarland region until 1935.

in 1922, and was by now an avid follower of Hitler. A Great War flying ace who had won the coveted Blue Max medal, Göring was a natural in Hitler's eyes to take on the supreme leadership of the party's thugs, the SA. In July, Göring made it clear to the SA district leaders that "there is not yet sufficient clarity in respect to the various patriotic groups. . . . Competition between these groups is to be avoided at all costs."[17]

Essentially, the NSDAP did not control many of the Freikorps troops. The Vereinigte Vaterländischen Verbände (VVM) and Hermannsbund were loosely connected with the party and it was assumed that they would soon join the NSDAP fold. However, Ehrhardt's Viking Bund wanted nothing more than to take out the NSDAP and declared war on the party.[18] It was mere detail to Adolf Hitler—a detail his heavy Göring could handle.

Hitler was pleased by Germany's plight. An avid believer in astrological signs, he thumbed his horoscope eagerly in the papers and learned that now was the time to act. He decided to organize a mass rally of a new Deutscher Kampfbund (the Association for the German Struggle) at Nuremberg at the beginning of September and have himself elected its president. It would become the first of his long series of "German Days" to commemorate the party's victories. "The unification of all battle associations into one great patriotic German Battle League absolutely guarantees the victory of our movement," Hitler ranted during his acceptance speech.[19]

However, Bavaria's virtual dictator, Gustav von Kahr, became seriously concerned that the loudmouth upstart Hitler would ruin his own plans to declare Bavaria a separate country from the rest of Germany and restore the Wittelsbach monarchy. "Propaganda must be adjusted to the broad masses in content and form," Hitler declared, "and its soundness is to be measured exclusively by its effective result."[20] Kahr was right to worry.

Hitler decided to concentrate all his activity in Munich. There, "training of a community of unconditionally reliable supporters and development of a school for the subsequent dissemination of the idea" would be formed. Once the Munich leadership was irrevocably accepted, they could branch out across Bavaria and on to Berlin.[21] Thereafter, nothing would stop the juggernaut.

Life was an eternal struggle to Hitler, an "endless ladder."[22] For Germany to win its struggle and see its Aryan supermen and superwomen prevail, he created his own warped philosophy—a crude and brutal social and cultural Darwinism. His was a "world where one creature feeds on the other and where the death of the weaker implies the life of the stronger."

Yet even this determined philosophy did not go far enough for Hitler. Corrupting the great German philosophers from Schopenhauer to Nietzsche and writers from Schiller and Goethe, as well as Nordic myth, Hitler cobbled together an ersatz Aryan history, a grand mythology of legend with which his people could readily identify. In a passage redolent of Adam and Eve's fall from grace, "the Aryan gave up the purity of his blood, and therefore, lost his sojourn in the paradise which he had made for himself."

The Aryan had been at the heart of the great cultures of the past, Hitler argued, until the dilution of Aryan blood. Indeed, until then, the Aryans were the "culture bearers" from whom stemmed "everything we admire on this earth today—science and art, technology and inventions. . . . If they perish the beauty of this earth will sink into the grave with them."[23] The Aryan was the "Prometheus of mankind . . . kindling anew that fire of knowledge which illumined the night of silent mysteries and thus caused man to climb the path to mastery. . . . It was he who laid the foundations and erected the walls of every great structure in human culture."[24]

Of course, the Jews were at the heart of this impurity. So were Freemasons, Slavs, and Russians. Hitler believed the eternal Jew dragged down all that was great "into the gutter. . . . Culturally, he contaminates art, literature, the theater, makes a mockery of natural feeling, overthrows all concepts of beauty and sublimity, of the noble and the good, and instead drags men down into the sphere of his own base nature."[25] The assimilation of Jews into the Aryan culture was the source of all Germany's problems. It went against the laws of nature, like the mating of a fox with a goose.[26]

∽

Unaware of the danger Hitler represented, Hildebrand lectured part-time that autumn on art in Chemnitz at its school of art. Although aged twenty-nine, he remained at a loose end. Certainly, Cornelius as a concerned father who enjoyed his son's and daughter-in-law's company, did everything in his power to see his son established as an art historian closer to home, but to no avail.

The man who held the reins of power for all art historians' jobs in
Saxony was Dresden's Gemäldegalerie director, Hans Posse—a generation
younger than Cornelius, and a man who already demonstrated a covetousness and meanness of spirit. As can often be the case between aca-
demics, battle lines were drawn. Posse's feet were firmly planted in the
Pinder camp. Still more galling, Pinder wrote about the German baroque
in his recent book of the same title, detracting from Cornelius's own
work. If Cornelius had approached Posse cap in hand, he would have been
disappointed to discover that young Nikolaus Pevsner had just been
awarded the only internship granted at Dresden's Gemäldegalerie. It was
a plum position, since Dresden's picture gallery was deemed one of the
best for Renaissance art in all Germany.[27] Pevsner was seven years younger
than Hildebrand, making this snub sting in the Gurlitt household like an
oozing sore.

Not only did Pevsner bag the top junior job available in the whole of
Saxony, but to earn his crust of bread he was almost immediately hired on
as an art reporter and critic for the *Dresdner Anzeiger*, one of Dresden's
two daily newspapers, producing some forty articles in the first year.[28]

⁂

In the fall of 1923 the Freikorps groups wanted to march on Berlin, in the
hope of spilling some blood, preferably Hitler's, along the way. Kahr diverted them in October by sending them into neighboring Thuringia and
Saxony and removing the local leftist governments.[29] Saxony's two thousand NSDAP members waited in anticipation of filling the void. Göring
and his SA knew what to do. Captain Ernst Röhm had his own Freikorps
command. At last, *Der Tag*—the Day—had come. It was November 9.

Kahr knew that Hitler was up to something. Hitler's plan to ambush
Kahr, Reichswehr Major General Lossow, and Hans Ritter von Seisser, head
of the Bavarian State Police, to prevent them from announcing the reinstatement of the Wittelsbach monarchy had to be abandoned at the eleventh hour. A second opportunity should present itself, however, for the
night of November 10–11, when combined Battle Leagues would meet and
march to protest the anniversary of the armistice. At short notice, Kahr
announced in the press on the morning of November 8 that he would be
publishing the forthcoming program of the Bavarian government. Hitler

was in an unspeakably foul temper. Throughout the day of the eighth, Kahr refused to see him.

Ever calculating and opportunistic, Hitler swiftly revised his plan. He'd attend Kahr's Bürgerbräukeller (Bürgerbräu beer hall) meeting, and take over Bavaria's government by force. After listening to Kahr speak for half an hour, Hitler stood on a table and fired his revolver into the air, proclaiming, "The National Revolution has begun! This building is occupied by six hundred heavily armed men. No one may leave the hall. Unless there is immediate quiet I shall have a machine gun posted in the gallery."[30]

Kahr, Lossow, and Seisser were herded into a back room. Initially they refused to comply with Hitler's demands. Yet Hitler had a trump card: General Ludendorff. The putsch had been presented to the former head of Germany's military, and if it was successful, Ludendorff would have a place in Hitler's government. That was all it took. Ludendorff persuaded Kahr, Lossow, and Seisser that they would need to lend their support to the upstart Hitler. They all rejoined the bemused audience in the main hall, where it was announced that "the November criminals [the founders of Weimar] had been overthrown."[31] During the speech, Hess, aided by an army of storm troopers, prevented other cabinet members from slipping away.

Still, revolutions are never that straightforward. As the meeting broke up, rumors of street fighting reached Hitler. He immediately decided to drive to the scene and join the fray. Meanwhile, the ambushed triumvirate escaped and repudiated their support for Hitler—demanding instead the rebels' arrests.

Battle was joined shortly after midday on November 9. Röhm was reported captured at the War Ministry. Hitler and Ludendorff were determined to free him. As Hitler and his men funneled through the narrow Residenzstrasse just beyond the Feldherrnhalle into Odeonsplatz, they were met by over a hundred armed police. Some say Hitler fired the first shot, others the police. Göring was felled by a bullet to his thigh. By the time the gunfire abated a minute later, three police and sixteen Nazis lay dead or dying. Hitler was injured while fleeing.

Despite being the first to scamper to safety, Hitler was arrested two days later at Putzi Hanfstaengl's home. Göring was smuggled across the border into Austria to convalesce in his wife's arms at a hospital in Innsbruck. Hess, too, went into hiding.[32]

Kahr, Lossow, and Seisser immediately outlawed the NSDAP. They believed that national socialism was dead and Hitler utterly humiliated. They could hardly know that the date, November 9—*Die Neunte Elfte,* the ninth of the eleventh—would become one of the most important dates in the Nazi calendar and a national holiday from 1939.

GURLITT FAMILY

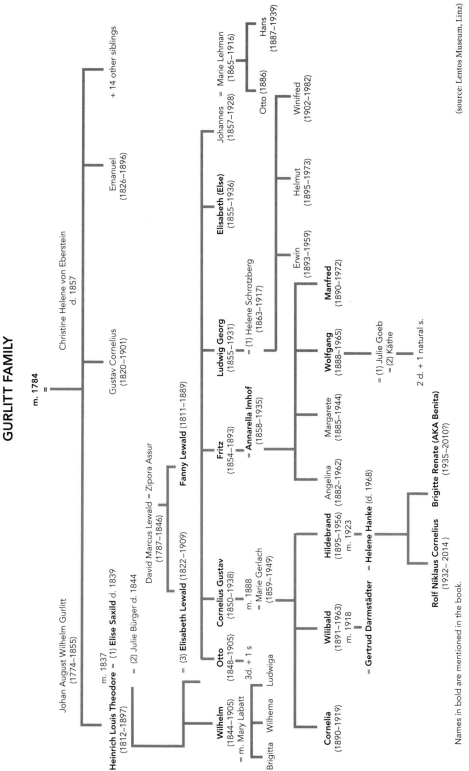

(source: Lentos Museum, Linz)

Names in bold are mentioned in the book.

Hildebrand and Cornelia circa 1917

Marie Gerlach Gurlitt as a young woman

Cornelius Gurlitt Senior
in full regalia

The three Gurlitt siblings circa 1917.
From left to right: Hildebrand, Cornelia, and Wilibald.

The Kaitzer Strasse home in Dresden, where Hildebrand grew up

Kaitzer Strasse home in Dresden today. The original Gurlitt home was firebombed on the night of February 13, 1945. This apartment building was built in its place in the 1960s.

External view of Schloss Niederschönhausen, where "degenerate" art was stored awaiting sale to foreign buyers

Looted artworks at Schloss Niederschönhausen with works by Delaunay, Chagall, Ensor, Picasso, and van Gogh

Original March 1944 invoice approved for export, signed by Hermsen and with the official stamp

(author photograph, courtesy of ANF)

The same invoice, but doctored with paintings substituted, amounts changed, and *without* the official stamp

(author photograph, courtesy of ANF)

Castle Aschbach front entrance at the end of the war. It remains substantially unchanged today.

Castle Aschbach dining room interior at the end of the war

Kurt Kirchbach's Jurid-Werke factory shortly after the war, rebranded "Cosid." Kirchbach abandoned the factory, fleeing to Switzerland at the end of the war, before resettling in Düsseldorf in the early 1950s.

Assembly line interior of Kirchbach's Jurid-Werke factory during the Nazi era. Kirchbach manufactured all German brake linings during the Great War.

11

∽∾

HOPES AND DREAMS

> Money is human happiness in the abstract; he . . . who is
> no longer capable of enjoying human happiness . . . devotes
> his whole heart to money.
>
> —ARTHUR SCHOPENHAUER

MONEY, OR RATHER ITS LACK OF VALUE, WAS THE BANE OF THE
Gurlitt's—and Germany's—existence. Within three days of the Hitler
putsch, President Ebert appointed Hjalmar Schacht the Reich's currency
commissar. The exchange rate stood at a mind-blowing 26 trillion marks
to one dollar.

By 1921, Schacht was deemed a genius, and the investment firm of
Databank that employed him had benefited from his elevated status. Still,
within the year, the bank's directors abandoned Schacht for its new swaggering executive board member, Jakob Goldschmidt, a Jew, who also
owned a brokerage house and investment bank. Goldschmidt's "views of
banking were diametrically opposed to mine," Schacht wrote in his mem-
oirs.[1] Schacht's distaste for Goldschmidt's dramatic risk taking drove him
to distraction, giving rise to Schacht's previously suppressed antipathy
toward Jews. Once, when Goldschmidt lost all sense of proportion, Schacht
admonished, "For God's sake, Goldschmidt, calm down. This situation
must not be handled with Jewish hyperactivity, but with Aryan calm."[2]

Schacht knew that Germany's inability to pay reparations had caused the occupation of the Ruhr by France and Belgium, the armed revolt in Lithuania, and countless riots and looting incidents throughout the country in reaction to the untenable hyperinflation. Confidence needed to be restored at once. A new kind of mark was needed. Alongside the near-worthless official mark existed all sorts of industrial, private marks, called *Notgeld* (emergency money), such as those from the conglomerates of Krupp and Thyssen and other large companies. Their *Notgeld* put them in a position of exceptional power, since it was backed by their own output and foreign exchange.

Then there was the matter of the Reichstag's poor leadership. Schacht declared publicly that inaction was no longer possible and immediately attracted Stresemann to his ideas. A compromise solution the Rentenmark, was swiftly agreed to by Stresemann. The Rentenmark would be based on all of Germany's land values, which in turn were mortgaged against Germany's remaining gold reserves. Stresemann's agreement to the proposal in the Reichstag was contingent on his reciprocal demand that he must be granted complete control of all matters concerning the new currency by parliament. The Reichstag hastily accepted.[3] Schacht was immediately appointed to the finance ministry to spearhead the Rentenmark's use, despite the Reichstag's cries against him as an appropriate candidate. Stresemann had outwitted the Reichstag.

On the morning of November 13, 1923, Schacht took his secretary of long standing to their new office—a janitor's cupboard that reeked of carbolic—at the Finance Ministry. From their windowless aerie they directed Germany's financial rescue. Schacht refused any salary, but insisted that his secretary, Clara, be paid six hundred marks per month.[4]

As Schacht sat down in his eyeless closet, the official printing presses could no longer keep pace with demand. With the exchange for the equivalent of one dollar in the trillions, the Finance Ministry had issued orders that the mark should only be printed on one side to hasten the process. Two days later, the presses stopped momentarily while the plates were replaced with those of the new Rentenmark. One Rentenmark equaled one trillion inflated old marks.

Schacht's sole concern remained reestablishing confidence in the mark. To do that, he knew he needed to create trust in *him* as the embodiment of the new German resolve. The Reichsbank and Reichstag had lost credibility internationally as well as nationally. As Schacht told the *Saturday Evening Post*, "I have tried to make German money scarce and valuable."[5] Days later, the ruthless *Raffkes* found that they no longer had sellers they could plunder. The piratical speculation with foreign currency was over. On November 20, a fixed exchange rate was announced at approximately the prewar gold mark value of 4.2 to the dollar.*

♐

Against this background, Cornelius feared if Hildebrand did not concentrate on making his own future and lose his innate laziness, life would pass him by, especially in hard financial times. Aged twenty-nine, Hildebrand had yet to fulfill his dream of becoming a museum director despite his father's growing international recognition in the world of architecture.

In February 1924, Hitler was put on trial with nine of his cohorts for the treasonous beer-hall putsch. He used it as a showcase for his oratorical skills, knowing that his words would be reprinted across the world's newswires. It was a gilded opportunity, especially since he had the Bavarian justice minister firmly in his pocket. Hitler interrupted the proceedings as often as he liked, cross-examining witnesses and regaling his audience with more than one lengthy, passionate monologue. "I alone bear the responsibility," Hitler stated with his chin thrust out like Karl Harrer. "But I am not a criminal because of that. . . . There is no such thing as high treason against the traitors of 1918."[6] Evidently, either he forgot or chose to ignore that Ludendorff, who stood in the dock with him, was the greatest of those traitors.

Ludendorff's defense was to call Hitler an unemployed, unscrupulous demagogue who believed that a mere "drummer" in the army could be the country's leader. "How petty are the thoughts of small men!" Hitler exclaimed. "I wanted to become the destroyer of Marxism. I am going to achieve this task." Evoking the greatness of Wagner, he babbled on about Fate having decreed his role. "The man who is born to be a dictator is not compelled. . . . He is not driven forward, but drives himself. There is nothing immodest about this."[7]

---

* 18 marks = 1 pound sterling

Hitler predicted that "the hour will come when the masses, who today stand in the street with our swastika banner, will unite with those who fired upon them. . . . For it is not you, gentlemen, who pass judgment on us. That judgment is spoken by the eternal court of history."[8]

Ludendorff was acquitted with the slightest of finger wagging, admonishing him to choose his friends better. Hitler and the others were found guilty, with Hitler's sentence being five years' imprisonment in the fortress of Landsberg. Despite the apparent severity of the sentence, Hitler would be eligible for parole within six months. Less than nine months after he was sentenced, on December 20, Hitler was released.

His time at Landsberg was spent fruitfully in planning the future. Treated as a revered guest, Hitler dictated his book, first to his chauffeur, then to Rudolf Hess from his "cell" with its superb view over the River Lech. Originally entitled *Four and a Half Years of Struggle Against Lies, Stupidity and Cowardice*, this foundation for Nazism and the cult of Hitler would be given a catchier title by Hitler's former adjutant and current business manager of Nazi publications, Max Amann. Instead, it would be infamously called *Mein Kampf*.

∽

That same autumn, Cornelius was summoned to meet President Ebert. At their Berlin meeting he was informed that, as the longstanding president of the architectural association he had been invited to the United States to head a large German delegation for the World Architects' Congress in New York City in April 1925. The trip would be entirely paid for by the government, and because the delegation represented Germany, it would go in style, visiting some ten or so cities.

Certainly, it would be the opportunity of a lifetime if Hildebrand could cover the event, Cornelius mused. Fortunately, due to his prior coverage of arts subjects and his father's preeminent role in the American voyage, Hildebrand had little trouble in convincing the *Frankfurter Allgemeine Zeitung* to hire him to cover the story as an insider.

The tour would begin in New York—the heart of the American art trade—and provide some invaluable insight and contacts for Hildebrand in the years to come. He was poised, or so he thought, to bring Weimar culture to the world.

12

~~~~~

FROM NEW YORK TO ZWICKAU

I'm an international "Star"—The trip will pay to install
electricity, replaster and paint the house.
—CORNELIUS GURLITT, March 1925

ON APRIL 3, CORNELIUS AND HILDEBRAND EMBARKED ON THE
SS *Westphalia* from Hamburg to New York as part of a twenty-five-man
contingent of German architects. The early-spring North Atlantic crossing
was desperately cold, with storm-tossed seas delaying their arrival in New
York by a full day. Disembarking at one of New York's West Side piers on
April 17, Hildebrand described himself as a teacher to immigration officials.
He also told a second lie—the second of hundreds to American officials
over the next twenty years—that he was living at his father's home.

Neither Marie nor Helene accompanied their husbands. It was decided that Helene would move in with the ever-fretful Marie while the men
were away.[1] They received "beautiful reports" daily, dated April 18–20,
all seemingly having come on the same steamer. "I have to gather all my
strength for when Cornelius and Hildebrand return," Marie wrote
breathlessly, "probably on 20th May. I've made up the beds in Eitl's atelier
and hung her paintings, all with a heavy heart."[2] Cornelia's ghost was never
far away.

~~~

Predictably, Cornelius took an instant dislike to New York City. Hildebrand kept his own counsel. New York was brash, quarrelsome, with the noise of echoing jackhammers that expanded the already huge skyscape, Cornelius wrote home. He saw no beauty in the built environment. The tooting of car horns, automobiles thundering at speed over cobbled streets, the pollution, the roar of police and fire sirens, the speed of life and the vast sums of money spent on nonsense made him long for the peacefulness of Dresden. The eleven-hour sightseeing tour of the city behind three policemen on motorcycles holding back traffic was pure purgatory for the old man. He hastened to write to Marie that they had seen less of the excellent New York had to offer and more of the vulgar. Americans, Cornelius lamented, loved money too much and were too flamboyant.[3]

New York's officials would have proudly explained the first zoning law in existence in America—the New York zoning law of 1916. This regulated the configuration of all skyscrapers until 1960, and enshrined in law that light and air were to meet the ground at all times, giving New York its unique profile. Cornelius was, nonetheless, unmoved.[4]

Meanwhile, Hildebrand made it his duty to discover the city. This new, improved, determined Hildebrand had, perhaps, a financially motivated wife to consider. Or maybe his laziness evaporated when Helene pointed out that he was a victim of the academic jealousy between Pinder, Posse, and his father? Or was it quite simply that he sensed there was real money to be made from modern art as a dealer? Whatever his innermost thoughts, he undoubtedly saw money everywhere in New York.

This was his unique opportunity to understand the ever-expanding American art market—ostensibly for the newspaper articles he was writing—while also making useful contacts for his own future. After visiting the world-famous Metropolitan Museum of Art, Hildebrand dashed over to J. B. Neumann's gallery, the New Art Circle, located on West Fifty-seventh Street.* Neumann was German, a recent immigrant to New York and a devotee of Edvard Munch, Max Beckmann, Paul Klee, and Dresden-born Max Pechstein. His business partner, Karl Nierendorf, remained in Germany to manage the Neumann-Nierendorf Gallery in

---

* The Met was the first museum in the world to acquire a painting by Henri Matisse, in 1910.

Berlin.[5] Within ten years, Nierendorf and dozens of other Jewish gallery owners would attempt to join Neumann—or die doing so.

In Neumann, Hildebrand found a kind, generous man and indefatigable champion of modern art. As a dealer and publisher with broad German and European experience, Neumann offered a kaleidoscope of ideas and perspectives to the hungry Hildebrand. Most likely Neumann would have shared the drawing of himself that Dresdner Otto Dix had given him, and informed Hildebrand that he intended to promote American modern art in Germany and German art in America.[6] Neumann would show his generosity to another fledgling art academic in 1926: the future director of the Museum of Modern Art, Alfred H. Barr.[7] Five years later, Hildebrand made Neumann's ideas about cross-border exhibitions his own.

∽

Another must-see on Hildebrand's list was Alfred Stieglitz's exhibition at the Anderson Galleries. Stieglitz was the leader of the Photo-Secession movement in New York, and with Edward Steichen in 1905 set up Gallery 291—known simply as "291"—on Fifth Avenue. Stieglitz, above all others, strove to make photography an accepted and collectable art form in the United States. His latest show at the Anderson Galleries, entitled *Alfred Stieglitz Presents Seven Americans: 159 Paintings, Photographs and Things, Recent and Never Before Publicly Shown*, was a runaway success. The Anderson Galleries immediately gave Stieglitz a permanent exhibition there.[8]

Born only four years after Cornelius, in 1864, Stieglitz was one of the most important figures in American visual arts for more than twenty years when Hildebrand saw his work in New York. It was an illuminating initiation to the huge significance of photography, which Gurlitt would never forget, especially since American art was not yet popular in Europe.

What Hildebrand found especially fascinating about 1925 New York was that names which were present and appreciated in Germany, like Picasso and Cézanne, were not yet accepted in New York art circles. Both painters and other Postimpressionists and Cubists were on sale at his cousin's gallery in Berlin for more than a dozen years. Matisse, who was feverishly collected by the influential Stein family living in Paris since the early 1900s, was known and loved throughout Europe. It was Stieglitz who'd requested that Leo Stein write an article for his periodical *Camera Work*, but had to settle for Gertrude's short texts on Matisse and Picasso instead.[9] The significance of having a great patron collecting an artist's works was not lost on the cash-strapped Hildebrand.

The German architects toured the United States like dust devils, swirling through relative "backwaters" like Boston, Chicago, Detroit, Saint Louis, Philadelphia, and Washington, DC. In each city, presumably, the routine was much the same. Cornelius and his architects would be whirled through grand city tours and asked unctuously to lecture on German architecture while Hildebrand darted between the scheduled events, museums, and galleries. Unfortunately, neither Hildebrand nor Cornelius provided posterity with any detail of their epic journey.[10]

∽

Finally, in Germany that September, Hildebrand got his big break. He and his wife moved 115 miles away, to the industrial Saxon town of Zwickau. At long last, he had secured a position as the director of the small König-Albert-Museum there. It was a bitter pill for Cornelius to swallow, having set his hopes on Hildebrand securing a museum position in the higher-profile city of Dresden.

Whether there was a "discussion" about the move can only be surmised. Chances are that there were several. Still, it was a museum job. Zwickau's mayor, Richard Holz, had offered the younger Gurlitt a job based on a talk Hildebrand had given in nearby Chemnitz and on the glowing reports received from the school of art there. It would be some while, if ever, before Cornelius would come to terms with the shock move.

Marie, too, tried to put on a brave face. Hildebrand was already at work in Zwickau when she wrote to her sister-in-law that Helene's dancing classes commenced on October 1, and that her daughter-in-law would leave Dresden on September 22, since their accommodation in Zwickau needed redecoration. "Hildebrand will need to be in Dresden from time to time," Marie consoled herself, "since exhibitions will travel here from Zwickau." At least, she added, Zwickau was closer than Freiburg, where Wilibald had settled.[11]

That autumn, the political complexion of Saxony changed, too. Zwickau had become an NSDAP stronghold four years earlier, with a large following among the lacemaking and bobbin manufacturers. Although the NSDAP was still outlawed, supporters found ways around the problem. A temporary movement called the Völkisch-Soziale Block (VSB), an ersatz organization of the NSDAP, was founded by industrialists Fritz Tittmann in Zwickau and Martin Mutschmann, a lacemaker, in the southern part of the province at Plauen. Mutschmann soon became the preeminent Nazi in Saxony, and would remain so for the next twenty years.

The NSDAP's outlaw status did not last long. The Nazi Party newspaper, the *Völkischer Beobachter*, resumed publication in February 1925. Hitler was released from prison the previous December, and feverishly toured Germany, fully funded by his patron Stinnes and other industrialists. In June, a relatively unknown journalist wrote a front-page article, "The Idea and Sacrifice," dedicated to an imaginary, unknown Communist who had seen the errors of his ways and joined the Nazi Party—the *real* party representing the workers' struggle. His name was Joseph Goebbels.

Both Goebbels and Hitler were in Saxony in 1925 at the same time that Hildebrand took up his position. Goebbels had become a rising star in journalism and already held a true veneration for Hitler. After he read Hitler's *Mein Kampf*, he wrote in his diary, "Führer was more than a man. He was half plebeian, half God, perhaps even Christ."[12] On November 5, 1925, Goebbels met Hitler at Braunschweig just before they were both due to speak at a meeting of their followers.

Mesmerized by Hitler's big blue eyes—they were like shining stars, he claimed—Goebbels could hardly believe what he saw and heard that night: "With wit, irony, humor, sarcasm, with seriousness, and glowing with passion. That man has got everything to be a king. A born people's tribune. The coming dictator."[13]

In mid-November, Goebbels traveled to Gauleiter Martin Mutschmann's hometown of Plauen, in southwest Saxony. After Goebbels met Mutschmann, he described him as "a decent, brutal leader." The following day, Goebbels continued his grueling schedule, traveling on to Chemnitz, where two thousand Communists interrupted the speeches before brawling broke out, reportedly killing two people. Next, Goebbels spoke at Zwickau—the heartland of Germany's automotive and lacemaking industries. There he met Hitler again, "to his great joy." Goebbels wrote in his diary that "he greets me like an old friend. And looks after me. How I love him! He gives me his photograph!"[14]

This was no chance meeting. Hitler had heard that the little man with the clubfoot had a deep, melodious voice. He also heard that Goebbels could grip a packed hall and persuade his listeners to become members of the party. The führer was there to witness Goebbels in action personally; to see what use he could make of him in the days and years ahead. Goebbels passed the test and became part of the inner circle, contributing the key phrase, which he'd taken from a book by Moeller van den Bruck, *Das Dritte Reich*—The Third Reich.[15]

☙

While Goebbels and Hitler toured Saxony, Gurlitt prepared his first-ever museum exhibition. There is no surviving public record of whether he went to hear the Nazi leaders speak; however, given the publicity Hitler generated, it would have been in keeping with Hildebrand's curiosity to go along to hear the man whom people were already calling the führer.

13

ᏯᎢᏯᎢᏯ

THE MYSTERIOUS MR. KIRCHBACH

Patron: One who countenances, supports or protects. Commonly a wretch who supports with insolence, and is paid with flattery.

—SAMUEL JOHNSON

TO SUCCEED, HILDEBRAND NEEDED THREE THINGS: A PROPER JOB at a museum to build his credentials, to publish academic articles on artistic subjects, and, above all, a patron. It is easy to forget that every museum, just like every artist, needs at least one patron. In Germany, patronage came through the auspices of well-respected galleries, where the gallery owner would agree to exhibit and act as an agent for the artist's works for a fee from 10 to 25 percent.

Others were fortunate enough to have the regional Kunstverein, or artists' association, exhibit for them. These associations were effectively quasi-dealers and agents as well as quasi-museums—writing intelligent articles about the artists and portraying their work in the most favorable light while advertising their exhibitions at the association. As the Kunstvereine were essentially state-funded, it was the German taxpayer who was the patron.

For museums, life was simpler. European museums were funded by the state and run as private fiefdoms by their directors, with all the rights, privileges, and responsibilities inherent in that relationship, for the portrayal of civilizational and cultural heritage in their communities. Still, museum directors had to create a sparkling universe that would become a magnet for visitors, gallery owners, and artists, too.

∽

Hildebrand Gurlitt's patron came from the most unlikely of places and proved to be *the* turning point in his life. As a first step, however, he needed to assess Zwickau's holdings and arrange special loans with gallery owners, artists, other museums, and private collectors, like his parents' nearby Jewish neighbor Fritz Glaser, who owned over sixty Dix paintings. As with museums today, Gurlitt knew that creating an original themed show would attract visitors, and German modern art was already his passion. The trip to the United States had given him a fresh perspective on how to capitalize on that love, as well as on future trends. With his father's connections—and his own made during the war and afterward—he hoped to put Zwickau on the artistic map.

The German art market in the second half of the 1920s was changing rapidly. The great art dealers like Alfred Flechtheim and J. B. Neumann had moved their center of operations—Flechtheim from Düsseldorf to Berlin and Neumann from Berlin to New York. Where Neumann's move was opportunistic, Flechtheim's was political.

Düsseldorf was in the French-occupied Ruhr, and Flechtheim was on the French political war-criminals list, since he had served as the administrative head of the *Flamenpolitik* units in Brussels.[1] Having worked for Flechtheim during the war, Gurlitt was keen to renew the acquaintance now that he had a job. On the back of meeting Neumann in New York, it was especially easy. The revived acquaintance gave Gurlitt an opportunity to network with others in Flechtheim's circle, too, like his young and debonair assistant Karl Buchholz. Other Berliners were courted, too—Walter Feilchenfeldt and Grete Ring, who took over Paul Cassirer's gallery in 1926 following Cassirer's suicide attempt, and Karl Nierendorf, who ran the Neumann-Nierendorf Berlin gallery, to name a few.[2]

Neumann's Munich art gallery specialized in graphics and was now run by Günther Franke, who would often deal with Gurlitt in the years ahead. In much the same way, Flechtheim's Düsseldorf gallery was operated by the man he and Buchholz had trained, Alex Vömel. Other key dealers in Bavaria were Anna Caspari and Maria Almas-Dietrich, in Munich, and Karl Haberstock, originally from Augsburg.

Flechtheim also had international contacts in London, specifically with the Marlborough Gallery, as well as a partnership in Paris with Daniel-Henry Kahnweiler of Galerie Simon. Hildebrand soon found another attraction to Flechtheim: his legendary parties replete with movie stars, artists, financial barons, musicians, cabaret dancers—essentially anyone who thought they were someone in Weimar's increasingly decadent culture. As Gurlitt knew, "The future of Germany is being tentatively anticipated by Berlin. The man who wants to gather hope should look there."[3]

On a personal level, Hildebrand was aware that his father opposed his new strategy for success. It smacked of the mercenary, of the brash commercial—perhaps even, heaven forfend, of the American. He saw that his parents were aging and could no longer comprehend the new order of this alien world. The loss of the war, hyperinflation, and political instability had all taken their toll.[4]

Cornelius disliked the very idea of modern Berlin—often likened to a desirable woman. It had a racy, almost immoral cultural energy. Frequently referred to as cold, coquettish, arrogant, snobbish, parvenu, uncultivated, and common, Berlin became the symbol of something every man "wanted to own, for if he owned Berlin, he would own the world."[5]

Berlin's rawness worried Cornelius. After all, hadn't he fretted over his son's mental health since 1915? Besides, diving into Berlin's depths as Hildebrand had determined to do was not a road to scholarship. It was simply unnecessary to circulate among such people with a predatory intent or vulgarity of spirit. Yet Gurlitt *needed* to rebel against this intransigent "old guard" viewpoint to succeed. Over the next ten years, Hildebrand purposely cultivated a more distant relationship with his father, where he said little and explained less.[6] It was time to come of age.

&

Gurlitt agreed with his University of Frankfurt cohort, playwright and winner of the coveted Georg Büchner prize Carl Zuckmeyer, who borrowed from the French king Henry IV, "Berlin was worth more than a mass. This city gobbled up talents and human energies with unexampled appetite . . . with tornado-like powers."[7]

In 1929, Zuckmeyer rose to fame as the scriptwriter for the film adaptation of Heinrich Mann's novel *Professor Unrat*. The film's title was *Der blaue Engel—The Blue Angel*—and starred Marlene Dietrich. Hildebrand's long-envied cousin, Wolfgang, had already imbibed at Zuckmeyer's starry table; and to Hildebrand's mind, Wolfgang *owed it* to him to open up the world of Berlin.[8] It would be a partial payment of the family debt to introduce him into the cutthroat art world there.

Any Berlin art dealer of worth had his own pet collectors and artists. Wolfgang was no exception. Like Flechtheim, he had made a specialty of selling French modern art, much as his own father, Fritz, had done in the late 1880s. Still, Hildebrand knew it would be difficult to win Wolfgang's confidence. It was also doubtful that Hildebrand knew that Wolfgang had never returned nineteen Henri Matisse paintings loaned by Michael and Sarah Stein in June 1914 for an exhibition at his gallery.[9]

Even if Hildebrand had found out, he might have shrugged and agreed with Wolfgang that the nineteen Matisse paintings were victims of the Great War. Besides, the art world was colonized by shady deals and highly selective secrecy. Treachery was the common currency. Relationships were jealously guarded, and no one told anyone else the absolute truth for fear of being outmaneuvered or discredited.

∽

Berlin remained Gurlitt's artistic priority, even from the wilds of Zwickau. Helene was no longer able to teach due to an injury, and the daily grind of how to pay their living expenses overshadowed any grand plans. While Hildebrand achieved a great deal in a short period of time with his exhibitions and lectures, he had already discovered that changing Zwickau's staid institution known for its classical sculptures would be difficult during the ascendancy of the Nazi Party. He was still borrowing from his mother, who delayed the installation of heating and electricity for the Dresden house as a result. "We have a lot of obligations," Marie wrote in August 1926. "We need to husband our resources."[10]

More worrying, the gauleiter of Saxony, Martin Mutschmann, a devoted Hitler acolyte, was already interested in what should be allowed in exhibitions at Zwickau. He also determined what did or did not make "good art." This shouldn't have surprised Gurlitt, since the basic tenet of Hitler's philosophy in the arts was about the degeneracy of culture. Everything from prostitution—that "disgrace against humanity"—to education at German *Gymnasiien* was deemed "a mockery of the Greek model" that contributed to "the emergence of sexual ideas." The responsible catalyst for the collapse of culture in society was naturally Jewish bolshevism. "It is no accident," Hitler claimed, "that the Bolshevistic wave never found better soil than in places inhabited by a population degenerated by hunger and constant undernourishment: in Central Germany, Saxony, and the Ruhr." In a blunt stab at the cognoscenti, he continued, "the so-called intelligentsia no longer offers any serious resistance to the Jewish disease, for the simple reason that this intelligentsia is itself completely degenerate."[11]

Perhaps Cornelius had read *Mein Kampf* by the late 1920s. If not, it certainly made for poor scholarship in view of his support for Hitler until 1936.[12] If Hildebrand had read it at this juncture, he chose to ignore damning statements about his beloved contemporary art. In 1923, Hitler maintained that art bolshevism was the cultural and spiritual expression of the movement as a whole.[13] As Albert Einstein would later say, "If the facts don't fit the theory, change the facts."

"Even before the turn of the century," Hitler cried, "an element began to intrude into our art which . . . could be regarded as entirely foreign and unknown."[14] This was no mere aberration of taste as in the past. It was the dissolution of German culture. Hitler called anyone who refused to see his viewpoint as an "accomplice in the slow prostitution of our future." A cleansing of German culture was essential in the theater, art, literature, cinema, press, posters, and even window displays. Failing this, the "rotting world" would be suffocated by "the stifling perfume of our modern eroticism, just as it must be freed from all unmanly, prudish hypocrisy."[15]

As early as 1924, Weimar culture was branded as "degenerate" by Hitler. This hid a deep-seated hatred masquerading as a philosophy from which he would never stray. *Mein Kampf* was more than a mere book. It was Hitler's manifesto. If he came to power, he would carry out his vision. Indeed, on February 27, 1925, in his first speech upon his release from Landsberg, Hitler laid down the gauntlet. The enemies of the NSDAP were the Weimar Republic, Marxists, and Jews. "To this struggle of ours there are only two possible issues: either the enemy passes over our bodies or we pass over theirs!"[16]

⌘

It may seem rotten luck that at precisely that very moment Gurlitt was trying to build an independent life as an art historian and museum director. In 1925, there were twenty-seven thousand members of the NSDAP. Dividing the country into thirty-two main districts, or *Gaue*,* Hitler had appointed his gauleiters to each one, with Martin Mutschmann leading Saxony. Two years later, NSDAP membership nearly trebled, to 178,000.

In October 1926 Joseph Goebbels became the gauleiter of Berlin. It was the gauleiters' task to rejuvenate the party locally: clear out the violent rowdies who'd been putting off the "silent majority" and eradicate the Babylon that Germany had become. Thus, from the outset, Gurlitt found Mutschmann standing in the way of educating the inhabitants of Zwickau to the new horizons of modern art.

Yet all was not lost. Gurlitt's quick intellect and arrogance readily embraced the concept of eternal affability toward artists, gallery owners, and collectors. He was charm and persuasiveness personified. His exhibitions had special receptions providing enviable hospitality to schmooze the local great and good. Gurlitt's flair for the modern, his contacts in the art world among living artists, his cultivated good taste, and his familial credentials were his unique selling points. His confidence, newfound energy, and apparent generosity of spirit were certain to attract connoisseurs.

The most important of Gurlitt's nurtured aficionados was the wealthy industrialist Kurt Kirchbach. Kirchbach and his twin brother, Ernst, were born and raised in Dresden. Their father, Karl, had invented a new process for industrial and automotive seals and set up a factory in 1910 in the small town of Coswig, between Dresden and Zwickau. When war was declared in 1914, Germany found that it could no longer provide *any* seals for automobile or tank engines, as the British manufacturer Ferodo had a

---

* This roughly corresponded to the thirty-two electoral districts.

virtual stranglehold on the German market. Naturally, Ferodo refused to ship any equipment after the outbreak of war.

The brothers, in charge of the business since their father's death in 1913, saw their opportunity, and rescued Germany's War Department. Their genius was having come up with a type of woven asbestos, taking advantage of the local expertise in lacemaking, and creating molded and cured seals for any imaginable use. They delivered the first brake pads and seals ever made in Germany within months of the war's outbreak. By the end of the war, they were fabulously wealthy.

With enough money to back further inventions, they developed specialist friction-resistant resins and new perforated seals. Their wealth multiplied exponentially. Sadly, Ernst died in early 1920, toward the end of the horrendous outbreak of Spanish flu that killed around fifty million people worldwide.[17]

By the time Kurt Kirchbach met Hildebrand, he was married and had taken a business partner, Hans Kattwinkel, and the company was branching out into automotive clutch facings, exporting to the rest of Europe and the United States under the trademark Jurid. With hyperinflation, Kirchbach had decided not only that they would demand to be paid in foreign exchange whenever possible, but that he would also make a range of investments to help protect his personal wealth.

How, when, or why Kurt Kirchbach and Gurlitt began to work together is unclear.[18] Yet within a very short time of his arrival in Zwickau, Hildebrand and Kirchbach became very friendly, and Kirchbach asked him to help acquire art for investment purposes—as a paid consultant. It was a phenomenal opportunity, and one to which Gurlitt devoted a great deal of time and effort.

∽

Key to Hildebrand's success would be his ability to create a collection that Kurt Kirchbach could simply adore. This meant getting to know each other well, and, above all else, trusting one another. As anyone in business knows, having a wealthy client who entrusts one with an intimate and expensive project creates a special bond and places that person in a certain position of power. Hildebrand saw not only the advantages for his short-term monetary gain and stability, but also the endless possibilities for

Kirchbach to help him prize open the inner-sanctum doors of other wealthy industrialists.

By the late 1920s, Kirchbach manufactured original automotive clutch linings and brakes for the entire German automotive industry. Kirchbach's contacts were international, and reached the highest echelons of German industry. Gustav Krupp and Fritz Thyssen were important business associates. Philipp Reemtsma, of Reemtsma Cigarettenfabriken, was a personal friend. If Gurlitt could stick close to Kirchbach, his entire future in the art world as the "impeccable eye" of Germany's wealthy would be assured.

Consequently, after long and enjoyable consultations with his patron—for Kirchbach was far more than a client by 1926—it was agreed that their first foray into the art world would be in the realm of photography. It had the advantage of newness, grossly undervalued by many in Germany, and, as Gurlitt had seen in New York, was becoming vastly popular in the United States. It had the additional advantage in his patron's eyes of being a phenomenal visual documentary of the previous tumultuous twenty years. The Kurt Kirchbach collection of over six hundred photographs—or, as it would later curiously become known, the Helene Anderson Collection—would become the most significant avant-garde photographic collection of the 1920s. Among the many photographic artists were Man Ray, El Lissitzky, Edward Weston, László Moholy-Nagy, Umbo, and Albert Renger-Patzsch. It was as if Stieglitz had whispered a wish list of his preferred European photographers to collect.[19]

Of course, this was only the beginning. A superb modern-art collection followed over the long years of their friendship. Lovis Corinth, Egon Schiele, Max Beckmann, and Max Liebermann became the cornerstones of Kirchbach's collection of 234 modern-art masterpieces.[20] Gurlitt had not only made an unimpeachable name for himself with this collection, but also solidified his reputation as a loyal and steadfast friend to Kirchbach. They would come to rely heavily on one another in the years ahead.

14

THE ROOT OF EVIL

The dominant fashion is to look to the racial factor as
the *deus ex machina* of the human drama.

—CHRISTOPHER DAWSON, *The Age of Gods* (1928)

IT'S NOT WHAT YOU KNOW, BUT WHO YOU KNOW, THE SAYING GOES.
Thanks to Kurt Kirchbach, Gurlitt could do business as the first among
equals. Despite the rise of the Nazi Party throughout the 1920s, and
Mutschmann's often loud displeasure, towns as far away as Hagen, in
Westphalia, sought Gurlitt's advice.[1]

In 1925, it hardly mattered that modern art was scorned by Hitler and
the Nazis. Indeed, throughout the 1920s contemporary art prices held their
value. Museums continued to buy works direct from artists or the stocks
of German art dealers. Most popular among the German Expressionists
and Impressionists were Franz Marc, Otto Dix, Max Liebermann, and
Max Beckmann.[2] So long as the good times rolled on, so would Gurlitt's
rise within the established order.

Still Gurlitt's luck was on the wane again. Helene's health was a concern, and her long stay of five months in the hospital had proven costly.
Money was an ever rarer commodity than before. "I have sold a few things
to help out the children financially," Marie wrote. "Cornelius has sold two
figures from the garden—it was not easy for us, but our burden in taxes
has been heavy. . . . It will be so wonderful to see Helene and Putz again."[3]

Hildebrand was no stay-at-home husband able or willing to nurse his wife after her two operations. Instead, he juggled the day job with advising Kirchbach and visiting Helene in hospital. Yet, despite his newfound vigor, he hadn't realized he was battling against forces far greater than he could ever conceive.

With President Ebert's sudden death, the seventy-seven-year-old Field Marshal Paul von Hindenburg had been coaxed from retirement to become Germany's new president. Stresemann, who had done all the groundwork in international relations, was very busy indeed. The Locarno treaties assured Germany's western borders and the withdrawal of French troops from the cordon sanitaire* in the Rhineland. The pièce de résistance was Germany's admission to the League of Nations. Hope prevailed, certainly among the English, that Franco-German relations would improve to the point where France would also release its cordon sanitaire of alliances against Germany in the East—and that eventually—there would be a peaceful surrender of the Sudetenland of Czechoslovakia, the Polish Corridor, and the Free City of Danzig.

Nonetheless, the issue of reparations was far from resolved at Locarno. American banks and businesses had been piling on short-term loans to Germans; then the borrowers immediately plowed part of the cash into a falsely buoyant stock market for purely speculative purposes. Margin purchases and quick profits characterized investments in the "new era of hope." Meanwhile, Germany remained obliged to continue its reparations payments with borrowed funds, digging a deeper and deeper pit for itself. Schacht announced on May 11, 1927, that the Reichsbank considered that the commercial banks' reserves were too low.† Two days later, Schacht suspended all Reichsbank credit, creating the "Black Friday" of May 13.[4] As the US secretary of the treasury's agent general explained, "Germans are not going to get their payments under the Dawes Plan reduced because they have been buying securities on margin at much more than their correct value and now have to sell them at a sacrifice when the banks call their loans."[5]

Actually, all Europe was drunk on easy money and revolution. Ev-

---

* This was the term used internationally for the French Occupation and French Alliances in the East.
† This was one of the causes of the 2007 banking meltdown.

erywhere, the rich speculated with a fraction of their own money that they "invested" in the stock markets. Britain had survived its ten-day General Strike of 1926, which saw the inexorable rise of a new force in politics—the Labour Party—and confirmation that the social structure of the country had irretrievably changed. Most people feared that Britain—the stalwart of European democracy—would turn toward the left like France.* At the same time, the French franc slid in value against the dollar and was worth only two cents. The French budget spiraled out of control. Joseph Stalin seized power in the Soviet Union, keen to expand Russian influence and communism. Suddenly, the Russian Bear was standing on his hind legs, growling.

To make matters worse, Schacht, of course, was implacable at the Young Conference in February 1929 that was called at his urging and aimed at reducing reparations payments. Schacht worried about Germany's close ties to the American economy and German indebtedness to the United States. Meanwhile, the *New York Times* had printed the previous December that Stresemann and Schacht were at loggerheads. In fact, Schacht went too far, demanding the return of Germany's colonies, redefining Poland's boundaries (making it landlocked), *and* demanding further reductions in reparations payments.

Viewed as a current-affairs gambit, Schacht's demands had risked everything, and he was thoroughly trounced at the negotiating table. The German delegate and industrialist Albert Voegler of United Steelworks stormed out of the conference and proclaimed to the government that there were insufficient safeguards for Germany.[6] Of course, Voegler also told his industrialist friends Gustav Krupp, Fritz Thyssen, and Kurt Kirchbach what happened. Rather than resign, Schacht capitulated and signed the agreement on June 7, 1929, under tremendous government pressure.†

Schacht's rapid surrender was heavily criticized by the conglomerates of Krupp and Thyssen. The government was agog. Kirchbach, who depended

---

* One of the causes of the ten-day work stoppage was the declining wage and quality of life of some 800,000 miners. A total of 1.7 million workers went on strike, primarily in transport and heavy industries, in sympathy for the miners.
† The most enduring outcome of the Young Conference was the establishment of the Bank for International Settlements, located in Basel, Switzerland, which would oversee reparations payments.

on steel from Thyssen, was firmly against the agreement, opposing any steps that might adversely affect heavy industry.

Yet Krupp's and Thyssen's criticisms were playing to an audience. Schacht's manner was reported as "vehement, intolerant . . . excitable and dogmatic. The most tactless, the most aggressive and the most irascible person I have seen in public life. But he was fundamentally right."[7] Nonetheless, like the two great industrialist families, Schacht had lost faith and confidence in the Weimar Republic.

Schacht was also aware that Fritz Thyssen was the president of the supervisory board of the Vereinigte Stahlwerke (United Steelworks), and a major donor to the Nazi Party, handing over cash to Hitler personally. Emil Kirdorf, the king of coal in the Ruhr region, did the same.[8] They led the industrialist backing for Hitler. United Steelworks was the second-largest coal and steel company in the world after US Steel Corporation.[9]

The Thyssen connection mustn't be underestimated. By 1929, Hitler was certainly living beyond his means, and declared to the tax officials that his personal links to German big business made this possible. In fact, on Hitler's tax returns he stated that his profession was "writer" and the only income declared was his royalties from *Mein Kampf.* He was heavily in debt, if his tax returns are to be believed, and those debts were cleared absolutely in 1929.[10]

A year earlier, Fritz Thyssen financed the new Nazi headquarters in Munich, named the Brown House, acting as the guarantor for the RM 350,000 loan made through the family's Dutch bank. Pandering to Hermann Göring's increasing self-aggrandizement, Thyssen also provided three gifts totaling RM 150,000 to "enlarge" Göring's apartment and make improvements.[11] It was a relationship that would flourish with tender attention over the coming years, and contribute to the exponential growth of the Thyssen companies. Big business, led by Fritz Thyssen personally, had abandoned Weimar.

⁓

October 1929 proved disastrous. Stresemann died at the beginning of the month, and on October 24 the US stock market crashed. Instantly, American loans were demanded back, and Germany—as well as the rest of the world—was plunged into a deep depression. Before the year was out, over six million Germans were unemployed. Previously booming factories had fallen silent. Bread lines snaked through cities. Petty crime was on the increase. Youth unemployment was rampant. Widespread misery enveloped the country. Schacht's predictions of Armageddon had come true.

Evil thrives on misery, and Adolf Hitler was positively blooming. "Never in my life," he wrote, "have I been so well disposed and inwardly contented as in these days."[12] For Hitler, abject human suffering was the root cause of his future opportunities. He knew from the previous failed attempts at snatching power that his day could come only *with* the support of financial institutions and the military. The forthcoming election was tailor-made for his purposes.

∾

The cornerstone of Hitler's campaign to win the hearts of the German people centered on the emotional. He believed that only art—in whatever form—could touch the German people's souls. He'd imbibed the essence of racial hatred and art espoused in Dr. Hans Günther's theories in 1923 in *Rassenkunde des Deutschen Volkes* (The Racial Science of the German People) and Günther's 1926 book *Rasse und Stil* (Race and Style). Others, like Ottmar Rutz (*Menschheitstypen und Kunst*, 1921) and Dr. Ferdinand Clauss (*Die nordische Seele*, 1923, and *Rasse und Seele*, 1926), were also instrumental. Still, it was Günther's *Rasse und Stil* that coherently united art and the racist in an unholy alliance.[13] Hitler, the eternal thieving magpie, took the relationship to heart as his very own.

Essentially, these racial theories about art perverted the artist's intent and the humanist ideal at the core of all expression. While pigeonholing the psychological catalyst that ignited all creativity, the racists were able to forge a philosophy stoked in the fires of hell based on hatred and a twisted interpretation of all human creative endeavor. When the architect Professor Paul Schultz-Naumburg's book *Kunst and Rasse* was published, in 1928, he wrote, "Art is capable of expressing not alone its physical principle, but it also tries to secure supremacy in every way for its own spiritual law. The battle of *Weltanschauung* to a large extent is fought out in the field of art."[14] It was a mirror of Hitler's thoughts.

Yet the dubious distinction of being the first to express racist notions in art is reserved for the Jewish writer Max Nordau and his *Entartung*, published in 1892. He claimed that *Entartung*, or degeneration, would soon become a byword for all that was un-German. It was a concept that raged like a brush fire in a windstorm through Germany in late 1920s Weimar.[15]

∽

In the midst of this furor, Gurlitt continued to advise Kirchbach on his collection. It was a means not only of acquiring wealth and guaranteeing foreign exchange but also of elevating Kirchbach onto the same platform culturally as his business associates Krupp and Thyssen. Kirchbach, as a leading importer of raw materials from Norway, also helped Gurlitt organize the Zwickau showcase of German Expressionist artists in Oslo.

The Thyssen connection would prove lucrative for Gurlitt in the future, particularly as it also provided him with entrée into an international circle of experts, like Sir Joseph Duveen, who advised the Colnaghi Gallery in London and the groundbreaking American-born art historian Bernard Berenson.* These men dealt extensively with American collectors, whom Duveen had the foresight to see "had the money" where Europe only had the art.[16] Duveen and Berenson (codenamed "Doris" by Duveen) had the most coveted American private client list imaginable, which included Isabella Stewart Gardner, Henry J. Frick, Andrew W. Mellon, and J. P. Morgan.

Still, it was the allegedly "secret" side deal between Duveen and the Harvard-educated Berenson that intrigued Gurlitt. They lived in ruthless times, and it had been rumored in the trade that Berenson had cut a deal with Duveen whereby he would earn a commission of 25 percent of the purchase price of an artwork if Berenson merely gave it his seal of approval.[17] It was a recipe that Gurlitt would seek to replicate.

The Berenson contact made Gurlitt wide-eyed. The first known painting to be purchased by Heinrich Thyssen, according to the Thyssen-Bornemisza archive, was a landscape painted by Rembrandt's friend Jan Lievens in 1635 entitled *Rest on the Flight into Egypt*. Thyssen's dealer Ru-

---

* Bernard Berenson was the advisor to Thyssen and the art historian who had "decrypted" Renaissance art for collectors and auction houses by introducing his "scientific method," referring to paintings being "school of" or "Anonymous Master" or "studio of."

dolf Heinemann and "BB" (as Berenson was known to friends) were not worried in the slightest that it was bought without any provenance whatsoever.[18] Gurlitt, like others, had taken note.

∞

With the crash of 1929, Gurlitt entered the murky world of buying art from once-wealthy people desperate to convert their investments into cash—whether it was to pay their margin calls or simply to afford to live. This was when Gurlitt advised Kirchbach to begin to acquire German Expressionist artists from willing, recently impoverished sellers—or the starving artists themselves. This may have had little to do with the changing political landscape or Gurlitt's usual foresight, and everything to do with raw opportunism.

Still, the first half of 1929 was one of personal hardship. Gurlitt was left dangling by the mayor of Hagen, in Westphalia, regarding his possible appointment as their cultural advisor—not from any malice of the mayor but rather for his untimely long-term illness.[19] That June, Helene's brother was critically ill in hospital. He was a ship's engineer and his vessel had been shipwrecked, leaving him swimming in the Baltic for three days before he was rescued. Gurlitt "used his contacts" to have him brought to Zwickau so he could be near Helene. Yet, he soon died of pneumonia and was buried in Dresden in a plot near to Cornelia.[20]

Less than three weeks later, "Hildebrand has all kinds of trouble, as the city of Zwickau faces bankruptcy and the museum will have to close," Cornelius penned in a letter. "The mayor announced this to him and also expressed his regret and called his [Hildebrand's] exhibitions a 'shining testimony.' How he will determine his future is anyone's guess, but he's in good spirits."[21]

How indeed. Mutschmann was outraged by the Oslo art exhibition. It was one thing to have to deal with this "syphilitic" art inside Germany, quite another to show it to the world. Marie, too, became worried. That October she wrote that "poor Hildebrand has a lot of trouble and excitement in the museum, the city has no money, and the museum will be closed and the position of director withdrawn. . . . They have had such a terrible year." Indeed, eleven months earlier Hildebrand had been seriously ill with appendicitis and needed to be operated on twice, spending four weeks in hospital.

Then Helene's grandmother died, in April, followed two months later by the death of her brother. There was also the tragic death of Marie's sister-in-law,* who was killed by a hit-and-run driver.[22]

Obviously, Hildebrand was telling his parents only what he wanted them to believe: that he'd been the object of a systematic smear campaign by Gauleiter Mutschmann and Oberbürgermeister Richard Holz had quite evidently slipped his mind.

∽

In 1928, the Nazi Party ideologue Alfred Rosenberg—a former architectural student who had written the unreadable *Myth of the Twentieth Century*, which mistook all ideas about race and art for philosophy—had founded the Kampfbund für deutsche Kultur with Hitler as the cultural seat of power of the Nazi Party.[†] Organized as an onslaught against modern art while taking advantage of the change in the political landscape, it was aimed at the hearts and minds—the emotional core—in maintaining and nurturing all that was truly German.

Art would henceforth become the bludgeon to create the new Nazi mythology and the key to social integration in Hitler's new, improved "collective society."[23] The raw emotional power of each individual's reaction to art was raised to the level of high Nazi doctrine. This, Hitler felt, was intrinsic to his ultimate success.

The *Diktat* of Versailles had oppressed Germany. Of course, Hitler blamed the Jews and Bolsheviks. It was a simple message, repeated time and again. A message that hit home. Hitler's whirlwind campaign and message moved the German people. They felt that they had an ally. They also felt, wrongly, that in Hitler there was someone who felt their pain.

When the results were in, Hitler's NSDAP had won a staggering 107 seats in the Reichstag, making it the second-largest party.[‡] Hitler's inner sanctum was filled to overflowing with men who believed, as he did, that the perfect model for their new collective society would be the complete absorption of Germany's art into the permanent fabric of the State.[24]

---

* Her brother Oskar's wife.
† The Association for the Struggle of German Culture.
‡ 6,409,600 Germans voted NSDAP and 4,592,000 voted Communist (whose seats increased to 77).
  Source: *The Rise and Fall of the Third Reich*, 138

Gone were the days when Hitler could be derided as the leader of some lunatic fringe. When the NSDAP won Saxony by a significant margin, Mutschmann swung into gear. The *Ortsgruppe*, or regional Nazi group, in Zwickau ousted Gurlitt on April 1, 1930, after the umpteenth assault on his character.[25] Still the cover-up continued, this time on a national scale. Cited by Mutschmann to the NSDAP as the paradigm of progressive museum work, Gurlitt was nevertheless officially removed from his position for the "poor financial state" of his institution. Unofficially he was sacked for his love of modern art, a fact that Oberbürgermeister Richard Holz went to great length to affirm.[26]

When the Reichsverband Bildender Künstler (Federal Association of Artists) heard about Gurlitt's dismissal, a furor erupted. Only months earlier, the Nationalgalerie in Berlin had been heavily criticized for raising substantial funds to acquire paintings by van Gogh, and thus leaving German artists to misery in the Depression. In Gurlitt, they had an ally who bought from living German artists not only for his museum, but also for Kirchbach and other private collectors. Soon some fifty museum directors petitioned the government in protest. Surely it was their task to support contemporary German art, was it not?

Unsurprisingly, when Hitler came to power, in January 1933, these fifty names would come to regret their solidarity with Gurlitt. They were all put onto a special list, for future retribution.

Gurlitt, meanwhile, had no alternative but to pack his bags and return to Dresden with his wife. Still, he had no intention of living hand to mouth or hearing his father's endless suggestions about his future for long. He'd had a foretaste of success through Kirchbach's patronage and he wanted more. To achieve that, he would need to be flexible in his opinions, be outwardly charming, and appear to act without guile.

15

⌘

CHAMELEONS AND CRICKETS

Art is man's way of re-creating the world after God.
—The character Gottlieb in *The Master* (1919)

GURLITT SENSED THAT THOSE WHO COULD NOT ADAPT TO THE changing times would be devoured by them. His usual perspicacity had been on high alert since the art market tumbled with the crash of 1929. Museum purchases made up approximately 50 percent of the entire German market in 1928, but fell to around 28 percent in less than a year.[1] By 1931, museums made up a mere 18 percent.

Some dealers, such as Berliner Ferdinand Möller, went bankrupt during the 1923–24 hyperinflation and were barely making a comeback. Others, such as Curt Valentin, an associate of Alfred Flechtheim in 1930, complained openly about the misery of the art galleries, with their falling prices and rising expenses in photography, advertising, catalogue printing, and transportation.[2]

The market was unpredictable. Prices fluctuated wildly depending on the desperation of the seller and the type of art. This was precisely when Gurlitt needed to be out in the market buying. In Kirchbach, he had a benefactor who trusted his judgment and understood the advantages and bargains on offer through other peoples' misery. Of course, Cornelius's disapproval made Hildebrand disguise his art dealing.[3]

Nearly a year later, in March 1931, Hildebrand and Helene were still based in Dresden—and he hadn't yet told his father the truth. Cornelius blithely wrote to his sister-in-law that Hildebrand "holds a lot of lectures and supports himself and his very dear wife. Housing issues aside, they want to move to Berlin where more earning potential is possible."[4]

Hildebrand may have tried to discuss the subject. If he did, Cornelius most likely brushed him aside, reciting the problems that Hildebrand's uncle Fritz once faced and his cousin Wolfgang's current financial difficulties. If Hildebrand persisted, the old man may have gone on about Hildebrand's fragile nerves and said that he was better suited for a life in academia. Then again, knowing his father's feelings on the subjects of commercial art dealing and his mental health, Hildebrand may have felt that silence would prove a better cure.

∽

During his thirteen-month hiatus from museum life, Hildebrand surreptitiously dealt in art for Kirchbach and those to whom he was introduced. His art trade with Wolfgang dates from this period, too.* Acquisitions of German Expressionists—Nolde, Beckmann, Liebermann, and Schiele— were the most popular with both Gurlitt and Kirchbach. With the growth of the NSDAP, Gurlitt believed the contemporary art market would remain volatile. The opportunity to buy low in Germany and sell high to Americans was irresistible. It was precisely what Neumann, Duveen, and Berenson had been doing for years.

The Museum of Modern Art had opened the year before in New York, thanks to the drive, donations, and friendship of three women: Lillie P. Bliss, Mary Quinn Sullivan, and Abby Rockefeller.[5] Peggy Guggenheim, the "Prophetess of the Blue Four"—Lyonel Feininger, Paul Klee, Alexey von Jawlensky, and Wassily Kandinsky—was buying other artists' works in droves.[6] The long-awaited springboard of German Expressionists into America was achieved in 1929, too, when the Institute of Arts in Detroit bought

---

* While the German government and the Kunstmuseum Bern steadfastly refuse to publish Gurlitt's papers, the redacted accounts published online by Bern show that Wolfgang was an early and important trading partner.

its first Beckmann. If Gurlitt did not hop on board, the train would leave without him.

Like Kirchbach, Hildebrand agreed that the biggest threat to the art market was not the Depression, but the rise of communism. The 1930 election had shown a rise in Communist voters to 4,592,000, increasing in their seats at the Reichstag from 54 to 77.[7] The right-wing Nationalists dropped by half, paving the way for them to open discussions with the NSDAP. Gurlitt's "shifting sands" morality helped him to reason that he was powerless to change the times in which he lived, except to make the most of them.

The times, however, were changing beyond all reckoning. Within two years, *everything* Germans saw or heard was carefully and ruthlessly purged of all foreign influences. Everything from advertisements to imported foods would be censored to remove the foreign or critical elements according to the tastes of one man. For many of us today, it is nearly impossible to imagine a world where the penalty for criticism was torture and death. Gurlitt knew that if he did not adapt to the new order, he would become live bait, a cricket, for those who'd become chameleons.

∽

In the autumn of 1930, a young architect who studied under Professor Heinrich Tessenow at the Institute of Technology in Berlin-Charlottenburg, and who heard Cornelius Gurlitt lecture there, was at a turning point in his life. He had been relatively apolitical until then, though his father had been deeply distressed by the gains the Communists had made in the September elections. Like Tessenow, he believed that "It is in our nature to love our native land. . . . True culture comes only from the maternal womb of a nation."[8] His name was Albert Speer.

Speer went to hear Hitler speak one evening at a beer hall at the behest of some of his students. Like some aging rock star, Hitler entered the room amid cries of near-hysterical enthusiasm. "On posters and in caricatures, I had seen him in military tunic, with shoulder straps, swastika armband, and hair flapping over his forehead," Speer wrote. "But here he was wearing a well-fitted blue suit and looking markedly respectable. Everything about him bore out the note of reasonable modesty."[9] Speer was witnessing Hitler's uncanny gift for turning chameleon.

Speer expected to hear some lunatic speaking. Instead, he heard an impassioned plea against the dangers of communism and how it would rob Germany of hope and full employment and plunge their beloved nation into perpetual insecurity. Hitler succeeded at a stroke in sensing what his audience needed to hear, and how to deliver the defining message. He unified student and lecturer, small shopkeeper and the unemployed, and even provided them with a scapegoat—the international Jew. Speer was shocked at how impressive Hitler was. As for the anti-Semitism, it had been going on for so long in Germany that it was hardly something new. Besides, like everyone, Speer had "Jewish friends" and claimed he didn't see the danger.[10]

As if sleepwalking, Speer claimed that he entered "Hitler's party" because of the hypnotic impression Hitler made on him. He claimed, too, that he had done so without reading *Mein Kampf* or Rosenberg's *Myth of the Twentieth Century*, blaming this serious misstep on his lack of political schooling.[11] Gurlitt could claim no such lacuna.

∽

Gurlitt was the first museum director to become a victim of Nazi ideology concerning modern art. Whether it was through the support he had received from other museum directors or some introductions or assistance Kirchbach had provided behind the scenes, he was appointed at long last as director of the Hamburg Kunstverein.

"We are very pleased with Hildebrand's choice, and the dear young people look forward to finally being able to getting back to their own apartment," Marie wrote in April 1931.[12] The Kunstverein was located in the chic area near the Elbe on Neue Rabenstrasse. Still, Hildebrand complained to his mother after they moved into the apartment that the Kunstverein was short of money and couldn't pay him an appropriate salary.[13] The financial arrangement regarding commissions from paintings sold or indeed what private deal he had with Kirchbach at this time remained a secret.[14]

In October 1931, Gurlitt went to Gothenburg, in Sweden, for the exhibition he'd arranged of a young Hamburg artist. How did he manage an international exhibition of a little-known German Expressionist in such a short period of time? Again, Kirchbach seemingly flung the doors open wide with his very substantial Swedish connections made from years of

importing premium quality Swedish iron ore.[15] Gurlitt's relationship with
the Zwickau industrialist was so close that when Kirchbach and his wife
had growing marital difficulties, Kirchbach confided in Cornelius that
Hildebrand was like an adopted son to him.[16]

In the first week of December, Frau Kirchbach visited the Kaitzer
Strasse home in Dresden as a houseguest for an entire week. It was she
who told Cornelius and Marie how Hildebrand and Helene were *really*
doing—and that she'd been to the "Gurlittfest" in Altona as well. Perhaps
they had mixed feelings hearing about Hildebrand's opening of another
exhibition and the success of Manfred Gurlitt's opera.* They were forced,
after all, to visualize it through this polite but distant woman's eyes.[17] Even
more upsetting was the unmistakable fact that Hildebrand and Helene
were becoming increasingly detached from their humdrum lives and ever
closer to the Kirchbachs. By the end of 1932, Kirchbach gave Hildebrand
enough money to bail out Wolfgang Gurlitt from looming bankruptcy. It
always paid to have a Berlin gallery in one's back pocket.

✎

In the summer of 1931, Hitler began to raise cash to fight—and win—the
1932 elections. According to his press chief, Otto Dietrich, "the Führer
suddenly decided to concentrate systematically on cultivating the influential industrial magnates."[18] He would leave his rabble-rousers Goebbels
and Hitler's second-in-command Gregor Strasser to whip up the masses
while he crisscrossed Germany meeting privately, often one-on-one,
with Germany's industrialists. The "hit list" was long and the usual suspects
were already on board—Fritz Thyssen, Emil Kirdorf, and Albert Voegler.

Kirdorf, Germany's coal baron and an early convert, presided over
Hitler's slush fund, secretly known as "the Ruhr Treasury." Others, like
Georg von Schnitzler, a director of I. G. Farben, and August Rosterg, of the
potash industry, said they would support Hitler. Soon Deutsche Bank,
Dresdner Bank, and Commerz Bank followed. Hitler's Munich-based SS
chief, Heinrich Himmler, had his own Freundeskreis der Wirtschaft (Circle
of Friends of the Economy), which would raise millions for the party.[19]
Lesser names like Kurt Kirchbach were also contributors, as Germany faced

---

* Manfred was a first cousin, younger brother of Wolfgang.

a stark choice in 1932 between going Communist or lurching to the right and the NSDAP.

Schacht, too, became involved on the periphery, though he hadn't joined the Nazi Party. He met with the heads of I. G. Farben, Bosch, and Siemens, who remained lukewarm toward Hitler as a personality. Friedrich Flick, the coal and iron magnate, gave a token fifty thousand marks to Hitler.* Wilhelm Keppler, another Nazi industrialist, pressed those involved in heavy industry to join through his fund-raising arm Keppler Kreis (Keppler Circle).[20]

At this crucial time, another fund-raiser worked tirelessly, too. Hermann Göring returned to Germany in 1927 following a general political amnesty. He'd spent a great deal of his time in exile in Sweden, and married a Swedish woman who was, sadly, epileptic and contracted tuberculosis. Fritz Thyssen and other industrialists were his good friends, and soon Göring became an advisor to Lufthansa. No longer the dashing pilot of World War I, Göring would prove nonetheless invaluable in raising the Nazi profile among German aristocrats like Prince Philipp von Hessen, Queen Victoria's great-grandson and the son-in-law of Victor Emmanuel III, king of Italy. Above all, Göring was most useful in helping to win over the military.

A little over a month before the 1932 elections, Hitler became a German citizen, enabling him to stand for president if he wished. On February 22, 1932, Hitler allowed Goebbels to declare his candidacy for president of Germany in opposition to the elderly Hindenburg.[21] As the campaign progressed, Hitler—later nicknamed "the Bohemian Corporal" by President Hindenburg—shed his recent lethargy and ran a merciless campaign of public appearances and speeches around the country, often chartering a Lufthansa aircraft. Just as the mythical gods descended from Valhalla, Goebbels used the analogy to describe "the Führer over Germany" swooping down to relieve his people's suffering.[22]

Ernst Röhm, the leader of Hitler's 400,000 men of the SA, threw a cordon of his thugs around Berlin on the eve of the first election. The word "putsch" haunted the air again, according to Goebbels. Yet the results of the first March 13 ballot showed Hindenburg with just under the required

---

* Less evenhandedly, he donated 1.8 million to reelect Hindenburg.

majority to form a new government—with 49.6 percent of the vote. Hitler won 30.1 percent, and the Communist candidate Ernst Thaelmann had 13.2 percent. The influential businessman Alfred Hugenberg withdrew his German National People's Party candidate for the second round, scheduled in a month's time, rather than enter into a coalition with the NSDAP. Nonetheless, Hitler hoped to sweep up enough votes to beat Hindenburg, but was disappointed when Hindenburg won an outright majority of 53 percent on April 10, 1932—with a million fewer votes cast.[23] Two weeks later, in the local Prussian elections, the Nazis were returned as the region's largest party, with 38.3 percent of the vote.[24]

∽

All the while, the depression was deepening. Schacht was fighting his own economic fires, with the failure of his old bank alongside other institutions. Coupled with Hitler's continued onslaught against the republic, the inevitable happened, and in May 1932 the rats deserted the rotting ship. General Kurt von Schleicher refused to head the Ministry of Defense unless Hindenburg hired a new captain. Chancellor Heinrich Bruening was forced to resign, and with him what was left of Weimar was lost. That June, the Reichstag was dissolved.

Röhm wanted to strike, but Hitler hesitated. Whether his indecision was caused by the suicide of his half-niece and alleged lover Geli Raubal the previous September or by problems within the party or both is difficult to judge. By this time, Hitler began to mistrust his undisputed "number two"—Gregor Strasser—who led the party along with Ludendorff while Hitler was incarcerated at Landsberg.

In fact, Hitler believed that no one trusted Strasser any longer, yet was loath to abandon him. Strasser, his brother Otto, and Ernst Röhm were the first to back him for the party leadership; but as far as they were concerned, the führer had changed its direction. They felt that a more socialist approach, in tune with the party's roots, would win them the election.

With nearly half a million men under arms in a private army, chaos reigned in Germany's streets. In Prussia alone, there were over four hundred pitched battles. In Hamburg and Altona, nineteen people were shot dead and 285 wounded. The new chancellor, Franz von Papen, who came from impoverished Wesphalian nobility and had virtually no political power base, banned all parades prior to the forthcoming elections in July and proclaimed martial law in Berlin.

Papen knew he had little choice but to accept a provisional cabinet headed by Hitler. "I regard your cabinet only as a temporary solution and will continue my efforts to make my party the strongest in the country," Papen told Hitler. When polling day came, the Nazis were the largest party in the Reichstag, with 230 seats.[25] Surely Hindenburg could not refuse to make Hitler chancellor now?

Yet that is precisely what happened. Hindenburg "regretted that Herr Hitler did not see himself in a position to support a national government appointed with the confidence of the Reich president, as he had agreed to do before the elections."[26] Naturally, Papen got the job as chancellor instead.

Hitler's riposte was to order his henchmen to prepare for an armed insurrection. While they plotted, he retired to his retreat at Obersalzberg. As Hitler withdrew from the limelight, Goebbels opened communications with the Center Party to sound them out about forming a coalition government. In August 1932, Goebbels went to Austria to strengthen the Nazi Party in Vienna.[27] When Hitler emerged from his splendid isolation, he claimed he'd been worried about the economy. He announced that he had "held occasional conversations with economics experts like Gottfried Feder and Carl Röver and their theories foretold a disastrous future."[28] Papen must go. Only Hitler had the mandate to lead Germany, he told the government.

Oddly, it was the Communist opposition and not the NSDAP that brought down Papen's government. The Communists tabled a motion for a vote of "no confidence" in the chancellor; and no matter how bitter the taste, the Nazis were obliged to vote alongside them.[29] The vote was 513 to 32 against the government. The Reichstag was again dissolved in September, when the new Reichstag president, Hermann Göring (representing the largest party), notoriously ignored Chancellor Papen while conducting the vote of "no confidence." Another election was scheduled, for November 1932.

∽

Rumors began to circulate that Gregor Strasser had clinched a deal with the provisional Chancellor Schleicher for the post of vice-chancellor.

Goebbels, who had been suspicious of Strasser for years, urged Hitler to act. After pacing the length and breadth of his villa—literally for hours—reflecting on his course of action, Hitler told Goebbels that if the party splintered, he would shoot himself.[30]

Hitler, of course, did no such thing. Shortly after Schleicher became chancellor, in December 1932, he attempted to split the Nazi Party by gathering Gregor Strasser to him. Strasser's brother Otto had already defected. As the head of the party organization, Strasser was in direct contact with all the local leaders and had earned their loyalty. When Strasser demanded that the NSDAP tolerate the Schleicher government, Göring and Goebbels persuaded Hitler not to listen. Two days later, Strasser and Hitler met privately. After a bitter row, Strasser formally resigned from the party. The fallout was greater within the party than outside it, primarily owing to paranoia about what Strasser might do. Near-superhuman efforts from Hitler and Goebbels were needed to keep the party together. Gregor Strasser's decision was a prelude to the Night of the Long Knives, two years later, when at least eighty-five former party members were killed, including Schleicher, Röhm, and Strasser.

∞

Though toppled, Papen had enjoyed a taste of power, and wanted more. A secret meeting was arranged between Papen and Hitler at the home of a Cologne banker who had donated to the Nazis.* Also present were Hitler's economic advisor Wilhelm Keppler, Rudolf Hess, and Heinrich Himmler. Hitler left his confederates in the parlor while he and Papen spoke privately for over two hours. It proved a turning point in both men's fortunes.

As a result of the new entente, Strasser instantly declined Schleicher's offer to become vice-chancellor, remaining loyal to Hitler, and crucially telling the führer the new chancellor's plan. Germany had been struggling without an effective government for two months, since the November elections.

When Goebbels led the NSDAP to victory in a local election at Lippe on January 15, 1933, Hindenburg's son, Oskar, and State Secretary Otto

---

* Each side claimed that it had initiated the groundbreaking contact.

Meissner broke the deadlock. Stealing out of the presidential palace by taxi, they were driven to the Berlin home of the phony aristocrat Joachim von Ribbentrop, who was also, coincidentally, an old army buddy of Papen's from the Turkish front in the 1914–18 war. Once there, Oskar von Hindenburg withdrew for a private talk with Hitler. Both men kept the content of their meeting an absolute secret, yet it was Meissner's impression that Oskar had fallen under a sort of enchantment by Hitler.[31]

On January 23, 1933, Schleicher reluctantly admitted to Hindenburg that he could not forge a government majority and asked to dissolve the Reichstag. Hindenburg refused. Five days later, Schleicher resigned. Hindenburg called Papen back and asked him to explore the possibilities of forming a legally constitutional government under Hitler.

Though Schleicher was finished, he tried to keep Hitler from assuming power by ordering the army to take over the capital, claiming that he'd been obliged by events to seize power from the Reichstag under emergency measures. Colonel Oskar von Hindenburg intervened. Acting as adjutant to his father the president, he asked General Werner von Blomberg (who led the army) where his loyalties lay. Blomberg went to the president to explain that he'd received contrary orders—one from General Schleicher and the other from his son. Hindenburg immediately swore the bewildered Blomberg in as defense minister and gave him the authority to put down any insurrection.[32]

Hitler gave credit where it was due, announcing shortly after becoming chancellor, on January 30, 1933, that "if in the days of the revolution the Army had not stood on our side, then we would not be here today."[33]

⁂

Yet these momentous events hardly seemed to concern Gurlitt. In May 1932 he'd gone to London on business, thanks once again to Kirchbach's thriving collection and his international links. Cornelius, true to form, advised his son, despite his own increased isolation from the outside world. "I was pleased how warmly he agreed with me about my views on art issues here." There was no real science to the academic theoretical knowledge, Cornelius believed, only talent—which was something unfathomable. Every artist made his own art, and it was up to Hildebrand to try to understand the artist rather than his art if he wished to succeed. As a final comment,

Cornelius duly noted that he was pleased that Hildebrand had made the time to visit his cousin Rose Gurlitt while visiting London.[34]

Evidently Gurlitt's London sojourn was a success. That July, he mounted an English art exhibition in Hamburg from works he'd personally selected in England. The British ambassador and the mayor of Hamburg spoke at the opening, and Hildebrand was asked to organize a return exhibition for Hamburg artists in London.[35]

Finally, in 1932, Hildebrand Gurlitt was prospering. Then, as if to ruin his good fortune, he began to have gastrointestinal problems, which were mistaken previously as a flaring up of his nervous condition. In fact, he was suffering from Crohn's disease and was told to eat a diet of nothing but pulpy, unsalted foods if he wanted to avoid an operation. Given that Helene was expecting their first child, good health was all the couple had on their minds. Meanwhile Germany's government reeled.[36]

On December 28, 1932, Helene gave birth to a healthy baby boy, whom they named Cornelius after Hildebrand's father. He would become known as Cornelius III to his grandfather, just like "in other princely families."[37]

That same baby Cornelius Gurlitt would become known to the world shortly before his eighty-first birthday, in 2013, as that strange recluse who'd hoarded the largest collection of alleged Nazi looted art discovered since 1945.

16

THE FIRST STOLEN LIVES

To save all, we must risk all.

—FRIEDRICH SCHILLER

BEING CHANCELLOR OF A MINORITY GOVERNMENT WAS HARDLY the fulfillment of Hitler's dream. Worse, the Ministry of Culture and its Department of Propaganda eluded his ministerial clutches.[1] How could he be expected to save Germany from a swarm of Communists when he'd been deprived of the hearts and minds of all Germans?

It simply wouldn't do. So, Hitler proclaimed that he could not work with the deputies elected to the Reichstag and called new elections for March 5, 1933. Although he had the men in the SS and the SA at the ready to seize power, Hitler was insistent that he *must* be duly elected. In the event of an election defeat, an armed insurrection by Röhm's and Himmler's military zealots was absolutely forbidden. It must be done legally. Throughout his twelve-year stranglehold on Europe, "legality" would loom as the fundamental cornerstone of his criminality—he would simply change the laws to suit his aims.

Still, no one bargained on his first act of outlawry. While Vice-Chancellor Papen dined with President Hindenburg at the Herrenklub on the night of February 27, 1933, he saw a red glow rising from the direction of the Reichstag. The shrill cry of sirens and people running in panic signaled that the parliament building was on fire. Papen bundled the aged Hindenburg to safety. When he returned, minutes later, he saw billowing clouds of gray smoke against the night sky, lit by flames licking at the Reichstag's roof. It was already too late to save the building.

Hitler spent that evening with the Goebbels family. Their meal was interrupted by an urgent telephone call from Hitler's friend Putzi Hanfstaengl with the news. By the time they reached the Reichstag, engulfed in flames, Göring was shouting to the dumbstruck crowd, "This is a Communist crime against the new government. We will show no mercy. Every Communist official must be shot. . . . Every Communist deputy must this very night be strung up."[2]

Was Göring stage-managing events? An underground passage from his Reichstag's President's Palace connected the central heating system directly to the Reichstag itself. Had this tunnel acted as the thoroughfare for Karl Ernst, a former hotel bellhop and Berlin's new SA leader, and his small contingent of storm troopers armed with self-igniting chemicals and gasoline? Had these men then made good their escape back into Göring's President's Palace?[3] One week before the election, the fire smacked of impeccable timing.

Equally, it is inconceivable that either Goebbels or Hitler were kept in the dark. It is also absurd to believe that they had left their chosen arsonist victim to chance. Marinus van der Lubbe, a simpleminded Dutch Communist with a long history of arson, had been groomed as their scapegoat. While the storm troopers were working in one part of the building, van der Lubbe was setting his sad campfires in another. Within two and a half minutes of this poor patsy entering, the Reichstag was already consumed by flames.[4]

Van der Lubbe was arrested by Göring as he exited. "Göring knew exactly how the fire had started," a Gestapo leader, Rudolf Diels, later said. In fact, Diels had told Göring "to prepare, prior to the fire, a list of people to be arrested immediately after it."[5] That night, Diels rounded up some four thousand Communist "agitators."

The next day, the Communist leader of the Reichstag, Ernst Torgler, surrendered to the Gestapo. A few days later, three Bulgarian Communists—

Georgi Dimitrov, Blagoi Popov, and Vasil Tanev—were also arrested, and were put on trial along with van der Lubbe at the Supreme Court in Leipzig. Dimitrov, who would later become prime minister of Bulgaria, destroyed Göring's version of events, and was able to secure an acquittal for himself and his fellow countrymen. Van der Lubbe, however, was less fortunate. He was found guilty and guillotined.[6] Other stolen lives soon followed.

⁂

Despite emergency powers granted to Hitler on February 28 to suspend portions of the constitution—including freedom of the press; the right to freedom of expression; lawful assembly; and other provisions guaranteeing personal liberty—Hitler failed to gain an absolute majority in the elections, winning only 288 seats. It was a disappointing result given the aggressive propaganda campaign waged. Billboards plastered with Nazi posters, radio programs broadcasting Hitler's, Goebbels's, and Göring's voices to the entire country, mass rallies, torchlight parades, forced entry into people's homes, and summary arrests had all failed to deliver what Hitler so dearly coveted—a clear mandate from the German people to save them. He had fallen short of the two-thirds majority required to establish his dictatorship legally.

The rest is well-trodden history. Hitler manipulated what remained of Hindenburg's ministers to do his bidding. On March 13, Joseph Goebbels became minister of propaganda. With a wave of the wand, the pair contrived their masterstroke, announcing the opening ceremony of the new Reichstag at the Garrison Church in Potsdam, that great shrine of Prussianism. It was here that Bismarck opened the first Reichstag of the united Germany in 1871. Here Frederick the Great was buried. It was the place of prayer of the Hohenzollern kings and the place where a young Hindenburg went on pilgrimage in 1866 as a young Guards officer. Naturally, Goebbels arranged for radio to broadcast the ceremony.

A visibly moved Hindenburg proclaimed, "May the old spirit of this celebrated shrine permeate the generation of today, may it liberate us from selfishness and party strife and bring us together in national self-consciousness to bless a proud and free Germany, united in herself."[7] If only . . .

∽

Cornelius Gurlitt urged his family to vote for Hitler in the March 1933 elections. Despite Hitler's anti-Semitic remarks, Cornelius wanted Hitler as chancellor because he "is a great man." He was happy to accept restrictions on his freedom in recognition of a "higher power" that would protect Germany.[8]

These "restrictions" referred to the Enabling Act, which Hitler put before the Reichstag on March 23. The duly elected delegates met for the first time at the Kroll Opera House that day, the only building in Berlin large enough to accommodate them. With the passing of the Enabling Act Law for Removing the Distress of People and Reich, Hitler swept away parliamentary democracy in Germany in five short, sharp paragraphs. Total authority over all legislation, the national budget, and any constitutional amendments was given to the cabinet for an emergency period of four years. The powers of the president would remain undisturbed, as would the status of the Reichstag. The federal structure, too, would remain unaltered. Churches and their relationships with the state would not be changed.

All who opposed the motion were shouted down. Still, Monsignor Ludwig Kaas, leader of the Center Party, was able to argue successfully that the presidential veto should remain. Kaas mustn't have known that Hindenburg was already descending into the shadows of senility. When the vote was taken, 441 delegates agreed against 84, all Social Democrats, who voted against the bill.

The gangsters had taken over the state, legally. Hindenburg would never exercise his right of veto. At last, Hitler was dictator, elected by a minority of Germans.

∽

Only days after Cornelius pledged his support for the Hitler dictatorship, Hildebrand wrote to an art dealer in Tenerife, Eduardo Westerdahl. As a respected Spanish art critic, painter, and writer and the publisher of the *Gaceta del Arte* (the Art Gazette), Westerdahl had contacted Gurlitt about the Surrealist movement. Could Gurlitt possibly send him some photographs and articles for his magazine? Hildebrand was thrilled to comply, since by 1933 he was a changed man. The "new, improved" Gurlitt was never one to miss an opportunity, so he asked whether Westerdahl would consider an exhibition; and if so, would he like to exhibit the work of a Hamburg artist? Gurlitt, of course, was happy to arrange for transportation by steamer free of charge to Westerdahl, and hoped he would respond, giving the size of his gallery and how much space might be made available for such an exhibition.[9]

Evidently, Westerdahl was delighted. In January 1933, Gurlitt wrote back concerning the transportation and packaging arrangements.[10] Six months later, Gurlitt apologized to Westerdahl for taking so long to reply to his April 2 letter due to "subversion" and other "outside things" that had distracted him.[11] The June letter states that in order to proceed with the export license, "you must write to me that you would like to exhibit the best examples of German Expressionism." Then Gurlitt instructed Westerdahl to lie. He must also declare "that these works are from the old tradition of established art (also of less extreme art, such as the smaller experimentations). Please make your wishes abundantly clear . . . as only then, will I be able to send you the paintings you desire."[12]

What caused a delay of two months between Westerdahl's April letter and Gurlitt's reply? Given that he instructed Westerdahl in the precise wording of an outright lie, "the old tradition of established art," there is only one possible cause. The Nazis were closing in on purveyors of the modern art so hated by Hitler.

Gurlitt, however, was not the only nervous art dealer in June 1933. The rough-and-tumble of the art world was becoming venomous. April 1—the day after Hitler's dictatorship began—was also the consummate art dealer Alfred Flechtheim's birthday and the day the Nazis began to specifically target him. Goebbels had appointed architect Eugen Hönig as the temporary leader of the Reichskammer der Bildenden Künste (RBK), or Reich Chamber for the Visual Arts, twenty-four hours earlier. It was Hönig who would lead the initial attack against the Jew Flechtheim.

Hönig proclaimed that the problem of inflation in the art world had *not* been caused by the world economic problem. Rather, inflation had crept in owing to that "element among art dealers who were raising prices . . . that there were those professing connoisseurship without having the moral competency." Hönig had chosen his words carefully, accusing Flechtheim,

the general director of the Staatlichen Museum in Berlin, Prussian senator of the Akademie der Künste Wilhelm Waetzold, and the Düsseldor-
fer Kunstakademie director Walter Kaesbach of being guilty of carrying
out "the whole art swindle."[13]

The sharp intakes of breath rippled across the international art mar-
kets. Flechtheim? Surely it was not for his art but rather for his obvious
Jewishness? Why else involve the senator for Prussian art and the
Düsseldorf-based Walter Kaesbach, who were Flechtheim's closest friends
in the government art sector? What about the Expressionist artists, like
Emil Nolde, who supported Hitler?

There was more to come. Ten days after Hönig's war of words directed
against Flechtheim, Göring ordered a search of the Bauhaus in Berlin,
claiming it was a fortress of subversives. At the end of term in July 1933, it
was closed. It was the beginning of the endgame.

∽

Kulturpolitik, or cultural politics, was implemented from March 31, 1933.
Over the next two years a dictatorial cultural bureaucracy took shape. Not
only was Goebbels's Reichs Ministry of Public Enlightenment and Propaganda involved, but so, too, were Interior Minister Wilhelm Frick and Education Minister Bernhard Rust. While provincial governments maintained
their jurisdiction during the first nine months of the Third Reich, Hitler
had already given the order to Göring to arrest Communist artists who remained in Germany.[14]

From the outset, overlapping of duties and interpretation of bailiwicks
remained vague. Alfred Rosenberg, the self-appointed spiritual leader of
the Nazis, had been ineffectual in grabbing his fair share of the propaganda
spoils from Goebbels. Meanwhile, Göring, Goebbels, and Robert Ley, head
of the National Labor Front, frequently skirmished in the field of artistic
expression. Education Minister Rust praised Nolde in private, but in public, Rust prevented Berlin's Nationalgalerie boss, Alois Schardt, from en-
dorsing modern art. Interior Minister Frick closed and then reopened the
exhibition of modern works at the Ferdinand Möller Gallery in Berlin—
actions that smacked of indecision or, worse, some sort of cronyism of
which Frick had been unaware.[15]

Cronyism usually meant protection by a powerful ally, but could also mean carrying out the Nazis' will. Möller was close to Rust and Goebbels, since he was allowed to continue to exhibit pro-modernist groups like Der Norden in his gallery well into the autumn of 1935. Yet his real safety stemmed from foreign ministers Konstantin von Neurath and later Joachim Ribbentrop.[16] Möller continued exhibiting, buying, and selling modern art unmolested while acting with implicit Nazi approval.[17]

Still, the art market represented only a fraction of Hitler's perceived enemies. Those most dangerous to Hitler's dictatorship, his political opponents, were handled under the Enabling Act, which allowed him to abolish the separate powers of the historic German states, and devastate Germany's core political infrastructure. At the same time, the SA was given the go-ahead to wield its sadistic, primitive urges on Germany's populace.

Some fifty thousand supposed "opponents" of the regime were arrested and imprisoned in institutions and ad hoc concentration camps. They were subjected to extreme violence and brutality. Then there were "the disappeared"—in the main, political opponents from the Center Party, Communists, and Social Democrats. Unlike earlier, the elimination of the opposition was carried out in public, to serve as a constant reminder of what antagonism of the regime really meant.[18]

⨎

Flechtheim's face became a ubiquitous symbol of the international Jew, as Hitler's poster boy—plastered onto posters, spread across newspapers, and distorted into the very image of the degeneration that Hitler associated with modern art. Karl Buchholz had wisely left Flechtheim's Berlin establishment to set up his own bookshop and gallery before 1933. Still, he remained loosely associated with his former boss through Curt Valentin, who became Flechtheim's manager when Buchholz left. Alex Vömel still ran the Flechtheim Düsseldorf gallery. Together, they would be the key individuals to "help" Flechtheim ship his most valuable paintings to safety in France, Switzerland, and England.

Nonetheless, as each day passed, Flechtheim heard and saw the atrocities taking place around him. Each day, he became more and more jittery, fearing that the Gestapo would burst in and take him away to some place of torture and steal his paintings and livelihood. The only thing keeping him in Berlin was his wife, Betty, who simply refused to leave *her* Berlin. Things would surely improve, she told her husband.

Hildebrand Gurlitt knew better. On August 31, he wrote to Eduardo Westerdahl from a new temporary address—13 Zesenstrasse. "I must advise you that after long and arduous indecision I have resigned from my position at the art association. I would not like to abandon our project together, but must first see through a different company if there is a future in German abstract art internationally. While this chapter is frozen, I hope that our plans are merely deferred."[19] What was this "different company"? "Today's Germany is so different intellectually," he continued, "that our former working practices are no longer valid."[20]

The letter hints that Gurlitt may have been shaken by the dilemma facing dealers like Flechtheim and artists like Nolde and Liebermann. Or was it that he saw an unprecedented opportunity to get extremely rich quickly? He was certainly intelligent enough to have understood the threat to anyone trading in modern art or whose livelihood depended on Jewish artists. The incident with Westerdahl had been a double blow: closing a new market and losing face with Flechtheim, who had agreed through Gurlitt to provide Westerdahl with photographs for his magazine as well as give the contact details for Kandinsky.[21]

~∞~

Whether Gurlitt had actually been attacked so early in the new regime seems unlikely, *except* for his support of modern art. Those with a Jewish grandparent—a second-degree *Mischling*, or mixed-breed—would need to wait until the September 15, 1935,* Nuremberg Laws. These restricted intermarriage between Jews and Gentiles and reduced Jews to "state subjects," stripping them of German citizenship. This makes his decision to resign from the Kunstverein in August 1933 a calculated means of survival based on a clear assessment of the prevailing Nazi winds.

Certainly, the effect of the cordon of Nazi laws squeezing the life force from Cornelius was a factor. Where the old man had voted for Hitler seven weeks earlier, he was now writing to his sister Else in words that would become a well-worn tale. Providing a long litany of Gurlitts who fought for

---

* Gurlitt's fortieth birthday.

Germany since 1870, Cornelius lamented that he was suddenly part of a "Jew-ridden family" expected to deny his own "dear and noble mother."[22] He wondered about the rest of the family and what was to become of them. Cornelius's last thought was of Rose, in England, and Manfred, whose life had become difficult because of his "latest Bolshevik opera."[23]

Cornelius hadn't known that Manfred's mother, the despised Annarella, had already taken up her son's cause with the Nazis, claiming that Manfred was not Fritz's son but rather the offspring of Willi Waldecker. Whether true or not, this removed the stain of Judaism. After her tale was coupled with Manfred's promise to join the Nazi Party and write music for the Nazis, Cornelius's nephew became part of the Nazi arts establishment, too.[24]

Then, days later, an outraged Cornelius fulminated, "My sons, I have to make statements, whether we are Aryans. This is very difficult, because no one knows what an Aryan is. Was our ancestor, the monk Matinus Gorlitius, a German or a Jew?"* Gorlitius was a good Lutheran and the superintendent in Brunswick. Their name derived from the village of Görlitz. Nearby Mount Gora, admittedly, had a Slavic name. Would Hitler next call them Slavs? "I and my sons, like all members of associations, have been asked to prove our Aryanism. How can I deny our beloved mother . . . ? We have given our lives to Germany . . . there are four Iron Crosses in the family."[25] These were the same arguments all Jews used as they argued that they were German.

⁓

Setting up in business as an art dealer took a great deal of capital, large premises, and reasonable safety from persecution. Even if no money was needed, only Kirchbach could provide Gurlitt with the protection required for himself and his family. It was Cornelius, again, who shed light on the situation with Hildebrand, albeit in a tone of disapproval. "Hildebrand leads a strange life. A very rich factory owner, who has a very difficult marriage relationship, has discovered that Hildebrand is the only nonselfish man he knows, and therefore takes a strong interest in helping him, paying him a salary and the ensuing expenses."[26]

Cornelius's New Year's letter was highly informative. "Hildebrand is

---

* Gorlitius was a correspondent of Martin Luther's in the sixteenth century.

having bizarre experiences. A wealthy industrialist in Dresden, Mr. Kirchbach, came to visit me to clarify the situation." Evidently, from the moment Cornelius heard about Hildebrand's resignation from the Kunstverein, he was befuddled by his son's new survival plan. Kirchbach arranged to visit Cornelius in person at Hildebrand's behest. By the time Cornelius wrote his letter, Kirchbach and Hildebrand were in Naples, and would remain there throughout the Christmas period.

Kirchbach also confided in Cornelius that "his wife was cheating on him." Cornelius advised him, since the marriage was destroyed, to sue for divorce. Yet Kirchbach refused to contemplate a legal end to the marriage for unspecified reasons. "Now he has chosen Hildebrand as his guardian angel, because his nerves are broken. They are now both in Naples, he mostly bedridden, but he promises to pay Hildebrand well. Hildebrand is to buy him a house in Dresden when they return." Hildebrand's maternal cousin, the real-estate agent Hans Gerlach, was on his way to join them to discuss possible alternatives. Meanwhile, "Helene stays at the house in Hamburg and maintains the gorgeous little Cornelius. She is an excellent woman."[27]

Cornelius was allowing his innate disapproval of commerce to cloud his judgment. Kirchbach and Hildebrand had worked out that to buy and sell art in the months and years ahead, they would need to acquire Renaissance or earlier art as a basis for trade with the Reich. Where better to establish such an incomparable historical collection than Italy, where Mussolini had been exercising his own form of cultural brutality for some years? It was even smarter that they worked from a base in Naples, the hotbed of the Camorra, which even the Sicilian Mafia feared. Kirchbach could not bear for his adoptive son Hildebrand to be dehumanized by the Nazis, and agreed that such a collection would seal his guarantee of Gurlitt's safety more than his own unassailable contribution to the war effort.

Since the Nazis no longer wanted Expressionist art, Gurlitt saw Kirchbach as his means to bring German Expressionism under their protective wings and out into the wider world. Hildebrand immediately saw the benefit of "saving modern art" while becoming rich. Kirchbach, for his part, would amass a magnificent contemporary-art collection to match his photographic collection, while sharing the company of a man he'd come to admire. It was a plan that would eventually be mirrored by the Nazis during the forthcoming conflagration.

PART III

WORLD WAR AND WILDERNESS

So foul a sky clears not without a storm.

—WILLIAM SHAKESPEARE,
King John

17

◇◇◇◇

CHAMBERS OF HORRORS

Newspapers are read differently now . . . between the lines.
—Victor Klemperer, *I Will Bear Witness*, April 7, 1933

"THE PROPHETS OF RACISM AND OF RACIST ART SOUNDED TO MOST of us in the Weimar Republic like lonely fanatics, condemned to everlasting frustration," eyewitness Hellmut Lehmann-Haupt wrote. "So many of us, young and old . . . missed one important fact: these mad prophets were gathering around them significant audiences of ever-mounting size."[1] The Nazis were no longer some small right-wing group that could be shrugged off blithely. Their politics of humiliation and exclusion had gripped the country.

Another eyewitness, Dresden Technical University academic, journalist, and diarist Victor Klemperer, knew from the outset that his earlier conversion to Protestantism was immaterial to the Nazis. His diaries, kept throughout the Nazi period, show a different Dresden from the one Cornelius Gurlitt portrayed. While many gritted their teeth and hoped, Klemperer felt shame wash over him. On the day Hitler became chancellor he remarked simply that he saw "a children's ball with the swastika" in a toy shop.[2] The führer intended to warp children's minds from the earliest age.

Those who opposed Hitler did so at their very real peril. The boycott of Jewish shops was announced on April 1. Dresden's student body announced that "the honor of German students forbids them to come into contact with Jews." Munich's Jewish professors had already been prevented from setting foot on the university campus. The rectors of Frankfurt University, the Technical University Brunswick, and Bonn University Hospital were arrested along with the Christian business editor of the *Frankfurter Zeitung*.[3] Klemperer mocked the Spanish Ministry of Education for offering Albert Einstein a professorship (which he accepted) as the most bizarre twist of history. As "Germany establishes *[la] limpieza de sangre*"—a purification of the blood first performed in the Spanish Inquisition—"Spain appoints the German Jew."[4]

Jews—whether assimilated or religious, captains of industry or peasants—were treated with equal disregard. Humiliation and torture were the Nazis' stock-in-trade. In Dortmund, ten days prior to the boycott of Jewish shops, SA and SS thugs dragged a butcher, Julius Rosenfeld, and his son through the streets to a brickyard. There the son was compelled to set fire to his father's beard with a burning newspaper for their captors' amusement. After five hours, the elder Rosenfeld was released on the condition that he return with a slaughtered ox for his tormenters as ransom for his son.[5]

These brutal acts and others, called *Einzelaktionen*, were commonplace before Hitler's seizure of power, known as *Machtergreifung*. Courts were emptied of judges and lawyers—either for their political views or their religion; doctors were not allowed to conduct medical research or treat certain patients. These *Einzelaktionen* were not spontaneous excesses, as the Nazis characterized them in an attempt to brush the subject aside, but rather part of a concentrated national propaganda campaign to terrify any opposition into submission.

Artists, too, were fighting for their existence. There were over 870 Jewish writers and editors in Germany in 1933 and an estimated 2,600 Jewish artists who were active in the visual arts and music. There were thousands more who were Communists or political opponents.[6] Even William Dodd, Roosevelt's rather green ambassador to Berlin, who arrived in the summer of 1933, couldn't fail to miss the intimidation and the irreparable cost to human life.[7] To claim ignorance of the arrests, disappearances, and propaganda or the rising violence throughout German society was nothing short of an outright lie to oneself and others.

∽

Joseph Goebbels, as the Third Reich's "culture czar," ran a stiletto-sharp propaganda machinery of state, as agreed with Hitler a year earlier.[8] Allowed to construct his own vast administration in the realms of the arts, propaganda, and *Kulturpolitik*, Goebbels was responsible for delivering Hitler's undiluted message. Within the first month of the *Machtergreifung*, Klemperer noted "the influence of the tremendous propaganda—films, broadcasting, newspapers, flags, ever more celebrations (today is the Day of the Nation, Adolf the Leader's birthday)?" He admired their expertise in advertising, filling the cinemas with films of Hitler's rallies "to 600,000 SA men . . . and always the Horst Wessel Song. And everyone knuckles under."[9]

Goebbels's private fiefdom, the Reichsministerium für Volksaufklärung und Propaganda—the Reich Ministry for Public Enlightenment and Propaganda, or RMVP for short—had become a mammoth organization by the beginning of 1934. Successfully poaching bits from other ministers' portfolios—broadcasting from the Postal Ministry, the Press Office from the Reich Chancellery, censorship from the Ministry of the Interior, and advertising from the Economics Ministry—made Goebbels extremely powerful. With the diversion of tax revenue from radio licenses, the RMVP became virtually self-funding, despite its rapid growth.[10]

Goebbels's unfettered access to Hitler and a friendship stretching back some twelve years proved too sharp a dagger for other ministers to effectively blunt. When Göring or Himmler or Ribbentrop complained about Goebbels's abrasive attitude and covetousness, Hitler seemed unnaturally pleased. There was nothing like dissent among his ministers to keep them from plotting against him. Besides, Goebbels had the added advantages of being a crack administrator, an arch plotter, and unquestionably loyal.

Yet Goebbels had a weak point. He actually liked modern art. When Albert Speer was sent to Goebbels's new home in June 1933 for a spot of interior-design work, he "borrowed a few watercolors by Nolde"—bright flower paintings—from Berlin's National Gallery. Goebbels and his wife, Magda, were thrilled with the choice—that is, until Hitler came to look at Speer's work. "The pictures have to go at once; they're simply impossible!" Hitler cried.[11] So, they did.

Speer felt that the combination of Goebbels's unbridled power and doglike servility to Hitler was bizarre. "There was something fantastic about the absolute authority Hitler could assert over his closest associates of many years, even in matters of taste. Goebbels had simply groveled before Hitler. . . . I, too, though altogether at home in modern art, tacitly accepted Hitler's pronouncement."[12]

It was this lack of aesthetic debate that prompted Goebbels to set up his powerful Reichskulturkammer (RKK), or Reich Chamber of Culture, in September 1933. The RKK would oversee the seven arts: visual art, music, literature, film, the press, radio, and theater. Each of the artistic divisions would have its own chamber. Attempting to prove that there was no hint of party politics, non-*völkisch* artists were recruited to head individual chambers. Fritz Lang took on film, modernist poet Stefan George headed literature, and Richard Strauss led the music chamber. Artists, art dealers, and those associated with any branch of the seven arts needed to become RKK members in order to work legally. So much for Hildebrand Gurlitt's resignation from the Kunstverein a month earlier. . . .

৩৯

Less than three weeks after Gurlitt's last letter to Eduardo Westerdahl in Tenerife, Flechtheim's Berlin gallery was "Aryanized" by Alfred E. Schulte. Valentin moved on to work with Buchholz instead of remaining under Schulte. Valentin was already aware that he'd need Buchholz's protection in the days ahead. After all, Valentin's mother had converted to Lutheranism from Judaism before he was born, making him a first-degree *Mischling*.[13]

Alfred Flechtheim, meanwhile, fled to Paris. Daniel-Henry Kahnweiler was Flechtheim's first hope for refuge. Kahnweiler claimed he was in no position to help. Flechtheim's other associate, Paul Rosenberg, would not help either, despite Flechtheim's continued pleas. Over the next three years, Flechtheim became the eponymous "wandering Jew," spending barely longer than two weeks in any one place—moving about trying to sell what remained of his art stocks wherever he thought he could to buy his freedom. He lived in constant fear.[14]

As a result of the export restrictions and close surveillance, Flechtheim was obliged to sell at unconscionably low prices, and Gurlitt was one of many salivating to take advantage of Flechtheim's financial and personal embarrassment.[15] By the summer of 1933, Flechtheim expressed his plight to George Grosz, who had fled to New York: "Regards to your wife & to [I.B.] Neumann, please. He shall pay me for the Beckmanns [I sent him], at least somewhat. I have no money at all."[16]

Flechtheim's predicament proved fortuitous for Buchholz, Valentin, Vömel, and even Gurlitt. Vömel, manager of Flechtheim's Düsseldorf gallery, wrote to his special friend and art dealer Christoph Bernoulli in Basel that he was making great alterations to the gallery, and "when it's all over the Düsseldorf gallery will be changed to Galerie Alex Vömel" from March 30.[17] Vömel had, however, rather jumped the proverbial gun. By sending the invitation to his *new, improved* Alfred Flechtheim Gallery to Flechtheim himself, the fugitive owner arranged to have his remaining stock swiftly transferred to Buchholz for safekeeping.[18] Of course, nothing would be safe.

There were others who would benefit from the new chamber of horrors in Hitler's Germany. Some victims, like Max Beckmann, were not Jewish. Others fell instead into "degenerate" categories of Communist, Freemason, and political opposition. Karl Nierendorf and I. B. Neumann were bludgeoned into dissolving their partnership, putting Neumann into severe financial distress, coming fast on the heels of the Depression. Nierendorf's Munich partnership with Günther Franke was henceforth called Gallery Nierendorf and Graphic Cabinet. Grete Ring and Walter Feilchenfeldt, who had taken over Paul Cassirer's Berlin gallery, abandoned their German art business altogether. Ring relocated to the Cassirer subsidiary in London, whereas Feilchenfeldt went first to Holland, then to England before finally settling in Switzerland. The name Cassirer continued in London, thanks in no small part to artworks channeled from Germany through the Amsterdam subsidiary run by Helmuth Luetjens.[19]

Yet a chink in the Nazi armor glared brightly to those who had the supreme will to survive. There were some auction houses that were mysteriously exempt from the onslaught. Lepke—one of the largest in Germany—and Graupe both were owned by Jews. Still, both non-Aryan firms were allowed to continue as before (until 1936) under new legislation called Toleration Regulations. In other words, Jews who brought much-needed foreign currency into the Reich would be allowed to go on trading. From 1936, Lepke was compelled to take on an Aryan partner, Hans Carl

Krueger. Hans W. Lange became the "Aryanized" firm of Paul Graupe in December 1937.[20] By that time, Lange was already a trading partner of Gurlitt's.

From March 1933, it became impossible for any auction house to sell works by Nolde, Heckel, Marc, Feininger, Dix, or Oskar Schlemmer. Soon Beckmann and Liebermann joined the crowd. The only way these artists could survive in Germany was through sales at private galleries, like Gurlitt's, or by surreptitiously exporting their works abroad.[21]

Gurlitt saw the unrivaled vistas amid the chaos. Both he and Helene immediately joined the RKK, becoming as friendly as possible with its members, especially Lange; and Goebbels's assistant, Rolf Hetsch; and the head of the RBK, Eugen Hönig, who had been Cornelius's student. With Kirchbach's money, a panicked art market, distressed sellers, and the trust of artists who were losing their representation in galleries daily, Gurlitt and Kirchbach earned fabulous amounts of money—in foreign currency. Gurlitt could make himself useful to the RMVP through Hetsch and the RBK through Hönig, with his new expertise in Renaissance art, while Kirchbach protected him from on high.

✑

Where Goebbels had been the mastermind behind the public's brainwashing against modern art, the Nazi Party ideologue Alfred Rosenberg was more at home in supporting the *völkisch* art movement. As the editor of the daily Nazi newspaper, the *Völkischer Beobachter*, and a member of the Kampfbund für deutsche Kultur (literally Combat League for German Culture), or the KDK, Rosenberg became the figurehead of *völkisch* groups, which were predominantly radical traditionalists.[22]

This *völkisch* movement, so admired by Hitler, idealized the German peasant and rejected all modern styles from the Impressionists forward into the twentieth century, often labeling these artworks as "cultural garbage" or "Jewish" or "Bolshevik." It was Rosenberg who popularized the simpler false precept of "Jewish Bolshevism." His main task was to "demonstrate the interdependence between race, culture, science, morals and soldierly values." One of his earliest adherents was Heinrich Himmler. From 1932, members of Rosenberg's KDK received an illustrated journal, the *Deutsche Kulturwacht*, or German Culture Watch, and its readers'

thoughts were molded by its reviews of the performing arts and literature.[23]

Museum directors who wanted to keep their jobs were in a quandary.
To survive, they knew exhibitions deploring modern art were essential. This
desire for survival—so inherent in the human mind—gave rise to art
exhibitions collectively known as Art Chambers of Horrors (*Schreckens-
kammern der Kunst*) or Exhibitions of Shame (*Schandaustellungen*). Some
museum directors chose other names, such as *Images of Cultural Bolshevism* (*Kulturbolschewistike Bilder*).[24] The works exhibited were drawn from
locally held public collections, concentrating on the "aberrations" created
by German artists.* Throughout the summer of 1933, more exhibitions
were announced, geared to specific audiences for educational purposes.
Still, the hidden message to the Nazi elite from the museum directors was
"These works were acquired by my predecessor(s) and I don't agree with
their policies."

✍

The Gurlitts were also direct beneficiaries of the new policy. Suddenly,
paintings by landscape painters like Hildebrand's grandfather Louis were
back in vogue. Architect Eugen Hönig, Goebbels's man in charge of the
RBK, had written to Cornelius on April 21, assuring him of his deep
admiration for the elder statesman and, paraphrasing the words of Shakespeare, when he wrote that "he was not a towering architect, but had greatness thrust upon him."[25] Cornelius was flattered. That December, while
preoccupied that no publisher would print his autobiography, he wrote his
sister Else that "the great crime of the German people is that they are so big
and powerful."[26]

Oddly, Cornelius failed to mention the furor created in Dresden by an
exhibition that September. Held in the inner courtyard of the Neues
Rathaus, it became known as the *Spiegelbilder des Verfalls in der Kunst*
(Mirror Images of Decadence in Art). This show traveled to twelve other
cities by 1937. Hitler declared that "this unique exhibition . . . ought to be
shown in as many German cities as possible."[27]

Since Dresden had been at the heart of German Expressionism, with the

---

* Other cities, such as Karlsruhe, preferred to exhibit approved art (*Government Art 1918–1933*).

Bridge and the Dresdner Sezession Gruppe in 1919 as well as the Association of Revolutionary Visual Artists of Germany, known by the acronym ASSO, the city had more images to put on show than other cities of similar size. Karlsruhe and Mannheim also mounted exhibitions, but it was Dresden that proved the forerunner of the most notorious exhibition of them all—the *Entartete Kunst* (*Degenerate Art*) exhibition in Munich in 1937.

Not only was the art on display stage-managed to look chaotic and reckless, unmasking the artists as mentally deranged in the eyes of the public, but the cruelest trick of all was that the public was invited "here to form its own opinion," according to the *Hakenkreuzbanner* (the Swastika Banner) of April 3, 1933. Whenever public outrage became muted, actors were hired to display "outrage" to visitors.

Artists were accused of mental illness as well as degeneracy. Some exhibitions even posted the sale prices to the museums in pre-1924 marks so that they seemed extortionate. Minors were frequently forbidden entry on the grounds that "obscene" paintings were on display. The exhibitions' educational purposes were underlined by the "model galleries" adjacent to the chambers of horrors where "healthy, stable art" instructed the public with its sane, contrasting example.

By 1935, having stirred up public outrage against artists and art dealers, museums began to actively rid themselves of the offending paintings. These were quickly snapped up at a fraction of their former price by the likes of Gurlitt, Buchholz, and Möller to use for bartering purposes, sales abroad, or future stock. Initially, the Folkwang Museum in Essen joined forces with Möller, while the Wallraf-Richartz-Museum in Cologne worked with Gurlitt.[28]

No one could pretend they hadn't seen the future in March 1933. *Deutscher Kunstbericht* (German Art Report), edited by Bettina Feistel-Rohmeder, clearly stated "what German artists" could expect from the new government: "That all products of cosmopolitan and Bolshevist purport be removed from German museums and collections. They were allowed to be shown 'in a heap' . . . [and] what sums were spent on them, together with the names of the gallery officials and ministers of culture who were responsible for acquiring them, after which these inartistic products can have but a single use, which is as fuel to heat public buildings."[29]

∽

Hermann Göring was among the first to recognize that artworks had a huge export-market potential, particularly in Britain, Switzerland, and the United States. It was a simple hop and skip from that realization to the use of contemporary art in his Four-Year Plan as a primary means of funding Germany's rearmament. His plan was intended to make Germany independent of all imports, launching an ill-conceived program of autarky. To achieve this utopian state of self-sufficiency, coal mines and other mineral-extraction operations abandoned long before as a result of lack of productivity were reactivated. Ersatz raw materials were produced, but never equaling or surpassing the world-market price. Schacht, now economic minister, made the blunder of believing that Germany planned to export these synthetic raw materials for foreign exchange.

The raw materials were always destined to be used to rearm. What Germany could not manufacture, it would need to buy with foreign exchange. Göring's Four-Year Plan flew in the face of all that Schacht had worked for, with the repudiation of his own "New Plan" of 1936. *Newsweek* reported that Schacht had rushed back to Berlin from his Easter holiday. "Reason: Adolf Hitler had given the Assistant Nazi-in-Chief, Air Minister Göring, absolute control over raw material imports *and* foreign exchange. . . . The disgruntled Economic Minister handed in his resignation. The Führer handed it back—and reminded the doctor that Adolf Hitler *is* Germany."[30]

Doubtless, too, Schacht was unaware of Hitler's intention to use Germany's wealth of contemporary fine art to obtain foreign exchange. Though before that would be allowed officially, Germany needed to get the 1936 Olympic Games out of the way and show the world that it was once again the physical and moral powerhouse of Europe.

18

THE FOUR HORSEMEN

Did we force ourselves on you or you on us?
—JOHANN WOLFGANG VON GOETHE, *Faust*

DISEASE, WAR, FAMINE, AND DEATH WOULD DESCEND, FIRST UPON Germany, then upon the world in the coming war. The four official riders of the apocalypse that befell Germany's contemporary art in 1937 were Hildebrand Gurlitt, Karl Buchholz, Ferdinand Möller, and Bernhard A. Böhmer. Yet Gurlitt alone was classed as a second-degree *Mischling*.

Well before 1937, like Karl Lueger in the Vienna of Hitler's youth, Vice-Chancellor Göring claimed he decided who was Jewish. Exceptions under the Toleration Act were based on prior service and future opportunity. Gurlitt was a most resourceful and intelligent dealer. Besides, with Hönig indebted to his father, Kirchbach an essential cog in the ever-grinding wheel of war machinery, and Hetsch a daily fellow traveler, Gurlitt had insured his future well.

Yet when Gauleiter Mutschmann demanded Cornelius's retirement from the architects' association in December 1935, the old man was utterly dismayed.[1] He lost the will to complete his autobiography.[2] Just a few days shy of Cornelius's eighty-sixth birthday, Wilibald was compelled to take a "leave of absence" from the University of Freiburg, too. Only Hildebrand's newfound illustrious position, in part conferred upon him by his relationship with the indispensable Kirchbach, bucked the family's misfortunes. Cornelius failed to grasp the reality of Hitler's Germany, even though it had been a long time in the making.

∽

From March 1933, no one was under the illusion that art was just some harmless pastime. What constituted art in any of its seven forms was of paramount significance to the essence of what made a "good" German. Two months later, Goebbels, as gauleiter of Berlin, demanded the resignations of Kollwitz, Beckmann, and Karl Hofer from the art academy. Robert Scholz, the Third Reich's most influential art critic, called for a "purge" of the racially alien elements in the arts.[3] Mutschmann hit out against Dix in Dresden. Klee was removed from his teaching post in Düsseldorf. Ten members of the Prussian Academy of Arts were expected to tender their "voluntary" resignations, including its much-lauded Jewish president, Max Liebermann.[4] Modern artists were warned to respect the *Malverbot* (prohibition to paint) if it was declared against them. An infraction could be determined by the mere whiff of turpentine or the touch of a wet paintbrush during a surprise visit by the Gestapo. The elderly Nazi sympathizer Emil Nolde, despite his sympathies, was shocked when he received his *Malverbot* order.

That October, Hitler personally laid the cornerstone of the Temple of German Art, or *Haus der Deutschen Kunst*, in Munich, which would exhibit art personally vetted by him. Carl Spitzweg, one of Hitler's favorite artists, would take pride of place with Lucas Cranach, Wilhelm von Kaulbach, and Böcklin. There should have been a few Louis Gurlitts there as well. Nowhere would the "representation of the true face of war" or "unfinished works" be present.[5]

Naturally, the purge of museum directors continued, with many of those who had supported Gurlitt earmarked in the cull. Dr. Lili Fischel was dismissed from Karlsruhe in 1933, replaced with a new director who ensured that all Impressionistic and Expressionistic paintings were displayed with pejorative labels. Stuttgart soon followed Karlsruhe's example.

In 1935, the valiant Gustav Hartlaub of the Mannheim museum was "caught" harboring outlawed modern art in the museum's cellars. In a show of medieval shame usually reserved for harlots, bawds, and thieves, the gauleiter arranged for these "degenerate" paintings, among them *Rabbi* by

Marc Chagall, to be loaded onto wagons and paraded through the streets of the city, prominently displaying the prices Hartlaub had paid with tax-payers' money. To seal his public humiliation, a large photograph of Hartlaub was also displayed.[6]

When museum directors evaded or blatantly ignored the imperatives thrust upon them, humiliation became the least of their worries. Carl Georg Heise was advised to "resign of his own wishes" in September 1933 or stand accused—falsely—of misappropriation of public funds and immoral conduct. When Count Klaus Baudissin, one of a clutch of Nazi art histori-ans, became the director of the Folkwang Museum in Essen, he ordered its fabulous rotunda, decorated with murals by Oskar Schlemmer, to be painted over.[7] Baudissin was delighted to accept 9,000 reichsmarks for Kandinsky's *Improvisation 28* from Ferdinand Möller, who promptly acted as intermediary in the sale of several Kandinsky paintings to the Guggen-heim Museum in New York.[8] Along with the Wallraf-Richartz-Museum, in Cologne, Gurlitt found a willing buyer at the Folkwang Museum in the years ahead.

✀

Shortly before the Olympic Games in 1936, the Nierendorf Gallery in Berlin held an exhibition of Franz Marc paintings. Marc was Jewish, yet had also won a coveted Iron Cross in the war. At the opening party,* the Gestapo stormed the gallery and closed down the exhibition on the basis that it endangered the Reich's *Kulturpolitik* and was a hazard to "public safety and order." Soon after, Berlin's Nationalgalerie director, Alois Schardt, emi-grated to the United States.[9]

During the Olympics, Schardt's replacement, Eberhard Hanfstaengl, hosted Berlin's *German Art Since Dürer* exhibition. Yet even this could not make up for Hanfstaengl's earlier transgression—a Max Liebermann exhibition. As soon as the tourists headed home, Education Minister Rust closed down the separate modern-art building of the Nationalgalerie at the Kronprinzenpalais. Similar moves were made throughout Germany. The time had come at long last to eliminate the "syphilitic" elements from society and German art.

---

* It is entirely possible that Gurlitt was there.

✑

Goebbels, undeniably, had a grand plan. All piecemeal art exhibitions, though well received, fell short of that final national push against degeneracy. Hitler's established architect, Paul Troost, was commissioned to build the Führerbau museum in Munich, dedicated to the best approved art. Goebbels's ego dictated that he must make his own grand contribution: a national exhibition of modern art. It would be called the Degenerate Art Exhibition—the *Entartete Kunst Austellung.*

The artworks to adorn this scornful stage set would be confiscated from German museums. Organized against the backdrop of growing anxiety about Hitler's brutality and refusal to acknowledge the existing boundaries between Germany, Poland, the Baltic states, and the Soviet Union—with Germans commonly demonstrating publicly in full war regalia—the huge effort that went into this exhibition seemed incongruous, even slightly mad, to many.[10]

Goebbels and Hetsch consulted with the Moravian-born critic Robert Scholz for suitable candidates to help put together the exhibition, selecting the mediocre artist Adolf Ziegler as the new president of the RKK. Ziegler was instructed on June 30, 1937, to begin preparations for the *Verfallskunst seit 1910* (Decadent Art Since 1910) exhibition. He led a five-man commission comprising the also-ran painter Wolfgang Willrich; Hitler's photographer and amateur art dealer Heinrich Hoffmann; his ruthless art dealer Karl Haberstock; Scholz, who also headed the Moritzburg Museum, in Halle (Saxony); and the antiquities dealer Max Täuber. Hitler decreed that none of the participants should engage in dealing art, as this might appear inappropriate.[11]

While the brief was to design an exhibition to contrast the "decadent" with the "approved," even Goebbels balked at Ziegler's and Willrich's zeal. A curator "of confidence" was appointed for the "weeding-out" process following the initial seizures to keep Ziegler and Willrich from overreaching themselves.[12] Eberhard Hanfstaengl, of the Nationalgalerie, refused to take part, thereby confirming his ignominious future. Instead, Hanfstaengl appointed Paul Ortwin Rave, his own curator, to the commission.

Ziegler, known to his many adversaries as the "Master of the Pubic Hair" for his particular detail of nudes, made his first swoop at Hannover on July 5 with his commissioners. The following day, Essen fell victim to their blitzkrieg. The day after, it was the turn of Hanfstaengl's contemporary-art museum, the Kronprinzenpalais.[13] At each museum, Willrich, wild-eyed, scribbled madly in his notorious notebook of death, detailing which artworks were to be purged. Ziegler and Willrich—the perfect representa-tion of the mediocre—relished their opportunity to openly revile and ridicule the modern greats.

Oddly, for a "Hitler-approved" operation, their confiscation of artworks was a blatant effrontery to the law. There were no agreements foisted on the plundered museums. Artworks were simply taken, with no promise of return, no insurance for the "loan," and no word about their ultimate fate. The cost to the Nationalgalerie alone was 141 artworks: sixty-four oils, four sculptures, and seventy-three drawings. Included among these were the paintings confiscated a year earlier at the Nierendorf Gallery by the Ge-stapo, wrongly described as "belonging to the Nationalgalerie." Clearly ownership had become a matter of opinion. Still, it would be only the first of thousands of such purges. Human lives had already been stolen. Millions more would follow.

⁓

The most compelling eyewitness account of these artistic ethnic cleansings was given by Paul Ortwin Rave, the commission curator. Art was no longer a mere matter of taste. It had been reduced to a false concept of racial impurity that needed eradicating in a manner that left no room for doubt.

The *Entartete Kunst* exhibition was purposely staged at an inappropri-ate venue, in the arcades of the Munich Hofgarten. It included six hundred expropriated artworks and opened on July 19, 1937, to an unprecedented number of visitors—free of charge—heralding its ultimate success. Rave described how the rooms were narrow and covered with trelliswork struc-tures overlaid with burlap.

"The paintings are attached to the partitions while the inscriptions are written on the burlap," Rave wrote. Windows immediately above the partitions, coupled with the narrowness of the rooms, made it awkward to view the displays. The main propaganda aim was served by the numerous inscriptions, like "Insolent mockery of the Divine under Centrist rule." Crucially, "the purchase price was indicated, a large red label was stuck to the artworks with a message 'Paid for by the taxes of the German working people.'"[14]

It was purposefully shambolic, to feed the viewers' revulsion, anger, and even nausea. As expected, Hitler, Göring, and Goebbels were elated. *Gebt mir vier Jahre Zeit* may have no longer been the title of the *Entartete Kunst* exhibition, but it remained the fulfillment of Hitler's prophecy. Between 1938 and 1941, it toured Berlin, Leipzig, Düsseldorf, Salzburg, Hamburg, Stettin (now Szczecin), Weimar, Vienna, Frankfurt, Chemnitz, Waldenburg (now Walbrzych, Silesia), and Halle (in Saxony) and was viewed by more than two million people.[15]

∽

Timing is everything in life, but was 1937 the time to implement the Four-Year Plan for art alongside Göring's Four-Year Plan for Germany? The reichsmark had again become unstable as a result of Germany's thirst for foreign exchange. Schacht, once omniscient in money matters, had taken to importing foreign goods, then blocking payments to the exporter. He would then attempt to negotiate barter agreements of German-manufactured goods as payment. Though pleasing to Hitler, it was nothing short of financial criminality.[16] Understandably, the more countries that became victims of this blocked-funds lark of Schacht's, the less confidence foreign nations had in the reichsmark.

Schacht's change of tack was ultimately brought about by Germany's race laws and the country's rearmament. On March 9, 1937, Hitler declared that an air force, which he called the Luftwaffe, would be built; and a week later, he announced conscription, the formation of twelve army corps with thirty-six divisions, and full laws governing military service. Article 173 of the Versailles Treaty was in shreds.[17]

Reportedly Hitler was so happy with Schacht (for a change) that on his birthday he sent his economics minister a magnificently framed painting. Schacht, ever the arrogant know-it-all, returned it to Hitler, thanking him for his "thoughtful choice" but advising that the painting was a fake. He kept the frame.[18]

Unsurprisingly, Schacht hated the new economic system. On November 29, at the Academy of Laws, he gave a heartfelt speech about the merits of capitalism and entrepreneurship. This flew in the face of what the

Nazi economists believed: that these were inventions and "instruments of" the international Jewish conspiracy. Of course, Schacht knew he had the backing of Germany's heavy industry before he dipped his toe into the scalding water, since the industrialists understood the need for hard currency to acquire superior materials from overseas.

Hitler literally banked on Schacht's previous good name. By the time the four art dealers were appointed to their tasks, Schacht had resigned as economics minister, although he remained the Reichsbank president— for a little while. He had finally learned that Hitler was unreliable and untruthful.[19]

◦‿◦

At the same time, Gurlitt, Buchholz, Möller, and Böhmer compiled a list of "internationally exploitable" artworks with the tacit approval of the RBK. A series of contracts with the dealers had already been agreed. The combined knowledge and contacts of these four men meant that nothing of worth could evade their grasp. Their real work, however, began immediately after the Munich exhibition.

By August, artists' works which were not represented in the exhibition were herded into warehouses. Any visual arts that "distorted" the human form, used unnatural colors, or were "unfinished," to use Hitler's terminology, were confiscated. If the artists were racially or politically unacceptable, their works were seized, irrespective of any Aryan credentials. Works by artists of other nationalities who fought against Germany in the war of 1914–18 were also plundered.

When Franz Hofmann, chairman of the confiscation committee, declared in March 1938 that Germany's museums needed to be purified, it was "old news." The confiscated art had been "safeguarded" already, to use the euphemism of the day. Any art that remained on display also became subject to the "Führer's prerogative."[20] For many years, scholars believed that approximately seventeen thousand works by more than a thousand artists had fallen victim to the four horsemen of this artistic apocalypse. Yet according to the Freie Universität of Berlin's database, set up by the Ferdinand Möller Foundation after the war, the number has been revised upward, to approximately twenty-one thousand.[21] The vast majority are graphic pieces, with approximately five thousand paintings and sculptures listed.

The Mannheimer Kunsthalle collection was utterly devastated by the seizure of some 584 artworks, owing to its high concentration of modern art. Düsseldorf's Staatliche Kunstsammlungen had nine hundred artworks plundered. The Frankfurter Städelgalerie lost 496, Breslauer Schlesische Museum 560, the Stuttgarter Galerie 283, the Chemnitzer Öffentliche Sammlung 366, and its Kunsthütte (art cottage) 275. Dresden's Staatsgalerie lost 150 works of art, its Stadtsmuseum 381, and its Kupferstichkabinett 365 prints and drawings. Hamburg's Kunsthalle had some 983 artworks sequestered, its Kunstgewebemuseum 269. In all, there were 101 public collections that were stripped of modern art. The scale of the looting was so vast that for its first year of operation a large grain warehouse at Berlin's Köpenikerstrasse was coopted for storage.[22]

Simultaneously, Hetsch began to draw up the inventory. Ziegler, acting on behalf of the Schlesische Museum, in Breslau, traded an expropriated Edvard Munch for a Caspar David Friedrich, expecting a sizable commission for the transaction.[23] Hermann Göring paid a visit to the warehouse and selected thirteen paintings for his own "use." There were four by van Gogh and Munch, three by Marc, and one each by Cézanne and Signac. He then instructed the dealer Sepp Angerer to sell or trade these for him abroad.[24] While Göring might have justified this theft as market testing, he never paid for these paintings—or *any* paintings he took, from anyone. Ever.

❧

In the midst of this sudden burst of activity, Cornelius Gurlitt died on March 25, 1938, aged eighty-eight. Two weeks earlier, on March 12, Germany had annexed Austria in what has become known to history as the Anschluss. Whether Cornelius thought this was as good a thing as he would have in 1914 is doubtful. He'd been stripped of all honors he held dear, as well as his membership in all architects' associations, some of which he'd led for most of his professional life. If Hildebrand hadn't intervened locally through the powerful Herr Kirchbach, chances are Cornelius would have had to wear the yellow Star of David in the streets.

Letters of condolence poured in to the home at Kaitzer Strasse, yet there is little more to tell. As is always the case, arrangements needed to be made and people notified. Given Hildebrand's prolonged absences from home for his work and Wilibald's distance from Dresden, the task of taking care of Marie most likely fell to Helene, now the mother of two children. Young Cornelius was only five at the time, and daughter Benita* only three.[25]

With Cornelius dead and Wilibald remote, the two touchstones for Hildebrand's moral compass had fallen silent. If Hildebrand and his brother corresponded after their father's death, these letters have not been made public. Hildebrand had successfully reasoned away his plundering activities as a means to save his family from public humiliation. None were made to wear the yellow Star of David. None of them were ever branded, as many others had been in their positions.

Nonetheless, without Cornelius as a constant reminder of Hildebrand's moral obligations to himself, his family, *and* the world of art, he appeared to have lost sight of the damage he was doing to his own reputation if there was ever to be a post-Nazi world. Given his earlier mental collapses and his innate high regard for his own capabilities, it would have been entirely in keeping to assume that he'd developed a strategy whereby he could claim that all he wanted to do was save the art he so loved.

---

* Her christened name was Renate, but the family called her Benita.

19

TRADECRAFT

No Emperor has the power to dictate to the heart.
—FRIEDRICH SCHILLER

THE ANSCHLUSS REVEALED A GENUINE TREASURE TROVE. VIENNA, the long-reviled city of Hitler's youth, paid dearly for having branded him an untalented vagrant. Its museums were raped of their riches. Some artworks were stored for redistribution in provincial towns, some taken back to Germany to warehouse as future barter currency. Others were plundered for the private collections of the Nazi hierarchy.

Jewish private collections like those of the Rothschild and Ephrussi families were attacked within twenty-four hours of the Anschluss. Images of Jewish women made to scrub the streets on their hands and knees, spat at and kicked by their Aryan overlords, were filmed for newsreels back home. Many were the wives and daughters of Vienna's elite. Robbed of their fortunes, they were then robbed of their dignity.

As the Third Reich's successes progressed, so did the fury of the art seizures in Germany and the Ostmark, as Austria was then called. Hitler installed the most deadly of his art historians and SS men, Kajetan Mühlmann, to carry out his orders as gauleiter of Vienna. Surprisingly, when Hitler was told of the scale of the confiscations from museums and private collections, he became temporarily queasy, fearing accusations of criminality against his government.

Proof of the führer's fears lay in the deluge of laws streaming from his pen that year. The Reichstag no longer had any power, and the opposition had emigrated, been killed, or been dealt with by other means. April 26 marked the enactment of the Ordinance for the Registration of Jewish Property valued in excess of RM 5,000. The May 31 law regarding "the confiscation of products of degenerate art" tidied things up quite neatly in the lucrative art world. Then, in the aftermath of *Kristallnacht*, on November 12 the First Ordinance on the Exclusion of Jews from German Economic Life was passed and Goebbels prohibited Jews from attending cultural events of any sort. On November 20 and 21, the Ordinance for the Attachment of the Property of the People's and State's Enemies and the "atonement tax" (*Sühneleistung*) completed the Jewish exclusion from *all* interaction in German life.[1]

Hitler also made sure the laws stipulated that all museum employees were employees of the state, assuring their silence. From now on "confiscation" meant legal expropriation. The Commission for the Seizure and Disposal of Degenerate Art (*Kommission zur Verwertung beschlagnahmter Werke entarteter Kunst*) was in charge of the disposal of all the confiscated art and worked closely with Gurlitt and the others. Their main contact was none other than Rolf Hetsch.[2] The deal struck with Gurlitt, Buchholz, Möller, and Böhmer was based on a license to determine which artworks were valuable enough to sell abroad for foreign exchange, and which ones represented a positive valuation within Germany. With such rich pickings, the four official dealers were soon overwhelmed.

Others, including Karl Haberstock, Karl Meder, Max Täuber, and Gurlitt's cousin Wolfgang, were drafted to help in the disposal battle campaign.[3] Yet this was no free-for-all. Six gangs were created by Hetsch to "conscientiously" determine the artworks' value on a sliding scale. The four official dealers remained responsible for the hoard at Köpenikerstrasse, and were hardly minded to share the profits of their endeavors except on a "needs must" basis.

The dealers knew they enjoyed an elevated status above the sixty or so other dealers engaged in similarly approved activities. They were equally aware that one false move could topple them from their pedestals. As with all men Hitler promoted to lofty heights, these four would become each other's best friends on the surface and worst enemies beneath. Trust was a commodity in very short supply in the Third Reich.

∽

Soon the grain warehouse held 1,290 paintings, 160 sculptures, and 7,350 watercolors, drawings, and art prints, as well as 3,360 pages and 230 maps. The average large city museum displays four thousand artworks, making the Köpenikerstrasse warehouse one of the largest "museums" in Germany.[4] The art dealers began to ply their trade immediately, contacting their associates abroad. The backs of the artworks were stripped of all inscriptions in order to keep their questionable provenance secret.

Still, they couldn't shift the art quickly enough. More room was required. They also needed to be mindful not to flood the market, as prices would fall. So, in August 1938, the most valuable 780 paintings and sculptures and 3,500 watercolors, drawings, and graphic works were transferred to Schloss Niederschönhausen, just outside Berlin.[5]

One of the first museum directors to go on a shopping spree at the Schloss was Georg Schmidt of the Basel Kunstmuseum. The four official dealers were allowed to buy for their own accounts and clients, so long as it was in foreign currency. Gurlitt acquired a Max Beckmann portrait for the princely sum of one Swiss franc. Soon after, he bought several paintings by Munch.[6] Buchholz was less mean in his valuations: he spent $160 on the Kirchner *Strassenszene* and sold it on through Valentin to the Museum of Modern Art in New York.[7] Valentin worked tirelessly to keep his partner at the front of the wolf pack, whipping up enthusiasm with private collectors, galleries, and museums in the United States. Previously, Buchholz had written to the Propagandaministerium that he had "a request from a major American institution for paintings by Kokoschka. . . . Over and above this inquiry, I would also be interested in an inventory of the entire stock."[8]

Möller pulled his own strings at the top, writing to Ribbentrop's wife at the beginning of November 1938 regarding the proposed forthcoming sale of degenerate art in Lucerne through the Fischer Gallery: "I should nonetheless like to point out how unfavorable an impression would arise if this auction were allowed to go ahead. . . . From the point of view of foreign policy, this auction could be felt as an insult to those states to which the artists in question belong." In a predictable attempt at psychological manipulation, Möller saved the crux of his message for last: "If it should prove impossible to avoid disposing of these things, the German dealers could still be entrusted with the task of selling . . . to foreign collectors on their own initiative, without causing too much of a sensation, and of handing over the whole of the foreign currency that they receive."[9]

Despite Ribbentrop's intervention, the deal was sealed with the Lucerne art dealer and auctioneer Theodor Fischer. All that remained was the selection of paintings to be sold. Goebbels, meanwhile, decided that since the grain store was needed for its intended purpose before the winter of 1939, whatever could not be sold at Lucerne would be set alight in "a bonfire as a symbolic propaganda action" intended to mirror the book burnings of 1933 that targeted "un-German" authors.

Meanwhile Buchholz's gallery on Berlin's Leipziger Strasse and a warehouse on Wilhelmstrasse that had been used by Wolfgang Gurlitt were also coopted to supplement the space at Niederschönhausen.[10] At the end of February the order came to destroy the artworks remaining at the grain store. On March 20, some five thousand artworks were allegedly burned in the courtyard of Berlin's central fire station. Chances are the four art dealers took anything deemed to be of value first.

The highly prescient Gurlitt, the sophisticated and wily Buchholz, the seasoned art dealer Möller, and the Güstrow-based sculptor-turned-dealer Böhmer all knew the risks they were taking in trying to corner the market for the expropriated artworks. Each had also developed his own subsidiary networks that he felt he could, more or less, trust.[11] Wolfgang Gurlitt, Theodor Fischer, Curt Valentin, Harald Holst Halvorsen, and Aage Vilstrup were their most preferred partners in the initial stages of the sales.[12] Valentin was allowed to leave Germany in 1937, armed with a letter from the ministry licensing him to sell German art in foreign countries and set up as Buchholz's New York partner in Manhattan. An estimated 85 percent of Buchholz's profits would come through Valentin's endeavors.[13]

∽

All "degenerate" art was not, however, fully in the government's control. Some remained with dealers or still resided with private collectors. With the *Malverbot* extended to all nonapproved contemporary artists in the previous year, Max Beckmann joined others, like Max J. Friedlander, former privy councillor of the German Empire and Gemäldegalerie director, in Holland. This meant that the dealers had to be wary of expatriate German painters and artists devaluing their own supply. Hetsch, in an effort to protect the value of the hoarded collection, ordered that all modern art must be surrendered to those who acted as temporary, local government depositories: Günther Franke in Munich, Fritz Carl Valentien* in Stuttgart, Alex Vömel in Düsseldorf, and Wolfgang Gurlitt in Berlin. These quasi-official depositories were instructed to forward the art for triage and preparation for sale.[14]

While the four dealers were officially prohibited from selling direct to Germans, they created a black market nonetheless by ignoring the interdiction. Over the twelve years of Nazi rule, they became adept at understanding precisely where the best price could be obtained in their own financial interests. Still, the government's expropriation from private citizens paradoxically added to the dealers' problems. Confiscation from wealthy Jews had long been labeled as *redemption* of Jewish assets. Taking money or valuables from those who were classified as "Jewish" (whether practicing Christians or nonpracticing Jews) was a *redeeming* process for the perpetrator, akin to an act of religious salvation. Since Jews were no longer citizens of the Reich according to the Nuremberg Laws, they were illegally in possession of assets that formed part of the *Volksvermögen*, or "the People's Property." Whatever had been owned by the Jewish population was considered plundered or exploitative assets to be returned to the German people.

Often these assets were taken as *Fluchtgut*—escape goods—in the form of exit or emigration taxes. Compulsory payments to flee the country somehow magically equated to the person's entire wealth, making them immigrant paupers in their new homelands. As these *Fluchtgüter* were converted into cash, they were transferred to a special account at the Reichsvereinigung (Reich Federation).[15]

A similar system had been set up with the Reich Chancellery for the sale of all *entartete Kunst* (degenerate art), commonly called "the EK

---

* Not to be confused with Curt Valentin.

account." The big mistake made, however, was that only all *net* proceeds from the sale of the artworks were to be deposited. This meant that the dealers first made their sales—either directly overseas or by a series of convoluted transactions involving swaps and barter—and then took their commission, which ranged, in principle, from five to 25 percent, before transferring the net amounts into the EK account. It was a system rife with abuse. By 1939, the four dealers became adept, too, at stealing from Hitler.

✐

It is wrong to assume that all "sales" were simple buy-and-sell transactions. Often artworks were bartered for other "approved" works or for other undervalued "degenerate" art abroad. How to buy in foreign markets was also tricky due to the inconvertibility of the reichsmark. Vast sums had been blocked in Germany, awaiting counterparty transactions in foreign currency abroad. The ever-enterprising Swiss helped enormously with a solution. Ferdinand Möller wrote, "As you know, in selling to America, there is the opportunity to sell through the agency of the Trust of the Treuhand-Gesellschaft in Zurich. This will save approximately one-third of the purchase price. Naturally, for the client, a price reduction of 33% is interesting, and it is that which makes the Swiss Trust attractive."[16]

The discounted rate made the Swiss trust system the agent of choice for the four dealers. Before the Anschluss, the Norwegian Harald Halvorsen had agreed on a purchase price of RM 5,000 for eighteen works by Munch. RM 4,500 was paid in blocked currency and RM 500 paid in unblocked, or hard, currency. In 1938, Möller used the same method when he transacted a subsequent sale to Halvorsen. Later, Halvorsen bought more works by Munch taken from German museums through Gurlitt on the same basis.[17] In all the cases described the Swiss trust called the Schweizerische Verrechnungsstelle (SVSt) was the crucial component of the dealers' profitable trades. Thanks to the Swiss, art became the resolution of all foreign-country trades where payments had been blocked by the Nazis. As early as December 1935, the requirement for hard cash increased to 50 percent of the purchase price.[18]

In this complex trust arrangement with the Swiss, nothing was straightforward. To illustrate using one of the Halvorsen acquisitions: Essentially, the German government released reichsmarks blocked from earlier unrelated transactions at a 10 percent discount to the Swiss and Halvorsen paid the Swiss only 10 percent on top. The SVSt as intermediary then repaid the Germans in highly coveted Swiss francs or other foreign currency using standard clearinghouse methods at market rates, and taking a commission on both sides of the transaction. The more foreign currency obtained in these art deals, the better it was for Germany.

Other issues affected the discount rate or percentages of unblocked versus blocked reichsmarks used, including the willingness of foreign governments to trade with Germany and the availability or scarcity of paintings. The relationship to hard cash made art a pure trading commodity that could release blocked reichsmarks originally intended to pay for raw materials or other purchases by Germany. At a stroke Switzerland became the money launderer to Hitler's increasingly criminal regime, and art the method of payment for war matériel.

Still, fingers should not be wagged exclusively at Switzerland. England and the United States were deeply involved in similar complex financial undertakings prior to the SVSt, in the mid-1930s. In 1936, Otto Fischer, head of the Swiss museums, had exclusively used England and the United States to finance his purchases. His first acquisition through the SVSt was, however, the highly dubious acquisition of Lovis Corinth paintings from his widow for the Basel Kunstmuseum using 65 percent blocked reichsmarks.[19]

As early as 1939, Hildebrand Gurlitt and Karl Buchholz had begun trading together through these Swiss channels as well as through other agencies. With the help of the SVSt, in the period between 1937 and 1941 the four official dealers sold some 8,700 artworks in Switzerland.[20] Finally, Hildebrand Gurlitt had arrived at the treasure house of the world.

20

⟨⟫

THE TREASURE HOUSES

> We have a good opportunity to sell these pictures for
> Germany in Switzerland, a most important and precious
> thing to obtain.
>
> —WOLFGANG GURLITT to Basel Kunstmuseum, April 1942

WHILE DECLARING THAT "GERMANY NEITHER INTENDS NOR WISHES
to interfere in the internal affairs of Austria, to annex Austria or to conclude
an Anschluss," the Germans were welcomed as conquering heroes into
Vienna on March 12, 1938.

Overshadowed by the swarm of Luftwaffe planes overhead, thousands
fled to the British embassy on that day and in the days and weeks that
followed. Horror stories of women in labor breaking the embassy's windows
so their children could be born on British soil or their needlessly prolonging
their interviews, once inside, in the hope that they would go into labor were
legion. Others, fleeing certain death as Jews or Freemasons or Communists,
waited in the embassy queues that snaked for nearly a mile through Vienna's streets.

Britain's Parliament urgently provided emergency legislation. Captain
Thomas Kendrick, the naval man in charge of British intelligence at the
embassy in Vienna, along with the Reverend Hugh Grimes, of the Anglican
Church, immediately instituted underground activities that included is-

suing false passports, backdated baptismal certificates, and other decep-
tions worthy of the best spies.[1]

Slightly less than eight months later, allegedly in retribution for the
murder of a German legation secretary in Paris by the young Jew Herschel
Grynszpan, a well-planned assault against Jews was given the green light.[2]
While publicized as public outrage against Grynszpan's heinous act, the
groundswell of hatred against the Jews seemed more of a loving remem-
brance dedicated to the führer on the fifteenth anniversary of his failed
Munich putsch. On the night of November 9–10, the SA and ordinary German and Austrian citizens took part in *Kristallnacht* (Night of Broken
Glass)—a pogrom of all physical edifices that housed Judaism within and
the Jewish people.[3]

In London, the *Times* headline read "A Black Day for Germany,"
whereas the *Daily Telegraph* reported "German Mobs' Vengeance on Jews."[4]
While reportedly "only ninety-five people" were killed, more than thirty
thousand Jews were arrested in Germany and Austria. Over a thousand
synagogues were burned down, and all the Judaica within was either
destroyed or looted. In Germany, to prevent a black market devaluing
Jewish assets, the Ordinance on Utilization of Jewish Assets was published
a few weeks later, on December 3.[5] Some of the cultural property and
artworks reached the hands of Hildebrand Gurlitt.

∽

The wealthy wood-importing family of Friedmann owned four agricultural
and hunting estates near Breslau (now Wroclaw, Poland) producing sugar
beet. David Friedmann was the main beneficiary of the riches of the family
business. His sister Marie Hildegarde was amply provided for by her share
of the inheritance and her lawyer husband, Dr. Georg Garnowski. In
November 1938, the Garnowskis had two boys—Klaus, aged fourteen, and
Hans, aged eighteen. Friedmann's father had been appointed general
counsel for Germany to Venezuela under the Weimar Republic for his role
as the most significant importer of exotic hardwoods to Germany. Fortunately for him, he died shortly after Hitler became chancellor.

That October, Friedmann agreed to sell the family hunting lodge
to General Paul von Kleist—who less than a year later commanded the

Twenty-Second Panzer Corps invading Poland. The hunting lodge was envisaged as Kleist's playground and haven from the coming war. Friedmann's brother-in-law, Georg Garnowski, was acting as Friedmann's lawyer. The date for the closing was set for the morning of November 10 at Friedmann's home on one of the neighboring estates. However, during the devastation of *Kristallnacht*, Garnowski was arrested by the Gestapo.

Frantic with worry, Marie Hildegarde telephoned her brother. Of course the property closing for the hunting estate would need to be postponed. Marie Hildegarde then had the inspiration to call Kleist directly. Surely such a powerful man could help her husband? Surely his arrest must be some dreadful mistake—he was a good German, after all, she pleaded. Kleist reassured her. He would have Georg released. She must go to her brother's home, where they would meet as planned.

So Marie packed up warm underwear and socks for her husband, presuming that he had been kept in squalid conditions overnight, and drove with her younger son, Klaus, to her brother's home. In the tense hours that followed, Klaus languished beneath the Max Liebermann oil painting *Two Riders on the Beach*, waiting fretfully for his father. He loved horses and the painting.

True to his word, Kleist arrived in his chauffeured car, followed by Georg, who had been driven from the prison by two SS guards. Kleist allowed the reunited couple to embrace while he patted young Klaus on the head and comforted him, "See your father is unharmed." Klaus was then sent back to wait in the small study where *Two Riders on the Beach* hung. While Kleist's closing went ahead without any further hitches, Klaus saw another world, another time in the painting.

After the completion of the sale, they all sat down to a full three-course lunch together. Then the men played a little skat.* By late afternoon it was time to leave, and Georg said his good-byes to his son, wife, and brother-in-law. That's when Klaus learned that his father was only on day release. Georg was driven directly to the Buchenwald concentration camp, where he remained for three weeks. The idea behind this short stint in a concentration camp was not to murder, but to humiliate, annihilate any resis-

---

* Popular three-handed German card game with bidding.

tance to the Nazi will, and, above all, to take possession of any of the detainees' personal wealth.

On August 23, 1939—one week before the declaration of war by Great Britain and France for the invasion of Poland—Klaus was put onto a *Kinder* transport bound for Sweden. His brother Hans had escaped to Holland separately. Aged fifteen, Klaus would never see his uncle or parents again. The next time he would hear of the *Two Riders on the Beach* was November 3, 2013, when the news broke that Hildebrand Gurlitt's son, Cornelius, owned the painting, among some 1,406 others.[6]

∽

Throughout 1939, Gauleiter Kajetan Mühlmann raped Vienna of its treasures. Sales to Switzerland progressed by the thousands. By spring, Hitler's future war plans were made clear to the perspicacious Gurlitt and clever Buchholz through a memo sent from Hans-Heinrich Lammers at the Reich Chancellery that all the depositories were to protect the art from any bomb damage by "making bombproof basements" at their establishments.[7]

The specter of war had long been foreshadowed, and the four dealers had time to prepare themselves. Yet "saving" art may not have been their top priority, even at this stage. The horrors of the Third Reich were already abundantly clear, even though the mass deportations to the East would only begin in 1941. Personal survival, especially for the second-degree *Mischling* Gurlitt, depended on fail-safe protection.

With Cornelius's death, Hildebrand treated Kirchbach increasingly as a surrogate father, returning his many kindnesses with like generosity.[8] Their relationship would continue until death, and would be so close that Gurlitt never mentioned Kirchbach's name to his captors. On July 15, 1940, Gurlitt arranged for Kirchbach's registration of worldwide patents for his esoterically named "Jurid" process in the relative safety of Uruguay, with Buchholz's assistance. From now on, payments for use of his patents were made directly to his Uruguayan account, most likely in dollars, Swiss francs, or pounds sterling. Payment in coveted foreign exchange was always preferable, and also eliminated any risk of sequestration.

❧

Of course, 1939 plunged Europe into another world war, thereby renaming the Great War forever as the First World War, with this new one unabashedly christened as the sequel with the number "Two" or "Second."

Yet this monstrous year for humanity proved a momentous year for the art world. The often reviled Nazi Party member and art dealer Karl Haberstock devised a plan to elevate art trades upon the world stage. He had two cracking ideas with which he hoped to topple the "four horsemen," and thereby control the German art market. The first was an international auction in Switzerland, the second the realization of Hitler's dreams.

Hitler had been toying with creating a temple to the arts in his hometown of Linz for decades. Indeed, he had redesigned all of Linz himself many times over on paper. Haberstock was, if nothing else, a wizard of organization, and suggested to Hitler that he knew just the man for the job as Linz's director. Understandably, the führer's Linz project lagged behind the redesign of Munich and Berlin, where Hitler already employed a dozen architects on their major projects.[9]

Hitler envisaged Linz's improvements with a suspension bridge and impressive public buildings embracing both sides of the Danube as it wended through the city. At the apex of his plan was the district headquarters for the Nazi Party, which would house a bell tower with a crypt for his burial place. There would be a picture gallery, a library, a museum of armaments, an exhibition building, a military headquarters, a stadium, and a town hall. While Hitler fell into excited raptures over the project, explaining how Linz would be the German Budapest, Haberstock pointed out that Hitler's museum seemed a rather poor relation.[10] Until then, apparently, Hitler hadn't realized that the planned museum was merely on the same scale as museums in other cities. It took little, if any, convincing for the führer to see the opportunities a "supermuseum" would create—particularly if he was in charge of the selection of artworks.

Still, Hitler had a war to orchestrate. Of course, Haberstock agreed, the museum building needn't be built before making acquisitions. There was ample room in the basement of the Führerbau in Munich in the interim. Haberstock put forward only one name as Linz's director: Hans Posse, director of Dresden's Gemäldegalerie. Not only was Posse the right man in terms of his experience, his expertise in Renaissance art, and his international reputation, but, most significantly in Haberstock's eyes, Posse would be eternally thankful to him. Once Posse was appointed, Haberstock hoped, the four dealers' days would be at an end.

Predictably, on June 21, 1939, Hitler announced that Posse had been appointed to the exalted position of director of the Sonderauftrag Linz (Special Project for Linz). Posse would liaise with Hitler and the architects for the revised plans of the building, but his primary function was to acquire art befitting Hitler's legacy. When construction was completed, the museum would be called the Führermuseum. Meanwhile, the offices of the Sonderauftrag Linz would remain at Dresden's Gemäldegalerie. The two art historians in Posse's service there, Robert Oertel and Gottfried Reimer, were appointed as his assistants for the Linz acquisitions.[11]

⚬∽⚬

While Haberstock moved to override the four dealers' importance with the appointment of Posse, there were other independent dealers who represented a danger to his plans. Walter Andreas Hofer, Hermann Göring's art agent, fed his master's insatiable appetite for art by supplying Göring's cavernous mansion Carinhall with treasures. Hofer had a well-oiled network with the crafty Lucerne-based Swiss art dealer and auctioneer Theodor Fischer, as well as with Fischer's Paris representative, the German expatriate Hans Wendland. This enabled Hofer to buy, sell, or barter on behalf of Göring with relative impunity.

Somehow, Haberstock also believed that he could override Hofer. Fischer was an old friend from their days at the Cassirer firm in Berlin, so Haberstock resolved to offer him a juicy bone—an auction of degenerate German art. Fischer leapt at the opportunity. Working for Göring privately as well as for the Nazi State made Fischer the preeminent auction house and art dealer for the Germans in Switzerland.[12] The advantages were clear; why sell a dozen paintings through complicated blocked-and-unblocked-currency-hedging methods when an international auction every month or so would bring in much more foreign exchange?

Yet Haberstock hadn't bargained on three major factors. The first was

that Hitler and his mass-media mogul Goebbels had been calling the
degenerate art "rubbish" publicly for years. They had also flooded the market
through a combination of confiscations from fleeing refugees and expropriation from museums and Jews. The May 1938 law legalizing expropriation by
the state solidified this impression abroad. Secondly, a decided reluctance by
some museums to buy artworks that had been brutally wrenched from their
legal homes had settled in. Finally, the four dealers knew the vicissitudes in
the art and currency markets and in the previous two years had become
adept at manipulating them to their advantage. They were supple in their
greed, where Haberstock had allowed it to cloud his vision.

∽

Trading at the Schloss continued regardless of Haberstock's machinations.
Georg Schmidt of the Basel Kunstmuseum was the hot prospect, acquiring
art throughout the spring. Separately, only 125 artworks were selected for
Lucerne, yet Gurlitt seemed keen to close a deal with Schmidt to buy direct in
Berlin. So he visited Schmidt in Basel on the Wednesday prior to the auction.

   Gurlitt told Schmidt that he'd help bid on the artists' work that most
appealed to the museum director during the auction. Separately, Buchholz
offered to represent the museum with the German government after the
auction of subsequent purchases. Following Gurlitt's visit, Schmidt wrote
to Buchholz that it had been agreed that the museum would purchase first
from those works still stored in Berlin, to better plan what funds might
remain available for the auction itself. Gurlitt and Buchholz had joined
forces, using the meeting in Basel as a final lever.

   As the more senior dealer, Buchholz took the lead in subsequent negotiations.[13] Schmidt selected thirteen paintings prior to the auction, including Corinth's *Ecce Homo*, Marc's *Tierschicksale* (*Fate of the Animals*),
and Kokoschka's *Die Windsbraut* (*The Tempest*), for a purchase price of
18,000 Swiss francs.[14] It was the first documented sale negotiated with
Buchholz and Gurlitt acting in partnership. Others followed.

∽

The Fischer Auction took place on the beautiful summer's day of June 30,
1939, at the Grand Hotel National overlooking the peaceful Lake Lucerne.
Museum directors around the world were torn between attending or

boycotting the proceedings, since it was rumored that the proceeds would fund Nazi expansionism and rearmament. The Basel Kunstmuseum had no such scruple. Neither did Switzerland's Zentralbibliothek. Schmidt had been granted an initial allocation of 50,000 Swiss francs.[15] While Alfred A. Barr of the Museum of Modern Art was in Paris at the time, refusing to attend, he would continue to buy purged modern art from German State collections through his friend Valentin and Buchholz through November 1941 and possibly beyond.[16]

The minor squall surrounding the auction rose to a thunderstorm in early June when Alfred Frankfurter, editor of *Art News* and advisor to the American banker and art collector Maurice Wertheim, cabled Fischer: "To counteract rumors suggest you cable confidentially not for publication actual ownership June 30 sale and whether money obtained goes to Germany STOP Believe would stimulate American bids."[17] The less-than-truthful Fischer replied that all payments were to be made to his gallery for distribution to German museums for new acquisitions and that a competitor in Paris was responsible for the nasty rumors.

That "competitor" was the exiled Paul Westheim, a German Jewish publisher banished to France, who knew precisely how the German government intended to recirculate the money. Fischer also claimed that a group of dealers were colluding in a ring that was the result of Westheim's outcry, and that their malicious influence had spread to New York. Potential bidders were contacted directly, but to no avail. By the time the 125 artworks were previewed, the unsubstantiated gossip had soured several heavy hitters from attending.

Fischer penned a panicked series of letters to the Propagandaministerium protesting about Schmidt's buying direct from Buchholz and Gurlitt in Berlin. Before he had a reply, he wrote again, asking permission to lower reserves to a margin of 20 percent below the reserve prices for the six most prized works by Gauguin, van Gogh, and Marc and three by Picasso. He also asked for a full week after the auction to find buyers for the unsold works.

The reply was emphatic. Fischer could lower the reserves on three less valuable works and seek buyers for unsold works after the auction. However, it was out of the question for the most valuable paintings to be sold for less than the reserve price. Furthermore, it was deemed inappropriate for the Propagandaministerium to be represented except by an unknown junior official. Neither Hofmann nor Hetsch would be present. Haberstock, too, was ordered to stay away.[18] Gurlitt, however, was there.

At three o'clock, the auction began. Seated among the 350 guests were Swiss collectors like Emil Bührle; the *Art News* editor Alfred Frankfurter, bidding on behalf of Maurice Wertheim; and painter Henri Matisse's son Pierre, who was an art dealer in New York and Paris. Pierre was interested primarily in his father's painting *Bathers with a Turtle*, as were Saint Louis, Missouri's Joseph Pulitzer, Jr., and his bride, Louise, who were on their honeymoon. Pulitzer had persuaded Matisse to bid on the painting for him. Film director Josef von Sternberg and New York dealers Karl Nierendorf and Curt Valentin were also present. The museums from various American cities snuck in alongside their Antwerp, Basel, Bern, Brussels, and Liège counterparts. There was also a smattering of English, French, Swiss, and German collectors, and journalists were there to report on the proceedings. The auction took place in German, French, and English, and the bidding was set in Swiss francs. No advance credit arrangements needed to be made, and anonymity was guaranteed—a very Swiss specialty.[19]

Just as the auction began, a bellhop dashed in and whispered to Frankfurter that he had an urgent telephone call. Exceptionally, after the painting on the block fell under the hammer, Fischer announced that they would wait for Frankfurter's return. Murmurs spread through the crowd. Even today, experts have differing theories about what was said in that phone call. Had Frankfurter been threatened? By whom? Or had he been warned off acquiring any other paintings, save lot 45? Whatever was said remains a mystery, but it was a pale and shaken Frankfurter who reentered the auction room several minutes later.[20]

The auction continued, punctuated only by Fischer's monotone droning on in three languages until lot 45, Vincent van Gogh's *Self-Portrait*, came onto the auction block. Frankfurter became suddenly animated, and deftly outbid his nearest Belgian rivals, paying an equivalent of $40,000 for the painting. He promptly submitted his bidder's card, took the painting away, and called for his car. He swiftly placed it in the trunk and drove away as if scalded by the experience.[21]

∽

"Jews boycotted the auction," Fischer later complained to Haberstock; only "two-thirds of the works were sold."[22] Of the 125 lots, thirty-eight did not meet their reserves. Picasso's *Absinthe Drinker* did not sell and became the vortex of an international incident. Its original donor to the Hamburger Kunsthalle demanded to have a right of first refusal to buy the painting back. Instead, for the next two years, it hung in the German embassy in Bern while the ensuing litigation was resolved. It was ruled that the donor had no further claim on the painting. "I want to avoid at all costs a situation in which our payment will be blocked in Switzerland," Haberstock wrote heatedly to Fischer. "If there's any danger of this, the sale must be handled in such a way that the painting would be first returned to us and the payment made directly in English pounds to us at the Reichsbank to the account 'EK.'"[23]

Valentin, meanwhile, had temporarily reprieved Alfred H. Barr from his worst demons. "I am just as glad not to have the museum's name or my own associated with the auction," Barr wrote to his manager, Thomas Mabry, on July 1, knowing that he planned to acquire four significant artworks through Valentin from the auction: Derain's *Valley of the Lot at Vers*, sequestered from Cologne; Lehmbruck's sculpture *Kneeling Woman*, from Berlin's Nationalgalerie; Klee's *Around the Fish*, purloined from Dresden's Gemäldegalerie; and the Essen Folkwang Museum's *Blue Window*, by Matisse.[24] Barr had, of course, previously arranged to purchase Kirschner's *Strassenszene* through Valentin, for which Buchholz had paid $160 at the Schloss.

Barr knew he was allowing his heart to rule his head. The outrage felt by artists like Beckmann and Picasso and French dealers was nothing compared with the furor in the European—and particularly French—press. Yet the morality of his acquiring art at the expense of German museums and private collectors forced to flee Germany penniless was overwhelmed by the absolute need to possess these works for *his* museum. With this clearly in mind, he instructed Mabry in that same July 1 letter that "I think it very important that our releases . . . should state that [the works] have been purchased from the Buchholz Gallery, New York."[25]

Barr not only paid Valentin his commission on all transactions, but also sent museum trustees to shop in the Buchholz Gallery in New York, popping in personally once a week to "say hello." Had Valentin told Barr that Buchholz, one of the four official dealers for Hitler, was his business partner? Or that Buchholz had provided an initial stock from the grain store and Schloss Niederschönhausen for the gallery when Valentin immigrated? Or even that he had been given a letter by the Nazis authorizing him to sell these artworks in the United States?[26] This authorization had been granted in mid-November 1936 in response to Valentin's September 22 request to immigrate to New York to sell German art in America. It was no different from the authorization given to Hitler's other "approved" dealers.

The original of Valentin's authorization is housed at the Archive of American Art, part of the Smithsonian, in Washington, DC. Valentin had given the letter to his faithful assistant, Jane Wade, with the handwritten note "1936 permit to continue buying pictures in Germany" appended at the bottom. On the next line, he wrote to Wade, "Can be destroyed."[27] "Can" and "must" are two different instructions, and so Wade held on to the document.

While Valentin may not have confided these darkest secrets to Barr, MoMA's director must have suspected the closeness of Valentin's relationship with Buchholz. Over a decade later, Barr implied to an Associated Press journalist that MoMA had actually boycotted the auction, losing (to Gurlitt) the best Munch that had ever been sold.[28] During the war he might have assuaged his conscience by funding Varian Fry's emergency efforts to save the German and French intelligentsia through Fry's base in Marseilles. Or perhaps he was simply helping Fry as an old Harvard classmate.

Eighteen years later, Barr defended his actions to Kenneth Donahue, the curator at the Ringling Museum of Art, in Sarasota, Florida, who was wrestling with the same moral dilemma. "I frankly thought it was a good thing for the Germans as a whole," Barr rationalized, "to have some reminder of their collective guilt and folly." That was bad enough. Yet Barr went on to reassure Donahue. "You're safe on the first count (legal); your conscience must guide you on the second (moral)."[29]

∽

The total proceeds from Fischer's June 1939 auction were 500,000 Swiss francs. Compared with other specialist auctions of the period in the main capital cities of the world, it was a meager result. Of the thirty-eight unsold works, only *The Absinthe Drinker* found a home in Switzerland. The thirty-seven that remained were returned to the Propagandaministerium in Germany only in 1941.

Gurlitt, Buchholz, Möller, and Böhmer would profit, however, from Fischer's losses. It was Böhmer who eventually bailed out Fischer in 1941, selling Picasso's *Absinthe Drinker* on behalf of the Propagandaministerium to Fischer for an estimated 24,000 Swiss francs against a trade for Anthony van Dyck's *Madonna and Child*, appraised at a value of 150,000 Swiss francs. This same van Dyck had been purloined from the Max Emden Collection a short while earlier at an appraisal value of 60,000 Swiss francs. Fischer sold it on to Otto Huber for 25,000 Swiss francs.[30] Böhmer's commission was 10 percent based on a revised valuation for the picture at 110,000 Swiss francs. At the auction that June, Böhmer purchased Corinth's *Self-Portrait* for less than half of its estimated value.

❧

That summer Posse's Sonderauftrag Linz dominated the European art market. On September 1, 1939, Hitler invaded Poland, and days later World War II began. By June 1940, Hitler had spread his net throughout Eastern Europe and successfully invaded Denmark, Norway, Holland, Belgium, and Luxembourg, and carved up France. Czechoslovakia had been slowly strangled by the annexation of the Sudetenland in 1938 and the ultimate invasion of the whole country on March 15, 1939. After the fall of France, Great Britain alone stood against Germany in Europe—teetering on the edge of destruction until lend-lease for war matériel was signed with the United States in March 1941—ending the shadowboxing surrounding American neutrality. On June 22, 1941, Hitler's Operation Barbarossa for the invasion of the Soviet Union began. There was no longer any delusion about Hitler's aims.

❧

Until the end of 1941, Gurlitt, Buchholz, Möller, and Böhmer worked primarily for the Propagandaministerium for thousands of transactions involving the confiscated art. Gurlitt's own incomplete and redacted ledgers show this clearly. Thousands of works of art that the Reich had expropriated were never found. Until recently, all were believed lost. Among the missing works was Max Liebermann's *The Lion Tamer*, which would be rediscovered only in 2011, at a Stuttgart auction. The unnamed seller was Gurlitt's son, Cornelius.

21

⌖

THE POSSE YEARS

While Man's desires and aspirations stir,
He cannot choose but err.

—JOHANN WOLFGANG VON GOETHE, *Faust*

IMPENDING WAR INEVITABLY LED TO THE SQUIRRELING-AWAY OF art treasures throughout Europe. London's National Gallery moved the bulk of its holdings to remote Wales. Belgium asked for asylum for its priceless van Eyck Ghent Altarpiece in France. Knowing that France was the Continental prize Hitler most coveted, the Musées Nationaux spread its riches between dozens of former royal châteaus in the Loire. Belgium's Altarpiece was moved to the south. Noted collectors were also given the opportunity to safeguard their collections alongside those of the Louvre. Many, including the Rothschilds, whose cousins had suffered so badly in Austria, were glad of the help. British subject Alphonse Kann sent a portion of his collection to the château at Brissac. The American Nazi sympathizer Florence Gould put her valuable tapestries in storage at the American embassy.[1]

∽

Since the Fischer Auction, there was a new master whom *all* art dealers in the Third Reich wanted to serve—Dr. Hans Posse, the weak-chinned, thin-lipped son of Dresden, who had been the director at the Gemäldegalerie since 1913. He was talented, opinionated, and starry-eyed at the unparalleled potential of the new role conferred on him: amassing riches for Hitler's übermuseum.

During the war of 1914–18, Posse was responsible for Raphael's magnificent *Portrait of a Youth* from the Czartoryski Collection of the National Galerie in Cracow, which had been evacuated to Dresden by German Monuments Men for safekeeping.[2] Perhaps one of Posse's greatest selling points to Hitler was that he refused to return the Raphael painting until 1920, once the harsh sentence of the Versailles *Diktat* was passed on Germany.[3] Covetousness in the name of the Reich was always applauded. When Gauleiter Mutschmann attempted to oust Posse for alleged anti-Nazi sentiments in 1933, he was immediately and personally reinstated by Hitler—at the quiet urging of Haberstock. Posse's true crime was the acquisition of modern art.[4]

Gurlitt knew that Posse hadn't warmed to him while they lived in the same cliquey art community in Dresden. Hildebrand blamed Posse's coldness on some perceived snub in the unending feud between Posse's friend Pinder, in Leipzig, and his father. Notwithstanding this, it seems more likely that Posse couldn't abide Hildebrand's high opinion of himself. Whatever the cause, Gurlitt sensed that the only way to ensure his exalted position for the future was to work for the Propagandaministerium *and* Posse. First, however, he'd need to break Haberstock's stranglehold of gratitude on Posse.

In fact, Haberstock and Posse coordinated their efforts since the Anschluss. Posse traveled to Vienna to see German troops parading victoriously through the city. While the Gestapo interrogated and tortured private collectors from their base at Vienna's Hotel Metropole, Posse personally impounded the collections of Alphonse and Louis de Rothschild. Together with the Nazi Kunsthistorisches director with the unfortunate name von Baldass, Posse plundered thousands of artworks from private collectors who either fled without their beloved possessions or who were made to sign them over for their freedom, like the Ephrussi family.

These artworks were then taken to the Hofburg Palace (used as Vienna's depository) before being redistributed to the Kunsthistorisches Museum and smaller museums throughout Austria, or sold at the state-owned auction house, the Dorotheum. As if by magic, however, some reappeared in the hands of the official four dealers of the Third Reich.

Gurlitt and his colleagues had been trading in Austria before the Anschluss. Yet, theoretically, once Austria was part of Germany this should have been forbidden. Their mandate was to sell for foreign exchange *and* they were not licensed to sell to Germans, which the Austrians had become. They carried on regardless. If Barr salivated over a few modern masterpieces, how were lesser mortals supposed to act?

Their presumed dilemma was resolved in general by Switzerland, and in particular by the SVSt trust. Dr. Hans Herbst, the Dorotheum's director, was able to sell to Switzerland, the nonoccupied territories of Europe, and the United States. Over the next six years, he would become one of Gurlitt's primary contacts and sources for transactions—both privately and on behalf of the Sonderauftrag Linz.[5] Schmidt of the Basel Kunstmuseum would be another.

As with many of the artworks sold by Valentin in the United States, Gurlitt relied heavily on Switzerland as the intermediary for barter and sales transactions involving blocked (discounted) and unblocked reichsmarks to obtain much-coveted foreign currency. As Valentin himself wrote to refugee art dealer Galka Scheyer in California in 1939, "By the way, it is not too difficult to get pictures from Europe. I received shipments from Switzerland, from France, from England und [*sic*] even from Klee himself."[6]

For Gurlitt to join the treasure hunt, sooner or later a base of operations in Austria would be de rigueur. He had bailed out Wolfgang from insolvency in the early 1930s, not for family loyalty but to exercise a hold over him. Wolfgang had bought himself a small single-story chalet down a country lane nestled on the outskirts of the sleepy Alpine village of Bad Aussee in Austria. Situated only an hour or so from Linz, it was the perfect location for Hildebrand's uses, too. Yet it must have been the topic of many a hushed family conversation, for Wolfgang often lived there with his first and second wives after it became unsafe in Berlin in 1943. Soon his mistress joined them, too.

Gurlitt also kept a nasty secret: that Wolfgang had tried to circumvent him. At the end of 1938, Wolfgang had written to Theodor Fischer in Lucerne offering his "superior" services to the Swiss art dealer and auctioneer. Fischer replied that he already had a relationship with Wolfgang's cousin Hildebrand and the Propagandaministerium. Wolfgang's assistance would be surplus to his requirements.[7] Only once they ironed out their difficulties did Gurlitt finally arrange for Wolfgang to receive the coveted official authorization to trade internationally on behalf of the Third Reich, on February 7, 1940, so long as it was on his terms.[8]

༺༻

When war was declared in Europe on September 3, 1939, Austria became merely the first of many rich countries the Nazis would plunder. As the blitzkrieg thundered through Poland, Posse harked back to his previously safeguarded charge—Raphael's *Portrait of a Young Man*. The thought of keeping it safe again proved intoxicating. The Raphael, however, would be only the fingertip of his desires.

By mid-October, Kajetan Mühlmann's field of operations moved into Poland. He secured three of the incomparable Czartoryski Collection's masterpieces for Berlin: the Raphael, da Vinci's *Lady with the Ermine*, and Rembrandt's *Portrait of Martin Soolmans*. Over the coming years these would travel several times between borders as Allied air raids struck at the heart of the Third Reich. The Raphael, however, would always voyage cradled lovingly by Mühlmann.[9] It was last seen in the offices of Gauleiter Hans Frank of Poland in 1945.

Poland lost most of its treasures in the first year of Nazi occupation. The Veit Stoss Altar and its glorious panels fashioned by Hans von Kulmbach were stolen from the Marienkirche, in Krakow, and moved to Berlin. In late November 1939, Posse made his first—and only—inspection trip of the Polish collections to determine if there were other treasures worthy of Linz. Aside from the artworks already plundered and "several works of the National Museum in Warsaw," Posse sighed, "there is not very much which could enlarge the German stock of great art. The Polish store of applied art is richer and more varied" and could be consigned to his assistants for handling.[10]

Posse's snide remark excluded, naturally, the twenty-seven drawings by Albrecht Dürer at the Lvov Museum, as well as the work of other German masters which remained in Soviet hands. The order to retrieve these as soon as the war permitted was issued, since the Dürers were looted by Napoleon in Vienna and were deemed part of Germany's patrimony. Within six days of the German attack on the Soviet Union in June 1941, while battles still cracked hotly within earshot, Mühlmann was sent into the fray on the express orders of Göring to retrieve the drawings and bring them to the reichsmarschall at Carinhall straightaway. The next day, they were in Hitler's possession and would remain with him always.[11]

∽

By 1940, Gurlitt had learned to be alert to every opportunity to endear himself to the Nazi elite. On December 10, he wrote to Posse that he'd heard the Linz director was looking for a suitable present for the reichs-marschall. Apparently, Gurlitt had come across just the thing—a snip at RM 25,000. The proposed gift required swift action. After all, it could hardly be possible to buy it more inexpensively.[12]

The gift was intended as a present for Christmas 1940. It was "framed beautifully and would make a wonderful addition to the reichsmarschall's collection. The old stained glass window from an early German artist also had very beautiful gold-work."[13] Naturally, Gurlitt's sales pitch claimed he'd stumbled on it for a museum client. That very Friday afternoon he planned to meet some men who were anxious to see it, as it was precisely what they'd been looking for. Still, if it was something Posse would like to consider, the director could count on Gurlitt for his utter discretion in the matter. Posse could even reverse the charges if he wished to discuss the matter by telephone.[14]

Of course, Gurlitt knew about the tradition that had already sprung up among the Nazi hierarchy of expensive gift giving at Christmas, on their birthdays, or as New Year's presents. Gifts to Hitler, Göring, and Goebbels on these occasions were intended as tributes to their greatness. Since 1933, art became increasingly significant in these overblown ceremonies of homage; and anyone who was able to acquire the highly unusual grew in stature with the recipient.[15] As Gurlitt's letter arrived only a few short weeks before Christmas, an old stained-glass window with intricate goldwork did not demand the question "From where did it come" or indeed invite comment about the price, but rather "How soon may I see it?"

However, two days later Posse replied that "with the best will . . . I can't acquire it for this price." Doubtless, Posse knew it was an inferior example at any price. Yet, Posse's second paragraph shows a new willingness to deal with Gurlitt. "There is an exceptional stained glass window with eight images from the St. Lorenzen Kirche near St. Marien im Mürztal I can recommend (4.5m high x 1.3m wide). This can be found at the Kunsthaus Malméde in Cologne. . . . It is truly a rare and eclectic object."[16] Posse had set a Machiavellian test.

This stained-glass window, eventually bought through Gurlitt, formed part of Göring's enormous tally of looted art. Believing he was part of the inner circle at last, Gurlitt offered Posse one of his own grandfather's paintings—*Acropolis,* a landscape of the Greek ruin—weeks later, on January 15, 1941. The price was, again, that all-too-familiar RM 25,000. Posse hesitated.

Two months later, Gurlitt wrote to Posse to say that the painting had sold at auction in Frankfurt for RM 6,275 on March 6—evidently forgetting the huge price tag he had previously demanded. At the bottom of Gurlitt's letter, Posse wrote, "Write to Professor Albert Speer." Then, on March 21, Posse penned his letter to Gurlitt: "I've just returned from a long journey to see a letter from Professor Speer that he bought the Louis Gurlitt. Would you be so kind as to send him an invoice to his home: Berlin-Charlottenburg, Lindenallee, 18?"[17] At a stroke, Posse had rumbled Gurlitt, demonstrating his superior market knowledge and that he knew Gurlitt had tried to swindle him—twice. Posse clearly understood who Gurlitt was *and* had the trump card against him, which he might need in the future.

With the requisite written proof that Gurlitt had tried to dupe him, Posse knew what kind of beast the man was and became confident that Gurlitt could be controlled by threats and blackmail if needed. By that point, too, Posse had tired of Haberstock's increasingly outrageous demands. To his mind, Haberstock compared less favorably to the malleable Gurlitt. Then Posse had a brainstorm. Let the two dealers fight it out like gladiators in the arena. Consequently, he set up Gurlitt in opposition to the criminally deceitful Haberstock from January 1941.

Haberstock had already come up against the opposition of the Reich Chancellery officials, owing to his unsavory reputation and "illegal" business transactions in 1940, and had been prevented from conducting further business in Holland. However, Haberstock would not be denied his part in the rich pickings, reminding Posse of the debt owed to him. So Posse retaliated by limiting Haberstock to French territory only—just weeks before he signed the travel papers for Gurlitt that set the two men up in opposition to each other. The country was big enough for the egos of both art dealers, was it not? Haberstock could continue to act as Posse's main dealer in France in much the same way Prince Philipp of Hessen had been working for Posse in Italy. Both Haberstock and Gurlitt would be held in check knowing that the other was looking over his shoulder. It was a most Machiavellian plan.

✍

Once the blitzkrieg rattled through the Western Zone in May–June 1940, with its occupation of Belgium, Holland, and Luxembourg, some art dealers demonstrated considerable concern for the safety of the artists—in many cases their bread and butter—who'd taken refuge in these countries. Gurlitt was *not* among their number.

On June 14, 1940, Karl Buchholz penned a letter to Max Beckmann, in exile in Amsterdam since 1937. "It has been so long since we've written to one another," Buchholz lamented a month after Holland's surrender. "I had a letter today from Valentin [from New York] saying he needs to buy more pictures from you and he hopes you're still working. Perhaps you could send a selection of new oils direct to New York."[18] Buchholz was explicit: He could no longer send artworks direct to the United States from Germany, whereas there hadn't been any such restriction by the artist himself in Holland.[19] Valentin, too, was worried, having also written to Beckmann, on June 8.[20] As if to underline the danger to Beckmann of continuing to paint despite the *Malverbot*, the envelopes of these letters were stamped by the German censors, showing that they had both been opened.

Until then, Buchholz had caught glimpses of Beckmann's welfare from officials traveling through Holland, ever hopeful that soon he would be able to exhibit Beckmann's work again in Germany. In his letter, Buchholz promised to send "a man" to Beckmann. That man would be Erhard Goepel, who not only represented Posse in the Netherlands for Linz, but also for the feared Dienststelle Mühlmann. From 1941 until the end of 1944, Goepel also worked closely with Gurlitt in the Netherlands, Belgium, and France.[21]

In Germany, Gurlitt, too, was quietly exhibiting and selling Beckmann's art, along with many other Expressionists from his private Kunstkabinett located within his own home. In the front room were nineteenth-century "approved" artworks; the back room was chock-full of degenerate art. According to Beckmann, Gurlitt had been the last to exhibit his works before he was forced into exile.[22] Due to the discreet atmosphere created, thanks in no small part to Gurlitt's attractive wife Helene, dealers and collectors were able to congregate, discuss modern art, and, most importantly, buy modern art even if they were German.

∽

Gurlitt's Kunstkabinett was not registered as a business in his own name. Until 1940, it had been in Helene's name, in a successful move to "Aryanize" the family business. Yet, once war broke out, Gurlitt transferred the ownership of the Kunstkabinett to a Hamburg art dealer, Frau Ingeborg Hertmann.[23] Gurlitt wanted to hedge his outward involvement in art trades if Germany lost this war, and Helene's involvement in the business did not achieve that goal. Between 1940 and 1942, Inge Hertmann was the owner of record of the Gurlitt Kunstkabinett. Yet she was more often than not referred to as Gurlitt's secretary. In her own words, she became "a confidante, gaining insight into Dr. Gurlitt both privately as well as in the business."[24]

Privately, Hertmann thought Gurlitt was the most secretive and greedy of men. Still, she described Helene as the more grasping of the two. Everything he said or did was about creating the right illusions about his business for both artists and potential clients, while, in fact, all that interested Gurlitt was generating the greatest profit. For many, Gurlitt's attitude might seem like "good business," but given how the artworks were acquired, it displayed a distinct lack of morality. Although Gurlitt made "absolutely derogatory statements" about the Nazi regime, he "donned their cloak during the entire time," Hertmann claimed, in order to benefit from "the advantages afforded to him." As time went on, more and more of his letters and invoices were signed *Heil Hitler!*" His rapacious and less scrupulous cousin, Wolfgang, never once used the expression.[25]

In fact, Gurlitt "often dropped into the conversation that he was working with Dr. Hetsch of the Propagandaministerium, Reichsleiter [*sic*] Speer, Goebbels etc. With Speer, Gurlitt had both personal as well as business relationships."[26] Gurlitt bought cheaply and sold high. He had wide-ranging business relationships, and often sold to some of Germany's top industrialists.

"Herr Reemtsma's secretary," Inge Hertmann claimed, "heard Gurlitt voice that in 1942/1943 he worked for the führer himself."[27]

Hertmann was genuinely outraged at the enormous profits that Gurlitt made on the sale of art. "While at the Kunsthalle [Kunstverein] in Hamburg he had purchased several Liebermann paintings very inexpensively and sold these on for unheard of profits." Considering that Liebermann's widow had been forced to sell their villa in the beautiful southwest Berlin suburb of Wannsee in 1940 for a pittance, Gurlitt's attitude showed extreme callousness to the memory of a man who, during his lifetime, had been the mainstay of the German Expressionist movement.*

To make matters worse, Gurlitt had acquired Liebermann's *Two Riders on the Beach* from the Aryan auctioneer and art dealer Hans W. Lange in 1942.[28] Still, he did nothing to save Liebermann's widow, Martha, who in 1943, aged eighty-five and bedridden by a stroke, killed herself when she received notice that she would shortly be deported to Theresienstadt.

Hertmann highlighted another example, too. "Concerning the Jews, when Litzmann went into exile," she explained, "he gave Gurlitt his paintings to sell. I recall that he wrote to Gurlitt afterward, please send us the money from the sales, we are starving. Gurlitt instructed me in a calm and casual manner to send ten reichsmarks to the Jews and to use the services of a Herr Werner to send them the money."[29]

Hertmann had more damning things to say against Gurlitt, too. It seemed that Gurlitt was directing art operations for the Abwehr during the Posse years. "With Messrs Abbs and Gieseler, who are already dead," Hertmann told police in late November 1947, "Gurlitt nurtured very profitable deals in extremely private conversations. I heard that these two men were, as far as one can know, spies from the Abwehr and had a commission from Gurlitt for [taking] wagonloads [of art] to Holland."[30]

Indeed, while she worked in the Kunstkabinett, "Gurlitt spent more and more time in Paris, stopping at 14, rue St Simon, and had connections with the art dealers Ader, Aubry, and André Schoeller, 15 rue Théeran [*sic*]. André Schoeller was an expert in French Expressionism. With these men, and many others, Gurlitt nurtured extravagant deals."

---

* Liebermann died in 1935. His death, however, was not announced in the Nazi-controlled media, owing to his Expressionism and Judaism.

Cornelius Gurlitt's now notorious fifth-floor Munich apartment,
where the world's press camped out in November/December 2013

Nazi propaganda
against Jewish
artists and art
dealers "In
the shadow of
Jehovah"

Völkischer Beobachter, Nazi party newspaper—"Historic Day for German Art"

Cornelius Gurlitt's Salzburg home. The only other semi-derelict property in the area is directly opposite. Did Cornelius own both?

Exterior of Hôtel Drouot today, Paris

Dorotheum auction
house, Vienna

This painting was looted from Alfred Flechtheim by Hildebrand Gurlitt. When it sold at auction, the Gurlitt mystery began to unravel.

A Monuments woman researching art provenance in Altaussee salt mine

Max Liebermann painting *Two Riders on the Beach* as shown in the news conference in November 2013; it once belonged to David Friedmann and is the second painting to be restored from the Gurlitt art hoard.

Hildebrand's cousin, Wolfgang Gurlitt, painted by Lovis Corinth. Wolfgang, too, was an unscrupulous looter but he never signed his letters "Heil Hitler!" unlike Hildebrand.

Louis Gurlitt
1812 Altona – 1897 Naundorf / D

Aequer Berge (Vorappenin in der ital. Region Lazio), 1856
Aequi Mountains (Preapennines in the Italian region Lazio),
1856
Öl auf Leinwand / oil on canvas
erworben / acquired 1953

Aequi Mountains 1856 by Louis Gurlitt
(1812–1897), on display at the Lentos Museum,
Linz. It is one of the few reminders of the museum's
associations with Wolfgang.

Cornelius Gurlitt
attempting to go grocery
shopping in 2013.
The revelations of his
father's role in the Nazi
looting shocked him.

One of the areas where art was stored at Altaussee— two kilometers underground

Painting of Alfred Flechtheim by Otto Dix, Nationalgalerie, Berlin. Flechtheim became Hitler's symbol of the hated Jew.

Hildebrand Gurlitt in Zwickau, 1930, during his only period as a museum director (1925–1930)

Henri Matisse's painting *The Open Window,* now called *Woman Seated by the Open Window,* which once belonged to Paul Rosenberg, and is the first painting to be restored to the rightful heirs

Despite her disillusionment and disgust, Gurlitt had chosen his Aryan partner well. Hertmann knew that if she spoke out to those who might care about such things in the Third Reich, Gurlitt would denounce her. Understandably, she said as much to the police after the war, adding that she was forced to "keep her mouth shut." After all Inge Hertmann was married to a Jew. "Such things as I am portraying here occurred regularly," she told the police, "as if rolling off an assembly line. For me today, these things need to be reemphasized. Gurlitt always acted for indecipherable reasons."[31] She hadn't appreciated that his natural penchant for privacy had been hard-wired into him from childhood by his father; or that he had, in turn, further developed this art of concealment to pass on to his own children.

∽

Hertmann's affidavit in 1947 claimed that she'd protested directly to Gurlitt countless times about his callous and unscrupulous behavior during her tenure. From Gurlitt's perspective, obviously Inge Hertmann had to go. Fortunately, Gurlitt already had a new Aryan partner in mind through the auspices of his next-door neighbor, Wilhelm Hermsen, the Dutch chemist who lived at 5 Alte Rabenstrasse. It was Wilhelm who introduced Gurlitt to his relations Theo and Jean—whose specialty was the transportation of fine mahogany furniture.[32] Little else is known about precisely how this partnership came about; only that Theo agreed to replace Ingeborg Hertmann sometime before November 1942, and that together, Hildebrand Gurlitt and Theo Hermsen would make a killing in France.

22

SWALLOWING THE TREASURE

Character is simply a habit long continued.

—PLUTARCH

HILDEBRAND GURLITT HAD BEEN BEAVERING AWAY FROM 1938 for the Third Reich, ranging from the seemingly innocuous "museum commissions" on up to the Propagandaministerium, the Abwehr (Military Intelligence), and the Sonderauftrag Linz. While his claim to Reemtsma's secretary that he worked for Hitler may appear to have been a boast, it was the truth. From the moment Hitler appointed Posse, there was no difference made *ever* between the führer's private collection and the one intended for Linz.[1]

Gurlitt's and Hermsen's laissez-passer, signed by Posse, was issued along with directives to the Nazi occupation forces to provide adequate means to transport the paintings back to Germany. Gurlitt's international banking arrangements to pay for any art acquired from one of the "provinces" of the Nazi occupation were handled by Linz in conjunction with Dr. Hans-Heinrich Lammers, head of the Reich Chancellery. Where possible, Gurlitt bought inexpensively in reichsmarks or local currency, selling on in dollars, Swiss francs, or British pounds and making a double killing on the transaction. His operations expanded rapidly, with Hermsen running things from Paris in conjunction with the larger transports handled by

Gustav Knauer, located at 8 rue Halévy. Over the next few years, Hermsen, an expatriate Dutchman who had been living in Germany, would also need a guardian angel—a role Gurlitt was destined to fulfill.

~∽~

Since Holland and Belgium had fallen to the advancing war machine within days,* only France remained free from Hitler's sway on the Continent. Rotterdam was still burning when Kajetan Mühlmann, in full SS regalia, swooped down on the Netherlands with his team of dealers and art historians to begin thieving.[2] Rather than consolidate the new territories in northern Europe as in the East, Hitler's forces simultaneously attacked France. A piecemeal approach to conquering Western Europe would not be tolerated.

The shock and awe that the blitzkrieg created was legend. There would be no heroic Battle of the Marne in this war, Commander in Chief Weygand told the government. Maréchal Pétain agreed. By three a.m. on June 10, outriders had cleared the way for the government cavalcade to reach the small town of Gien on the River Loire, following the national art collection into exile. In the six weeks since the Western Campaign had begun, over 112,000 French soldiers had died and another estimated 225,000 were wounded.[3]

The gains made by the Wehrmacht and Luftwaffe were so rapid that millions fled with less than an hour to spare before the front line engulfed their homes. Those who had the time packed up scant belongings onto carts or took to the roads acting as their own packhorses. Others left unfinished meals on the table, grabbing a cherished family photograph as they escaped. The northeast city of Lille, with its bustling industrial population of 200,000, lost over 90 percent of its residents in an afternoon.

The British Expeditionary Force, along with surviving French and Belgian fighters, retreated helter-skelter to Dunkirk, where, miraculously, a ragtag flotilla of small ships had joined ships of the Royal Navy and merchant marine. The vessels were commanded by their courageous owners—ordinary British men and women—who had answered the SOS

---

* This campaign was known as *Fall Gelb*, the Yellow Campaign, and the battle for France as *Fall Rot*, or the Red Campaign.

from radio broadcasts.* Amazingly, they managed to rescue some 340,000 men. An estimated forty thousand were sadly left behind—killed or captured by the Wehrmacht or Luftwaffe. Somehow, the British convoys had snatched a moral victory from the jaws of defeat.[4]

Everywhere, the main roads were choked with millions of refugees. The days of early June were called "the Exodus," with the displaced achieving biblical proportions. People from all walks of life crisscrossed the country searching for safety and escape. One week after the last of the Dunkirk soldiers were rescued, Goebbels authorized his first propaganda broadcast of German radio in French.[5]

Despite the terrible news, it was a stupefied country that heard the voice of Maréchal Henri Pétain—the old hero of Verdun in the last war—crackle over the airwaves on June 17, 1940, as if reading from a crumpled piece of paper. At the request of the president, he had taken over the leadership of the government of France. "It is with a heavy heart," Pétain continued, "that I tell you today that it is necessary to cease fighting" and that France was prepared to agree an armistice with Germany.[6] Pétain had made the announcement without consulting his generals in the field, not to mention Churchill, who had flown to France to meet the French leaders in person five days earlier.[7] The government fled into exile again, this time in French North Africa.

∽

Many believed that Paris had already lost two-thirds of its population. More than two million inhabitants had taken to the roads by the time the armistice was signed, on the evening of June 24.[8] Hitler reveled in the symbolism of forcing France to sign the armistice in the same railway carriage in the forest of Compiègne where Germany had been compelled to sign its humiliating surrender that led to the *Diktat* of Versailles.

The armistice agreement came into effect at 12:35 a.m. the next day. A separate armistice had been signed in which Pétain agreed that two-thirds of the country would be occupied by the Reich. A straight line from west of Cheverny at the Loire was drawn southward to the Spanish border.

---

* Much of British fleet was engaged in a number of naval theaters: in the Far East; in the Mediterranean; protecting convoys in the Atlantic; bringing food and armaments to Britain; and protecting British colonies.

Bordeaux and the Atlantic and Channel coasts of France were to remain part of the Occupied Zone.

France's Free Zone—or Vichy, as it was also known—would comprise, in geographic terms, approximately one-third of the country, extending eastward from the Loire River west of Cheverny to Switzerland, then south to the Mediterranean. The French regime was named after its capital, the spa town of Vichy, some sixty kilometers from Clermont-Ferrand in the Massif Centrale. Vichy had been chosen over Clermont-Ferrand itself because Vichy had enough hotels and cafés to accommodate the disheveled new racketeer government under the dubious auspices of Pétain and his shabby lieutenant, Pierre Laval.[9]

For Gurlitt, the armistice provided one significant clause: No assets could be transferred from the Occupied Zone to the Free Zone. The U.S. ambassador to France, William Bullitt, observed that the Nazis' "hope is that France may become Germany's favorite province—a new Gau which will develop into a new Gaul."[10]

Paris was infested with the leaders of each division of the armed forces and foreign services. The Luftwaffe took over the Ritz Hotel, the Gestapo the Hotel Le Meurice, across from the Jardins des Tuileries. The Kunstschutz and the Military Authority were headquartered at Hotel Majestic on Avenue Kléber. The office of the authorities to handle the Jewish question (IEQJ*) was safely ensconced at the former headquarters of the Jewish art dealer Paul Rosenberg at 21 rue de la Boétie. German ambassador Otto Abetz, theoretically a Francophile with a French wife, was assigned to the German embassy in Paris by Ribbentrop.

As in Vienna, the Rothschild collection was the first to be summoned to the ambassador's attention. The distinctive black cases with the Rothschild golden monogram soon arrived bearing their priceless "gifts." Indeed, the observant curator of the emptied Jeu de Paume Museum wrote in her journal, "The inestimable artistic treasures of Baron Edouard de Rothschild, torn from the Château de Ferrières or Hôtel de Tallyrand, soon joined other masterpieces from the collections of Seligmann, Wildenstein,

---

* Institut d'Études des Questions Juives.

Alphonse Kann, Rosenberg and Bernheim, whose names and addresses were placed on the list handed over to the Gestapo."[11] The observant curator's name was Rose Valland.

Abetz immediately charged three of his embassy employees—Karl Epting, Carl-Theodor Zeitschel, and Eberhard Freiherr von Künsberg—with the task of securing and transporting back to the Louvre all art belonging to French Jews which had been thoughtlessly stored among the national treasures in the French châteaus.[12] Both Zeitschel and Künsberg were agents of the military police and had strict instructions that any suitable works of art from these "safeguarded" Jewish collections would find homes in Germany.

The re-creation of the German 1914–18 Art and Monuments Protection Office, the Kunstschutz, was headed by the distinguished art historian Count Franz Wolff-Metternich. He had most recently been the provincial curator of the Rhine-Westphalia Museums, and was a direct descendant of the famous statesman who was so instrumental in the restructuring of Europe after Napoleon's defeat. Advised that he would be put in charge of preservation of monuments in Western Europe, Wolff-Metternich was rather surprised to learn that he would be responsible only to the Supreme Command.[13]

What no one in Germany realized was that Wolff-Metternich was strictly from the old school of thought. Private property was protected under article 47 of the 1907 Hague Convention and must be respected. Wolff-Metternich undertook his task with a diligence that befitted his highly respected name. Lists of monuments to be protected were drawn up; owners of châteaus were told to keep their valuable furniture securely under lock and key and safe from bombardments; riflemen were sent to protect the châteaus. Wolff-Metternich worked with the Duke of Noailles, head of historic buildings (*Demeures Historiques*), and the head of the Musées Nationaux, Jacques Jaujard.[14]

Yet even Wolff-Metternich hadn't bargained on the covetousness of his assistant Hermann Bunjes, an art historian who had previously studied sculpture under Louvre curator Marcel Aubert. Wolff-Metternich had also been unaware of Otto Kümmel's activities in Paris. From 1939, Kümmel was ordered by Goebbels to research all artworks and artifacts that might conceivably have been sold under duress or looted from Germany since

Napoleon's day. Kümmel's lengthy tome was entitled *Memorandum and Lists of Art Looted by the French in the Rhineland in 1794*. It was deemed such a success that a follow-up project was commissioned for all art in foreign ownership since 1500.[15]

In August 1940, Goebbels, acting with Hitler's express authorization, had taken over a project from Education Minister Rust to reclaim all German art in the West under an act called Reclamation of Cultural Goods from Enemy States (*Rückforderung von Kulturgütern von Feindstaaten*). Goebbels would personally oversee Kümmel's follow-on assignment and wrote to all foreign representatives of the Education Ministry, the Foreign Office, and Gaue branches of the RBK on August 13, 1940, that this relentless search for cultural objects of importance "which . . . have found their way into the hands of our present enemy" was essential in the conclusion of "upcoming treaties" and feasibly "all . . . the conditions of a lawful change of ownership." Essentially, Goebbels planned to take Kümmel's work beyond the research phase into seizure of all art of German origin or deemed Germanic in character from the Napoleonic Wars.[16]

✑

Vying for his own position in France, Alfred Rosenberg, who had been repeatedly discredited by Goebbels in his attempts to head Hitler's cultural ideology if not its bureaucracy, finally found his niche. Under a direct order from the führer on July 5, 1940, Rosenberg was authorized to collect all archives and libraries of the declared enemies of the Third Reich. When Rosenberg tried to stretch the order to apply to artworks, Wolff-Metternich's Kunstschutz became alarmed, and issued a prohibition to move any artwork without the written permission of the regional military commander.[17] Undeterred, Rosenberg reorganized his staff into one of the most effective wartime plundering organizations, called the Einsatzstab Reichsleiter Rosenberg (Action Staff of Reichsleiter Rosenberg), or ERR.

Gerhard Utikal emerged as Rosenberg's bureaucratic mastermind headquartered in Berlin, weaving an intricate web of handpicked staff and special commandos to loot art. The Dienststelle Westen (Western Office), headed by Kurt von Behr, in France, soon became all-powerful. By the end of August 1940, some 1,244 cases of written material from the Jewish,

Polish, Turgenev, and Rothschild archives and libraries were transported to ideological training centers in Germany.[18]

Evidently, there were conflicting forces at work in occupied France, but that was to be expected from Hitler whose modus operandi consistently set his divisional chiefs against one another. From the outset, Ambassador Abetz told his agents to ignore Wolff-Metternich. Wolff-Metternich, in turn, ordered his people to beware of the art booty that the Foreign Office and its ambassador seemed determined to take. Then, on September 17, Field Marshal Wilhelm Keitel empowered the ERR to secure all "ownerless" cultural property—including any object given to the French by the enemies of the Third Reich since the outbreak of the war—on the führer's personal order. The same order was given to several German occupying departments charged with plundering Belgium and Holland. The word "ownerless" was of course another euphemism for property-left-behind-by-fleeing-imprisoned-or-dead-people.

Yet at the heart of this descent into barbarity was Hitler's utter and steely determination to control the confiscation of all the art in the occupied territories. Just as he had controlled the *Kulturpolitik* in Germany since 1933, he must do the same in the countries he'd acquired. Hitler knew that he could never achieve this with Wolff-Metternich, who by virtue of his name alone was absolutely unassailable to the aristocracy serving in the army and air force. Rosenberg and his associate Kurt von Behr, on the other hand, were ruthless and eager to be Hitler's creatures. While Wolff-Metternich had limited success in protecting French patrimony, he would prove less fortunate with private collections.

❧

First located at the Louvre, Behr's ERR operations soon moved to the Jeu de Paume Museum nearby.* There, collections belonging to fifteen dealers and Jewish collectors were hastily unpacked.[19] Jaujard asked Rose Valland, who had been the volunteer guardian of the empty modern-art museum, to make as complete an inventory as possible of the art passing through

---

* Jeu de Paume, literally meaning "game of the palm," was a medieval form of tennis played by the French kings. When the Louvre was the royal palace, the Jeu de Paume was its indoor tennis court.

the museum, noting, in particular, where the pieces were subsequently expedited. It was a difficult task for anyone trained in espionage—an impossible one for an ordinary civilian curator on no pay.

"I didn't as yet understand quite clearly the reasons which pushed me toward my decision," Valland wrote on November 1, 1940, when Hermann Bunjes ordered her to stop taking a French inventory. "I hadn't the slightest notion of how I could justify my presence. . . . I was overtaken by my determination not to leave my post. The agreement of my bosses took away the last of my doubts, and I knew what to do."[20]

Bunjes had already been seduced by the idea of working for Reichsmarschall Göring, for whom, unknown to Valland, an art exhibition was being prepared. Nonetheless, she dutifully noted down that the artworks were transported by the Luftwaffe at the end of October, and that Behr wore a Red Cross uniform. She also saw that the paintings were arranged as if for an exhibition. Then, on November 3, a vast array of chrysanthemums—the flower of funerals in France—was brought in, as well as potted palms, rugs, decorative arts, and champagne to celebrate the arrival of Reichsmarschall Göring himself. Appearing in a long cashmere coat and fedora hat, Göring seemed an odd fat figure standing near the magnificent French treasures and the impeccably dressed German officers who cowered before him.[21]

Göring's personal art dealers, Walter Andreas Hofer and Sepp Angerer, had reconnoitered Paris earlier, and ordered their selections be taken to the Jeu de Paume. Even Göring was stunned by what he saw, and spent the whole day at the museum. When he asked if that was all and was told that there was more in storage, Göring delayed his departure until he could see *all* the treasures. It came as an absolute surprise that there were even more masterpieces than he had seen during his "buying spree" in Holland.[22]

Here were riches simply beyond his imagining. Vermeer's *Astronomer*, owned by the Rothschilds, Rembrandt's *Boy with a Red Beret*, van Dyck's *Portrait of a Lady*, and other artworks had him drooling with greed. On the afternoon of November 5, Göring issued an order declaring that the "safeguarded artworks" which the Wehrmacht and ERR had protected were henceforth divided into several groupings. The führer's choices would always come first—whether for the führer personally or for the Sonderauftrag Linz. Next the reichsmarschall as second-in-command would have the right to "objects which would complete" his collections at Carinhall, which would one day, too, become a national museum. The third category would be made available as "useful" objects for Rosenberg's anti-Semitic think tanks. Next, the German museums could look at acquiring what remained, with the dregs left over going to the French museums or sold on the open market.[23] Of course, that wasn't what happened next.

By the time the Nazi gift-giving season began in December 1940, Göring had forbidden Count Wolff-Metternich or his assistant Dr. Bernhard von Tieschowitz from interfering any further with his activities in France. He even amended his November 5 order to read, "Further confiscation of Jewish art property will be effected in the manner heretofore adopted by the ERR under my [Göring's] direction." Wolff-Metternich immediately fired Bunjes, who had been so obviously favored by the reichsmarschall. He was promptly rehired by the ERR.

While Göring made his selection of an initial lot of fifty-nine paintings, Hitler did not officially authorize the removal of any artworks from France until New Year's Eve 1940. Hans Posse selected the Vermeer *Astronomer* and Boucher's famous portrait of Madame de Pompadour, as well as works by Franz Hals and Rembrandt. All of Hitler's and Göring's choices were transported to Germany on February 9, 1941, on Göring's private train. Göring would make nineteen more plundering visits to Paris prior to the liberation.[24]

Even Maréchal Pétain joined in the gift-giving spirit. He had decided to give Francisco Franco a number of Spanish masterpieces from the French national collections as a gesture of goodwill, a gesture meant to send a message that Franco should remain neutral in matters concerning France. Nonetheless, Jaujard was having none of it. Instead, he arranged for several Visigothic crowns found near Toledo, a Murillo painting, and an ancient statue, the *Dama de Elche*, to be exchanged for items of similar value from the Spanish collections. Pétain was furious that his gift had been subsumed into a squalid trade by the traitorous Jaujard and his associates.[25]

⚶

Hildebrand Gurlitt, like dozens of other German dealers, had been active in this period, too. At the end of September 1940, Bunjes approved the resumption of auctions in Paris on three conditions: (a) that all artworks valued in excess of FF 100,000 be specifically highlighted in the catalogue, (b) that the names and addresses of the buyers of such items be reported to him in a timely manner, and (c) that he receive a copy of every catalogue from every sale.

What is striking is that Bunjes had allowed auctions to resume without the usual Aryanization of Jewish art galleries having been approved by the military occupiers. All known Jewish art-gallery owners and dealers had been targeted, with their galleries effectively impounded by the Gestapo from July 4, 1940, when Otto Abetz took up his ambassadorship.[26] Yet it would be another two years before the Wildenstein Gallery would be Aryanized by Roger Dequoy with the assistance of Karl Haberstock.[27] Granted, many Jewish art dealers and artists had fled before the occupation, but their galleries' new Aryan owners or mere managers had not necessarily been those whom the Nazis would have wanted.

Daniel-Henry Kahnweiler, formerly of Galerie Simon and an ex-trading partner of both Alfred Flechtheim and Paul Rosenberg, had sold his gallery to his sister-in-law, Louise Leiris, a good Catholic from Burgundy who managed the business while Kahnweiler hid in Vichy until the liberation. Nonetheless, Kahnweiler kept abreast of the art world through correspondence with friends like Curt Valentin in New York.[28] Interestingly, in one of Kahnweiler's letters he laments the "death of poor Bettie," referring to Betty Flechtheim's suicide just before her deportation to a concentration camp.[29] Flechtheim himself had died a haunted and broken man in London in 1937.

The occupiers lamented that there was often little choice but to accept a French person as an Aryan, despite the fact that they were patently not of German descent. Many were appointed as provisional managers or directors of firms where the Jewish owner had died or fled, like Claude Charpentier in the case of Galerie Bernheim & Cie. Charpentier also owned a lucrative auction business a stone's throw from the larger, state-owned Hôtel Drouot, and had become good friends with Gurlitt, Goepel, and the new associate, Hermsen.

Charpentier was advised that the death of Bernheim, in 1939, and the disappearance of his partner Levy, in June 1940, meant that there were many unpaid debts that needed his immediate attention, including FF 56,000 in unpaid rent. The building had been damaged by the occupation of young Communists in 1941, and repairs were required, too. The only paintings that remained in the gallery were apparently not the property of Mr. Levy, but had been left there instead for safekeeping by the various artists Levy represented.[30] It was left up to Charpentier to clear up the mess. Naturally, the artists' paintings were sold without consulting them.

Incredibly, refugee German Jewish art dealers continued to make a killing in the French market, too. Among them were Hugo Engel and Allan Loebl. Gurlitt worked extensively with both men in Paris, as well as with Engel's son Hubert in Nice (in the Free Zone). So did members of the ERR, including Gustav Rochlitz and Bruno Lohse, who took over the running of the ERR from Behr in 1942.

Both Engel and Loebl were exempted from wearing the yellow Star of David by the order of Hans Posse. In fact, both had been working in France, according to Posse, for "ten long years" and had provided him with very useful information regarding the whereabouts of certain paintings.[31] After the war, Gurlitt freely admitted during his interrogations that he'd worked with both men. Why not? They had been made to suffer, just as he had, he claimed, because they were Jews. What Gurlitt omitted to say was that their status as exempt from wearing the yellow Star of David had been arranged through Haberstock—with whom he also swore he had never done business—on behalf of Posse.[32]

Haberstock personally had a bit of a false start to his Parisian operations. He had hooked his star to Maria Almas-Dietrich's, since she was the only art dealer who could sell directly to the führer without the prior approval of Hitler's increasingly powerful deputy, Martin Bormann, or Hans Posse.* Maria Dietrich's daughter and Dietrich, too, were close personal friends of Eva Braun, who had protected them both from the ignominy of Dietrich's ex-husband being a Turkish Jew. Dietrich also had the foresight to become Heinrich Hoffmann's mistress.

Still, Almas-Dietrich knew little about art, being more inclined to enjoying a whale of a time living the high life in Paris. She bought fake Guardi oil sketches, paintings, and much more. Many were obvious fakes—

---

* Bormann effectively took on Rudolf Hess's role after Hess's ill-conceived "peace mission" ended with his capture in Scotland in May 1941.

like the Vigée-LeBrun, Guardi, School of David, and Rottenhammer, which were returned to the art dealer Roger Dequoy by an irate Bormann.[33] Many others were of poor quality or badly restored.

⨳

Like artists living in Holland and Belgium, those living in France were not prevented from painting. Indeed, Picasso, who had initially taken to the roads like millions of others, felt the unrelenting cry of Paris and could not resist returning. Whereas Matisse, in ill health and unable to work in the Free Zone, described the German occupation of Paris as a type of narcosis deadening French artists into a stupor. Pierre Bonnard said he returned to Nice to recover his equilibrium.[34]

Picasso, on the other hand, had a different nemesis than Hitler—Generalissimo Francisco Franco of Spain. Although Picasso's work was highly rated on the degenerate-art scales, even the ERR recognized that a Picasso had tremendous worth in terms of foreign exchange or artistic swaps. Picasso, too, was cognizant that he was an international figure of enormous stature. So long as his work held its value, he would be allowed to paint. In fact, he painted some 1,473 artworks between the outbreak of the war and the liberation of Paris.[35]

Yet artists and collectors faced other dangers, too. When the Devisen-schutzkommando (Currency Control Command Unit) prized open his bank vault, Picasso confounded the soldiers so much with his outrageous stories that they took nothing. He then persuaded them that the neighboring vault belonging to Georges Braques was also his. The sister of the world-famous Art-Nouveau jeweler Henri Vever stood silently as she observed the soldiers' bemusement at the hundreds of Rembrandt etchings that her brother had collected when they came to plunder his vault. The Devisenschutzkom-mando concluded in its report that Vever's vault contained so many etchings that they simply had to be fakes. Once again, they had walked away empty-handed.[36]

As for exhibitions, the Nazis took an entirely different view in France than they had elsewhere. Only Jewish or Masonic artists were in danger, meaning that Chagall and Modigliani were generally not shown. No German degenerate artists could be shown publicly either, nor were any anti-German works. Yet the Musée National d'Art Moderne was opened in August 1942 with works by Braque, Dufy, Léger, and Matisse alongside sculptures by the French collaborationist Aristide Maillol. Cubist exhibitions took place at Galerie Charpentier and the Salon des Tuileries. Of course, any works available for sale on the black market by German Expressionists or other outlawed artists sold well, if quietly.[37] The occupiers were determined that the cultural life of Paris should not be diminished by their presence.

23

࿓

VIAU

Opportunity makes a Thief.

—FRANCIS BACON

THE ART MARKET IN PARIS THROUGHOUT 1941 WAS POSITIVELY booming. In the winter season of 1941–42, Hôtel Drouot alone sold over a million objects for the highest prices since its records began, in 1824.[1] Gurlitt had made his first sales to Posse: the stained-glass window and a Hobbema from the Sedelmeyer collection with a manuscript from Hofstede de Groot.[2] The year 1942 promised to be even better.

Yet 1942 was a personal watershed for Gurlitt, too. In the bombing raids by the British RAF during the night of July 26–27, his home and private gallery were destroyed.[3] It would prove a providential loss. Though he would claim in 1946 that everything had been destroyed—from papers to paintings—he also claimed that all the furniture and priceless rugs that had been moved to safety in the closing months of the war had belonged to him in Hamburg.[4]

Given Gurlitt's uncanny foresight and will to do more than merely survive, once the bombing of Hamburg had begun, in January 1942, he almost certainly moved his family and valuables to the relative safety of Dresden. There, the armaments industry was insignificant, and Helene and the children could live with his aged mother in relative peace. Besides, while

Gurlitt traveled in search of booty, his father figure Kurt Kirchbach could also look in on the family whenever possible.

Nineteen forty-two offered other horizons, too. Gurlitt knew that Hans Posse was terminally ill with cancer. It was imperative that he make a big splash in the Paris market to be able to trump Haberstock and gain pre-eminence before Posse's successor was named. Gurlitt had his chance on December 11, when the most spectacular auction took place at Hôtel Drouot. The entire collection of the deceased dentist Georges Viau was on sale. Everyone who was anyone simply had to be there.

Viau had grown up at the Romanov imperial court, where his father was the imperial dentist. Working and living in Paris as an adult, he collected, sold, and collected ever more Impressionists. He was personal friends with many artists, such as Degas and Sisley. In provenance terms, his works were without fault, since he often bought from the artist directly. Viau was famous for his exquisite taste, and Paris had been waiting for his collection to come to market since his death, in 1939.

Finally the day arrived. Gurlitt stayed at the Hotel Saint Simon, as usual,* while Hermsen, who was not as yet known, stayed at a discreet pension at 8 rue de la Grange Batalière, just one block away from the auction house.[5] They arrived in plenty of time for the viewings on Thursday, December 10, most likely ignoring one another, so Hermsen could pick up on gossip kept from Gurlitt. Besides, Hermsen's French was more than likely better than Gurlitt's.[6]

Some six hundred people were seated in high expectation on the Friday. Soon they were hemmed in by hundreds of others standing and gawping around the fringes of the cavernous auction room. Of course, no Jews had been allowed to attend. That interdiction had been firmly understood by Étienne Ader, the Viau auctioneer, after his earlier auction at Versailles had been halted for selling Jewish collections *and* allowing the Jews themselves to attend.[7]

Since the matter of writing to the Kunstschutz† notifying them of sales in excess of FF 100,000 had become a daily routine, Étienne Ader had pre-

---

* This is the address that Ingeborg Hertmann had given to the police after the war.
† By the end of 1942 the ERR had beaten the Kunstschutz, with Dr. Bunjes as the contact person.

viously agreed with Bunjes that only items exceeding FF 1 million would require notification. Gurlitt acquired the following lots in his own name:

Lot 78	Cézanne—*Vallée de l'Arc de la Montagne—St Victoire*	FF 5,000,000
Lot 81	Corot—*Landscape*	FF 1,210,000
Lot 83	Daumier—*Portrait d'un ami de l'artiste*	FF 1,320,000
Lot 109	Pissarro—*Route de Coeur-Volant—à Louveciennes*	FF 1,610,000

All of these paintings were considered degenerate art by the Nazis. According to the required export-licenses, these were not the only paintings that had been purchased by Gurlitt that day. Several more under the million-franc reportable purchase price were bought by Gurlitt and Hermsen, too.[8] An estimated 12 million francs in all had been splurged in one auction by the pair.[9] Even more extraordinary was that there were no other major works acquired by other Nazi art agents—not even Haberstock—although Böhmer was certainly a buyer of art below the million-franc mark.

The Viau sale was big news, smashing all previous records, netting some FF 53.8 million in total before taxes. The most expensive painting in the sale was the Cézanne bought by Gurlitt.[10] Where it had been valued by Ader only for somewhere between FF 800,000 and FF 1 million, it sold for five times its estimated maximum worth. Gurlitt was certainly facing some stiff competition from another bidder.

Yet who was Gurlitt representing? He had spent over FF 9 million on just four paintings. When taking into account that another fifteen drawings and eleven paintings were also bought (two of which on behalf of Hans W. Lange in Berlin), Gurlitt was the single largest buyer at the Viau auction.[11] The sums he was paying—and the amounts in excess of market value—could have been authorized by Posse on behalf of Sonderauftrag Linz or a consortium of wealthy industrialists. After all, Gurlitt had been introduced by Kirchbach to the cream of German industrial society and had been buying on their behalf for years.

According to the new protocols, Gurlitt had to submit the artworks to the Louvre's Fine Arts Department for inspection prior to any export license being granted. Jaujard's team alone could determine if the art impinged on France's patrimony. A negative opinion theoretically meant that the art would not be able to leave the country. Yet when Louis Hautecoeur, one of Jaujard's curators, tried to examine Gurlitt's purchases, he discovered that Gurlitt had already packed them in crates for shipment back to Germany.

Then Hautecoeur was advised that Gurlitt was planning to take the paintings as part of his personal baggage immediately. Hautecoeur knew that one simply did not argue with Nazi efficiency in person without suffering the consequences. Instead, he fulminated in a two-page letter back to Hermann Bunjes of the ERR. "You have guaranteed that we will be granted a minimum access to the artworks to be inspected," he wrote, and yet in the case of these paintings "they had already been crated and loaded onto trucks. I am therefore confirming the contents of our letter dated January 14, 1943, in which I made it clear" that if these minimum guaranteed conditions for inspection were not met, the artworks in question would receive an "unfavorable opinion of the Department of Fine Art. These inspections must be carried out under the supervision of customs officials. However, most of these exporters refuse to comply. It is unacceptable that these inspections are carried out at the exporters' residences since substitutions may be made."[12]

Around the same time, in February 1943, Gurlitt submitted the fifteen drawings to inspector Michel Martin of the Fine Arts Department of the French Museums, and received his export authorization. Evidently, he never intended to submit the fifteen paintings he had purchased at the Viau auction to the scrutiny of Hautecoeur.

As was so often the case over the next two years, Gurlitt and Hermsen were highly selective in what they *chose* to share with the authorities. In 1943 alone, they would "officially" buy some forty-six artworks in Paris. Yet the words "officially" and "buy" carry a somewhat woolly warning: *Gurlitt hadn't paid for any of the artworks at the Viau auction.*

As auctioneer Ader explained in his January 26, 1943, letter to Jaujard and Hautecoeur, "The delivery of the authorization to export is principally intended as <u>payment</u> for monies received by me from Société Générale and Crédit Lyonnais for Mr. Gurlitt's (and Lange's) purchases. It appears that this authorization is not indispensable to Mr. Gurlitt to transport the paintings."[13] As Hautecoeur would write in the margin of the letter, "*Alors?*"—"So?"

Ader continues in an apologetic rather than unctuous tone. "In these conditions would it not be possible to exceptionally grant the export-license without these formalities of inspecting the pictures at customs, so that I could regularize the funds received from the banks?"[14] In other words, without the delivery of the export-license, Ader would be unable to have the "payment" released to him by the two banks for his own account.

Today in these circumstances, the auction house sells subject to obtaining an export-license from the government authorities concerned and does not release the artwork to the new owner without it. In the event the license is not forthcoming because the object is deemed too significant to the patrimony of the country, then the government procures the resident new buyer to match or better the offer within a specific time frame. In this case, without the paintings, Ader was out of luck. He could, however, demand payment for the drawings which had received their export-license. Whether Ader created a scene at Gurlitt's hotel, pleading with him to unpack the paintings and let Ader negotiate obtaining the export-licenses, or even at the customs yard on rue Halévy where Gustav Knauer's trucks were preparing to depart, is sadly unknown.

Undoubtedly, Gurlitt was made aware of Ader's plight and most likely shrugged and said that these events were most unfortunate, yet beyond his control. After all, Gurlitt would have argued, he had a timetable to keep—there was a war on—and it was the transport companies that dictated the movement of goods. No export-license was ever granted for the paintings, and Ader was never paid the FF 9.1 million owed to him. The additional 15 percent sales tax and 10 percent luxury tax, too, were in doubt.

There is another bizarre twist to the tale. Mrs. Louis Viau, the daughter-in-law of the deceased, purchased an artwork for over a million francs: lot 74, a Corot pastel, for FF 2.23 million.[15] This raises the question as to *who* the real seller was and the circumstances of the sale. Had the Viau heirs been taxed beyond endurance by the Nazi occupiers and forced to sell the artworks? Naturally, whoever the seller of the art was—whether the Nazi occupation officials or the estate of Georges Viau—that seller was nine million francs the poorer and the auctioneers suffered tremendous losses of commission.

∽

The Viau auction marked a turning point for Gurlitt. Not only had he left the country without payment or export-license, but he was also officially buying for Linz. Posse may have initially commissioned him to buy the paintings—presumably for swap purposes at Linz—but Posse had died in Berlin on December 7, when Gurlitt was already in Paris.

For reasons that have never adequately been explained, a noted anti-Nazi and friend of Gurlitt, Dr. Hermann Voss, was selected personally by the führer and Martin Bormann to replace Posse.[16] Earlier, Voss had been rejected for the position as director of the Kaiser Friedrich Museum on the grounds of his "cosmopolitan and democratic tendencies, and friendship with many Jewish colleagues." He was antiwar and had even uttered the blasphemous plea for God to deliver an "unfortunate France from the Teutons."[17]

Voss and Gurlitt had known each other for many years, with Gurlitt selling art to Voss's museum at Wiesbaden.[18] They both adored Botticelli above all other classical artists, and had a similar *Weltanschauung*. Like Gurlitt, Voss did not trust Karl Haberstock. A new era was dawning. A question remained, however: Did Gurlitt deliver *any* of those unlikely fifteen paintings to Linz, or barter or keep them, or deliver them to one or more of his industrialist clients? The answer could mean that Voss knew from the outset what Gurlitt had planned and either turned a blind eye, was too busy, or was part of Gurlitt's postwar plan.

24

KING RAFFKE

For a man to achieve all that is demanded of him he must
regard himself as greater than he is.

—JOHANN WOLFGANG VON GOETHE

VOSS'S APPOINTMENT HAD BEEN ANNOUNCED BEFORE GURLITT
returned to Germany. He would formally take over as head of Dresden's
Gemäldegalerie and Sonderauftrag Linz from March 1943 on a monthly
salary of RM 1,000, while also maintaining his directorship at the Wiesbaden Museum without salary. Still, Voss had been keen to get his feet
under the table.

Only four days after Posse's death and the same day as the Viau auction
in Paris, a letter was sent from the Gemäldegalerie in Dresden on behalf of
Voss asking Gurlitt to keep Gottfried Reimer informed of the status of
ongoing assignments, including the payments received. The letter asked
Gurlitt to "be specific"[1] when Gurlitt and Voss finally met up officially. In
February, there was a great deal to discuss, not the least of which was how
they could work most effectively together.

While 1942 had been a bumper year for the European and American
art markets, it had also brought the United States firmly into the war, and
heralded Rommel's rout in North Africa and the Wehrmacht's defeat at
Stalingrad. After the Wehrmacht's storming through Europe without loss

of territory since 1939, these events should have been enough to give any-one as insightful as Gurlitt pause and ask, *What if . . . ?*

While Gurlitt may have keenly anticipated events during the war of 1914–18, in this second war he had focused his mind exclusively on a killing of another sort. Despite the Reich's military setbacks—foreshadowed by the failure of the Battle of Britain in 1940 and Churchill's success at engineering lend-lease with Roosevelt—Gurlitt was too busy climbing the proverbial greasy pole over the backs of his competitors to allow the war to stop him.

In this war, Gurlitt grew a rhinoceros's hide and donned blinkers to the horrors that surrounded him. He ignored his part in stealing riches from tortured men and women forced to sell their treasures for the price of mere trinkets. After all, he had, in his own mind, been a victim, too. First he was ousted by the fanatical Gauleiter Mutschmann from his museum directorship at Zwickau. Then he was "forced" to resign from the Hamburg Kunstverein as a second-degree *Mischling*. Still, he'd allowed himself to be contaminated by the regime's lawlessness, brutalizing others, and had no idea that he, too, had become one of the arts army perpetrating Nazi criminality. His goal was to lead that army. Simply put, Gurlitt had become dehumanized.

Even so, Gurlitt's corruption began in childhood with the misguided principle that he came from a family that knew best how to safeguard art for art's sake. In the 1914–18 war, this wrongheaded idea was reinforced by his stint working as a German Monuments Man in Belgium and giving lectures on the superiority of German art. Then, in strict contravention of his father's wishes, and as a means of survival, Gurlitt had metaphorically folded his poker hand within months of his finally getting his first job as a museum curator, and turned his back on any notions of becoming a great scholar for the financial rewards of being an art dealer. What he never admitted was that once he'd begun to act as dealer for Kurt Kirchbach, in the mid-1920s, he'd felt the exhilaration of power. With power came the craving to greedily nurture it.

In fact, from 1929 throughout the Depression, when so many people were forced to sell their valuables for a pittance, Gurlitt had exploited their situations without mercy, believing that he simply scented a fine deal. He had become an adept art plunderer before Hitler's rise. When the anti-Semitic racial restrictions became clear in 1935, they created an art market for the taking, literally. Gurlitt not only painlessly renegotiated his personal position, but protected his wider family from threats, arrests, intimidation, humiliation, and loss of their personal property and private treasures. How? While hundreds of Jewish and politically undesirable art dealers had their lives stolen, Gurlitt prospered. Even his cousin Wolfgang had suffered no negative repercussions, whereas Wolfgang's younger brother, Manfred, had been targeted until he became a member of the Nazi Party. Why?

The answer to both questions is: friends in high places. Kirchbach, the surrogate father figure, was the *only* manufacturer of brake pads and linings for the transportation industry, feeding the insatiable Wehrmacht and Luftwaffe with their needs. He was essential to the war effort. Other key industrialists, too, were Gurlitt's clients. Yet the most significant friendship came from his father's former student of architecture, and Hitler's favorite architect, Albert Speer. Through his vast knowledge of art and the market, his charm and intellect, Gurlitt had assured his place among the victors, not the victims.

⌘

As the deportations began eastward, Gurlitt took to his role as art plunderer for the state with the zeal of the converted. When the *rafles*—lightning raids on homes displacing frightened people and their valuable property—began in France in May 1941, Gurlitt was buying art at auctions that were forbidden to Jews. Yet they sold Jewish valuables. He also traveled freely between the Free Zone of Vichy and occupied France. His second-degree-*Mischling* status gave him a good cover story with vulnerable sellers, was airbrushed as required with prospective buyers, and—importantly for him—provided his conscience with a plausible salve for his treachery. Even the officials of the Musées Nationaux who frequently condemned him thought that Gurlitt was most charming.[2]

With Hermann Voss as the new director of Linz, Gurlitt saw the unique opportunity to dominate the entire art market. Voss held the largest purse strings, and trusted him. Through his cousin Wolfgang, who was friendly with August Eigruber, the mobster gauleiter of Oberdonau, which included Linz, Hildebrand had unprecedented access to knowledge of the Reich's plans to safeguard the looted art. Posse had set him up in opposition to

Haberstock in France, Belgium, and the Netherlands; then Voss refused to countenance any dealings with the old fox Haberstock. At last, Gurlitt could be the king *Raffke*—the king profiteer—and could successfully feather his own nest for what was promising to be an increasingly precarious future.

⁓

Before November 1941, there is little official correspondence to link Gurlitt with widespread plundering operations in France. Nonetheless, he had been actively selling to French clients since his appointment to the German purges of art in 1938 and had significant contacts there.

Given the running battles between Wolff-Metternich's Kunstschutz and the ERR, it was only a matter of time before the names ERR and Kunstschutz became interchangeable, on Wolf-Metternich's reassignment in 1942. As French Jews were arrested or fled for their lives, their belongings—irrespective of any fail-safe hiding places—were systematically looted. Even the most miserable possessions found a home at the M-Aktion division of the ERR—from children's toys to hairbrushes. The more valuable assets were raked through by the ERR in the name of Hitler, under the ubiquitous and rapacious eye of Göring.[3]

From September 1941, Gestapo looting sorties with specially coopted Luftwaffe officers were made into Vichy France. According to the traitorous French admiral Darlan, "The seizure of Jewish possessions is a political and nonmilitary decision."[4] The valuables of the dispossessed in Vichy were safeguarded as part of the "punitive measures" legally put in place by the French.[5]

One of the more notorious examples of such a punitive measure was Göring's seizure of the world's most unique collection of priceless enamel and gold miniature boxes and gilded miniature paintings, along with the Rothschild jewels, under special Luftwaffe guard. As Bunjes reported in an outright lie, "We have not discovered amid the art objects on deposit with the state, one which belonged to the Jews, even one of the great Jewish collections known throughout the entire world."[6]

By the middle of 1941, Göring's dominance of the ERR meant that the organization held all other offices competing for France's riches in its sway—from the Foreign Office to the Gestapo and Kunstschutz. Art was successfully torn from the safe depositories in the Loire châteaux where the national collections and the great private collections were held. Eventually many collections were taken to the Jeu de Paume. In almost all cases, Göring's Luftwaffe or the Gestapo provided the transportation. A veritable factory "manufacturing" looted art was in full flow, with German experts supplying professional triage services for the wounded artworks, the degenerate art going to Göring or the likes of Gurlitt for swaps with the treasured art reserved according to Göring's November 1940 instructions—enshrining Hitler's and Linz's primacy.

During 1940–42, much of the stolen art was recorded by the tenacious Rose Valland under the noses of her Gestapo guards and vigilant eyes of Bunjes and Behr. By the time Voss made his first trip to Paris, in early April 1943, Walter Borchers had been appointed Germany's head of the Jeu de Paume. The imposing and tremendously plausible liar Bruno Lohse, Göring's personal friend, was appointed as head of the Special Commission (Leiter des Sonderstabs) in Paris. Oddly, despite their apparent conflicting duties, Valland overheard Lohse whisper to Borchers to hide a painting from the school of Gérard of *Léda au cygne** from the Walter Strauss collection, closing with the remark "It will be for just us."[7] Valland scribbled this in her journal above the entry that a famous drawing by Rembrandt, *Portrait du père de l'artiste,*† previously noted in the collection, had vanished. Valland suspected Lohse.

The rabidly anti-Semitic art critic Robert Scholz was their superior, working alongside Utikal, primarily from Berlin. In 1943, it was Scholz's Parisian poodle, Günther Schiedlausky, who finally raised the alarm about Lohse. Documented inventories left the Jeu de Paume, but never arrived in Germany. Among the missing paintings were two from the Seligmann collection.[8] Voss's April visit resulted in Hitler's deputy, Martin Bormann, personally intervening. Sideswiping the ERR and Göring with a series of orders, Bormann transferred the plundering operations from the ERR to the agents of the Linz staff for further processing and observation.[9] Henceforth, Gurlitt's exalted position put him in indirect conflict or contact, depending on the viewpoint, with Bruno Lohse and the ERR in

---

* *Leda on the Swan*—approximate size 2m x 1.5m.
† *Portrait of the Father of the Artist.*

France. Even Lohse's actions, in theory only, would have to be approved by Gurlitt.[10]

⁓

In the distant village of Laguenne, located in the Limousin region of Vichy, one of the most treasured collections of Dutch old masters had been hidden away in the local branch of Banque Jordaan, some two kilometers from Tulle. On April 10, 1943, the bank's director was ordered to contact the prefecture of the Departement of Corrèze. None other than Louis Darquier de Pellepoix, the Vichy director of Jewish Affairs, had ordered the removal of the world-renowned Schloss Collection and its deposit in his bank. Apparently, even Vichy's head of government, Pierre Laval, the fat racketeer always sporting a white tie, had his fingers in this rich pie.

The bank director hesitated and bravely replied that he'd have to notify his superiors, which he did by coded message. Five days later, the police commissioner presented himself at the bank with five gendarmes in tow, notifying the manager of his mission to "safeguard" the premises and not allow either person or property to enter or leave. At seven a.m. the next day, a relief guard was placed around the bank. Then, at two p.m., a German truck with armed soldiers from Paris pulled in to take away the priceless collection. The hapless bank director watched, powerless, as the truck headed off in the direction of Limoges.[11]

"The Schloss Collection," so the telegram number 2603 stated, "is currently the richest collection of fine Old Dutch Masters in the world. It has six Rembrandts, masterpieces painted by Rubens, van Dyck, Jan Steen, Pieter de Hoch and several other revered artists. It has been developed over many long years and enjoys an international reputation. Its acquisition for the Linz museum would be an extraordinary gain."[12] In fact there were exactly 568 Old Masters: 262 were designated for Linz, only after 284 were safeguarded by the Louvre. An additional twenty-two had simply vanished.[13]

Officially, Voss had been the head of Linz for six weeks. The telegram was sent from the German embassy in Paris only days after his first visit there. The heist, however, had been in the making for some while. Haberstock had been scouring France since 1940, and even had a meeting with a "strange lady with a German-Jewish name" at the Hotel Negresco, overlooking the Baie des Anges, in the winter of 1940–41. Gurlitt, too, had set Herbert Engel on the trail of the collection, also in Nice. Gurlitt's associate and subordinate art dealer in France, Erhard Goepel,* had been in the hunt, too; and it was Goepel who finally located it. Yet it was Lohse who would handle the division of the spoils once it reached the vault of Banque Dreyfus in Paris.

This heist cemented Gurlitt's relationship with Lohse. Goepel had already been working with Gurlitt in acquiring early Italian Renaissance artworks valued at over 2.5 million Belgian francs from the time of the country's occupation.[14] Though Gurlitt was never specifically named as the one involved in the selection of art to be given to Linz or which "lesser" works would go up for auction, Gurlitt's fingerprints are all over the transactions that followed.[15] Besides, France was officially *his* bailiwick.

Cleverly, the method of "payment" was levied against the "occupation credits" that France had to pay Germany. The amount payable was round-tripped from the French Treasury to the occupiers and back again. Some FF 42 million was paid in this way against the total FF 50 million purchase price. This was a favored method that Gurlitt used for payments if required. It was an extension of the preferred blocked and unblocked reichsmarks used in the Swiss trades.

❧

Lohse, as the new head of the ERR Paris, needed to negotiate his way through the highly charged interests on behalf of Göring, Bormann (for Hitler), Ambassador Abetz, and Abel Bonnard, minister of fine art for Vichy. Since Lohse had his heart set on larceny rather than administration, purloining a landscape by van Goyen on April 6 in the backseat of his car,[16] he had entirely misread the situation.

Essentially, Hitler was furious about two matters. First, there was absolutely no *legal* pretext—always dear to Hitler's heart—for the outright seizure of the Schloss Collection in Vichy. More worrying, Lohse had permitted the Musées Nationaux the "pick of the litter"—leaving Hitler

---

* Goepel also worked for the Dienststelle Mühlmann in the Netherlands on Robert Oertel's recommendation.

with the sour taste that he had been granted the gristled leftovers. For the most powerful man in Europe, it was an insult beyond imagining.

From Berlin, Utikal abandoned Goepel and Lohse. So did Göring, since his fortunes had begun to wane with Hitler over his own art plundering. Even Alfred Rosenberg entered into the fray, disowning Lohse and Goepel, calling them "overzealous representatives."[17] Voss, however, received only a slap on the wrist for his part in the caper. It was only the method of payment that rescued him from further admonition. Secretly, however, the audacious coup was admired, and would trailblaze new pastures in Vichy.

Once the 262 Dutch old masters from the Schloss Collection arrived at the Führerbau in Munich, on May 27, 1943, they were never recovered. Only those acquired in the preemptive strike by Jaujard at the Louvre would be returned to their owner, Alphonse Schloss, after the war.[18]

∾

On the same day the Führerbau accepted the Schloss Collection, a plume of noxious smoke billowed high above the Jeu de Paume. It was the first bonfire of the vanities raging on the terraces of the Tuileries. Just as in Florence in 1497, when the Dominican priest Savonarola decided that the Florentines had become degenerate in their worship of cosmetics, art, and even printed books, so seemingly the ERR had determined that the art of Klee, Picasso, Léger, Ernst, and others was unfit to see the light of another day. Anything that played to the artist's vanity rather than exhibit good artistic taste was doomed and burned that May afternoon. Or so the ERR claimed. Rose Valland believed that between five hundred and six hundred modern artworks were lost that day, but all she saw—or was allowed to see—was the smoky column rising far above Cleopatra's Needle in Place de la Concorde. No reliable witness to the conflagration has ever come forward.[19]

Apparently, it all began with a damning interim report penned by Scholz to Hitler for his birthday on April 20, 1943. Scholz wrote that the ERR must continue their custodianship of safeguarded assets from French Jews under his guidance. Scholz—the great Nazi editor and keeper of purity of art in the Reich since the mid-1930s—stated that he would come to Paris and set their house in order. Scholz may have been the first to suspect that

Lohse and his associates had taken it upon themselves to "destroy" fac-similes of modern art and their frames so the originals could be sold for their private accounts in a discreet neutral locale, like Switzerland, Por-tugal, or Spain.*

On July 19, French and German directors and curators were convened at the Louvre, including Dr. Borchers and others stationed at the Jeu de Paume. A mock trial, again reminiscent of Savonarola's public sermons, dictated that the masterpieces of Courbet, Monet, Degas, Manet would be spared—by Hitler's personal order—but only to serve as swaps to bolster the economy of the Third Reich. Pragmatically, they were commodities superior to reichsmarks.

The artworks of Bonnard and Vuillard, Matisse, Braque, Dufy, Marie Laurencin, and Derain were evaluated by Scholz for their commercial rather than aesthetic value. The sentences were then passed and the men of the ERR brandished their knives, mercilessly slashing the condemned enemy alien art. Once their destruction was complete, the shreds were shipped in dozens of truckloads and set alight in the garden of the Jeu de Paume.[20]

৶৹

Such was the state of the French art market in the summer of 1943. By the autumn, Gottfried Reimer, who had faithfully served Hans Posse, too, was unhappy with the ongoing enigma surrounding missing artworks which had begun under Posse and continued under Voss.

Fearful that someone would think he was involved, Reimer wrote to Hans Reger, the architect responsible for the Linz inventory at the Füh-rerbau in Munich, that he'd noticed in his index of paintings for 1943 that there were several discrepancies. While some paintings hadn't been re-ported as shipped to Dresden or Munich, others had also not been indi-cated as Party Chancellery purchases. "They were also not included in the catalogue, and yet payment had been made. . . . These problems are *viru-lent*," Reimer wrote, likening the anomalies to an epidemic.

Reimer clarified how he made the discovery. Accounts payable from Voss for all art purchased reduced Linz's financial warranties for swaps as well as blocked and unblocked reichsmarks. This financial link enabled

---

* Karl Buchholz had set up in Lisbon.

Reimer to clearly see that paintings were missing when auditing his quarterly accounts and comparing these with the index of art acquired. When alarm bells sounded, Reimer then compared the arrival date with the dates the art had been sent. Even more paintings seemed to be missing. He then compared these with the dates of acquisition, the names of the dealers involved, and the paintings' names and sizes. "In this way," Reimer confirmed, "we night comptrollers could see approximately that the artworks *which had already long before been paid for had not yet arrived at the Führerbau [or Dresden]*. By these measures, we then similarly could differentiate between earlier and new arrivals."[21]

So, paintings had gone missing. The use of the word "virulent" by Reimer meant that this was no haphazard occurrence, nor was it the fault of the transporter. Paintings approved for acquisition by Voss—many through Gurlitt—simply did not arrive. The implication was that Gurlitt had siphoned off some artworks. So, Gurlitt was stealing from Hitler.

୶

Even more astounding was Gurlitt's phony accounting. The best example dates from March 27, 1944, when Tieschowitz of the Kunstschutz signed off on an invoice for customs purposes made out to Gurlitt. The invoice was for FF 4.3 million (RM 215,000), with twelve paintings itemized. It was stamped with the official stamp of the Military Governor's Office and was given the export license number 13678.

However, there is a second invoice of the same date, with the same export number, detailing *six of the same* twelve paintings on the first invoice, and providing two *new* paintings to the list. The prices of the existing six paintings have also been inflated. Instead of the official stamp on this second invoice, the wording is only typewritten.

On the second unstamped invoice to the Sonderauftrag Linz, the paintings by the Dutch Golden Age painters Jan Weenix, his cousin Melchior d'Hondecoeter, and Cornelius van Poelenburgh as well as the modernist Dutch painter Dolf Breetvelt are missing. Two new paintings are provided in their places, one by Stevens for RM 40,000 and another by Gottlieb for RM 34,000.* The most probable explanation is that only six of

---

* Please see both invoices in the illustrations section.

the original twelve paintings were sent to Linz, along with the two additional substitutions, which were extremely inflated in value. The missing
paintings were all small Dutch masters, able to be easily disguised in personal baggage.

The wording on the authorization to export between France and
Germany specifically stated that it was only valid for the itemized contents *and* for the agreed value.[22] The pencil annotations on the first invoice appear to be Hermsen's, since he sent along a cover letter referring
to these and stating that he had rewritten the invoice as "those paintings
indicated in pencil are not in France, the others having already been
sent to Germany."

Later, Hermsen wrote to Gurlitt that Jaujard's team of experts had
inspected the paintings but that it was a "lunatic proposition" to remove
paintings just so the Kunstschutz could resell these a short while later.[23]
So, the paintings were not "already sent to Germany" after all. This revised
statement by Hermsen implies that it was either Kurt von Behr, the former
head of the ERR, Hermann Bunjes, or Göring's personal and "special" agent
Bruno Lohse who was responsible for the swap. Both Bunjes and Lohse
were members of the Luftwaffe and took orders from the reichsmarschall.
Yet Hermsen's remark refers only to two of the paintings destined for Gurlitt
and Linz—not the six that were ultimately removed.

Given the date in March 1944, it is unlikely that Behr was involved. By
then he was engrossed in the unsavory activities of the M-Aktion division
of the ERR, recycling euphemistically named "ownerless" property from
occupied France back to bombed-out Germans. Similarly, it is hardly likely
that the destination was Linz or Hitler personally, since as early as Voss's
appointment, in March 1943, the ERR was a highly compromised agency
that had worked with Göring in pillaging over seven hundred works of art
for Carinhall without payment.[24]

The export file is tantalizingly incomplete. Gurlitt replies on April 5
about the reworked invoice, breathlessly saying, "Please find out who bought
the painting. There is suddenly a great deal of interest in this, because we
had it." Was Reimer querying its whereabouts? Gurlitt concludes his note
to Hermsen with the elusive remark "I am sending to Holland RM 100,000
to the address indicated" without stating specifically what the money was
for or identifying the address.[25] The cryptic nature of the financial dealings

between the two men becomes positively mysterious when considering that the envelope had no postage stamp or postmark, leading to the probability that it had been sent in the diplomatic pouch, as Gurlitt was elsewhere at the time.

∽

Voss's other assistant, Robert Oertel, was also alarmed. For reasons he could not fathom, Gurlitt's foreign-exchange payments were given top priority.[26] It was Voss himself who informed Oertel that Gurlitt's and the Dorotheum's requests for payments must be immediately honored. Indeed, Gurlitt often acted as the agent for the Dorotheum.[27]

Both assistants worried that the manner in which Linz acquired its art had fundamentally changed. Dating from Voss's appointment, Gurlitt achieved a position of preeminence in the French art market. Haberstock had been sidelined. Theo Hermsen worked exclusively for and with Gurlitt; together, they expanded their network of potential buyers. Both acted in concert with Hans Herbst of the Dorotheum in Vienna, with all three parties selling art variously through Gurlitt to the Wallraf-Richartz-Museum in Cologne and the Kunsthalle in Hamburg.

Gurlitt's rise was specifically due to his execution of commissions on behalf of Voss. These were, in turn, based on a myth that the Gurlitt-Hermsen partnership was extremely effective in obtaining these export permits legally from France.[28] In many cases (as for the Viau auction) the requisite export-licenses from France were crucial in order for the foreign exchange authorizations to clear. Yet much of their success in obtaining official papers was nothing more than puffery.

In reality, Jaujard's office was thoroughly fed up with Gurlitt and Hermsen. The minutes of a meeting on February 11, 1944, state categorically that "at several occasions in the past, this exporter has not observed the formalities demanded in export matters." The French representative Mr. Montremy was at pains to remind Dr. Korth (who was Haberstock's secretary) that incidents like these represented an outright flouting of the July 9, 1943, accord between the French and Germans. In the spirit of that agreement, Gurlitt's "oversights" had been omitted from the report. "Nonetheless," the minutes continue, "the license for the two Houdon sculptures will be granted to Mr. Hermsen on the condition that from this point forward he agrees to adhere to the letter of the agreement as demanded by the French authorities."[29]

Dr. Korth was described in all the French documents as Haberstock's secretary, yet in these same meeting minutes he also appeared to have the final veto over any change in the new laws governing fine art, at least according to the French. Consequently, Haberstock's secretary was, on the face of it, in a position of extreme power over Gurlitt and his transactions. Nothing could be farther from the truth.

In fact, between November 14, 1942, and August 18, 1944, the Gurlitt-Hermsen partnership made 116 export applications for an estimated value of FF 453,939,700.* Thirty-three of the export applications were refused in whole or in part. The artworks included approximately 526 paintings, fifty-five drawings and pastels, twenty-six tapestries, and nine sculptures. More often than not the artworks were exported without approval.[30] This represents two hundred paintings more than Hitler's dealer Maria Dietrich,† who bought some 320 paintings for the führer. As a partial statistic, it makes Gurlitt the leading official buyer of French art by far.[31]

Chances are that the official export applications represented a mere fraction of the artworks Gurlitt plundered from France. Whether it was one-tenth, one-hundredth, or even one-thousandth of the total was dependent solely on other factors emerging on the larger canvas of the French occupation. As ever, the chameleon Gurlitt adapted to the circumstances in which he operated.

⁓

From March 1943, Voss had ultimate control over all imports that were deemed part of the führer's booty.[32] Like all administrators in the other occupied territories, Korth may have received direct orders from Bormann,‡ but the specific knowledge and art market which they were plundering came from Voss and his agents. Of course, Korth reported back directly to

---

* Worth approximately $90,787,940 in 1944 when converted from New Francs or $1,226,545,069 in 2014 values (1 US$ in 1944 = $13.51 in 2014).

† She had long before dropped the Turkish-Jewish "Almas" from her name.

‡ In the interrogation of Georg Josef Eidenschink at Moosburg Detention Camp after the war, he declared that Korth worked directly for Hitler. If true, then he served two masters with different purposes in Haberstock and Hitler.

Haberstock on the state of the French market, too. Although the French incessantly complained about exporters ignoring the legal exportation safeguards agreed between occupier and occupied—and more often than not about Hermsen and Gurlitt—the partnership remained the largest single applicant for the export of French artworks to Germany by a huge margin.[33]

In some cases, like the export application of six paintings by German and Dutch artists as well as a fine Gobelins tapestry, the French Department of Fine Arts lamented that "in view of the fact that these are all made exclusively by foreign artists, it seems [according to prior agreements] that the Musées Nationaux are unable to voice an objection to granting the license."[34] Only rarely was an export license granted without it being phrased in the negative.

From 1943, when seeking approval for artworks to be exported, the exporter had to place the proposed items with their transport company under the auspices of French Customs officials. From that moment, the French inspectors of the Musées Nationaux had only three weeks to decide whether or not the artworks were suitable for export. The Gurlitt and Hermsen file was spiced with constant remarks that they were "undermining the customs officials" or "avoiding inspections" or "acting in bad faith" or "paintings had already been exported" or they were "nonresponsive to letters, visits and telephone calls."[35]

Gurlitt also reveled in the system he and Hermsen had set up, which protected his cherished invisibility. From 1943, Gurlitt often acted as agent for some better-known art plunderers, such as Gustav Rochlitz, Albert Speer, and Joseph Goebbels; however, in many instances, his name does not appear on the manifests.[36] The export applications were more often than not made by Theo Hermsen for the account of Gurlitt. As the outcome of the war became clearer and the pace of the looting operation expanded exponentially, a sort of "shorthand" between Hermsen and Gurlitt became the norm. Hermsen would request the export for the account of the Dorotheum or Mr. Schmidt or Dr. Voss or Linz or Goepel, often omitting the name of Gurlitt completely. Yet whenever there was a problem associated with a given permit, Gurlitt personally intervened.

The pace of their operations accelerated wildly from January 1, 1944. Prior to D-day, according to the French dossiers, thirty-four separate export licenses for Dresden were made on behalf of Linz, representing approximately three hundred paintings.* Yet, according to the German archives, there are only twenty-nine invoices and notifications, with a number of the paintings missing. Still, this is only a small part of the discrepancies between the two archives.

Between D-day, on June 6, and August 18—the last date of an application by Gurlitt—an additional forty-four export license applications were made. Paris was liberated on August 25, placing Gurlitt in the beleaguered city just a week before its liberation. Goepel was clearly Gurlitt's subordinate in several of these transactions, often acting as Gurlitt's personal courier back to Germany.[37]

The most compelling evidence of Gurlitt's complete transformation from a "savior" of art into a man who stole the lives of the rightful owners remains that he did *not* stay in Paris to surrender and meet the Allied Monuments Men when they arrived. Even if he hadn't known about them firsthand—which seems unlikely—Goepel would have told him about the special Monuments, Fine Arts, and Archives soldiers comprising the top American and British museum curators and scholars as they plowed through northern France and Belgium. Then again, if he had remained in Paris, surely the Musées Nationaux and Rose Valland would have disabused the Monuments Men of Gurlitt's purported innocence.

Gurlitt's reasons for rushing back home were abundantly clear. There was more loot left in Germany to stash away, and he had no intention of returning anything.

---

* Not all of the export applications state what type of art was being exported or indeed the quantity.

25

QUICK, THE ALLIES ARE COMING!

Rich preys make true men thieves.

—WILLIAM SHAKESPEARE, *Venus and Adonis*

D-DAY, JUNE 6, 1944. WHILE OVER A MILLION MEN COMPRISING American, British, Canadian, Free French, Polish, and other Allied troops fought their ways into France from the hard-won bridgeheads in Normandy, art and other assets had already begun their journeys to secret caches throughout the Third Reich and beyond. The Nazi hierarchy outwardly projected the illusion of victory, while quietly preparing to send their personal treasures to safe havens. Goebbels, Ribbentrop, and Himmler availed themselves of the services of Buchholz's "bookshop" in Lisbon, even providing him with a secretary as a trustworthy gatekeeper.[1] Göring arranged to pack up his art and furniture from Carinhall to ship southward to Berchtesgaden.

Evacuation plans for all the art acquired by Hitler and Linz, as the two were inseparable, were put in place from March 1943. Unofficially, and secretly, Linz officials had made arrangements through the existing city museum director Justus Schmidt to recommend a suitable mine in the Austrian countryside in which to hide at least six thousand artworks. Since Schmidt was personally appointed by Hitler and had been working closely with Wolfgang Gurlitt for many years, he could hardly fail to recommend the Altaussee salt mine, equidistant from Salzburg, Linz, and Hitler's retreat at Berchtesgaden. It was also less than a five-minute drive from Wolfgang's chalet. The beauty of the salt mine was that it had been in operation for centuries and its deep horizons* afforded a uniquely perfect atmosphere, with a balanced acidity in the air, a constant temperature of seven degrees Celsius (forty-five degrees Fahrenheit), and a steady humidity of 63 percent.[2]

∞

Finally, in the same month, the first response from America for the protection of monuments and art was mooted to George Stout, the head of conservation at Harvard's Fogg Museum. Paul Sachs, Stout's boss and a family heir to the bank that bore his name after Goldman's, had been saddled with the responsibility of selecting the Americans who would lead the country's conservation corps.[3] While the American contingent is most famous today, it was far from the first group to try saving Europe's cultural heritage. European countries had long been aware of the dangers. In the Netherlands, the government had drafted "An International Convention for the Protection of Historic Buildings and Works of Art in Time of War" in January 1939.

In 1941, when the vast scale of the thievery was first recognized, the British passed legislation to prevent art seized in the Netherlands and Belgium from being sold in Britain or the United States. A year later, the British warned the world that looted art was being threaded through neutrals like Switzerland, Portugal, and Spain, targeting the Americas (both North and South) and financing the Nazi war machine with the proceeds.

When the Allies began to make inroads into the territories previously held by the Third Reich, the scale of the art looting astounded many. On January 5, 1943, sixteen governments of the United Nations and the Free French Committee signed a declaration called the "Inter-Allied Declaration against Acts of Dispossession Committed in Territories under Enemy Occupational Control." All signatories agreed that they would do their "utmost to defeat the methods of dispossession" practiced by the Nazis and Axis Powers against countries and peoples whom they had "so wantonly assaulted and despoiled."[4]

Yet none of this mattered to Gurlitt in August 1944. Some of his greatest work was yet to come.

---

* The various levels are called horizons.

By April that year, Gurlitt had unbridled control. He wrote his own authorization passes between France, Holland, and Germany, notifying Oertel or Reimer of the specifics he required. One of these states simply that Dr. Hildebrand Gurlitt works "under the instructions" of the Sonderauftrag Linz; that he is "always importing these artworks to Dresden and other cities"; and most of all, that it is imperative that Dr. Gurlitt "has priority on the Reichsbahn."[5] The authorization was stamped without changing a word.

Still, Reimer and Oertel had become increasingly uneasy. Amounts invoiced and transfer requests often reached into the millions of francs every three or four days. It was difficult to keep track of what had been acquired, what had not, the destination of the artworks (Linz, Dresden, Munich), and, indeed, whether they were for other museums around Germany. Goepel seemed to be on a whirligig, spinning between Amsterdam, Paris, Brussels, and Dresden, delivering hundreds of paintings in the spring of 1944.

The salt mine at Altaussee had been rented by the Third Reich from January 1943. Meticulous records show how much the rental, full salaries, and maintenance of the entire mine cost per quarter. Even the workforces required to adapt the salt mine to its new role in life—the felling of trees for fresh lumber from the pine forests above ground, transportation costs, the building of racks to house the artworks, medical costs for miners, the employment of local art historians—form an entire day-by-day journal of the financial history behind just one of Hitler's hideaways.[6]

The same punctilious bookkeeping existed for other mines rented out to the Reich. Hallein, Heilbronn, Jagstfeld, Kochendorf, Laufen, and Merkers—which comprised the Dietlas, Menzengraben, and Philippstal mines—were other salt mines used, along with the Siegen copper mine and the Heimboldshausen potassium mine, as repositories for looted artworks. Each had its specific use. Some had their special depositors. Hallein became known as "Himmler's Cave."[7] Local castles, such as Weesenstein, near Dresden, and private castles near Bamberg, such as Schloss von Pölnitz, were used as local repositories. Monasteries, like the baroque monastery at Ettal, which housed collections from the State Library, and the Carthusian monastery at Buxheim, which doubled as a restoration laboratory for the ERR, were coopted. Former royal palaces, too—the most famous of which being Ludwig II's fairy-tale castle Neuschwanstein, near Füssen— housed several thousand works of art.

During this freewheeling, chaotic time, Gurlitt arranged for some of the paintings he possessed to be sent to Curt Valentin in America for sale through Buchholz. Dollars were needed in addition to Swiss francs to maximize his profits. The reichsmark was no longer a currency that anyone wanted to trade in. He could hardly have imagined that his Käthe Kollwitz artworks, initially acquired in memory of his sister, would be sequestered by the Office of Alien Property and the FBI in New York.

∽

On May 20, 1944, Hermann Voss signed an authorization for Gurlitt to travel to Paris to "purchase artworks worth RM 2,000,000. . . . This is of great cultural political interest." Voss expected that Gurlitt's assignment would require him to "sequester transportation." His authorization de- clared that Voss expected the full cooperation of the various departments of the Third Reich. It was, naturally, signed *"Heil Hitler! Voss."*[8] Forty- six of Gurlitt's export-license applications were filed on the basis of this single authorization.

It covered export applications that in turn represented at least 241 paintings, thirty-seven tapestries, thirty-nine drawings, and two pastels. In other words, the applications covered a little less than half of all of Gurlitt's "official" booty. Armed with such a sweeping yet vague permit from Voss personally, Gurlitt had effectively received carte blanche to run roughshod over whatever system had been previously agreed. From this point, he not only created a black market for himself, but also ran one for other, less fortunate, dealers. His price was a cut of the booty or the profits after the war.

Everyone piled on the bandwagon: Gustav Rochlitz, Hans Wendland, Herbert Engel, Theodor Fischer, and even the delightful Maria Dietrich. Naturally, as with all black-market transactions, much was hidden—and still less documented.[9] Anyone who was involved in the plunder of France wanted to board a vessel impervious to destruction.

Just as the dealers sensed the defeat of the Third Reich, so the French curators sensed an Allied liberation. While nothing appears in the files to reveal an official "go slow" policy, the usual three-week deadline for making a determination on the artworks placed at customs was widely ig-nored.[10] One of these applications, number 28561, of August 8, 1944, is of particular interest. Seven paintings by van Ruysdael, Fragonard, Nattier, and others were examined, but only the Nattier was refused export. All were bought on behalf of the Dorotheum through Theo Hermsen, and yet were invoiced to Linz. None arrived in Germany or Austria. The Nattier went missing, too.

A similar but different incident occurred with application number 27684. This consignment of seven paintings and two pastels included works by Cranach, Bouilly, Lampi, and Ricci worth approximately FF 5.2 million. Before the paintings could be inspected, the Bouilly had vanished. In a fury, the Louvre inspector refused an export license for the Cranach, which he knew the Reich held dear. The only problem is that by the time the decision had been made the entire consignment was already en route to Germany.[11]

The inevitable, of course, happened. When the consignment arrived in Germany, one of the paintings—the Ricci—had disappeared. It was hoped that it had been mistakenly sent to Neuschwanstein. "It was supposed to have been sent to Munich," Oertel huffed in a letter to the former ERR man Schiedlausky, who was now stationed at the castle.[12] Oertel suggested that Schiedlausky bring it to Munich personally, but it was not at the castle either. Oertel thundered in dismay. He needed to find out how such a valuable work of art could simply melt away.

On further investigation, Oertel discovered that Gurlitt had used Rochlitz as his courier to bring the Ricci and other paintings to Germany. Oertel wrote vengefully to Gurlitt, the more time that lapsed between the sale of the Ricci and other missing paintings, the less likely they were to find them. Gurlitt claimed these had been personally transported by Rochlitz to Germany. Oertel replied, "I can no longer certify all [art] and withdraw the covenant of the Sonderauftrag Linz from these artworks."[13] There was no salutation at the end of the note, only the icy facts. Gurlitt would need to locate the missing art if he wanted to receive payment. He had been rumbled once again.

Gurlitt's accounts now came under heavy scrutiny, often receiving notes with stipulating phrases like "the first three of your paintings have already been accounted for in an orderly manner . . . however the last three cannot be certified as having been delivered to us." Alternative phrasing, "to make myself crystal clear" and "I have already passed these paintings" and "your previous invoice for RM 75,000 has already been disputed," litter the pages of the archives.[14]

Yet Gurlitt remained at large and continued to work closely with Voss. Somehow, Rochlitz alone shouldered the blame, and attempted to defend himself against Gurlitt's "lies." In a falling-out among thieves, Gurlitt made a statement under oath through a Hamburg lawyer attesting to his innocence, implicating Rochlitz. Oertel was obliged to back down.

◦∕◦

In October 1944, Voss personally wrote three separate authorizations for Gurlitt: the first for an advance of RM 500,000 to go to Hungary; the second, to travel to Holland and Belgium to repatriate German artworks; and the third, to return with artworks from France. Naturally, every courtesy was to be extended, and whatever transportation arrangements he would require. Even Martin Bormann availed himself of Gurlitt's undoubted expertise in spiriting away art. Bormann's authorization for Gurlitt specified that "the Wehrmacht and civil authorities lend Dr. H. Gurlitt whatever assistance he requires as he is working on a special mission for the Sonderauftrag Linz."[15] Speer, too, availed himself of Gurlitt's talents.

From the autumn of 1944, Gurlitt brought back art from sundry occupied territories and concealed it on behalf of Hitler, Bormann, Linz, Speer, and other Nazis. Not only were mines and castles required, but also safe havens in the neutral countries of Portugal, Spain, Sweden, and Switzerland. Yet only in Switzerland would the art be entirely safe from prying eyes. Portugal and Spain provided important export springboards to the United States and South America, clogging Buchholz's network with looted art, cash, jewels, and gold. Swiss banks, too, had their vaults overflowing with art, gold, diamonds, and cash to protect the hierarchy of the Third Reich.

While the Allies closed in, they were conscious of the movements of capital and valuables into these safe havens, but powerless to do anything about it. Eventually, Allen Dulles,* who oversaw Project Safehaven from his Bern headquarters of the Office of Strategic Services (OSS), was empowered to stop the exodus of these funds and treasures lest they be put at the disposal of a possible Fourth Reich.

All of 1944 and early 1945 would be used by Gurlitt to ensure that his own arrangements were secure, including a good story to tell the Allies. Meanwhile, he knew that the Soviets were closing in on Dresden. He returned there before the end of January 1945 to bring all the art he had squirreled away into its final exile, safe from the looming Soviet sphere of influence. His son Cornelius Gurlitt recalled in 2013 helping his father remove *Two Riders on the Beach* from the living-room wall.

---

* Dulles would later become the first civilian head of the Central Intelligence Agency (CIA).

26

౷

SURRENDERED . . . OR CAPTURED?

From now on, every single thing demands decision, and
every action responsibility.

—Martin Heidegger

ON MONDAY, FEBRUARY 12, ALL ARYANS IN BRESLAU WERE EVACUATED,
leaving only its handful of Jews to face the approaching Soviet army.
BBC Radio announced that all residents in Saxony should gather provisions for three weeks and bury them. The warning advised never to keep
these in their homes for fear of marauding Soviets or, worse, desperate
Wehrmacht deserters. On Saturday, a reported seven hundred deserters
from Hitler's army struck Dresden—more than twice the number of Jews
left alive. By Monday, there were seventeen thousand. Rebellions were
whispered as having taken place in Berlin, too.[1]

The next day destroyed Dresden. Was Gurlitt truly an eyewitness
to the events on the fiery Tuesday night of February 13–14, 1945, as he
claimed? That night, firestorms from Allied bombs reduced the entire
city center and Old Town to ashes, killing somewhere between 22,500
and 25,000 people.[2] The "Florence on the Elbe," as Dresden had been
called in guidebooks, was no more. More than 3,900 tons of high-explosive
bombs—40 percent of which were incendiary devices—were dropped
on the magnificent baroque provincial capital. Until then, Germany's

seventh-largest city had remained entirely unscathed and was a place of safety for refugees from other bombed-out towns.

At 9:39 p.m., the air raid sirens blared. Despite the late hour, the sky was suddenly darkened with a vast bombing formation—*ein dicker Hund*, or "fat dog." The locals shrieked in the streets while scampering for refuge.[3] The Reich air defense had issued a warning some twenty minutes earlier, but with only ten Messerschmitt-BF110 night fighters on the airfield, the sirens were Dresden's only real defense.* If Gurlitt had been there, he would have prayed that the bombers were headed for Leipzig instead.

Dresden had only the optics manufacturer Zeiss-Ikon operating in the armaments industry on its outskirts. Still, it had been shut a year earlier as there were too "few remaining Jews" to work as slave laborers.[4] On that very morning—February 13—the order was given for the last of Dresden's few hundred Jews to report for a "work assignment outside Dresden"—the local euphemism for Theresienstadt. They were to assemble at Zeughausplatz—where the synagogue had stood until the earlier firestorm of *Kristallnacht*. They were also told to bring blankets and provisions for travel. The only Jew in all of Dresden to be spared was Victor Klemperer. Even he did not know why.[5]

When the massive forest of magnesium parachute flares—*Weihnachtsbäume*, or "Christmas trees"—illuminated the night sky, most believed their luck had finally run dry. By early morning on February 14—not only Valentine's Day but also Ash Wednesday—the city, with its resplendent Old Town, had become an inferno, with temperatures peaking at 2,700 degrees Fahrenheit. Thousands screamed as they ran through the streets, their bodies melting in the heat. Those who rushed into the Altmarkt Square were instantly cremated.

Gurlitt knew as early as the defeats of 1942 that this would be a war to the bitter end. He'd had three years to prepare for post-Nazi life, just as the Nazis had prepared for their war from 1934 to 1938. More significantly, since September 4, 1943, he had protected his private collection previously on view at Kaitzer Strasse at Schloss Weesenstein. This included his prized Breughel, *Flower and Fruit Wreath*, and Dürer drawings.[6] He was in good

---

* There had been eighty-four heavy anti-aircraft guns around Dresden until the summer of 1944, but these were withdrawn to the ever-nearer eastern front by February 1945.

company. Hermann Voss, Erhard Goepel, Robert Oertel, and other select art historians took advantage of the same privileges.[7]

꧁

It is interesting to pause and consider how Cornelius and Benita would have seen the preparations, and their house stripped of all its beautiful art. Cornelius remembered helping his father to pack up. Both children would have felt some deep connection to the art. It was what their ephemeral father figure battled for, returning home to his family only between art salvaging operations. Even though Cornelius was only twelve years old, it is not too far-fetched to think that Hildebrand tried to mold his son in his own image. Nor is it too speculative to presume that the key to Cornelius's personality in later life came from this period—from the artworks his father plundered to his father's hero stories—and the boy's relationship to both.

It is easy to imagine Cornelius, like young Klaus Garnowski, contemplating the paintings on display in his grandmother's home, and loving them. Unlike Klaus Garnowski, when Cornelius looked at *Two Riders on the Beach* he felt the need to protect it from a disconnected world on the run. His father's paintings offered him solace in a world where there was none, other than in his relationship with his sister.

꧁

Hildebrand's world had no place for such childhood considerations. He and his fellow art dealers would need to reply in detail to questions tediously repeated by the Allies regarding their role in "safeguarding" public and private property under the Nazis. Voss and Gurlitt agreed long before that the American sector would be the safest place to take refuge. After all, it was the American market which Gurlitt and others had targeted throughout the 1930s and early 1940s, and they could, if required, obtain—so they thought—letters of recommendation from important museum directors there.

Besides, Gurlitt had been careful. His name hardly appeared on the manifests. Better yet, he already knew that Theo Hermsen was untraceable.[8] Gurlitt's own story was clear: he would portray himself as a victim. His wife and children were compelled to stay behind with his mother while he was forced to conduct business on behalf of the Reich. The implied threat to their welfare was clear. He would play on his victimization by the Nazis and his *Mischling* status. He'd show that he was also a victim of the Allies for the destruction of his home—indeed, twice over, once in Hamburg and once in the city of his birth.

Although the Gurlitts' Kaitzer Strasse home was destroyed that fateful February evening, the personal devastation suffered by the Gurlitts was negligible, due to his timely prescience. He had lived on a knife edge since Saxony's murderous regional governor, Martin Mutschmann, rose to power and targeted him in 1925 for his lack of appreciation for *völkisch* art. In the twenty intervening years, foresight had become a sixth sense.

Yet as he breathed the air choked with fire, smoke, and smuts of human flesh, in the days after the bombing, what must have truly broken his hardened heart was the sight of Dresden's magnificent buildings reduced to smoldering rubble from the firebombing. This alone made his sense of loss absolute. How could his exquisite baroque city, whose monuments and buildings his father had so painstakingly conserved and catalogued, be reduced to this charred wasteland in one foul night? Recalling this personal grief in the days ahead would help him to perform his role of victim well.

His decision—so long in the preparation—had been made. The responsibility for all that had happened in the plundering of art during the Third Reich was not of his making. The Nazi litany of thieving would not be laid at his feet. Only the stewardship of his widely dispersed collection mattered now. The Allies, indeed the world, would thank him for his preservation of all the modern art he had saved. He had averted a catastrophe for humanity by safeguarding it. That he had also prevented a personal financial disaster was merely fortuitous. His various caches within Germany might sustain the odd direct bombing hit, but the bulk of his vast fortune and stealthily shielded artworks had been scattered long before, secure in safe havens in Austria and Switzerland. Some, too, had been exported to the United States through Buchholz in Portugal.

∽

While Dresden still burned, its Jews escaped into the countryside with their deportation papers tucked snugly in their rucksacks. Over the coming days, they trickled back to find lost loved ones. Notes fluttered on the smoky breeze, while others were still posted on unhinged doors and ruined walls:

"We're still alive" and "We're at Auntie's" and "Find blankets and bring them to" and "We've run to our favorite place in the forest," and more. As the young Jewish slave laborer Henny Brenner stumbled across the Elbe on the bomb-damaged Loschwitz Bridge to relative safety in the districts that remained intact, she could hardly contemplate what new horrors they might be escaping to under the Soviets.[9]

Gurlitt's story was that on the morning of February 16, he struggled through the debris-laden, chaotic streets to move his terrified family to the temporary home of his eighty-six-year-old mother, who had been living with family at Possendorf. The likelihood, however, was that they, too, had been safely tucked away at the Possendorf farm. Food had been scarce, and anyone with an ounce of farsightedness and access to a motor vehicle had fled to small villages and farms long before that night. Though only some ten miles south of Dresden, all roads that remained passable were choked with refugees wedged into wood-fueled trucks, pedaling bicycles, carried in wheelbarrows, or meekly escaping on foot. Exits from Dresden were all but inaccessible, and it would have taken all day to make the ten-mile journey.

Most high-ranking Nazi officials had abandoned Dresden before the bombing—before the roads became inundated with the latest human wave. Mutschmann had saved all his valuables from his villa, even rescuing his carpets, before fleeing. Of course, he neglected to warn all of Dresden's inhabitants. This must mean that there had been an advance warning for those who were important to the crumbling regime.[10] Men like Mutschmann. Men like Gurlitt.

Seeing Dresden reduced to ashes and the plumes of smoke and fire reaching to the skies on the morning after the raid, Gurlitt would have reflected on the final touches to his contingency plans. The war was all but over. Like many who needed to face unsavory questions, Gurlitt knew the Allies would be overwhelmed with the shocking scope of the Nazi destruction. Then there would also be the physical rebuilding expected of these conquerors of a defeated Germany, requiring monumental organization and oversight. Though they might try, he was confident that the Allies would be unable to reconstruct the details of his own opaque role within the Nazi machinery that safeguarded artworks. That is, if all the art dealers stuck together and their secret documents had been "destroyed."

He also knew there were more significant mass murderers to pursue—those who had devised and run the death camps.

All of the dealers' Nazi prewar and wartime histories were so interwoven that if any one of them snagged the silken thread of half truths, they would all find themselves on the wrong side of the Art Looting Investigation Unit he understood the Americans had instituted to probe into the ERR, Dienststelle Mühlmann, and even Sonderauftrag Linz. That he had worked directly for Hitler, Goebbels, Göring, Bormann, Speer, and others needed careful thought prior to any Allied interrogation. Then, he might have worried about what would happen if Buchholz were captured. What if they discovered that the dealers had targeted the United States for sales of looted art from the outset?

Gurlitt needn't have worried about Buchholz. He had been flown in Göring's personal plane to Madrid on May 5, 1945, to establish another of his bookshops and art galleries at number 3, Avenida General Mola. Buchholz was living well, if illegally at number 83, Avenida General Mola, out of the reach of Allied interrogators in neutral Spain.[11]

⁓

Timing remained crucial. The Red Army was rapidly approaching Dresden, and Gurlitt had no intention of surrendering in a Soviet-controlled zone. BBC Radio talked about the Allies "shaking hands" in Berlin, but Gurlitt firmly believed that the Soviets would claim vast swaths of Germany for their own and—in a wicked twist of fate—encircle Berlin for their own Communist lebensraum.

Indeed, Gurlitt warned the other dealers countless times that they'd never be able to recover the bulk of their collections if they were found behind the Red Army lines.[12] Hadn't they realized that the Soviets were in no mood to listen to bedtime stories about whether this German or that one had subscribed to whichever of the Nazi ideologies?

To the Soviets, all Germans were loathsome; and Stalin let it be known to his advancing general Zhukov that the more raping, killing, and pillaging that went on, the better. If the art dealers thought that they would be safe from the Red Army excesses spreading westward faster than their war machine, they were assuredly mistaken. The czar's former palaces at

Tsarskoe Selo, near Leningrad,* had been ravaged by the Third Reich, and millions of Russians were dead.[13] Yet Böhmer and Möller were slow to comprehend the depth of Soviet hatred for the German people and remained in Güstrow and east Prussia respectively.

Gurlitt's supportive wife, Helene, was another matter. It took no such explanations for her to understand the gravity of the situation. She had been a sleeping partner with him from the beginning. She had looked after the collection while her husband was traveling—which was more often than not the way of things. She understood why he packed a few things to go away again after the bombing of Dresden. If his children, Cornelius and Benita, whined that he was leaving them alone again, or that they were afraid, Gurlitt would have explained his duty to visit Professor Voss without delay to protect Germany's cultural heritage. That he was collecting his Dresden-held collection, too, soon became apparent.

Ultimately, the most critical part of his plan rested on the cooperation of Hermann Voss. Only Voss could ensure Gurlitt's strategy for escape from prosecution and help avoid some unanticipated blunder. Voss's home in Dresden had been hit, too, but like Gurlitt, he was safely ensconced outside the city. Claiming illness, Voss was at Schloss Weesenstein—around fifteen miles away on back roads and farm tracks from Possendorf.

Gurlitt knew he'd have only this one last meeting to discuss the thousands of questions and anodyne answers that needed to be agreed on with Voss. After all, what stories would Haberstock or Böhmer or Möller or Buchholz or Dietrich or any of the other art dealers come up with to defend their actions? Would they reveal something they shouldn't about their personal collections that could implicate him in their wrongdoing? He'd bought and sold art with them all, never questioning any provenance. Then there was the matter of what they might say about their little shop at Schloss Niederschönhausen, just outside Berlin, where more than twenty-one thousand safeguarded artworks were eventually sold.

What could he say about the artworks from private collections? Did

---

* Saint Petersburg became Petrograd and the name was changed again once the Bolsheviks took control in the October Revolution, to Leningrad—then again, back to Saint Petersburg, with Glasnost.

his mind wander to the Chinese tapestries he had purloined from the Goldschmidt-Rothschild collection?[14] These must be denied, of course. Whatever had been settled between the dealers before the Dresden bombing, Gurlitt realized at this point that he couldn't trust any of them to keep their mouths shut.

⸎

When Gurlitt reached Schloss Weesenstein, his rattled friend Voss was, of course, delighted to see him. After commiserating about the destruction of Dresden, the two former museum directors planned their futures. Their discussions lasted much of that day and the next, and it was agreed that Gurlitt must make his way to Mainfranken, or Lower Franconia, which BBC Radio had declared safe from bombings. It was a racing certainty that it would also be controlled by the Americans.

Voss agreed he'd handle communications with the other art dealers and urge them to escape to Franconia, too, while Gurlitt made his way south and west. Voss assured Gurlitt that he'd send word ahead to the ancestral home of the medieval baronial family of Pölnitz at Aschbach, near Schlüsselfeld. It had all been arranged. After all, Gerhard von Pölnitz was also complicit in the safeguarding of artworks for the Church and the Reich, and had flown many of Göring's purchases from Paris and to hiding places abroad. Had Pölnitz flown Buchholz to Madrid? Chances are, given what followed, that Pölnitz had also flown several shipments for Gurlitt to Germany and Switzerland, too.

Finding adequate transport and open roads was Gurlitt's next task. Money was, of course, no object, since he carried significant sums in foreign exchange at all times.[15] Fortunately, he hadn't too far to look. The firm of Posselt proved most amenable to his urgent demand, swayed by the unexpected sight of folding money in US dollars. Posselt agreed to lend Gurlitt the use of a large truck and trailer that eventually needed to go to Nuremberg.

Within weeks of arriving at his mother's refuge at Possendorf, Hildebrand, Helene, and their two children waved good-bye to Hildebrand's mother. Had he offered to take his mother with them? Had she refused? Whatever happened, she would be trapped behind the Red Army lines and he would never see her again.

As the Gurlitts climbed aboard their truck and trailer, the children were laid onto mattresses by the wood-burning stove.* It would be Cornelius's job to top up the fire when his father shouted back to him. With all the crates on board, there was hardly any room left for the two children. It would have been quite an experience—claustrophobic, terrifying, and exhilarating.

Their parents most likely told them that they were embarking on a great adventure and were traveling to a beautiful castle where they would all be safe. Three days later, after a harrowing journey, picking their way through the imploding German countryside, they arrived at the castle home of Baron Pölnitz at the tiny village of Aschbach bei Schlüsselfeld, in Upper Franconia. There, the Gurlitts were met by Hildebrand's alleged nemesis Karl Haberstock, Baron and Baroness Gerhard von Pölnitz, their sons Peter and Ludwig, and the baron's French mistress, Jane Weil. Here, Gurlitt and his family patiently awaited his "surrender."

✍

From the children's viewpoint, their adventure was a watershed. For as long as they could remember, their father had flitted in and out of their lives like some incredibly rare butterfly—frightfully important and extremely sought-after for his knowledge. Throughout the war, he had never stayed long enough for them to comprehend his affairs. Cornelius, for all that his grandfather had lauded him as a bonny lad befitting royalty, had become a quiet and withdrawn boy, connecting emotionally only with his sister, Benita. He was intelligent and also a talented artist, but as time marched on, his apparent shyness and father's devastating secrets would impel him into the life of a loner. It was these next few months and years that would scar him forever.

Already, Cornelius's life had been stolen by his father.[16]

---

* By this time gasoline was generally unavailable to civilians and most vehicles had been converted to wood-burning stoves as means of propulsion.

PART IV

THE STOLEN LIVES

The Lord God, merciful and gracious ... who will by no means clear the guilty, visiting the iniquity of the fathers on the children and the children's children, to the third and the fourth generation.

—Exodus 34:7

27

◎~~~◎

HOUSE ARREST

Leave your sons well instructed rather than rich, for the hopes of the instructed are better than the wealth of the ignorant.

—Epictetus

ON APRIL 30, 1945, HITLER SHOT HIMSELF AFTER HIS NEW BRIDE, Eva Braun, took a cyanide capsule. In accordance with Hitler's will, Bormann had their bodies brought to the garden outside the führer's bunker and set alight. Inside the bunker, Speer's model of the Linz Führermuseum, so often contemplated by Hitler in his final days, remained abandoned. Since the Nazi Party was Hitler's sole beneficiary, as party chairman Bormann either had taken the artworks from the bunker with him or had previously arranged for them to be secreted away.

Bormann, however, escaped. For more than twenty years, many believed he had survived and fled to Paraguay.[1] Gurlitt heard the rumors about putting Bormann on trial in absentia alongside twenty-three leaders of the Third Reich. Doubtless Gurlitt was unaware that Bormann had arranged for his ardently Nazi wife, Gerda, and their nine children to flee Berlin by abducting another five youngsters so that she could claim she was the director of a children's home conveying her young charges to safety.[2] Though many searched for Bormann's whereabouts or remains, he appeared to have vanished amid the chaos of the battle for Berlin. Did this mean that Gurlitt, as custodian of Hitler's and Bormann's art, which he had secreted in Switzerland, would remain its guardian until the party chairman instructed him? Was Voss in the loop?

∞

Gurlitt's interrogator, First Lieutenant Dwight McKay, had no idea about his secrets. McKay had already learned, however, that justice was as ephemeral as a purloined jewel in the Third Reich. If Hitler didn't like what he came across, he made an edict changing the law and—poof—it was illegal. His minions changed the law's shape and meaning so it couldn't be recognized, and inserted it into a new jewel of their own making for their own nefarious purposes. Still, McKay would think like that, since he was a lawyer from Illinois, from a long line of Midwest lawyers.

It had been six years since McKay graduated from University of Chicago Law School. He'd been working for only two years when he enlisted after Pearl Harbor in December 1941. From the moment the Allies landed in Normandy, McKay was assigned to General Patton's Third Army Judge Advocate's Section to track down war criminals. Eventually, his outfit was detailed to sniffing out German art looters and stationed near Frankfurt between the collection points set up at Wiesbaden and Marburg by the Allies.[3]

That's how he found himself a stranger in a ravaged and alien country, asked by the US government to determine (a) who were war criminals, (b) what atrocities they were alleged to have committed, and (c) whether they should be brought to Nuremberg to stand trial. He was thirty years old and some 4,400 miles from home. He knew next to nothing about art—except the names of some famous artists—but was learning quickly how the Nazis used art to achieve their war aims. What McKay found most shocking was that he truly cared about people and right and wrong—and none of that seemed relevant to Hitler's Germany. He was thunderstruck by what the Nazis had done to their own people and the rest of Europe.[4] Never mind what they had done to the law.

McKay's unit had been investigating the German art looters for about a month before they were tipped off that one of Hitler's main dealers for the Führermuseum was in the vicinity. When he checked the name of Hildebrand Gurlitt on his "most wanted" list, the inevitable red flag stared back at him. The list had been compiled through a variety of sources: the Roberts Commission, the French Musées Nationaux and their equivalent in all other occupied territories, the Army Services Forces Manual M-352-17B Civil Affairs, and input from individual officers of the Art Looting Intelligence Unit (ALIU). The "most wanted" list from the Allied armies for crimes against humanity was consulted separately.

According to McKay's report, Gurlitt was "captured" at Schloss Frankenberg at Aschbach bei Schlüsselfeld, the ancestral home of the von Pölnitz family. When the American jeeps rolled into the small village, the mayor greeted them, and informed the soldiers that the "schloss"—where the main street rises behind the lake—was now home to Nazis who'd arrived with many trucks. Soon after, McKay was on the scene.

Gurlitt's collection of 117* paintings, nineteen drawings, and seventy-two various objets d'art were among the hundreds of crates cosseted in the castle. Naturally, Gurlitt was placed under house arrest and his collection taken into custody by McKay and his team. The collection was shipped to the imposing Neue Residenz high atop the city of Bamberg, some twenty miles distant. McKay's next job was to depose Gurlitt, make his preliminary judgment, then wait for the ALIU to take over from there.[5]

For three grueling days, from June 8 to 10, 1945, McKay interviewed the forty-nine-year-old Gurlitt.[6] It had been forty days since Hitler and Goebbels had committed suicide. The "bush telegraph" between the art dealers told Gurlitt that other dealers had been arrested, too. Haberstock and Pölnitz had been taken elsewhere for questioning. Each was now weaving his own tale.

McKay noted that Gurlitt was soft-spoken, wore spectacles, and was nervous and taciturn. His replies were to the point and translated with accuracy, so Gurlitt attested, by the US Army sergeant translator number 5 of German Jewish origin, Paul S. Bauer.[7] McKay also knew that a smart witness said as little as possible.

The American began his questioning with standard biographical information: name, date of birth, wife's name, children's names, current address. To lull Gurlitt into a sense of security, McKay then asked him about

---

* One painting was looted from the Wiesbaden Collecting Point—never to be returned. A Rodin drawing was erroneously returned to France, and was claimed to have "never arrived."

his parents. Gurlitt's reply led McKay to believe that his prisoner had a highly inflated opinion of himself, since his face lit up when describing his father as the former president of the Union of German Architects and president of the German City Planning Academy—and that he had "rediscovered" the significance of baroque architecture.[8]

When it came to his mother, Gurlitt laid it on with a trowel. Naturally, he did not call his mother by his youthful biting nickname for her—Madame Privy Councillor.[9] Instead, he played on his second-degree-*Mischling* status, and the prominence of his Jewish grandmother's family. McKay appeared unmoved, simply noting down the facts as Gurlitt told them.[10]

Undeterred, Gurlitt continued, no longer reticent, sensing perhaps that if he told this lawyer more about his distinguished family, his interrogation would be over. So McKay was regaled with stories of Gurlitt's renowned landscape-painter grandfather and an uncle who was an eminent composer in England. McKay must see surely, Gurlitt added in a suitably timid voice, that he came from a long line of influential artists.[11] Gurlitt finished with the sad story of his father's final disillusionment— omitting of course to mention that Cornelius had voted for Hitler. He also forgot to say that he freely signed *"Heil Hitler!"* on his correspondence. Nor did he mention Wolfgang's brother, Manfred, a Nazi Party member who had emigrated to Japan, especially as America was still at war in the Far East.

Of course, McKay was not to know that much of Gurlitt's tale was a well-rehearsed lie, even though he suspected he hadn't been told the truth. He also hadn't received any files confirming that Gurlitt had stowed some of his personal valuables, along with those of the Gemäldegalerie, at Schloss Weesenstein.

∞

Next McKay asked about Gurlitt's own professional achievements. Understandably, to evoke sympathy, Gurlitt began with the Great War and how he'd been wounded three times between 1914 and 1918. He omitted any mention that he had "safeguarded" art in the West or written propaganda dispatches from the eastern front. Questions relating to Wilhelmine Germany were not asked as a rule, but in McKay's limited experience, they were frequently answered. Every Nazi of a certain age had to prove that they had served the kaiser loyally, too, as if this would somehow exonerate them from the most heinous crimes under Hitler.

Gurlitt painted a dismal picture of his suffering after the Great War: how his personal friendships (non-Nazi, inevitably) and hard work eventually led to his directorship of the City Art Gallery in Zwickau from 1925. That skirted over six years of personal history and limited "professional achievements."

It had long before been agreed with Kirchbach that Gurlitt would never mention his name to his interrogators. Meanwhile, Gurlitt had learned that Kirchbach's Coswig factory remained unscathed; however, it was firmly within the Soviet sector. To his relief, Kirchbach and his wife escaped to Basel in the final days of the war, and would remain there until the dust settled.[12] All was proceeding according to their postwar plan.

When McKay asked about Zwickau, Gurlitt became tight-lipped, stating merely, "Through developing this small museum into a living updated institution for workmen I incurred the enmity of the Nazis and was dismissed already in 1930."[13] McKay was no fool and knew that the Nazis had grabbed power only in 1933, yet when he pressed Gurlitt on this obvious sin of commission, McKay's prisoner refused to say more. For some unknown reason, McKay did not note down that there were three years that were not adequately explained by Gurlitt.

Next, McKay asked the obvious question: So what did you do next? Gurlitt's hard-luck story continued. "I gave lessons of the history of art in the Academy of applied Art in Dresden, published a book about Käthe Kollwitz . . . and wrote articles for the *Vossische* and *Frankfurter Zeitungen*."[14]

Gurlitt claimed that he was "called to Hamburg as director of the Kunstverein" in 1930, making his establishment a haven for modern art—including modern English artists. He talked about the Swedish and English exhibitions, but said he was denounced when he "sawed off the flagpole" of the Kunstverein to avoid flying "the swastica [sic] flag." This incident led to his downfall and seemed to surprise Gurlitt since Hamburg had been a mecca for "free-thinking artists" until then, he added verbosely. He had no choice but to become an art dealer to survive. McKay already knew that Gurlitt had survived quite well—he had RM 250,000 in bonds and another RM 250,000 in cash on deposit in Germany.[15]

✐

McKay, and later on, Monuments Man interrogator James S. Plaut saw Gurlitt's tax returns, which showed a remarkable rise in his declared income from the time of the Anschluss:

RM 20,789 in 1938   RM 15,253 in 1939
RM 25,358 in 1940   RM 44,452 in 1941
RM 41,001 in 1942   RM 176,855 in 1943
RM 159,999 in 1944   and zero in 1945.[16]

His bonds and deposits with the banking firm of Ree in Hamburg showed only a portion of his wealth. Gurlitt's Dresden bank account had an additional RM 40,000 in cash. Then there were the artworks—"which are here in this castle"—worth between RM 40,000 and RM 80,000.[17] His interrogators also knew that Dresdner Bank had been the primary conduit for all transfers from the Reich Chancellery.

Given that the Sonderauftrag Linz had paid Gurlitt in excess of RM 22 million from the end of 1942 to 1944 in France alone, even with a meager 5 percent commission, Gurlitt ought to have been declaring at least RM 1 million in income in the years 1943–4.[18] That, of course, doesn't take into account paintings he sold to industrialists like Kirchbach, Thyssen, and Reemtsma. Evidently, the money was never deposited in a German bank account—nor was anything like his *real* income declared on his German tax returns. In other words, Hildebrand Gurlitt had defrauded Hitler, not only of works of art, but also of tax revenue. McKay and all the Monuments Men were in good company when Gurlitt duped them. The question remains: Where did he stash the cash and art?

✐

Unaware of the tax fraud, McKay soldiered on interrogating Gurlitt. He next asked where Gurlitt had been at the outbreak of the war. "In 1939, I was in Switzerland, then Paris,"[19] Gurlitt replied. McKay's eyebrows may have metaphorically risen at this point, but first he needed a declaration by Gurlitt about belonging to the Nazi Party: "Since 1919, I have never been a soldier. My wife and I [were] never a member of the party or any other Nazi institution (except like all other art dealers in the Reichskammer der bildenden Künste). No connection whatsoever to any party official, as an art dealer only cooperation with my former colleagues, the directors of Museums, never sworn in on the Fuhrer [sic]. Never voted for the Nazis, likewise not my wife. Was never in a position to denounce my fre [sic] opinion."[20]

McKay knew Gurlitt was lying, but had no evidence—at least yet—to prove it. So McKay asked, "Tell me about your trips to Paris."[21]

The reply was not immediately forthcoming. Gurlitt insisted that he "knew nothing" (the rehearsed refrain that rang out time and again from many collaborators). He had told McKay all he could remember. Gurlitt signed a sworn statement that his first trip to Paris was in 1941, where previously he had stated that he went to Paris in 1939. When called out on this by McKay, Gurlitt replied that the 1941 trip was not for himself but for the German museums—the first of ten business trips between 1941 and 1944 undertaken for Dr. Hans Posse, and then, on Posse's death, for Professor Hermann Voss.[22]

McKay had the admission he wanted. This tied Gurlitt directly to the primary safeguarding campaign wielded to fill Hitler's Linz museum. McKay extracted a testimony that was far short of the truth, but nonetheless quite revealing: "I was paid by transfers through the clearinghouse. Up to 1942 they were unrestricted for my use." Gurlitt made purchases for private clients and then "later only for the Führermuseum" through different dealers, but only very rarely "from private persons. In total I acquired about two hundred paintings in France and have given them to museums. I have sold little to private persons."[23] Given? As previously stated, he exported a minimum of 526 paintings, fifty-five drawings, two pastels, nine sculptures, and twenty-six tapestries in that period through Knauer, according to the Musées Nationaux.

McKay noted down the contradictions, querying them with a question mark in the margin. He had, of course, no access to the information that littered the Archives Nationales de France's AJ 40 files on the spoliation of France by German art dealers. For his part, McKay hoped, however, that Gurlitt would become talkative about his acquisitions for Voss and the Führermuseum from France. The outcome would determine if Gurlitt could be classed as a "war criminal."

"I was sent to Paris on the endorsements of former colleagues . . .

Directors [*sic*] of great museums," Gurlitt explained. "This I liked very much, because on account of the bombs and the always increasing Nazi-terror. . . . There was furthermore the danger that I, as quarter Jew, should have been forced to work for the Organization Todt."[24] Though McKay had been in the job of interrogating art looters for only a month, he was already well versed in the story. Still, had his prisoner dealt in looted art? Gurlitt blatantly lied, Never. Never? Never, came the reply again.

Had Gurlitt somehow kidded himself? Had he forgotten about *Two Horses on the Beach* by Max Liebermann, stolen from David Friedmann and sold to him through Hans W. Lange? Or what about the Chinese tapestries from the Goldschmidt-Rothschild collection? Or his newly acquired Matisse from the Paul Rosenberg collection, which now resided in a bank vault? Of course not.

Interestingly, until this point, Gurlitt hadn't painted any pictures of the bonfires of books and artworks, nor had he expressed the predicament of the artists. Later interrogations claiming that this had been the impetus behind his actions crumble when his first transcript is read. Gurlitt stressed in the main that he had been compelled to become an art dealer and only dealt in works of art with a good provenance.

∽

Even more bizarre was Gurlitt's statement under oath that Hermann Voss—not Hans Posse—was responsible for his role as one of the four official art dealers to empty German museums of their modern art. This was natural enough, he explained, since the Gurlitt name was well respected in art and architecture circles.[25] Again, this was pure invention by Gurlitt. At the time that Voss allegedly recommended him to Goebbels, Voss had applied to immigrate to Britain. Since Voss had not requested political asylum, his application was refused. Voss had no alternative but to return to work in Germany in 1935 and keep quiet about his personal views. It was only his vast knowledge of German baroque and Italian Renaissance art (he had worked at the German Institute in Florence during the 1914–18 war) that kept him in employment.[26]

Still, McKay was no art expert and simply noted everything down. Gurlitt skipped over the years 1941–42, claiming that he had "never spoken to any superior officials of Voss, nor ever written to them."[27] His friendship with Albert Speer, or buying and selling art for Hitler, Goebbels, Göring, and Ribbentrop was never mentioned. Nor was how Hitler treated his personal and Linz collections as one and the same.

Gurlitt claimed that the way it worked was simple. Voss instructed Gurlitt where to go to acquire art and Gurlitt obeyed. "I did not have closer insights to the office of Reichsleiter Bormann," Gurlitt lied fancifully. "Payments were made from the Reichskanzlei over to Bankhaus Schickler, Delbruk [sic] in Berlin. My bills were made out to Professor Voss, commissioner for the Museum Linz."[28]

Was Gurlitt aware of what the führer bought? McKay asked. Gurlitt said he was aware that Dietrich, the photographer Hoffmann, and others were active in this regard. "For these purchases there was no laid-out plan, while Professor Voss wished to have a museum collection put on a scientific and historic base."[29] Here Gurlitt was referring to the 1939 mammoth project undertaken by Dr. Otto Kümmel, then director of the Berlin Museums.[30]

McKay zeroed in on the main question that troubled the Allies, asking Gurlitt how it worked with the pictures from the Jewish collections. Gurlitt of course had "no personal knowledge." He had only heard rumors of sequestrations and forced sales. As expected, McKay's concerns related to the unremitting violations of article 46 of the 1907 Hague Convention. Gurlitt admitted to having heard that "Jewish-owned art treasures in France were seized by a law," then went on to claim that he hadn't ever "seen [it] with my eyes."

Immediately contradicting himself, Gurlitt stated, "I know that the German Ambassador used a Baroque Writing [sic] desk, which came from the Rothschild collection. I also saw marvelous French drawings from the 18th century in the room of the German embassy, which were said to come from the same source." Though Gurlitt had been told of a "rich palace" in Paris where Jewish art was collected and divided among different Nazi officials, he "never went to this building."[31] Pointing the finger at Bruno Lohse, Gurlitt claimed that he'd heard that Lohse was rapacious. Yet Gurlitt claimed he "always avoided to meet high Nazi Officials in Paris."

Perhaps McKay raised a metaphorical eyebrow again here. Gurlitt certainly felt he'd been caught in a lie and clarified: "I was only once to [*sic*] a large reception in the embassy together with hundreds of people." It was there that he heard the Gestapo bought paintings from private collectors or dealers "under pressure . . . which I heard very often, but I never could prove it or even get reliable information, as I otherwise should have gone after such an accusation and would have informed Professor Voss privately. I did notice . . . that I was not shown many pictures, which were reserved for other dealers."[32] Was this a poor translation, or was Gurlitt squirming?

∽

After three days of questioning, a weary McKay realized that he'd barely scratched the surface and filed his report. His final task was to secure Gurlitt's formal signature on the statement and indicate which works of art were his. This marked the beginning of the arduous task for Allied art experts to determine what had been legitimately acquired and what had been safeguarded or stolen. At no point in the process did Hildebrand Gurlitt indicate that he was safeguarding his collection for posterity or that he had "rescued" the modern art in his possession or indeed that he was warehousing it for others.

Later, while viewing his art collection at the Neue Residenz in Bamberg, Gurlitt seemed more relaxed as he identified a number of his grandfather's landscapes, a painting by Beckmann, and the Otto Dix self-portrait.[33] Max Liebermann's *Wagon on Sand Dunes*, Marc Chagall's *Allegorical Scene*, Max Beckmann's *The Lion Tamer*, Max Liebermann's *Two Riders on the Beach*, Edgar Degas's *Nude Woman Washing Herself*, Pablo Picasso's *Woman's Head*—all elicited equal joy. Some 115 paintings, nineteen drawings, and seventy-two various objets d'art were again sworn by Gurlitt to be his entire surviving collection—the rest had been destroyed during the firebombing of Dresden. Even his records were gone.[34] No one seemed to note that, miraculously, his tapestries and furniture had survived.

Nor did they find out that Gurlitt had sold two of the four most expensive paintings bought at the Viau auction in December 1942 to Hermann Reemtsma of Hamburg. Reemtsma acquired the Corot landscape and the Pissarro, having refused to take the FF 5 million Cézanne *Vallée*

de l'Arc de la Montagne—St Victoire, as Reemtsma believed that it, and the
Daumier, were fakes.*

႟

McKay's investigation was as complete as possible in the absence of cor-
roborative testimony. Whether to prosecute Gurlitt or not depended on
the outcome of the art experts' evaluations. Yet these would be mired in
red tape for years. As early as 1944, Henry Morgenthau, Jr., the US secretary
of the treasury under Roosevelt, had devised his plan to handle the daunt-
ing task ahead. Unofficially called the "Morgenthau Plan," it was signed
into law by President Truman as JCS 1067 on May 10, 1945. Among its
many functions, JCS 1067 provided for the denazification of Germany as
an integral part of rebuilding the country.[35]

By August 1945, "Morgenthau's Boys" were on the case of the looted
art, too. These men were expert treasury investigators loaned to the US
Army of Occupation to sniff out the looters and return stolen works to their
rightful owners or heirs. It was Morgenthau's Boys who made the horrific
connection between looting and the concentration camps. Yet they would
be withdrawn from their forensic searches by more political wrangling in
the months ahead, since their work overlapped with the work of Project
Safehaven, headed by Allen Dulles from Bern.

As for First Lieutenant Dwight McKay, he was transferred to Nuremberg in September to work on the prosecution of the biggest Nazi war
criminals—perhaps wearing a sly smile when thinking of Gurlitt and the
grilling he should face for years to come.

႟

Decades later, S. Lane Faison, the noted Monuments Man and naval
officer, remarked in a radio interview that he had the complex remit from
the Roberts Commission to write the "official history, as far as we could put
it together, of how Adolf Hitler's art collection was formed."[36] He worked in

---

* Georges Viau had an irrepressible hobby of "restoring" his Impressionist art, often overpainting
  quite badly. It is entirely possible that beneath his well-intended restorations, a real Cézanne and
  Daumier might be found.

a three-man team with Lieutenants James S. Plaut and Theodore Rousseau, Jr., to achieve that end, in a short period and with great aplomb.[37] These three men interviewed Haberstock, Gurlitt, Pölnitz, Voss, Lohse, Georg Büchner (head of the Bavarian galleries), Dietrich, Carl Buemming, and Herbst among the vast array of dealers and functionaries.

While the Monuments Men were gathering intelligence and writing up their reports, the United States Military Detachment to Bamberg G-222 issued an evacuation order, on November 21, 1945. Signed by Property Control Officer Wallace W. Johns, it read:

> To Whom It May Concern:
>
> Mr. Chaim Krut has been appointed custodian of the castle of Aschbach and all the properties belonging to it.
>
> The owner, Baron v. Poelnitz and family are hereby ordered to vacate the premises immediately. No furniture of any kind or equipment may be removed from the castle or the grounds. Anything which has been removed must be returned at once.
>
> This is an order of the Military Government.[38]

A political decision had been made to use the castle as a recuperation and recovery unit for concentration-camp victims. Baroness Pölnitz was apoplectic with rage, accusing "these people" of ruining her fine antiques. She would have to bear the ignominy until such time as the valuables could be removed to another location.

Meanwhile, Monuments Men declared that the Schloss had been used as a major depot for the museums in Nuremberg, Bamberg, and Kassel and that Pölnitz was in custody. Private individuals like General Fütterer and the German ambassador in Budapest had also housed their art collections there. "In residence is Herr Karl Haberstock from Berlin, the personal art dealer of Adolf Hitler and Herr Hildebrand Gurlitt from Hamburg and Dresden, another art dealer of the führer. Both of these collectors have great collections of works of art on the premises."[39] The wives, though not mentioned, were assuredly there as well.

As a result of the evacuation order, Gurlitt and his family were forced to move across the road to the less salubrious accommodation at 13a High Street, overlooking the scenic lake that dominates the tiny village.

Haberstock had been taken into custody and questioned in Munich as a material witness in the main war-crimes trials. Gurlitt remained under house arrest.

❧

Meanwhile, Lane Faison retreated to the London desk to write his great tome—Consolidated Interrogation Report no. 4—regarding Hitler's museum and library. It was dated December 15, 1945. Yet even Faison recognized that they hadn't all the facts at their disposal. A shorter, supplementary report was created after Faison was shown a mere eleven files from the office of Hans-Heinrich Lammers, chief of the Reich Chancellery. It was Lammers who personally questioned Gurlitt's acquisitions in the closing days of the war and also approved vast advances of cash on Gurlitt's rescue missions.

The Monuments Men had performed a vital piece of the investigative work in extremely difficult circumstances, and nothing should detract from their efforts. They were, save young Harry Ettlinger, all museum men and women—all highly trained—with a tremendous knowledge of the visual arts. None of them were, however, trained investigators. None were policemen or investment bankers. They learned their craft as art-looting investigators "on the job," interviewing their German counterparts effectively as fellow art historians.[40]

❧

Early in 2014, Jonathan Searle, formerly of Scotland Yard's Art Squad and the arresting officer of the twentieth century's greatest art fraudster/ provenance forger, John Drewe, and the talented artist/forger John Myatt, reviewed the Gurlitt interrogations. His comments were illuminating. Most significantly, in addition to highlighting the numerous repetitions in Dwight McKay's report ("the list of paintings from pages 12 to 33, frequently repeat the same information e.g., Degas *Nude Woman Washing herself* pp. 16, 29, and his *Two Nudes* pp. 16, 26; Fragonard's *Anne & the Holy Family* pp. 16, 23; Guardi's *Entry to a Monastery* pp. 15, 23, 29; Prud'hon's *Adam and Eve* pp. 18, 25, 32; David Teniers' *Landscape with skittles* pp. 16,30,49 etc. etc."), Searle pointed out that the interpreter Paul Bauer's poor command of English would have hampered McKay's investigation.

McKay's own lack of knowledge of the art market, Searle observed, was also a hindrance.[41]

The use of double negatives, the clumsy translation of Gurlitt's intentions in seeking refuge with Pölnitz, and, above all, the lack of financial due diligence to back up the interrogation leave much to be desired. Indeed, Searle points out, "The financial investigation side of this statement is negligible. Gurlitt makes a few estimates on his financial deals and then whines 'I was told, that I was a poor man before the Nazis came and that I now have money and a whole truck-load of paintings. To that I have to reply . . .' (p. 8). But he gives no figures." Searle rightly states that "there is no inventory or ledger anywhere for the purchase and sale of paintings, which is standard for any archive, and this team included the word Archives in its name 'Monuments, Fine Arts, and Archives Section' (MFAA)."

Searle states that there were "345 specialists attached to this outfit which is considerable, even taking into account the thousands of paintings etc. stolen."[42] Gurlitt was not interviewed directly by the one person who could have proven his lies—Rose Valland.

Searle's criticism continues:

This statement would be severely criticized today without a backup financial statement done by the investigating officer. More figures should have been given for the sale of paintings. There are very few and it reads like a financial black hole. It must be said that modern police investigation, certainly since the 1980s, is particularly geared toward financial investigation with specially trained "financial investigators" attached to every serious CID* team or squad—I was one myself. But this is just a fancy name for something that has always been looked into in the past. I should have thought it was obvious to a trained lawyer.[43]

As a former investment banker, I can attest that Searle's comments address many of the questions that I had as well during my research.

∽

---

* CID—Criminal Investigation Department.

In CIR no. 4, Faison went to great lengths to highlight that the files contain "complete statements of the special Linz accounts in Holland and Italy" and that the "exhaustive reports of the purchases made by H. GURLITT, GOEPEL, and the Dorotheum (Dr. HERBST) in France, Holland and Belgium" are included.[44]

Faison shared McKay's and Plaut's scepticism. There was something not quite right about Gurlitt's story. The main thrust of their findings concluded that Sonderauftrag Linz was a criminal organization and its adherents should be tried for war crimes.[45] Hildebrand Gurlitt would be held over under house arrest at Aschbach. The smidgen of information fed to Faison and his team in 1945 had shown Gurlitt to be a consummate liar. Finding the truth, however, would be another issue.

Jim Plaut and Theodore Rousseau believed that the answers were to be found in Switzerland, and so they set out to discover what really happened.

28

UNDER THE MICROSCOPE

There is nothing more deceptive than an obvious fact.

—ARTHUR CONAN DOYLE

EDWARD C. ACHESON, CHIEF OF ECONOMIC INTELLIGENCE OF THE
Secret Intelligence branch of the OSS, wrote a letter dated April 9, 1945,
classified "most secret" regarding Switzerland. Acheson, the younger
brother of the American assistant secretary of state for economic affairs
Dean G. Acheson, was no slouch. "There is an unsubstantiated rumor that
some Top Secret material has been received concerning the holdings of
some highly placed Nazis in Switzerland. How unsubstantiated is this
rumor?"[1]

That same day, Acheson penned a second letter, regarding Lichtenstein.
There were three query categories: how Swiss law applied there; what
holding companies had been or were being whitewashed; and how to get
to the ultimate beneficiaries of any holding company.[2] Acheson was on the
scent of the strict Swiss secrecy laws, which blanketed all bank transactions
for individuals, companies, and assets that could benefit the fallen Reich.

Acheson's role differed from that of Monuments Men Plaut, Faison, and
Rousseau. His task was to make sure that the stolen artworks would not be
used as part of some unknown German financial network to fund another
war. The Monuments Men wanted restitution and punishment, in that
order. Inevitable conflicts arose from the outset between the two groups.

To complicate matters further, Project Safehaven itself, as an interagency endeavor, was torn between its various agency overlords. Even the American embassies in Europe had incompatible aims with the other government bodies where looted art was concerned.

Though written on March 17, another unsigned attachment from the US embassy in London arrived on Acheson's desk in Bern on May 3, 1945. Apparently, a Matisse painting—*The Open Window*—had been tracked to Switzerland. The Monuments Men believed that Max Stocklin, a convicted art dealer imprisoned in Paris, had imported the painting stolen from the Paul Rosenberg collection at Floriac, near Bordeaux. Stocklin worked closely with the German occupation authorities and was particularly chummy with Rochlitz and Lohse. In fact, prior to the war, Stocklin and Rochlitz had assessed a range of highly valuable Jewish collections in France and Germany with an eye to confiscation.[3] Along with Lohse, they would collectively "buy" considerable quantities of valuables, with and without the knowledge of the Nazis in France.[4]

One of the most coveted of the collections assessed belonged to Paul Rosenberg. The author of the letter to Acheson* recounted his interview with the sculptor André Martin, who was then employed at the Galerie Neupert, in Zurich. The painting had been imported to Switzerland in an apparently legal manner by Stocklin, with the duty paid, approximately two years earlier. Stocklin assured Martin that the painting had been purchased at a Parisian gallery, but alas, he could not recall which one. Martin was to sell it on behalf of Stocklin, and so it was offered to the Bern Kunstmuseum and a Dr. Trussel, who was known to Acheson. The museum would purchase the painting only if it had a clear provenance proving that it was sold prior to the occupation of Paris in June 1940. Clearly, the museum suspected that it had been in the Rosenberg collection. Martin claimed he had no interest in the painting other than his commission in the event of a sale.[5]

Wing Commander Douglas Cooper, art historian, modern art collector, and indefatigable British Monuments Man, took over the file from there. His twenty-six-page report *Looted Works of Art in Switzerland* and his follow-on work with Paul Rosenberg personally in the days im-

---

* Probably Plaut or his British counterpart, Douglas Cooper.

mediately after the war show Cooper's doggedness and determination to help Rosenberg reclaim his looted art.[6] Cooper traced Matisse's *Open Window* through a series of twenty-eight exchanges made in Switzerland—all with the full knowledge of Hermann Göring.

Ten of these exchanges—with dealers Adolf Wuester, Max Stocklin, Arthur Pfannstiel, Galerie Neupert on behalf of Alfred Boedecker; Dr. Alexander von Frey; Galerie Almas-Dietrich, in Munich; and the Dik Gallery in Amsterdam—were for Hitler, Ribbentrop, and Bormann. The exchanges were designed to avoid the contravention of an edict issued by the Reich Chancellery minister Lammers on November 18, 1940, at the behest of Hitler, which decreed that *all* confiscated works of art were to be sent to Germany and placed at the disposal of the führer.[7]

As the armistice with France was signed with the French people—not with Freemasons or Jews who no longer enjoyed the French nationality—Jewish property was deemed "ownerless." Jewish assets were thereby free of any encumbrance and could be shipped to the Reich. Nevertheless, in the case of the outlawed modern art, importation to Germany simply would not do.

Still, why should valuable art "lie fallow" when such an "abundance of highly salable material" should go to the greater Nazi good? Ideology could be bent, Göring believed, as had often been the case in the interests of commercial realities that would better serve the Reich.[8] So the exchanges took place. The twenty-eight forensically examined by Cooper occurred between February 1941 and the end of 1943. All of these were fully disclosed to Göring, with eighteen of the twenty-eight exchanges arranged on his behalf with Gustav Rochlitz in Paris.

The exchanges were both direct and indirect and provide a useful catalogue of how things worked. The first of them involved Göring and Hofer on one side and the ubiquitous Swiss auctioneer Theodor Fischer, his Darmstadt partner Carl Buemming, and the firm of Bronner in Basel on the other. Göring and Hofer traded twenty-five Impressionist paintings, all withdrawn from the depository at Neuschwanstein, near Füssen, by Göring personally on July 12, 1941. These paintings were variously by Corot, Courbet, Cottet, Degas, van Gogh, Lucas, Manet, Monnier, Renoir, Rousseau, Rodin, and Sisley.

Fischer had selected all twenty-five paintings in Berlin. British collector

Alphonse Kann owned the Daumier, all the works by Degas, the Manet, the Rodin, the Renoir, and the Rousseau. The van Gogh belonged to British collector Alfred Lindon. In exchange, Fischer gave Göring six paintings: four Cranachs, a triptych by a Frankfurt master, and a painting of the Nuremberg school.

The second exchange, also a straight swap, was between Fischer's French agent, Hans Wendland, and Göring. Wendland gave a Rembrandt purchased in Marseilles in 1941 and two sixteenth-century Brussels tapestries in exchange for twenty-five Impressionist paintings.

The third exchange also involved Fischer, as did the fourth and eighth. The close financial connection between Wendland, Fischer, and Emil Bührle, at Galerie Neupert, was also detailed.[9]

Yet it was the sixth exchange that would embroil Gurlitt—albeit posthumously:

EXCHANGE No. 6 MAX STOECKLIN*[sic] of Paris with ERR (for the Reichs [sic] Chancellery):
STOECKLIN gave:-
WINANTS.   Woodland landscape.
ZEEMAN.   Small Fishing Harbour.
STOECKLIN received:-
MATISSE.   The open window[sic].   Coll. Rosenberg[10]

Cooper had interviewed André Martin of Zurich and knew that the painting was currently on sale at the Galerie Neupert there. The contract for the exchange was drawn up, without appraisal, on June 15, 1942, on behalf of the Reich Chancellery. Officially, the picture still "belonged" to Stocklin, who remained in a French prison. Cooper ended his report on the swap with the hopeful note, "There would seem to be no reason why it should not be seized."[11] Cooper naturally made Paul Rosenberg aware of the situation, and the latter planned to travel to Switzerland from New York as soon as the peace permitted.

∽

---

* Names were often spelled different ways in reports. I have adopted the French spelling of "Stocklin."

By spring 1945, Plaut, Faison, and Rousseau had the chief function of finding the stolen art and working toward its restitution. Once they were back in their home countries, it became the national governments' task to return the loot to its rightful owners—an often arduous and thankless job, particularly when the owners had been murdered.

Yet the Monuments Men's work became increasingly embroiled with Edward Acheson's duty to his Project Safehaven remit hunting for hidden enemy assets. On June 21, Acheson disseminated a report to the Western Allies entitled *Methods of Concealing German Capital*, pertaining specifically to Switzerland. Through the legal entity of a foundation "the transfer by a single person of legal identity to an association of individuals (fondation)" was permitted. The *fondation* had the right to manage *all* property, "and one single individual can have the right to execute all administrative acts on its behalf."[12] What Acheson's report does not state was that the *fondation* also created preferential tax status and was impossible to penetrate. This was the formula used both in Switzerland and in Germany after the war to protect looted art.

⁂

Throughout 1945, OSS Safehaven reports flooded the desks of the Macmillan Committee in London and the Roberts Commission in Washington, DC, regarding looted art in Argentina, Tunisia, Sweden, and Switzerland. Breughel and Rembrandt paintings were discovered in neutral Sweden amid myriad caches of other priceless artworks, gold, and cash.[13]

Plaut and Rousseau were more attuned, however, to "straw men" who were happy to act as a front for the German collectors and dealers hiding their booty in Switzerland.[14] These men would operate the vaults, bank accounts, *fondations*, or other means of investment on behalf of their German clients for a hefty monthly fee. It was this route that found personal favor with Hildebrand Gurlitt among others.

Simultaneously, that October, the French and British were closing in on Hugo Engel, one of Gurlitt's main negotiators in Paris. Engel had been reported as having sold five paintings to Karl Haberstock for FF 180,000 and several drawings to Maria Dietrich for FF 15,000 each. Other transactions were said to have occurred with a dealer called Kuetgens, who had sidelined a painting bound for the museum at Aix-la-Chapelle (Aachen).

Engel had also sold a Tiepolo to the Würzburg Museum through the dealer Moebuis for FF 30,000.[15] The investigation was ongoing, and the French officers would inform Cooper as soon as they had the names of other dealers with whom Engel worked.*

Plaut and Rousseau filed their report on looted art in Switzerland on December 9, 1945, based on their investigations between November 20 and the date of filing. Douglas Cooper was instrumental in helping them with their inquiries by introducing the pair to a certain Dr. Vodo of the Ministry of the Interior, who pledged to investigate the Fischer Gallery imports from France and Germany. Additionally, Plaut interviewed Oswald Rieckmann, who had been the chief of courier services at the German legation in Bern during the war. Rieckmann had delivered the diplomatic bags containing looted art to Göring's agent Hofer on arrival in Bern. Hofer would then pass on the art to Wendland and Fischer in Lucerne for sale or exchange.[16]

Plaut summoned Wendland, a German national, to the American embassy in Bern and made Wendland's precarious position abundantly clear—in particular that he could become the scapegoat for those art dealers holding Swiss passports. Wendland cooperated to the extent of providing Plaut with an introduction to Theodor Fischer and his two sons.

On meeting Fischer, Plaut felt that while no interrogation per se could take place, the outcome was "salutary." Fischer freely showed Plaut the confidential Allied report *Looted Works of Art in Switzerland*, dated October 1945, which the Americans and British had given in confidence to the Swiss government for action. It had been freely passed on to Fischer by a Mr. de Rahm of the Swiss Federal Political Department, Fischer said, who had proven most sympathetic to Fischer's current difficulties.[17]

Then the ax fell. Nine days after Plaut filed his report, he received a very cordial yet unwelcomed letter from Acheson. "Dear Jimmy," Acheson began, "the purpose of these lines is to bring you up to date concerning our recent activities. In view of the fact that it was agreed essentially in Washington to terminate the project in the first months of 1946, we have concentrated since mid-October on two principal objectives."

Was Acheson referring to Project Safehaven? Or was he specifically calling an end to the efforts of the Art Looting Investigation Unit (ALIU),

---

* Engel would buy his freedom in France by acting for the security services after the war.

which he now headed? As the letter continued, Plaut was left in no doubt. It was the latter. He had a month to complete all outstanding investigations in Europe and prepare material "for transmission, on termination of the project, to whatever agency is designated to carry on this work. This material will consist chiefly of a Primer of personalities with whom the project has been concerned."[18]

Faison's CIR no. 4 was due for release just before Christmas. This letter ordered CIR no. 3 to be incorporated into the "Primer" of personalities. Acheson acknowledged that the ALIU's work was far from finished, and that there were "pressing investigations which we will not even be able to touch, and it is going to be a real struggle to wind up satisfactorily those now in progress. The essential point is," Acheson lamented, "that the problem as a whole cannot possibly be unravelled [sic] fully in less than six months to a year. . . . There are strong grounds for our believing that the State Department has taken a receptive attitude toward the continuation of this work."[19]

What made Acheson think that there were "strong grounds" for believing that the ALIU's work would be allowed to continue? Could he have had a conversation with his brother, Dean, the assistant secretary of state for economic affairs, on the subject? Effectively, Plaut and the other American Monuments Men who remained in Europe were stood down from opening any further investigations. Continued follow-up of those files which had been opened would soon fall to others in the Office of the Military Government of the United States (OMGUS).

Edward Acheson, despite his lofty position within the OSS, hadn't the foresight to realize that the death of Roosevelt in April 1945 and the main crimes-against-humanity trials under way in Nuremberg had deadened the appetite for vengeance against mere racketeers like Gurlitt in the new Truman administration. Genocide and slave labor were the administration's main targets, with the twelve subsequent Nuremberg trials dragging on through October 1948. Only the Flick Trial (April–December 1947), the IG Farben Trial (August 1947–July 1948), the Krupp Trial (December 1947–July 1948), and the Ministries Trial (January 1948–April 1949) had the possibility of revealing Gurlitt's shady activities.[20] Gurlitt should have felt threatened, even though none of the art-historian mobsters had been put on trial. He had no way of knowing that the Truman administration did not wish to understand that art theft and genocide were intrinsically linked.

The ALIU was wound up in 1946—as was Project Safehaven. The many thousands of looted artworks in the American zone fell under the jurisdiction of the individual collecting point officers of the Monuments, Fine Arts, and Archives division of OMGUS. Faison's and Plaut's hopes of bringing the Sonderauftrag Linz into the limelight of an international war-crimes trial had been worn away to dust.

∽

At the same time as Plaut was reading Acheson's letter, Martin Bormann's wife, Gerda, had been found at the small village of Wolkenstein in the South Tyrol. It was only twenty-odd kilometers from General Karl Wolff's lair at Bolzano.* When she was arrested, the children whom her husband had kidnapped were, thankfully, returned to their parents, and her own children taken into care. During her interrogation, it was apparent that Gerda was extremely ill. She was taken to hospital after Christmas and diagnosed with terminal cancer. She died in April 1946 without referring to her husband's whereabouts or, indeed, making her husband's wishes clear regarding his art collection. This was extremely significant to the outcome of the Gurlitt investigation, as well as to Gurlitt's personal outlook for the future.

Separately, the nasty chief murderous looter of Austria, Poland, Holland, and Belgium, Kajetan Mühlmann, claimed that Bormann was uninterested in art. However, Gurlitt and others had sold art to him, and Bormann's collection was brought to safety at Altaussee before it was secreted in Switzerland. Bormann had approved Gurlitt's movements in the closing days of the war over any objections of Dr. Lammers, head of the Reich Chancellery. Most significantly, by virtue of the will Hitler signed in the bunker the day before his death, Bormann had total control over the entire Hitler collection, including that of Linz, on behalf of the Party.

---

* General Karl Wolff (SS head in Italy and the Tyrol) had instigated discussions with Allen Dulles in Bern for the surrender of the men of the SS under his control. This incident prompted what some call the first incident of the Cold War, called Operation Sunrise.

⁓

Despite the decision to disband the ALIU, 1946 brought new demands on Gurlitt to bear out his claims to innocence. The Culture Property Adviser's Office, a subsection of the US High Commissioner's Office in Germany, wanted him to confirm people with whom he'd conducted business, and who would be happy to put their own reputations on the line with regard to Gurlitt's character. The problem for Gurlitt was who to choose?

The Nuremberg trials were daily headlines until October that year. Like the rest of the world, Gurlitt claimed revulsion at the barbarism of the Third Reich. Moreover, it came as no surprise when Bormann was sentenced to death in absentia. Göring had famously committed suicide the day before he was to be hanged, and Gurlitt's friend Albert Speer—the architect who had become the minister for armaments and war production—had been sentenced to twenty years in Spandau Prison. Arrangements regarding Speer's collection in Switzerland would need to be made.

Whatever remained of Hitler's Reich was now run by the Allies, and Germany would become a divided nation for the next forty-five years. Relations between the Soviet Union and the British, French, and American zones were increasingly icy, too.[21] Western Allied military legislation overrode German laws—except, seemingly, the Nazi law of May 31, 1938, enacted retrospectively, regarding "the confiscation of products of degenerate art" by the Third Reich. Perhaps the Americans, the British, and the French believed that this law would allow them to legally confiscate whatever suspected looted art they found? Or, equally possible, perhaps the Allies simply believed that whatever legal structure existed before was null and void. It was a decision that would have a bearing on Gurlitt's son, Cornelius.

Gurlitt had been unaware until his house arrest that the Allies, including the Soviet Union, had signed the London Declaration on January 5, 1943, specifying that they would no longer recognize the transfer of property and valuables which had taken place in the occupied territories of the Third Reich, even if they seemed legal.[22] Gurlitt became anxious when he was advised that he needed to provide references before his case could be settled. He had the wit to recognize that he had been firmly placed within the denazification process for lesser criminals, and knew the danger that the choice of the "wrong" references represented. As each day brought new threats of war-crimes trials, and as Allied Control Council directives cascaded through the German legal system, Gurlitt became frozen with indecision regarding the people he should ask to stand up for him. He had every reason to be concerned, though he had no real insight to the fact that denazification of Germany depended heavily on former Nazis vouching for those who served them.

✑

Then, on October 15, 1946, Captain Jean Vlug, the Dutch Monuments Man associated with Faison, Plaut, and Rousseau, delivered a report to London Station. It seemed that Vlug didn't trust his report to be filed through normal channels, because he insisted that Faison's copy be hand-delivered to him personally. The report was a stunning piece of work detailing operations of Dienststelle Mühlmann in the Netherlands, Belgium, and France, with nearly 150 pages itemizing stolen property and where to find it.[23]

Like the ERR in France, the Dienststelle Mühlmann was a highly organized and ruthless art-looting operation, specializing in the removal of art objects from the Feindvermögen (Enemy Property Control). Various German art historians and experts performed triage operations, pooling their booty for sale in Germany to Hitler, Göring, Baldur von Schirach, Schirach's father-in-law and Hitler's photographer Heinrich Hoffmann, Fritz Todt, General Karl Wolff, Governor-General of Poland Hans Frank, General Kaltenbrunner, and Reichskommissar Seyss-Inquart.[24]

A letter from Hans Posse to Martin Bormann dated June 10, 1940, greedily noted, "Dr. Mühlmann, who in his capacity as special delegate for the safeguarding of art and cultural goods, has just returned from Holland and notified me to-day by telephone from Berlin that there is at present a particularly favorable opportunity to purchase valuable works of art from Dutch art-dealers and private property in German currency."[25]

The report also highlighted Erhard Goepel as working directly for Seyss-Inquart's adjutant, Schmidt. The vile and mendacious Kajetan Mühlmann was said to frequently visit Behr and Lohse in Paris. Mühlmann's equally ghastly half brother, Joseph, headed up the Paris operations of the

Dienststelle, and was often seen in the company of Gurlitt's cohorts Goe-pel, Gustav Rochlitz, and Hugo Engel. Similarly, Mühlmann sent several artworks to Herbst at the Dorotheum in Vienna. Vlug concluded that the activities of the Dienststelle Mühlmann constituted a war-crimes case.[26] Of course, Gurlitt was in the thick of this network.

It was Vlug who established that a number of French artworks pillaged from Paris were at Altaussee and Salzburg.[27] The Vlug report should have set alarm bells ringing with regard to Gurlitt, as Salzburg was another of his hideaways. Still, by the time it was received, the ALIU was disbanded, and winning the peace was deemed more important than an endless continuation of Nazi war-crimes trials.

⁂

Amazingly, Gurlitt engineered the release of some of his sequestered art-work after he made a final statement under oath regarding the buying and selling of art during the war. Of course, the fact that he declared that much of his collection had been *verbrannt* (burned) in the bombings of Hamburg and Dresden is now known to be utter fiction. Somehow he had made Edwin Rae, the chief of the Monuments, Fine Arts, and Archives section in Munich, believe that four of his paintings in fact belonged to his cousin Brigitta. These were released for her collection on November 7, 1946.[28] By the time Brigitta took possession, Gurlitt's antique furniture and tapes-tries had been added to the list of valuables to take away.

Toward the end of 1946, Gurlitt's references willing to attest to his good character were asked to respond to his pleas. Those whom he already knew to be safe—like Max Beckmann and several museum directors who had cleared the denazification processing—were among the fourteen names given. The best one was the lawyer Walter Clemens, in Hamburg. Maya Gotthelf, his former secretary in Dresden, who was half Jewish, made a fine case for his kindness to Jews. Yet Gurlitt knew, on reflection, that it would look odd if he didn't include the various museum directors for whom he bought art. So, he expanded his list to the museum directors at Kassel, Chemnitz, Karlsruhe, Cologne, and Zwickau. It was no accident that he omitted the Folkwang in Essen.

Naturally, Max Beckmann felt obliged to write on Gurlitt's behalf, since Gurlitt had shown and sold some of Beckmann's paintings after he'd been

forbidden to paint under the *Malverbot*. Even Gurlitt's pastor at Saint Peter's Church in Hamburg was asked to give a glowing report.[29] Still, it
rankled with Gurlitt that he was alleged to be a Nazi. In his mind, he was
an "art historian" and the Nazis took advantage of his situation. It was a
story he had been telling himself and his children for so long that it had
become the truth.

∽

Understandably, Voss's statement made to Faison at Altaussee in 1945 had
not implicated Gurlitt. On the contrary, Voss claimed that Gurlitt wanted
to save the art belonging to Voss's Wiesbaden museum when he fled to
Aschbach.[30] While Faison's original recommendation was that Voss be held
over for trial as a war criminal, he also recommended that Voss be put to
work with the art inventory at Munich—hardly a position for a man who
was not to be trusted.[31]

The general feeling between the detainee Gurlitt and his jailers was that
Gurlitt should be released from house arrest before Christmas; however,
many of his references arrived only in January. Yet when January came and
went without his freedom granted, Gurlitt decided on a bold action. Expecting he would be released in 1946, Gurlitt's minders agreed to allow him
to apply for work. If the paperwork came through, once a job offer was made
and accepted, his house arrest would be at an end. Still, Gurlitt also knew
it would take more than a mere job to regain his sequestered collection.
He'd need to prove that it hadn't been looted.

Then Gurlitt had a brainstorm. He decided to write to Rose Valland,
who as Captain Valland and French Monuments Woman was instrumental
in the return to France of thousands of works of looted art. His letter dated
February 10, 1947, not only showed his fears of imprisonment as a Nazi but
also requested that Valland provide him with a reference for a job in the
Rhineland. Apparently, they had met and spoken at some length during
one of Gurlitt's many interrogations at the Munich Collecting Point.

"As you know, I was left bereft of my position as the director of the
Hamburg Kunstverein when Hitler took power in 1933, particularly as I
championed degenerate art," Gurlitt began in poor French. "I have recently
been asked to apply as a candidate for the directorship of the Museum of
Krefeld in the Rhineland, an industrial town which was utterly annihilated

in the war. Thus, at last I will have the possibility to resume my old career as a museum director, which I was forced to leave since I was forbidden work as a lecturer or writer."[32] Since Krefeld was in the French zone, he hoped she would write him a fulsome reference.

Of course, work as a writer had not been forbidden to him and he had entered the trade of art dealer long before he went to Hamburg with the backing of Kurt Kirchbach. Still, memories tend to play nasty tricks with the truth.

Unctuously, desperately, Gurlitt spun his hard luck story to Valland. "You would be in a position to help a faithful friend of France and a true enemy of the Nazi regime. I have always intervened by word and deed for French art." He rambled on about how he loved Paris, how he admired French art. His plea to Valland included statements like "it is not without reason that my sister lived in Paris as a painter and artist" and similar pro-French irrelevancies about Wilibald's career and how "he's recently been asked to go to Bern" to work "in close cooperation with his French colleagues." Finally, Gurlitt delivered his pièce de résistance: "I am the son of Cornelius Gurlitt who wrote the first book in German about French baroque architecture and who edited several texts on French art."[33]

Valland had heard it all before. The soft strains of Gurlitt's violins playing a Hebraic theme continued: "All of us were attacked and hunted down during the period of the Third Reich and it is only through incomprehensible circumstances that I was able to save myself in France as an art dealer. In this manner I was able to avoid forced labor in the war industries or to be incorporated into the feared battalions of slave laborers in the Organization Todt. . . . I only want to be remembered for this [saving the art]."[34]

It is easy to understand why Rose Valland refused to reply, and why the job at Krefeld never came through. So, the search for gainful employment continued throughout 1947.

By this point, his father figure Kirchbach had resettled in Düsseldorf. As an archcapitalist and a man who had kept his hands clean of genocide during the war, Kirchbach had no intention of returning home to a bombed-out Dresden or his Soviet-held Coswig factory to live under a socialist regime. Fortunately, in the main through Gurlitt, Kirchbach had been able to bring his vast collection to safety in Basel before the war's end. The avaricious dealers Christoph Bernoulli and Alex Vömel, the "heir" to Flechtheim's business, naturally took a special interest in Kirchbach as a new arrival in Düsseldorf with a substantial art collection. These men, so crucial to the Buchholz escape route into Switzerland which then fed art through to Valentin in New York and South America, would soon be obliged, quite reluctantly, to include Gurlitt in their future thinking.

By 1947, Kirchbach made sufficient headway in revived industrialist circles to arrange Gurlitt's appointment as director of the Westphalian Kunstverein. It would be like old times. Gurlitt was delighted. Alex Vömel, the confirmed Nazi who never faced denazification queries, had reigned supreme in the industrial city for quite long enough. Vömel's mentor, Karl Buchholz, had escaped scottfree to Madrid, spared the ignominy of house arrest or questioning by lawyers or Monuments Men or Women. Unknown to Gurlitt or, indeed, Buchholz himself, the tall, distinguished-looking art dealer with his readily recognizable shock of gray hair, was seen by a French spy disembarking Göring's private plane in Madrid with enough art to begin yet another German bookshop in the Spanish capital. The French espionage report went on to state that Buchholz lived up the road from his proposed commercial premises, albeit without declaring himself to the authorities.[35] In Madrid, Buchholz was blessed with a significant former-Nazi network, including Göring's old school chum Alois Miedl, the Aryan owner of Jacques Goudstikker's fabulous art business in Amsterdam. Miedl was, of course, on the list of art dealers most wanted by the Dutch.

∽

Just as Gurlitt hoped to pack his bags, a supplementary police report arrived on the desk of the OMGUS. It was damning:

> Gurlitt had confessed relationships with Party [NSDAP] offices and from the time of the domination of the Third Reich derived tremendous benefit. Irrespective of his fanciful legal incapacity, he had throughout the state of emergency preyed on the Jews and had sophisticated dealings with men belonging to the Espionage and Abwehr

ministries. In the wider interest, he deserves further detention while investigations are underway relating to his acquisition practices of art abroad, notably in France.[36]

Ingeborg Hertmann, Gurlitt's Hamburg assistant, had told all she knew about his dealings until the end of 1942. However, the revelation had come too late. There would be no more trials for crimes against humanity. No new investigations. The only work that would be carried out now was that of restitution.

Gurlitt had been saved by heading to the American zone. The American OSS was the first organization to decide to cease operations with the intent of prosecution for vandalism against national patrimonies. Perhaps it was because of the growing hostility between the Soviets and the Western Allies, already engaged in the Cold War. Perhaps not. At the end of the day, by the time Gurlitt was released from his Aschbach aerie, the Iron Curtain had descended upon what was now called the German Democratic Republic (DDR). Access to any art or paperwork in the east of the country was out of the question.

During his captivity, it seems that Gurlitt had become quite chummy with the Monuments Men Breitenbach and Kormendi looking after him. Nothing had been *proven* against him, and so when he requested to move to the British zone for employment at the Düsseldorf Kunstverein, the request was granted. Kormendi made the handwritten notation on Gurlitt's file on March 22, 1948, that Gurlitt planned to move there.

Nonetheless, his collection was still held hostage, pending potential claims by France. On June 18, 1948, Gurlitt signed another oath—Declaration Number 01 345—which may have made his heart flutter: "One of the Art Officers of the Collecting Point Munich, whom I met last week in Munich, told me of his intention to visit me at Aschbach in a few days concerning this matter after his return from a trip to the former occupied areas in order to supply me with records."[37]

Still, Gurlitt knew where his *real* records were—and that they were safe. After three long years, he was a free man at last.

29

DÜSSELDORF

Then thieves and robbers range abroad unseen.
—WILLIAM SHAKESPEARE, *Richard II*

THE GURLITTS' DÜSSELDORF HOME AT ROTTERDAMER STRASSE 35 was understated and elegant. The children had been sent to board at their Steiner/Waldorf school near Stuttgart from 1945, thanks to efforts of their friend Karl Ballmer, a Swiss artist. Ballmer, along with his partner and collector Edith van Cleef, had met the Gurlitts in Hamburg, but the pair returned to Switzerland in 1938 after the Anschluss. Ballmer had made an easy convert of the Gurlitts to anthroposophy, the slightly perplexing philosophy Rudolf Steiner first put into practice forty years earlier. The philosophy, which advances the theory of an intellectually comprehensible spiritual world that is accessible through direct experience and inner development, spawned a gentler form of education in the postwar period.[1]

Meanwhile, the Gurlitt collection was still held hostage. Another inventory, in 1948–49, and more months of questioning still brought the property-control officers of the Collecting Point no closer to discovering the provenance of much of Gurlitt's art. They, like Plaut before them, knew that Gurlitt was covering something up, but couldn't *prove* it. Claims by the French had been either fulfilled or dismissed, except for two artworks. Perhaps they were overwhelmed by more than seven million art claims from survivors, collectors, and museums. Or maybe Gurlitt had simply proved too cunning. It would be more than five long years before Hildebrand Gurlitt would see much of his collection—but by then no one feared further punishment against those who had served Hitler's deadly whims.

∞

Düsseldorf provided the family with a new life, uncannily similar to the one at the Kunstverein in Hamburg. Old friendships were renewed, like the highly competitive one with Vömel, who had proudly served in the SA during the war.[2] Equally, new relationships were made. Young artists were sought out to exhibit.

Family and friends, too, had new lives. Wilibald was once more a university lecturer. Wolfgang had barely suffered—having agreed to lend his "entire collection" to the city of Linz in exchange for opening a gallery at the museum.[3] Surprisingly, Hermann Voss backed up Wolfgang's statement that he had never sold anything to Linz, demonstrating either a severe lapse of memory or, more likely, an unwillingness to point the finger.[4]

Manfred Gurlitt, Wolfgang's younger brother, had immigrated to Japan in 1939, working there as a conductor and composer. He remained there for the rest of his life. Dresden, Hitler, and the frenzied days at the end of the war were barely memories. Although he headed the "criminal organization" of Sonderauftrag Linz, Hermann Voss was set free in 1945. He lived in Munich writing about art, but would never again be a museum curator. Gurlitt's fellow dealers Böhmer and Möller met different ends. Böhmer committed suicide as the Soviets approached Güstrow. Möller protected his collection and opened a gallery in Cologne in 1949. Theo Hermsen, on the sole testimony of Gurlitt, was presumed dead.

∞

Gurlitt received the first direct shipment of his collection in 1950.[5] A total of eighty-one paintings and thirty-seven drawings were returned to him. Among the haul were Max Beckmann's *The Lion Tamer,* Max Liebermann's *Two Riders on the Beach* and *Wagon on the Dunes,* and a self-portrait by Otto Dix. Withheld from the first shipment were two paintings—Chagall's

Allegorical Scene (sometimes called *Mythological Scene*) and Picasso's *Woman with Two Noses*—since both were still pending further investigation subject to a French counterclaim. Worse, three artworks had gone missing, the Rodin drawing of Atlas among them.

With Bormann's disappearance unresolved, much of his capital tied up in looted art, and an overpowering desire to get "back into the game," Gurlitt lost patience. Finally, he turned to his friendly anthroposophist Karl Ballmer, the Swiss artist, writer, and publisher, to help him on the tricky matter concerning the provenance of his Chagall and Picasso. Ballmer was only too happy to comply, and immediately penned a letter attesting to his having given both to Gurlitt. On January 9, 1951, William G. Daniels, from the US Office of Economic Affairs, Property Division, wrote to Gurlitt that he accepted Ballmer's statement and that the two paintings would be shipped to him shortly.

Despite the successful claim of three other artworks by the French Monuments Men and Women against Gurlitt, they appear to have not been consulted in the matter. That Gurlitt had begun his story about the two paintings with the yarn that Chagall had given the painting to his sister, just as Picasso had given him the *Woman with Two Noses*, did not seem to matter either. No further comments or questions were noted in the file.

⁂

The past would be the past. It was time to relaunch his life and show the world he was unsinkable. It was time for a great exhibition; time to bring out his Beckmann paintings—along with those once owned by others. Only then could he begin to establish a proper provenance for them. Did it matter that he hadn't heard from the likes of Bormann, Speer, or others? Life had moved on.

Gurlitt decided to put on a Max Beckmann exhibition. While he hadn't written to Beckmann during the war, he now renewed contact with the aging artist, advising him of his future plans. He also thanked Beckmann for his adequate—if stiffly worded—character reference. Of course Beckmann would be his guest of honor, Gurlitt concluded. Beckmann declined, sending his son Peter as his representative instead.

The exhibition was a tremendous success. Yet from Peter's letters to his

father, it is obvious that neither one liked Gurlitt. Similarly, both Beckmanns seemed genuinely fond of Munich art dealer Günther Franke.
Unlike Gurlitt, Franke had been in close contact with Beckmann during
his exile in Holland. Beckmann's son was simply appalled by the way
Gurlitt swanned around the room unctuously greeting people. "Gurlitt
was overly pleasant, brimming over with enthusiasm about how amazing I was for having transported your pictures . . . like the Sphinx."[6] By
this, Beckmann implied that Gurlitt wanted to know his secret in bringing
art across borders without paying duty.

Notwithstanding his distaste for Gurlitt's behavior, Peter Beckmann
admitted that it was a "heavenly exhibition." Their friend Franke showed
extreme forbearance and did not complain, even though twenty-seven of
the paintings on show were his. At some point, Franke collared Beckmann,
mischievously dreaming up another, bigger, brighter exhibition, in Ven-
ice, for his twenty-seven paintings, which would put Gurlitt's show to
shame. "That soothes him obviously over this ghoul of a sanctimonious
Gurlitt treading on him with his unsettling monopoly on everything,"
Peter wrote indulgently.[7]

∾

During the next few years, Nazis convicted of crimes against humanity
began to trickle out of German prisons. Karl Rasche, an SS officer and
former spokesman of Dresdner Bank, was released from Landsberg in
August 1950. He died the following year on a commuter train in Basel,
aged fifty-nine. Emil Puhl, the economist well known to Gurlitt as
Schacht's successor and the man responsible for nonmonetary gold from
concentration-camp victims, was released in 1951.[8] He settled back in
Hamburg. Lutz von Krosigk, finance minister and the only minister to
serve during the whole of the Third Reich, was granted an amnesty in 1951.
Settling in Essen, he worked as an author and publicist after the war. His
boss, the icy-eyed Hans-Heinrich Lammers, head of the Reich Chancellery,
whom Hitler had ordered to be shot for his support of Göring, had become
a witness for the prosecution and was released in 1952. Lammers would
make Düsseldorf his new home.

As the 1950s progressed, so did the amnesties, and the senselessness of denazification. Only Hess, Speer, and Baldur von Schirach remained incarcerated.* Time marched on, and by 1954 Gurlitt was once again in the swing of things. He traveled to Brazil on business and certainly kept in touch with Buchholz, who had recently emigrated to Colombia.

His children were grown, and while Cornelius was extremely bright, he had not attained the full potential Hildebrand had expected. Was his disappointment redolent of his own father's toward him? In any event, Cornelius had no university degree, nor was he regularly employed. Aged twenty-one, Cornelius seemed unable to make friends easily. Yet he was a very talented painter, with many of the portraits of his beloved sister demonstrating his abilities to great effect.[9] Cornelius's extreme shyness was most likely a great frustration for Hildebrand, who saw himself as a man who could easily charm people. Still, Cornelius was his son, and Hildebrand and Helene had resolved that he would be the main heir to their fortune and custodian of their collection. Cornelius would slowly be taken into the world of art dealing—if it could possibly be achieved. There would be plenty of time in the years to come to groom him to carry out this crucial task.

⁂

The following year, Gurlitt became a major lender to a groundbreaking exhibition entitled *German Watercolors, Drawings and Prints 1905–1955, A Mid-Century Review,* which toured the United States. It was sponsored by the Federal Republic of Germany and circulated by the American Federation of the Arts. "Among the many lenders whose names are listed separately, and who all merit our sincerest thanks," Dr. Leonie Reygers, director of Museum an Ostwall, Dortmund, wrote, "Dr. H. Gurlitt, Director of the Art Association for the Rhineland and Westphalia is the major contributor to the exhibition which, owing to his generosity could be planned on an impressive scale."[10]

There were 112 pictures in all, with Gurlitt contributing twenty-two works from his "personal collection."[11] Among them were *The Lion Tamer*

---

* Karl Wolff was rearrested in 1962 when the trial of Adolf Eichmann presented evidence that he was responsible for the deportation of Italian Jews to concentration camps. In 1964, he was found guilty of the deportation of Jews to Treblinka and Auschwitz and the massacre of Italian partisans. He was released in 1969.

and *Zandvoort* by Max Beckmann. These would find their way onto the Lost Art Database in 2013.[12]

⌇

If Peter Beckmann's and Günther Franke's impressions of Gurlitt were widely shared in the art community, he must have been an insufferable man with whom to conduct business. Privately, it is easy to suppose that Alex Vömel may have not have been particularly welcoming to Gurlitt either. After all, it was a revitalized Gurlitt who was casually laundering his looted art in the open market. Certainly Erhard Goepel must have felt aggrieved that he was unable to obtain a position in a museum or art association while Gurlitt had succeeded.[13] Given the secrecy and jealousies of the art world, it is a highly plausible supposition.

Still, there would have been other people trickling back into the community in the 1950s who had reason to deeply resent Gurlitt's complete rehabilitation in the Federal Republic of Germany. Lammers in Düsseldorf, Krosigk in Essen, and Puhl in Hamburg are just three examples. Whether Bormann was still alive to wield a Nazi knife against Gurlitt is a matter of pure conjecture. Then there was Carl Neumann, who had bought the sensational fake Cézanne acquired by Gurlitt at the Viau auction, too.[14] Ferdinand Möller had died that January, Karl Haberstock in August. His victims numbered in the hundreds, his true friends were only his wife and brother. In his inexorable rise, Gurlitt had trod on many toes.

When Hildebrand Gurlitt was driving along the autobahn near Düsseldorf on the evening of November 9, 1956—that very special day in the Nazi calendar—he plowed into the back of a truck. His brakes had "failed." Gurlitt was killed instantly. His family was notified of the accident and Helene was called upon to identify the body. Did she ever once doubt its nature? Had she seen the irony of failing brakes and Gurlitt's thirty-year relationship with the king of brake manufacture in Germany, Kirchbach? Had she linked it to her husband's enemies or the date? Despite my asking for the police report of the accident, the authorities have not responded to my queries.[15]

⌇

Although Hildebrand Gurlitt had undoubtedly looted millions in plundered art throughout the war, he hadn't finished the work of educating his wife, his son, or his daughter in how to convert the hidden assets into cash. The man who wanted to be remembered for the false image of "saving degenerate art" would have his epitaph eventually rewritten by his untimely death.

30

AFTERMATH AND MUNICH

> If his lips are silent . . . betrayal oozes out of his every pore.
>
> —SIGMUND FREUD

LONG BEFORE HELENE GURLITT MOVED TO MUNICH, IN 1961, SHE had undertaken the laundering of her husband's booty. In the twelve years between Hildebrand's death and her own, she continued to share her version of the truth about the war years with her children—a version that would paint their father in the best possible light. When Hildebrand died, the "children," Cornelius and Benita, were twenty-three and twenty-one, respectively.

It was, however, nothing more than the familiar children's fairy tale "Hildebrand the Superhero of the Art World," which had been spun for them for as long as they could recall. The dizzying life they'd led throughout the war with a mostly absentee father had been the stuff of legend. The characterization of a latter-day elusive Scarlet Pimpernel "They seek him here, they seek him there, they seek him everywhere" could have applied to Hildebrand as he rattled through Europe amassing endangered art from the forces of evil. His escapades in the Great War were embellished, too, enhancing the fable.

Surrounded by great men of the art establishment in Germany in those heady days of the Third Reich, Cornelius, as son and heir, would have had no reason to question his father's crucial role in saving Europe's art from the horrid Nazis. His father had been privately lavish with his criticism of the regime. Even the term "house arrest" became something of a moving feast in the children's eyes while Hildebrand "helped the Allies with their inquiries," as they say in police dramas. Gurlitt and his wife were determined to keep the children as shielded as possible from the whole story, as any good parent would hope to do. The only problem with the myth was that it took over their lives, skewed reality, and made them all prisoners to the deep secret of their fabulous ill-gotten wealth.

∞

It would have been unlike Hildebrand Gurlitt if he had not thought up a plan to launder the looted art. He would also have been remiss if he hadn't noticed any ill will within the surviving Nazi or art communities. His oft-repeated argument that he had been made a victim of the regime as a *Mischling* had been recited so often that he believed it, and expected others to do the same. That men like Lammers had spent five years in prison would have been offset in Gurlitt's mind by his own term of three years under house arrest and the need to split up his family and send the children to the Steiner/Waldorf Odenwaldschule.[1]

Yet, with Hildebrand's sudden death, his work was left unfinished. Helene did not have the credibility within the art world to pull off his amazing feats of magic by slipping in a looted painting here, or a plundered drawing there. Nor was she capable of re-creating provenances that were credible. She could not insert art into exhibitions that would add to their provenance and value, as her husband had done. Instead, she was left with the pure and simple task of laundering the art as and when her cash reserves began to dwindle. It was a method she would pass on to Cornelius and Benita.

Periodically, Helene would sell a painting—effectively testing the market, seeing if any alarm bells sounded. The cash would be held in Switzerland, where the proceeds remained a secret—undeclared or underdeclared on her German income tax. Whether it was in a bank account or a safe deposit box was immaterial. The Swiss secrecy laws in those days were impenetrable for any reason whatsoever.[2]

Such was the case with Max Beckmann's *Bar, Brun* when it was first seen publicly in the Stuttgart gallery of Roman Norbert Ketterer in 1959. It had, however, previously appeared on the inventory list made at the Wiesbaden Collecting Point as *In the Bar* and it was returned to Gurlitt in 1950.[3] During his interrogations, Gurlitt had declared that the painting had been a gift from Beckmann and that he had "visited" Beckmann along with Erhard Goepel on September 13–14, 1944.[4]

This was Gurlitt's "Pimpernel Period," when he was desperately searching for the remainders of art left on the fringes of the crumbling Third Reich. Would Beckmann have "gifted" this to him when everyone in Holland was aware that freedom was around the corner? Was it a "thank you for your help," and if it was, was it for Goepel or Gurlitt or both? It is difficult to imagine, given Beckmann's later attitude, that the painting had been intended for Gurlitt.

Ketterer put the painting up for auction in 1960. It did not sell, according to the 1976 catalogue raisonné of Beckmann's work.[5] Nor did it sell during subsequent auctions in Helene Gurlitt's lifetime.

It is a rather mysterious painting, *Bar, Brun*. Beckmann painted it during his exile in Amsterdam. Although he had been outlawed by the Germans, he became part of a thriving expatriate community of Germans— even Jewish Germans of the museum world—living and working in the city under the Third Reich.* It was also an extremely prolific period for Beckmann, with many portraits painted of the people he met. Intriguingly, during this book's research some experts expressed a belief that these portraits represented "fellow members" of the Dutch resistance, while others—who should be equally in the know—claim that the portraits were of Dutch collaborators. Either story gives rise to further questions and interest in the painting.

Among the living, Helene and Goepel alone might have known the truth behind the painting's provenance. Helene must have despaired when it didn't sell in 1960 or at subsequent auctions. The question is, why was Helene in need of capital at this time? Had she run out of cash? Had the political climate regarding looted and modern art changed?

Other mysteries surround the move to Munich. In Cornelius Gurlitt's 2013 interview with *Der Spiegel*, he stated that he lived with his mother in the hundred-meter^2 (1,076-square-foot) apartment. Was he confused or

---

* Max J. Friedlander, former director of the Nationalgalerie in Berlin, being the main example.

dissembling? Since his Salzburg home had not as yet been discovered by investigators, it seems more than likely that it was the latter.

Some explanations can be found in the Munich city archives. On April 13, 1961, Helene moved from the Rotterdamer Strasse home in Düsseldorf to the now notorious fifth-floor flat at Artur-Kutscher-Platz, number 1, in Munich's Schwabing district. When she moved, she registered with the city authorities in accordance with the law. On the registration form, an entry indicated that Cornelius "lives in Salzburg." Benita's address is redacted from the document.[6]

So, Helene had decided to move to Munich—why? To be closer to friends like Erhard Goepel and Hermann Voss? According to a statement made by Cornelius in *Der Spiegel*, he never understood why his mother chose to move there, other than perhaps for her love of the bohemian reputation of the Schwabing district: "She had dreamed of a Bohemian lifestyle, and of affluent people who weren't interested in other people's money." Therein is the truth. In Düsseldorf, Helene felt exposed to public scrutiny. In Munich, she could blend in.

Or had that been the story that she chose to tell her son and daughter? Kirchbach lived in Düsseldorf and had remained the surrogate father of Hildebrand until the end. Still, his feelings about Hildebrand's sudden death or how he intended to support Helene from 1956 remain cloaked in forgotten memories. By the time Hildebrand had been released from his delightful idyll in Aschbach, Kirchbach had grown his business to DM 1 million and had 376 employees.[7] In 1950, he had two fellow shareholders and none of them had any children or heirs. Gurlitt could never run a brake-linings business, nor would he have been competent to do so. In 1953, it was a natural progression for the three aging shareholders to sell the entire business to their nearest competitor, Krupp AG.* A year later, the company was incorporated into the Krupp works in Hamburg.

From the moment Kirchbach sold his business, he split his time between Basel and Düsseldorf. The suspicion that he had sheltered his wealth in Switzerland was ever-present. Perhaps he also helped Helene once

---

* This was operated by Berthold von Bohlen und Halbach, Alfried Krupp's brother. Alfried had stood trial at Nuremberg for slave labor of Jews, some of them children, and was convicted. He was released in 1952.

Hildebrand had died, perhaps not.[8] Nevertheless, Kirchbach's own actions might well have become a blueprint for Helene, who was learning to handle the treasure trove on the hoof.

∽

Helene had only seven years of her new life. Although Cornelius was aged twenty-eight at the time of the move, it was evident that he was a man who did as he was told. Helene made all the family decisions—for them both. Benita had by this time married Dr. Nikolaus Frässle of Kornwestheim, near Stuttgart, and it is possible that Helene described her motive for the move as being closer to her daughter.

Whatever the truth, Cornelius shied away from the public's gaze, unlike his father. He was no man of action, but rather someone who had been taught to listen to his mother and trusted her to lead him. Another mystery surrounds the Munich address: Cornelius told *Der Spiegel* that his mother had bought two apartments on Artur-Kutscher-Platz. Yet none appears to have been sold and only one remained in 2013 when Cornelius became an international phantasmagorical man of mystery.

∽

On January 31, 1968, Helene Gurlitt died in a private clinic in Munich. She was cremated five days later and buried in cemetery plot Wald NT 11.00.[9] Cornelius was alone, save for his sister and brother-in-law. He seemed at a loss for what to do next. He didn't like Munich, since it was where Nazism had begun. Yet, he felt unable to pack up and move to his home in Salzburg. He had already tried to live with his sister temporarily and failed, before coming to stay with his mother. Cornelius had become stuck in a time warp. Unable to break with Munich and his mother's apartment, he began to periodically fetch artworks from the various caches and bring them to what had become, reluctantly for him, his home. When money was needed, he would sell one of the artworks to pay his bills—in cash.

Moving artworks was an activity that echoed in his memory and reminded him of his childhood. His playmates had always been the paintings by Beckmann, Chagall, and Liebermann. When his family moved from Hamburg to Dresden, they hung on the walls of the new home. When he graduated from secondary school in Düsseldorf, they hung once again on the family walls there.

When he was close to the paintings again, his friends, he could recall easier times when his father hung them in their new homes and showed him the backs of the paintings all bearing the "Gurlitt mark" of ownership. As a measure of protection against evil, he recalled how Hildebrand had hung the green-faced portrait by Ernst Ludwig Kirschner above Cornelius's bed—Hitler had always loathed green faces, Cornelius told *Der Spiegel*.[10]

❧

Cornelius began his retreat from reality before Helene's death. When he was questioned in 2013 about the "Munich hoard," as the 1,407 artworks found in his apartment were dubbed by the press, Cornelius admitted that he had stopped watching television when Germany's second television station—"the new station," Cornelius called it—began broadcasting in 1963. He had heard of computers and the Internet, but continued to book his hotels and taxis by post, arranged sometimes months in advance. He composed his letters on a typewriter and signed with a fountain pen, just as he had done in the 1960s.

Still, how had he remained invisible to the German government? How had he never filed a tax return, or come under other scrutiny? He had a residence in Salzburg, Austria, long before Helene's death, and had also become an Austrian citizen afterward. It is impossible to believe that the laundering operation had been a machination of his own making. He traveled exclusively between Germany, Austria, and Switzerland on an identity card, having diverged only once, as a young man, when he visited Paris with his sister.

Cornelius had no German bank accounts. He never collected a pension, declared any expenses on the German national health service, or paid property taxes in his own name. Everything that needed to be paid for in Germany was paid in cash—electricity, water, building charges. In fact, the apartment from which all the 1,407 artworks were confiscated didn't belong to him. Forty-five years after his mother's death, Cornelius Gurlitt was still living in an apartment registered in his mother's name.[11]

31

THE LION TAMER

The life of the dead is placed in the hands of the living.

—Cicero

CORNELIUS HAD ALWAYS WANTED TO PLEASE HIS FATHER. THAT'S why he studied art at the University of Cologne and attended lectures, as his father and uncle did, on philosophy and music theory. Hildebrand was trying to remake his son in his own image. Sadly for Cornelius, he was made of different stuff—perhaps better stuff, but nonetheless a disappointment to his father.

It had been obvious to both Hildebrand and Helene long before their deaths that neither Cornelius nor Benita would be in a position to take over his dealing in art with the same flair. Their son was a soft-spoken man of significant intellect, but who had equally withdrawn from society. Whether it was some form of autism or simply the knowledge that he could never fill his father's shoes, we shall never know.

Secrecy had been hardwired into Cornelius's genes. His grandfather, despite his presence in the art world, had been a very private man. His father had learned that trait at his father's knee and carried it into his secret, scheming life. Hildebrand would not leave it to chance that Cornelius—or indeed Benita—would live any other way. If they did, his reputation would be nothing more than a sham—and Hildebrand cared a great deal about his reputation and his legacy.

Cornelius's phobic protection of his "friends, the paintings" from the prying eyes of strangers was drummed into him from the earliest age to the point where he could not recall a time when the paintings hadn't been important to him. The family mantra was "Always the paintings" for his parents, and it became "Always the paintings first" for him.

Recalling his days as an eleven-year-old helping his father to pack away his "friends" from the family home in Dresden, Cornelius told *Der Spiegel*, "The family moved around a lot, always following a father who didn't have an easy time because he 'wasn't racially flawless.' But he always fought and was very clever."[1] Cornelius went on to cite the example of his father not owning his private Kunstkabinett as one of his clever ploys, not realizing that it had been common practice among outcasts in the Third Reich.

He was proud that his father hadn't complied with the law to register his art dealership in Dresden. This was hardly necessary, since Dresden was merely a convenience address that belonged to Hildebrand's mother and where he traded after having been bombed out in Hamburg. "My father was often driven out," the eighty-year-old Cornelius said, "he often fell but he always got back up on his feet again."[2] All the moving around under the auspices of a hero-like father, a famous man in Germany—a man seen by his son posing for photographs with Thomas Mann and Germany's first postwar president, Theodor Heuss—made Cornelius immensely proud. He even believed the malarkey he'd been fed that his father spoke fluent French and English, lamenting that "I only speak English, but slowly."[3] Overwhelmed, self-effacing, appreciative of beauty, and thankful to his father for his legacy, Cornelius Gurlitt was a man who thought he had always obeyed the law. He had no inkling of the mess his parents had left for him.

∽

Still, Cornelius had to live. From 1968, how to live would be best overseen by Benita and her husband. Yet it would be Cornelius who would need to do the running. While *Bar, Brun* hadn't succeeded in selling in his mother's lifetime, it had not excited any debate either. So he decided to try to sell the painting at other auctions—also without luck. Through Sotheby's in Munich, Cornelius arranged for the painting to be sent to auction at Sotheby's in London in 1980. There, too, it found no buyers.

Finally, three years later, in 1983, Marvin Fishman of Milwaukee bought *Bar, Brun* at Sotheby's auction in Munich for DM 550,000. Thirteen years after that, in 1996, the painting was sold to Robert Looker, who died in 2012 and whose heirs left the painting to the Los Angeles County Museum of Art (LACMA)—unfortunately on the same day that the *Focus* article about Cornelius scooped the world press.[4] LACMA's stalwart museum curator and the organizer of the groundbreaking 1991 *Degenerate Art* exhibition, Stephanie Barron, remained confident, however, that despite the Goepel and Gurlitt provenance, her research into the "gifted" painting had proved that it had not been looted or sold under duress.[5]

∽

It is likely that in the intervening years other paintings were sold by Cornelius, with the proceeds being kept either in cash in his Munich apartment or in Austria or at bank deposit boxes in Switzerland. Notwithstanding this, it would be the sale of *The Lion Tamer*, also by Max Beckmann, in 2011 that enabled the authorities to close in on the unsuspecting Cornelius.

∽

The Lion Tamer was on Hildebrand Gurlitt's inventory submitted to the Monuments Men in 1945 when he was placed under house arrest at Aschbach.[6] It was returned to Gurlitt in 1950, since no claim had been filed for the painting. However, the last owner of record, Alfred Flechtheim, had been branded and hounded from Germany—with friends like Buchholz, Valentin, Vömel, and Gurlitt taking chunks of his vast collection to "sell" or "hold" on his behalf. Flechtheim had become Hitler's poster boy, and worried himself into oblivion. He never sold *The Lion Tamer*. Flechtheim's nephew and heir—a tailor in London's East End—never knew it still existed and so was unable to make a claim.

∽

Life has moved on since those ad hoc days in the 1940s and 1950s when the onus was on the victims of the looting to determine when and where and how their worldly possessions had disappeared. Since the Washington Principles of 1998, publicly funded museums and galleries of all signatory countries are under an obligation to inspect their collections and make *any* potentially looted work of art from the Nazi era readily identifiable to the public.

This generally is interpreted as some sort of notice on a museum or gallery's website. They may even go the extra mile and register it on other lost-art websites such as the Art Loss Register. Yet there are more than a few problems with the system. Not only is there a proliferation of these lost-art websites, but increasingly the second and third generations of descendants of victims of the Holocaust and the Third Reich are unaware of the complete inventory of their ancestors who were murdered before the information could be passed on through wills or other documentation.

The more remote the knowledge base, the more often claimants will be unsuccessful in their claims. Finally, the Washington Principles do not cover private owners of looted art. To claim from a private owner, the claimant must—in almost all cases—sue for restitution. Notwithstanding these drawbacks, the beauty of the 1998 accord is that for the first time a statute of limitations was *theoretically* no longer a valid excuse to keep any looted artwork.[7] Paradoxically, this is also one of the reasons the agreement does not bind the current owners of the works who have bought them in good faith. In the words of the Washington Principles' architect, Stuart Eizenstat, it is an imperfect justice.

❧

Fortunately for Alfred Flechtheim's heirs, they had hired a New York lawyer, Mel Urbach, and his German partner based in Marburg, Germany, Markus Stoetzel, to help locate Flechtheim's exceptional collection. It was Stoetzel who made the breakthrough with *The Lion Tamer*.

According to the *Financial Times*, Stoetzel discovered the forthcoming sale only a few weeks prior to the auction due to take place at the Lempertz auction house in Cologne. In fact, it was to be the auction's highlight. Stoetzel, as part of his work as a lawyer recovering looted art, thumbs through auction catalogues from around the world. When he saw *The Lion Tamer* that November, he was stunned. He knew that most of the Flechtheim collection had been plundered by the Nazis and that at least twelve Beckmann pictures were still missing—including *The Lion Tamer*.[8]

By mid-November Stoetzel had written to Karl-Sax Feddersen at Lempertz to notify him that this picture had been part of the Flechtheim collection since June 1931 and that it had never been sold. In truly lawyerly fashion, Feddersen was put on notice that Stoetzel knew more about the painting's history than the auction house did. The gouache and pastel work on paper had been created during the period of exclusivity when Flechtheim and I. B. Neumann represented Beckmann and could *never* have belonged to the Gurlitt collection before January 30, 1933, as the gallery claimed in its catalogue.[9]

It took Feddersen some while to respond definitively to Stoetzel's letter, although apparently there were a number of telephone conversations. At first, Feddersen prevaricated. His client would not budge. Cornelius was never named as that client during the discussions, but it was somehow known to Stoetzel that it was Gurlitt's son or daughter who might be selling the picture. Stoetzel was forced to go into print a second time, adding the force of argument behind his initial letter that Flechtheim had been driven into penury by the middle of 1933, writing to Neumann in New York, "*Ich habe kein Geld*"—"I have no money." If he had sold the Beckmann only a few months earlier to Gurlitt, surely this would not be the case?[10]

Finally, only two days prior to the auction, Feddersen's unnamed client agreed to split the proceeds with Flechtheim's heirs. According to Stoetzel, it was proof that the Lempertz client was "willing to accept the fact that Mr Flechtheim was a persecuted Jew who had lost his collection under duress."[11] That was the victory Stoetzel sought to achieve. "In these cases, the most significant wrong to be righted," Stoetzel said, "is often the mere acknowledgment of the initial crime which always led to desperation and often to murder. We know Flechtheim was in effect murdered by the Nazis. What we seek for him and his heirs is justice."[12]

The split of the proceeds between Cornelius and the Flechtheim heirs was 60/40 in favor of the current owner. The painting sold for 720,000 euros* at the Lempertz auction on December 2, 2011, meaning that approximately 400,000 euros went to Cornelius. Feddersen was allowed to purr in public about the "wonderful picture" and how it was "one of the most beautiful pictures I have ever seen. A very, very impressive, large work."[13] Feddersen also said that his curiosity had been piqued by the famous name in the art world in Germany as the last owner of the painting and

---

* Approximately $908,000. Gurlitt's share was approximately $504,700 before auction commission.

asked if there were other artworks for sale. Apparently, Cornelius didn't answer him.

❧

The timing of the sale of *The Lion Tamer* may be significant, too. It was the first time Cornelius had gone to Lempertz, one of Germany's largest auction houses. Was he in a hurry to sell it to help pay for Benita's cancer treatment? Or was it simply part of the ongoing disposal of his father's hoard? Given that it was one of the artworks that were special to him as a boy, its sale would most likely have held a certain importance to him. It would be in character if he had decided to part with one of his dearest "friends" to help his sister—the only person with whom he felt a warm human connection. After all, Cornelius did say that he sold *The Lion Tamer* for medical expenses.

32

FEEDING FRENZY

I'm not as courageous as my father. He loved art and fought
for it.

—CORNELIUS GURLITT to *Der Spiegel*

THE BEGINNING OF THE END BEGAN ON WHAT SHOULD HAVE BEEN
a routine return trip from Switzerland. On September 22, 2010, Cornelius
was returning from Zurich to Munich on the EC 197 train. A customs official noticed the then seventy-eight-year-old avoiding his gaze, and when
he questioned Cornelius, felt he was acting suspiciously. Cornelius was
taken to the men's room and searched. Nine thousand euros in cash was
discovered. Cornelius hadn't committed any crime, since the limit for
declaring cash across borders in Europe is 10,000 euros.[1] Even so, it would
be the height of hubris to believe that Cornelius Gurlitt was not singled
out on that train.

The Zurich to Munich train is one of the prime places to find tax evaders of all nationalities. The shy and easily flustered Cornelius could not
stand up to the slightest scrutiny from a rough customs officer. His crime
was his apparent shiftiness, yet the officious official was forced to let him
go, reporting Cornelius's Munich address to his superiors since the 9,000
euros gave rise to reasonable cause of suspicion of tax evasion.

That was when the alarm bells blared. Cornelius Gurlitt, according to
all tax and income records in Germany, was a man who never existed.

Nearly two years later, on February 28, 2012, a team of perhaps as many as thirty people—customs investigators and lawyers from the Augsburg public prosecutor's office—burst into Cornelius's fifth-floor apartment by breaking the lock. The "strangers," as he called them, swarmed like angry wasps, advising him that they were government officials and were confiscating his collection.

For what seemed an eternity, but was in fact two days, Cornelius sat in his dressing gown in the corner while his "friends"—121 paintings and 1,285 drawings, watercolors, and prints—were boxed up, folded into blankets, and whisked away.[2] Even his father's papers were scooped up in the raid. He watched helplessly as his favorites were wrenched from their home. Max Liebermann's *Two Riders on the Beach*, which he had beheld for over four decades on the same wall, was taken from where it hung. Chagall's *Mythological Scene* was purloined from a locked wooden cabinet.[3] The apartment held a treasure trove of great German modern artists like Beckmann, Liebermann, and Marc, as well as Picasso and Chagall. There were also works by Fragonard, Dürer, and Impressionists Degas and Corot.

Desolate and alone in the empty apartment, Cornelius was bewildered, fulminating at the injustice. Not only were these strangers telling him that he had broken laws, but that his father had looted the art. In typical twenty-first-century "caring" fashion, a counselor from the local public-health services was sent to help Cornelius "talk about his feelings." It was, to use Cornelius's own word, "gruesome."[4] He had never talked about his feelings with anyone, except perhaps Benita. The counselor was dutifully sent away with the assurance that he had no intentions of committing suicide, but none the wiser about anything else.

∞

For the next nineteen months, experts appointed by the Bavarian government pored over the collection. Not once in that period did they question Cornelius, or indeed the auction house of Kornfeld he was said to have visited in Bern on that fateful trip. More significantly, they never tried to contact the potential claimants of the paintings, some of whom are now in their nineties. Cornelius fretted and missed his "friends"—but, unknown to the government, he had others stashed elsewhere.

When *Focus* magazine got the scoop of the decade breaking the news, in early November 2013, no one asked *how* they managed it. Until then, *Focus* was thought to be a small but good magazine, but *not* the type that was noted for breaking stories of international interest.[5] Some of those close to the Gurlitt case feel that money may have passed hands between a source at the customs warehouse where the artworks were stored and *Focus*. If not, then how did the magazine know?

Perhaps no one could have foreseen the media feeding frenzy that would result. In the weeks that followed, the world's press was parked outside Cornelius's apartment block, trying to tempt him out to talk with offers of cakes and other sweets they'd heard he loved, in an unedifying display of repellent behavior.

Still, there was more to the feeding frenzy than the search for a scoop or the story of how he could have so many valuable artworks in such a small apartment and remain unknown to the government. It quickly became a public-relations disaster and the throbbing heart of an international incident. Winfried Bausback, justice minister of Bavaria, claimed the first he'd heard of Gurlitt's hoard was from the press.

Bausback was inundated with press attention, but when the German federal government became involved, he immediately moved to create a task force under his ministry's authority to "expedite research into the artworks' provenance."[6] In light of the public outrage internationally, this task force was quickly expanded into one comprising international experts also responsible to Berlin's finance and culture ministries. Experts from around the globe were coopted onto what became known as the Gurlitt Task Force, thereby silencing them forever to public scrutiny.

⚭

Of course, Cornelius's already fragile health deteriorated, and heart surgery was desperately needed. By December 2013, at the request of his doctors, a Munich court appointed Christoph Edel as his guardian. Mr. Edel hired a spokesman, an art expert, and a specialist retinue of lawyers. They removed Cornelius to a secret location where he could receive proper medical care and not be hounded by the world's press. By February 2014, they filed a blistering complaint against the German government for violating his rights.

According to the document filed with the German prosecutor's office, the "seizure of Mr. Gurlitt's art collection (and various other items) was authorized by the Augsburg local court under section 94 of the German Code of Criminal Procedure (StPO)."[7] For such a seizure to be legal there must be probable cause—not a mere hunch, as was the case in this instance. This in turn means that any seizure order must clearly state the crime for which the items are to be seized, as well as which items are the subject of the seizure, and their relevance to the case. Finally, any seizure must be proportional to the stated criminal activity. All these reasons were missing in the case of Cornelius Gurlitt, and an appeal was lodged with the Augsburg courts on February 14, 2013, under section 304 StPO.[8]

Although negotiations were ongoing from January, they were riddled with setbacks. The appeal filed on February 14 made the government see the error of its ways, at least privately. Yet Edel, too, revealed a further cache of some sixty paintings at Cornelius's Salzburg home. What he hadn't made clear was that there were actually two derelict homes in Salzburg—one across the street from the other. Hence the reason for the return trip by investigators and the discovery of further paintings. Whether one of these was in Cornelius's name and the other in his sister's was never publicized. Yet, as these paintings were in Austria, they were not confiscated but merely sent to a secure warehouse awaiting Gurlitt's instructions.

Since Cornelius was a private individual and *not* subject to the Washington Principles, the German government could not compel him to give any of the art back to the mounting number of potential claimants. It is in no small part thanks to Cornelius's connection with Edel that he eventually changed his mind. A deal was struck with the government shortly before Easter, on April 7, 2013, in which the government agreed to restore all the art that was not suspect to Cornelius, in exchange for his agreeing to *give* back any works that were confirmed as having been looted. Cornelius further agreed to bind his heirs to the agreement. He could go in for his heart surgery with a clear conscience. Significantly, too, at a stroke, Cornelius had snatched the moral victory. The government was given precisely one year to accomplish its task.

Almost one month to the day after the deal was agreed, Cornelius went home to Munich. Though Tido Park, one of his criminal lawyers, had seen him the day before his death and thought he was recovering from his heart surgery, Cornelius died on May 6, 2014, with his medical team at his side.

⁓

Cornelius may have had trouble connecting with people, but he was no fool. Having been harassed beyond endurance by the government and press, he may well have seen the similarity between his predicament and his father's as it had been explained to him seventy years earlier. It was Cornelius's legacy to help the art survive the greed of the German government. Hospitalized at Ludwigsburg, near his brother-in-law, he summoned a notary. With Christoph Edel present, a will was certified to transfer Gurlitt's entire estate to the Kunstmuseum in Bern, Switzerland. The furor he created should have made Cornelius smile.[9]

The unsuspecting museum director, Mathias Frehner, was quick to claim that he hadn't ever had contact with Cornelius. Perhaps what was important to Cornelius was not an established relationship as much as Frehner's outspokenness regarding the restitution of looted art. Besides, Bern had been an old stomping ground of his father's in the days when he'd saved art. It had also been the location of one of Hildebrand's many undeclared bank accounts.[10] While Eberhard Kornfeld, the owner of the Bern auction house that Cornelius was allegedly visiting in September 2010, acknowledged that he knew Cornelius Gurlitt, and that Cornelius was a financial donor, he denied having any dealings with Cornelius after the sale of a painting for $48,757 from the collection in 1990.[11]

⁓

At the time of writing, nearly a year on from the *Focus* article, only a handful of paintings have been acknowledged by the Gurlitt Task Force as having been looted, including *The Open Window*, by Henri Matisse,* from the Paul Rosenberg collection, and *Two Riders on the Beach*, from the David Friedmann collection. The Task Force had only until April 6, 2015, to decide what should be done with the other 451 artworks on the lostart.de website. At the rate of less than five paintings assessed since February 2010, the government has woefully missed the deadline imposed by the agreement with Cornelius.

---

* Renamed *The Seated Woman* or *The Seated Woman by the Open Window* since the Gurlitt story broke in 2013.

Bern's Kunstmuseum announced at the end of November 2014 that it will accept the Gurlitt gift, but not any of the 451 remaining artworks suspected of having been looted. Perhaps that is what the German government hoped all along.

According to David Toren—formerly known as Klaus Garnowski—he received a communication from the task force stating that before they returned any artworks they wanted to mount an exhibition of the entire collection for the world to see. Toren was naturally aghast. Yet he had not come through his many ordeals without a wry sense of humor and thought that the Führerbau in Munich might be a suitable place. The humor belies an indescribable sense of frustration, lack of sympathy from the German government, and heartache at the length of time it may take before he might metaphorically see his painting again. David has been blind for seven years.

Until the painting is physically returned, David will not drop his lawsuit against the German and Bavarian governments. His connection with that painting is more than special. It was the painting that calmed him when he heard that his father had been arrested during *Kristallnacht*. It was the painting he turned to when he heard that his father was being sent to Buchenwald. Yet will the pain of restitution be too much to bear emotionally?

Chris Marinello, the lawyer for the Rosenberg family, who worked tirelessly for the restitution of the Matisse *Open Window* has been frustrated by the lack of communication from the task force, while fully understanding their monumental task. Prior to the announcement that the painting would be returned to the Rosenberg family, he had not been notified. It "continues the vein of disregard for due process and compassion that we have seen since the discovery of the Gurlitt hoard. . . . It is an unfortunate but entirely expected case of bureaucracy trumping empathy."[12]

∾

With the Bern Kunstmuseum's acceptance of the Cornelius Gurlitt legacy, an imperfect justice will be served. Still, the final outcome of the looted treasure will not be known for many years to come. Bern is, understandably, reluctant to accept the suspected looted artworks, which leaves their future in doubt. There were the original 1,407 artworks found in Cornelius's Munich flat, followed by some twenty-two further paintings in the possession of his brother-in-law, followed by another sixty-odd in Austria that burgeoned to over 250 fifty artworks. Then, belatedly, there was the Monet found in Cornelius's hospital bag after his death. By anyone's reckoning, the looted portion of the find must be worth somewhere around a billion dollars.

$$\infty$$

Yet is that all there is? Hildebrand had traveled to and from various caches from 1942 until his death. Many of these have been revealed, though there are still others to be discovered. In conversations with several Swiss bankers since the late 1990s, it has become apparent that Hildebrand held numerous bank safe deposit boxes as well as significant rental space in Swiss bank vaults. Then there were the artworks smuggled into Switzerland in the diplomatic pouches of the Third Reich.

As I said in the prologue, while still an investment banker I observed the name "RLITT" on a label beneath the frame of a nineteenth century landscape painting when a sliver of a sliding wall in a Swiss bank vault had remained slightly ajar in error. Without thinking, I asked the banker if the painting was by the nineteenth-century landscape painter Gurlitt. Pushing the wall tightly shut, he blustered at me about breaking Swiss bank-secrecy laws and declared, "No, that's the twentieth-century Nazi art dealer."[13]

Undoubtedly, there remain many more mysteries to unveil.

GLOSSARY

Abwehr	Military Intelligence
Alldeutscher Verband	Pan-German League
Alleinschulde	sole war guilt
Arbeitsgemeinschaften	labor associations
Arbeitskommandos	units of Black Reichswehr or Black Defense League
Demeures Historiques	Historic Buildings Commission
Der Blaue Reiter	Kandinsky's expressionist art movement from Munich
Deutschvölkischer Schutz und Trutzbund	German Nationalist Protection and Defiance Federation, more commonly known as the Organization Consul
Devisenschutzkommando	Currency Control Command Unit
Die Brücke	the Bridge Expressionist art movement, which originated in Dresden
Drang nach Osten	drive to the East
Einkreisung	encirclement
Einsatzstab Reichleiters Rosenberg	Special Commission for Reich Leader Rosenberg, ERR for short
Einzelaktionen	allegedly unrelated individual acts of brutality
Feindvermögen	Enemy Property Control
Flamenpolitik	Flemish cultural politics
Flottenverein	Naval League
Fluchtgut	objects of value sold at a discount to flee Nazi persecution

Freiheit	freedom
Freikorps	violent paramilitary groups formed from the former Imperial German Army
Fremdvölkisch	of an alien people
Freundeskreis der Wirtschaft	Circle of Friends of the Economy
Gauleiter	regional Nazi Party leader
Gebt mir vier Jahre Zeit	Give me four years' time, Hitler's warning to the modern art community
Gemäldegalerie	literally picture gallery, but also art museum
Institut d'Études des Questions Juives (IEQJ)	Institute for the Study of the Jewish Question
Italia Irredenta	territory of native Italian-speaking people in Austria-Hungary
Justizrat	justice councillor
Kampfbund für deutsche Kultur	Combat League for German Culture, abbreviated as KDK
Kriegesgefahr	a declaration of imminent danger of war
Kriegsmarine	German Imperial Navy
Kunstverein	art association, funded by the regions
Lederhosen	leather shorts
Machtergreifung	seizure of power by the Nazis
Malverbot	prohibition to paint
Mischling	of mixed race
Neue Künstler-Vereinigung München	New Artists' Association of Munich
Notgeld	emergency money
NSDAP	German abbreviation for the Nazi Party (National Socialist German Workers' Party)
Oberbürgermeister	lord mayor
OMGUS	Office of the Military Government of the United States
Ostwanderer	Eastern European immigrants
Raffkes	profiteers
Reichskammer der Bildenden Künste (RBK)	Reich Chamber for the Visual Arts
Reichswehr	National Defense Force
Sonderauftrag	Special Commission

Sturmabteilung	SA, storm troopers, brownshirts
Volk; völkisch	people; of the people (folk) or folkloric
Wehrverein	Defense League
Weltanschauung	worldview, but has come to mean the Nazi worldview

NOTES

Abbreviations

AAA	Archive of American Art, Washington DC
ANDE	Archives Nationales des Affaires Diplomatiques et Etrangères
ANF	Archives Nationales de France, Paris
BAB	Bundesarchiv Berlin
BAK	Bundesarchiv Koblenz
BP	Bernoulli Papers, University of Basel, Switzerland
CI	Courtauld Institute of Art
CDJC	Centre de Documentation Juive Contemporaine, Paris
CIR	Consolidated Interrogation Report(s) on file at NARA and Fold3.com
CL	Clinton Presidential Library, Little Rock, Arkansas
DIR	Detailed Interrogation Report(s) on file at NARA RG 260 and Fold3.com
FAZ	Frankfurter Allgemeine Zeitung
GETTY	The Getty Museum Reference Library, Los Angeles
IMT	International Military Tribunal
JSTOR	Online scholarly digital archive
LMD	Landeshauptstadt München Direktorium
NA	National Archives, London
NARA	National Archives and Research Administration, College Park, MD and Washington, DC
NPG	Nachlass Projekt-Gurlitt, Dresden Technical University
ODNB	Oxford Dictionary of National Biography
PC	Private collections, owners wish to remain anonymous
SKD	Archiv der Staatlichen Kunstsammlungen Dresden
SpK BA	Staatlicher Archiv Bayern (Coburg)
V&A	National Archive of Art, Victoria and Albert Museum, London

Prologue

1. 9/11 brought sweeping changes to bank and money-laundering regulations throughout the world. Switzerland's bank-secrecy laws, however, were eroded only when the US government refused to allow Swiss banks to participate in US markets at any level unless they revealed the assets of Americans seeking to evade US taxes. A number of bank directors were brought to trial as a result, and the secrecy laws are no longer as impenetrable as they had been.

1. New York, May 1944

1. spiderbites.nytimes.com/pay_1944/articles_1944_05_00004.html.
2. For the full list, consult Vesting Order 3711.
3. CL—Vesting Order 3711; NARA, RG 131, Office of Alien Property (OAP) Entry 65F-1063.
4. The first steps to found the FBI were made in 1908. Attorney General Charles Bonaparte announced the creation of the special force of sixty men in his Annual Report to Congress that fall. When lame-duck president Theodore Roosevelt weighed in on the side of Bonaparte, a fierce political battle ensued. Roosevelt declared, "The chief argument in favor of [the Secret Service] amendment was that congressmen themselves did not wish to be investigated." Source: www.fbi.gov/about-us/history /highlights-of-history/articles/birth.
5. www.fbi.gov/about-us/history/directors/hoover.
6. Under the Freedom of Information Act, I tried to obtain the file and was advised on appeal by the Justice Department that the FBI had destroyed it at the end of the twentieth century. In a conversation with Dr. Greg Bradsher, senior archivist at the National Archives in College Park, Maryland, he recalled being seconded to the FBI in the 1990s to stop the FBI from indiscriminately destroying documents of significant historic importance which could be transferred to the National Archives. He had no recollection of seeing the Valentin file.
7. BAK, B323/134, f. 53/286.
8. Ibid., f. 53/283.
9. Ibid., f. 48/255.

2. At the Beginning—Germany, 1907

1. 1907 was precisely thirty-seven years after the founding of the German Empire and thirty-seven years before Hildebrand Gurlitt's surrender to the Allies. For a riveting and award-winning account of young Joseph Stalin, read Simon Sebag Montefiore's *Young Stalin* (London, 2008). The book opens with an incredible retelling of Stalin's bank-robbery escapade in Tiflis.
2. According to Hildebrand in an autobiography written in 1955 intended to accompany his last art exhibition, he referred to his mother as "Madame Privy Councillor," presumably for her bossiness as well as her love of ceremony. See article entitled "A

Kind of Fief," www.spiegel.de, November 13, 2013. Also NPG, www.gurlitt.tu-dresden
.de, timeline for Cornelius Gurlitt.

3. I noted during my research that this bust is no longer in the Grosser Garten.

4. Louis was born in Schleswig-Holstein when it was Danish. He became German after
Denmark's loss of the region in 1864.

5. Gurlitt's statements to the Allies, Personalakte C. Gurlitt, Sächs Städtarchiv HStA
Dresden, 11125 Ministerium des Kultus und öffentlich Unterrichts, 15367.

6. There were no children by either of the first two marriages.

7. Stephen Games, *Pevsner—The Early Life, Germany and Art* (London: Continuum,
2010), 42; cf. Heinrich von Treitschke, "Unserer Aussichten," published in the
Prüssichen Jahrbüchern.

8. Avraham Barkai, *From Boycott to Annihilation: The Economic Struggle of German
Jews 1933–1943* (Hanover, NH: University Press of New England, 1989), 1.

9. Else was eleven years younger than Fanny, so only seven at the time. There is no record of the family's reaction to Fanny's conversion. However, conversion was common,
particularly as it allowed wealthy or genteel Jews to *become* German by marrying
gentiles.

10. Else's conversion certificate was obtained posthumously.

11. There are eighty-two surviving letters in the NPG between Cornelius and Wilhelm.

12. NPG, a constant theme in the family letters.

13. Ibid., 032/168.

14. Ibid., 056/023.

15. The Ephrussi family were fabulously wealthy, and like the Rothschilds, the sons were
sent to foreign countries to make their fortunes. For a wonderful portrait, read the
award-winning *The Hare with the Amber Eyes* by Edmund de Waal. French art dealer
Paul Durand-Ruel exiled himself to London—along with Claude Monet, Camille
Pissarro, and Charles-François Daubigny—during the Franco-Prussian War of 1870–
71. It was Durand-Ruel who popularized Impressionism throughout Europe and
America and famously said, "America does not laugh—it buys!"

16. For more on Tschudi and his pivotal role introducing French and modern art to
national museums, see Dictionary of Art Historians, www.dictionaryofarthistorians
.org/tschudih.html.

17. NPG, 032/090.

18. Ibid., 032/092.

19. Ibid., 032/090.

20. The date Wolfgang took control not stipulated.

21. "A Kind of Fief," November 13, 2013, www.spiegel.de.

22. Ibid.

23. Adolf Hitler, *Mein Kampf* (London: Pimlico, 1997), 116–17.

24. Barbara Butts, "Modern German Drawings 1875–1950," *Bulletin St. Louis Art Museum*, New Series (vol. 21, no. 2), 5.

3. From The Hague to Vienna

1. Stefan Zweig, *The World of Yesterday* (Kindle edition, Plunkett Lake Press e-book, 2012), 14–17.
2. Bertha became a member of the advisory council of the Carnegie Peace Foundation in 1911.
3. Barbara W. Tuchman, *The Proud Tower* (New York: Bantam Books, 1967), 271.
4. Ibid., 328.
5. Ibid., 325.
6. For the full text of the 1907 Hague Convention, see www.icrc.org/applic/ihl/ihl.nsf /52d68d14de6160e0c12563da005fdb1b/1d1726425f6955aec125641e0038bfd6.
7. Alan Bullock, *Hitler:A Study in Tyranny* (London: Book Club Associates, 1973 revised edition), 27; cf. Franz Jetzinger, *Hitler's Youth* (London 1958), 68–69.
8. Ibid., 30.
9. Charles de Jaeger, *The Linz File: Hitler's Plunder of Europe's Art* (Exeter: Webb & Bower, 1981), 11.
10. Lothar Machtan, *The Hidden Hitler* (Oxford: Perseus Press, 2001), 30; cf. August Kubizek's book *Adolf Hitler: Mein Jugenfreund* (Graz/Göttingen: 1953), 229, 203.
11. de Jaeger, *Linz File*, 12.
12. Bullock, *Hitler*, 30.
13. Linz is the provincial seat of government of the Upper Danube region. Its "artistic" tradition is rooted in music rather than visual arts: Anton Bruckner composed his symphonies while an organist at the cathedral; its town orchestra had a conductor who was a pupil of Liszt and who worked with Wagner. The singer Richard Tauber was born there. Another native son was Adolf Eichmann.
14. de Jaeger, *Linz File*,14.
15. Stefan Zweig, *The Society of the Crossed Keys* (London: Pushkin Press, 2013), 66.
16. Adolf Hitler, *Mein Kampf* (London: Pimlico, 1997), 48.
17. *Jugendstil* was called "Secessionist" in Germany.
18. Peter Vergo, *Art in Vienna 1898–1918* (London: Phaidon, 1975), 16.
19. Ibid., 34.
20. Ibid., 37.
21. Bullock, *Hitler*, 30; cf. Konrad Heiden, *Der Führer* (London: 1944), 48.
22. de Jaeger, *Linz File*, 14–15. These are the recollections of Professor Andersen, who sat next to Hitler during the examinations.
23. Hitler, *Mein Kampf*, 10–11.
24. Ibid., 20.

4. Cause and Effect

1. Christina Kott, *Préserver l'art de l'ennemi? Le patrimoine artistique en Belgique et en France occupées, 1914–1918* (Brussels: Peter Lang, 2006). Kott cites Cornelius Gurlitt's articles in the German art propaganda journal *Der Belfried* (*The Belfry*), 142–43.
2. Ibid., 317.

3. Barbara W. Tuchman, *The Guns of August* (New York: Ballantine Books, 1994), 11.
4. Ibid., 8.
5. F. Lee Benns and M. E. Seldon, *Europe 1914–1939* (New York: Meredith Publishing, 1965), 5.
6. Ibid., 9–11. *Italia Irredenta* was in conflict with Austria-Hungary in the Balkans and the Adriatic, making this an unnatural alliance.
7. Von Bülow imitated the effortless parliamentary stance of the aristocratic Arthur Balfour by clutching his coat lapels. Wagging tongues claimed he practiced this stance in front of the mirror at home.
8. Ibid., 30. King Leopold was a despicable man who had been responsible for all manner of atrocities in the Congo.
9. Ibid., 36.
10. Alan Bullock, *Hitler: A Study in Tyranny* (London: Book Club Associates, 1973 revised edition), 44.
11. Ibid., 45.
12. Ibid.
13. David Starr Jordan, "The Ways of Pangermany," *Scientific Monthly* 4, no. 1 (1917), 29.
14. Ibid., 29–31.
15. Barbara W. Tuchman, *The Proud Tower* (New York: Bantam Books, 1967), 272; cf. *World Population and Production*, W. S. and E. S. Woytinsky (New York: 1953), 530.
16. Ibid., 273.
17. Ibid., 275; cf. *Secret Letters of the Last Czar,* ed. E. J. Bing (New York: 1938), 131.
18. Brian Bond, *War and Society in Europe 1870–1970* (Stroud: Sutton Publishing, 1998), 56.
19. Ibid., 66.

5. War

1. NPG, 126/025.
2. Ibid., 031/045. Cornelia showed her works at Chemnitz in early June 1914.
3. Kolig was an exact contemporary of Kokoschka and from 1907 to 1912 had attended the Akademie der Bildenden Künste, which had refused Hitler at the exact same time. Oxford Art Online, www.oxfordartonline.com.ezproxy.londonlibrary.co.uk /subscriber/article/grove/art/T047206?q=Kolig%2C+Anton&search=quick&pos=1 &_start=1#firsthit.
4. Hubert Portz, *Zimmer frei für Cornelia Gurlitt, Lotte Wahle und Conrad Felixmüller,* Exhibition Catalogue Kunsthaus Désirée, Hochstadt, 26 April—14 June 2014 (Landau: Knecht Verlag, 2014), 29; Kolig letter; cf. Wilhelm Baum, *Kunstwerke sind Stationen auf dem Passionsweg zu einem verlorenen Paradies, Briefe und Dokumente zum "Nötscher Kreis"* (Klagenfurt: Kitab Verlag, 2004), 194n.
5. This painting was at Dr. Portz's unique exhibition at Hochstadt in Pfalz, Germany. I thank him for turning the painting over to expose this mark and putting me in touch with the owner.

6. Barbara W. Tuchman, *The Guns of August* (New York: Ballantine, 1990), 85.

7. Joyce Marlow, ed., *The Virago Book of Women and the Great War* (London: Virago Press, 1998), 19. A superb collection of the experiences of women throughout the war from all nations.

8. Ibid.; cf. *Outbreak of the World War*, collected by Karl Kautsky and edited by Max Montgelas and Walther Schucking, translated by Carnegie Endowment (New York: Oxford, 1924).

9. Winston S. Churchill, *The World Crisis 1911–1914* (London: Thornton Butterworth, 1923), 230. The italics are Churchill's.

10. Tuchman, *Guns of August*, 111–13.

11. Ibid., 90.

12. Ibid., 91–92.

13. She had previously been jailed for twenty days and fined $3,000 for contempt of court in the long-standing saga of the business hovering on bankruptcy. See Brisbane Papers, "Nellie Bly," Syracuse University of New York.

14. Brooke Kroeger, *Nellie Bly: Daredevil. Reporter. Feminist* (New York, 2013, Kindle edition).

15. Ibid.

16. Adolf Hitler, *Mein Kampf* (London: Pimlico, 1997), 148.

17. Tuchman, *Guns of August*, 144–45.

18. Ibid., 148–49.

19. Ibid., 145.

20. *Daily Telegraph*, www.telegraph.co.uk/ww1archive.

21. Margot Asquith, *The Autobiography of Margot Asquith* (London: Weidenfeld & Nicolson, 1995), 294–95.

22. Ibid., 143.

23. Kgl. Sächsische 23 Reserve-Division. This division was later triangularized, however, remained on the line in the Champagne region from August 1914 to July 1916. For movements of the German army, see *Histories of Two Hundred and Fifty-One Divisions of the German Army Which Participated in the War (1914–1918)*, compiled from records of Intelligence section of the General Staff, American Expeditionary Forces, Chaumont, France, 1919 (1920), 337–40.

24. Military records online at ancestry.com.

25. Other commanders included General Erich Ludendorff, Max Hoffmann, and Hermann von François. There were 78,000 Russians killed or wounded from the Second Army of 230,000 men and another 92,000 prisoners of war. On the German side, depending on the source, there were between 10,000 and 15,000 killed or wounded from the Eighth Army, which comprised 150,000 men.

26. BBC Radio 4, *On This Day 100 Years Ago* series.

27. NPG, 125/012.

28. Ibid.

29. Brisbane Papers, "Nellie Bly," *New York World* articles by Bly, University of Syracuse (NY) Library.

30. Kroeger, *Nellie Bly*, Kindle edition.

31. Ibid.

32. German military list no. 0365, February 15, 1915. It is not stated what Wilibald's injuries were. In letters with Hildebrand, it becomes apparent that Wilibald had a leg injury.

33. www.firstworldwar.com/source/champagne1915_falkenhayn.htm; cf. *Source Records of the Great War, Vol. III*, ed. Charles F. Horne (National Alumni, 1923).

34. Christopher Duffy, *Through German Eyes: The British & the Somme 1916* (London: Weidenfeld & Nicolson, 2006), 110; cf. Rintelen, 1933, 246.

6. Gurlitt's Struggle

1. Alan Bullock, *Hitler: A Study in Tyranny* (London: Book Club Associates, 1973 revised edition), 53; cf. Hitler's speech at Hamburg, August 17, 1934 in Norman Baynes, *The Speeches of Adolf Hitler* (Oxford: Oxford University Press, 1942), vol. I, 97.

2. Idea taken from the "Mend-Protokoll"; see below in *The Hidden Hitler*.

3. Ibid., 51. See also Lothar Machtan, *The Hidden Hitler*, 68.

4. Ibid., 67.

5. Bullock, *Hitler*, 52.

6. Both his war record and his letters are silent on this point.

7. NPG, 126/025.

8. Ibid.

9. Ibid.

10. NPG, 126/029.

11. Christina Kott, *Préserver l'art de l'ennemi? Le patrimoine artistique en Belgique et en France occupees, 1914–1918* (Brussels: Peter Lang, 2006), 19, note 6. Kott's study exposes the *purpose* of art conservation in occupied Belgium and France. She points up how scholarly research never questioned the aims of art preservation as anything but altruistic and an important progression toward the humanization of war. Given that Pan-Germanists and the military were heading up this occupation, she interrogates their motivations.

12. Ibid., 20; cf. Wilhelm Treue, *Kunstraub: Über die Schicksale von Kunstwerken im Krieg, Revolution und Frieden* (Düsseldorf: Drost, 1957), 295.

13. Kott, *Préserver*, 159, note 184. Clemen was repaid by the government through its subsidy of 8,000 marks for the production of 150 copies of his book.

14. Ibid., 42.

15. The first critical work of their efforts written in German is Thomas Goege's "*Kunstschutz und Propaganda im Ersten Weltkrieg, Paul Clemen als Kunstschutzbeauftragter an der Westfront*," in Udo Mainzer (ed.), Paul Clemen, Zur 125. Wiederkehr seines Geburtstages (1991), 149–68.

16. Ibid., 25.

17. Ibid., 25–26.

18. Ibid., 125, f/n no. 53. Also p. 158. The German title for this book is *Die Klosterbauten der Cistercienser in Belgien. Im Auftrage des Kaiserlich Deutschen Generalgouvernements in Belgien* (Berlin: Der Zirkel, 1919).

19. Ibid., 121, note 80.

20. Ibid., 117.

21. Ibid., 128–29; see note 68.

22. Ibid.; cf. Cornelius Gurlitt, "*Wallonien als Kunstland,*" *Der Belfried,* 1ère année, 1917, 500–501. While Gurlitt makes the point about artistic activity vs. birthplace, he makes his support of Pan-Germanism clear.

23. Kathrin Iselt, *Sonderbeauftragter des Führers: Der Kunsthistoriker und Museumsmann Hermann Voss (1884–1969)* (Köln: Böhlau Verlag, 2010), 47.

24. Hans Sluga, *Heidegger's Crisis: Philosophy and Politics in Nazi Germany* (Cambridge, MA: Harvard University Press, 1993), 83–85.

25. NPG, 126/044.

26. Ibid., 125/004.

27. Ibid., 126/044.

28. Ibid.

29. Hans Sluga, *Heidegger's Crisis*, 42–43.

30. Ibid.

31. Ibid., 44.

32. Ibid., 82.

33. NPG, 126/045.

34. Ibid., 125/019.

35. Ibid., 125/020.

36. Ibid., 126/045.

37. Ibid., 126/046. All underlines are original.

38. Ibid., 126/047. Professional translation of "On Life."

39. Ibid.

40. Ibid., 126/048.

41. Ibid., 126/051; 126/052; 126/053.

42. Ibid., 126/055.

7. Peace

1. www.oxforddnb.com.ezproxy.londonlibrary.co.uk/view/article/30553?docPos=6.

2. Jean-Jacques Becker, *The Great War and the French People* (Leamington Spa: Berg, 1985), 323.

3. William L. Shirer, *The Rise and Fall of the Third Reich* (London: Mandarin Paperback, 1996), 31.

4. Alan Bullock, *Hitler: A Study in Tyranny* (London: Book Club Associates, 1973 revised edition), 37.

5. Shirer, *Rise and Fall of the Third Reich*, 32n; cf. Telford Taylor in *Sword and Swastika*, 16.

6. Adolf Hitler, *Mein Kampf* (London: Pimlico, 1997), 185.

7. Peter Gay, *Weimar Culture: The Outsider as Insider* (New York: W. W. Norton & Company, 2001), 147–48. Also Shirer, *The Rise and Fall of the Third Reich*, 52.

8. Joyce Marlow, ed., *The Virago Book of Women and the Great War* (London: Virago Press, 1998), 375–76.

9. Shirer, *Rise and Fall of the Third Reich*, 34n; cf. Margaritte Ludendorff, *Als ich Ludendorffs Frau war*, 229.

10. Hitler, *Mein Kampf*, 185–87.

11. John Weitz, *Hitler's Banker—Hjalmar Horace Greeley Schacht* (New York: Warner Books, 1999), 54.

12. Ibid., 55–56.

13. NPG, 126/057.

14. See wwi.lib.byu.edu/index.php/President_Wilson's_Fourteen_Points.

15. Ibid.

16. Ibid.

17. The Freikorps was still thought to represent the "old imperial army," as Germany was left in limbo between the armistice and the signing of the Treaty of Versailles.

18. Robert G. L. Waite, *Vanguard of Nazism:The Free Corps Movement in Postwar Germany 1918–1923* (New York: W. W. Norton & Company, 1969), 62 and 62n; cf. E. J. Gumbel, *Vier Jahre politischer Mord* 5th ed. (Berlin, 1922), 12.

19. See *Mein Kampf*, 181n.

20. NPG, 126/059.

21. Ibid.

22. Ibid.

23. Frederick Taylor, *The Downfall of Money* (London: Bloomsbury, 2013), 99. Also Peter Grose, *Allen Dulles, Spymaster: The Life and Times of the First Civilian Director of the CIA* (London: André Deutsch, 2006), 58. John Foster Dulles would become secretary of state under President Eisenhower in 1953.

24. www.wwi.lib.byu.edu/index.php/Peace_Treaty_of_Versailles.

8. Aftermath

1. Robert G. L. Waite, *Vanguard of Nazism* (New York: W. W. Norton & Company, 1969), 22–23; cf. *In Stahlgewittern: Ein Kriegstagebuch*, 16th ed., Berlin, 1922, 257, 265 [Translated as *Storm of Steel*, Jünger's diary of World War I].

2. Ibid., 19; cf. Theodora Huber, *Die soziologische Seite der Jugendbewegung*, 12.

3. Psychoanalyst and historian Erik Erikson made this analysis. While this quote refers to Martin Luther (c. 1520), it is valid for the mental state of certain men who aspired to higher education after fighting a war. See Toby Thacker's *Joseph Goebbels*, 15–16, which quotes Erikson's *Young Man Luther: A Study in Psychoanalysis and History* (London: Faber & Faber, 1959), 12.

4. NPG, 126/066.

5. Ibid., 053/001.

6. Hermann Voss was *not* a direct descendant.

7. Justus Ulrich Mathias was born on December 14, 1917. Hildebrand was the child's godfather. Less than a year later, Felixmüller's son Luca was born. Felixmüller married another woman six months to the day after the birth of Justus. Hubert Portz, *Zimmer frei für Cornelia Gurlitt, Lotte Wahle und Conrad Felixmüller* (Landau: Knecht Verlag, 2014), 34.

8. Portz, *Zimmer*, 18, note 49.

9. NPG, 126/065; 126/070.

10. Ibid., 053/001.

11. Ibid., 126/067.

12. Portz, *Zimmer*, 22, note 72.

13. Ibid., 24.

14. Ibid., 126/084.

15. Ibid., 126/081.

16. Kollwitz lost her youngest son, Peter. Her monument entitled *Grieving Parents* is at the Vladslo German war cemetery.

17. Ibid., 126/079.

18. Adolf Hitler, *Mein Kampf* (London: Pimlico, 1997), 188–89.

19. Waite, *Vanguard of Nazism*, 90; cf. Toller, *Eine Jugend in Deutschland*, 232.

20. An estimated 400,000 men belonged to the Freikorps, making it the largest single power in Germany. See Arthur Rosenberg in his *Geschichte der Deutschen Republik* (Karlsbad, 1935), 75–76.

21. Hitler, *Mein Kampf*, 189n.

22. Ibid., 191.

23. William L. Shirer, *The Rise and Fall of the Third Reich* (London: Mandarin Paperback, 1996); cf. *Mein Kampf*, 210 and 213.

24. His executive committee number was 7, but his party number was 555.

25. Lothar Machtan, *The Hidden Hitler* (Oxford: Perseus Press, 2001), 106.

26. NPG, 126/080.

27. Ibid., 126/082; 126/083.

28. Ibid., 126/085.

29. Ibid., 126/087.

30. Ibid., 197/009.

31. Ibid.

9. Weimar Trembles

1. Robert G. L. Waite, *Vanguard of Nazism* (New York: W. W. Norton & Company, 1969), 129; cf. Von Salomon, *Die Geächteten* (Berlin: 1930), 115.

2. See Waite's *Vanguard of Nazism,* chapter 5, "The Baltic Adventure." The Freikorps invaded Latvia not only with the tacit approval of the Weimar government, but also with the explicit approval of the British, who feared a Soviet invasion of the region.

3. Ibid., 131.

4. NPG, 224/021.

5. Ibid., 033/011.

6. Prior to the Reichswehr's formation, in January 1921, it was known under two other guises: the Vorläufige Reichswehr (Provisional National Defense) and the Übergangsheer, or Transitional Army. The Freikorps was an unofficial army able to subvert the restrictions imposed by Versailles. Many of the former Freikorps members joined Hitler's NSDAP and the SA. See *Mein Kampf*, 476n. The criminal-justice system was a "state within a state" and administrator of the counterrevolutionary right-wing political groups. See Shirer, *The Rise and Fall of the Third Reich*, 60–61.

7. Frederick Taylor, *The Downfall of Money* (London: Bloomsbury, 2013), 133.

8. Ibid., 105; cf. "*Die Aufnahme der Friedensbedigungen*," in Troeltsch, *Die Fehlgeburt einer Republik*, 44. For exchange rates, see *The Downfall of Money*, appendix.

9. William L. Shirer, *The Rise and Fall of the Third Reich* (London: Mandarin Paperback, 1996), 64; cf. Lt. Gen. Friedrich von Rabenau, *Seeckt aus seinem Leben*, II, 342.

10. Waite, *Vanguard of Nazism*, 140–41.

11. Ibid., 141n. Details taken from Mann's memoires, *Mit Ehrhardt durch Deutschland*, 147–52, and Ehrhardt, *Kapitän Ehrhardt, Abenteuer und Schicksale*, 166–67.

12. Ibid., 142; cf. "An Eye-Witness in Berlin" in *The New Europe*, April 1, 1920, 274.

13. Taylor, *Downfall of Money*, 139.

14. Waite, *Vanguard of Nazism*, 164.

15. Shirer, *Rise and Fall of the Third Reich*, 60; "blackest page quote" cf. Franz L. Neumann, *Behemoth*, 23.

16. Shirer, *Rise and Fall of the Third Reich*; cf. *Mein Kampf*, 154, 225–26.

17. NPG, 033/012.

18. Ibid.

19. Ibid., 197/011.

20. Ibid., 197/013.

21. Ibid., 033/071.

22. Taylor, *Downfall of Money*, 184–85.

23. John Weitz, *Hitler's Banker* (London: Warner Books, 1999), 60.

24. Ibid., 364.

10. Rebels with a Cause

1. Robert G. L. Waite, *Vanguard of Nazism* (New York: W. W. Norton & Company, 1969), 239. Also Rabenau, *Seeckt aus seinem Leben* (Leipzig, 1940), II, 324.

2. NPG, 033/076.

3. Ibid., 126/142. Also www.dictionaryofarthistorians.org/pinderw.htm.

4. Ibid., 126/127.

5. Frederick Taylor, *The Downfall of Money* (London: Bloomsbury, 2013), 273–74.

6. Ibid., 275–76.

7. NPG, 126/150.

8. Peter Gay, *Weimar Culture: The Outsider as Insider* (New York: W. W. Norton &

Company, 2001), 105; cf. Bernard S. Myers, *The German Expressionists: A Genera-tion in Revolt* (New York: Frederick A. Praeger, 1966 ed.), 220.

9. Ibid., 105.

10. NPG, 224/215.

11. Ibid., 224/217 and 224/218.

12. Taylor, *Downfall of Money*, 366–67.

13. Alan Bullock, *Hitler: A Study in Tyranny* (London: Book Club Associates, 1973), 90–91.

14. Taylor, *Downfall of Money*, 338.

15. NPG, 033/063.

16. The owner of Sibyllen-Verlag was the great-granduncle of my dedicatees, Alexander and Gunther Hoyt.

17. Waite, *Vanguard of Nazism*, 255–256; cf. *Münchener Post*, August 20, 1923.

18. Ibid., 256.

19. Ibid., 256–57.

20. Adolf Hitler, *Mein Kampf* (London: Pimlico, 1992), 311.

21. Ibid., 316–17.

22. Ibid., 268.

23. Ibid., 262.

24. William L. Shirer, *The Rise and Fall of the Third Reich* (London: Mandarin Books, 1991), 86–87.

25. Hitler, *Mein Kampf*, 268, 296.

26. Ibid., 258–59.

27. Games, Stephen, *Pevsner—The Early Life: Germany and Art* (London: Continuum, 2010), 116.

28. Ibid., 129

29. Waite, *Vanguard of Nazism*, 257–58.

30. Shirer, *Rise and Fall of the Third Reich*, 67–68.

31. Ibid., 70.

32. Ibid., 74–75.

11. Hopes and Dreams

1. John Weitz, *Hitler's Banker* (London: Warner Books, 1999), 63; cf. Hjalmar Schacht, *76 Jahres meines Lebens*, 216.

2. Ibid., 64.

3. Ibid., 66–67.

4. Weitz, *Hitler's Banker*, 70.

5. Weitz, *Hitler's Banker*, 71; cf. *Review of Reviews* (November 1924), 541.

6. William L. Shirer, *The Rise and Fall of the Third Reich* (London: Mandarin Books, 1991), 76–77.

7. Ibid., 77.

8. Ibid., 77–78.

12. From New York to Zwickau

1. NPG, 121/040. See www.ancestry.com Microfilm publication NARA RG237, roll 3637.
2. Ibid.
3. Ibid.
4. www.ci.columbia.edu/0240s/0242_2/0242_2_s7_text.html.
5. Gesa Jeuthe, *Kunstwerte im Wandel: Die Preisentwicklung der deutschen Moderne im nationalen und internationalen Kunstmarkt 1925 bis 1955* (Berlin: Akademie Verlag, 2011), 33.
6. Sybil Gordon Kantor, *Alfred H. Barr, Jr., and the Intellectual Origins of the Museum of Modern Art* (Cambridge, MA: MIT Press, 2002), 93–94.
7. Ibid., 94.
8. www.getty.edu/art/gettyguide/artMakerDetails?maker=1851.
9. Janet Bishop, Cécile Debray, and Rebecca Rainbow, eds., *The Steins Collect: Matisse, Picasso, and the Parisian Avant-Garde* (New Haven: Yale University Press, 2011), 61.
10. Shortly afterward, Alfred H. Barr wrote in the *Harvard Crimson* that Boston was a "modern art pauper" because it had no examples of modern greats such as Cézanne, van Gogh, Seurat, Gauguin, Picasso, Matisse, Derain, or Bonnard. The *Boston Herald*, the *Boston Globe*, the *Boston Evening Transcript*, and *The Arts* rounded on both Barr and the artists mentioned. See Alice Goldfarb Marquis, *Alfred H. Barr, Jr.: Missionary for the Modern* (New York: Contemporary Books, 1989), 38–40.
11. NPG, 109/001.
12. Toby Thacker, *Joseph Goebbels: Life and Death* (London: Palgrave Macmillan, 2009), 58.
13. Ibid.
14. Ibid., 59.
15. Ibid., 61–62.

13. The Mysterious Mr. Kirchbach

1. Author interview with Markus Stoetzel (Flechtheim's German lawyer), Marburg, Germany, July 15, 2014.
2. Gesa Jeuthe, *Kunstwerte im Wandel—Die Preisentwicklung der Deutschen Moderne im Nationalen und Internationalen Kunstmarkt 1925 bis 1955* (Berlin: Akaedmie Verlag, 2011), 35.
3. Peter Gay, *Weimar Culture* (New York: W. W. Norton & Company, 2001), 132; cf. Heinrich Mann.
4. This is clear from the NPG letters.
5. Gay, *Weimar Culture*, 132.
6. See NPG letters 1925–1935.
7. Ibid.
8. The introduction to Berlin society and Alfred Flechtheim has been meticulously researched from several bibliographical sources and interviews where the interviewees asked not to be quoted. An especially helpful font of knowledge to quote was the

Eduardo Westerdahl Papers at the Getty Museum in Los Angeles. I thank Lois White of the Getty for her assistance. If the Gurlitt Papers in possession of the German government (as I write) are complete, they will bear out these relationships in greater detail.

9. Janet Bishop, Cécile Debray, and Rebecca Rainbow, eds., *The Steins Collect: Matisse, Picasso, and the Parisian Avant-Garde* (New Haven: Yale University Press, 2011), 161.

10. NPG, 121/042; 121/045 and 121/059.

11. Adolf Hitler, *Mein Kampf* (London: Pimlico, 1997), 228, 230.

12. Cornelius changed his mind about Hitler only *after* his shocking discovery that he was classed as a *Mischling* by the 1935 Nuremberg Laws.

13. Hitler, *Mein Kampf*, 235.

14. Ibid., 234.

15. Ibid., 232.

16. William L. Shirer, *The Rise and Fall of the Third Reich* (London: Mandarin Books, 1991), 119; cf. Baynes, ed., *The Speeches of Adolf Hitler*, vol. 1, 155–56.

17. www.deutsche-biographie.de/sfz41057.html.

18. The Gurlitt papers in possession of the German government should shed light on this.

19. www.photo.dresden.de/de/03/nachrichten/2008/c_82.php?lastpage=zur%20Ergebnisliste. See also www.faz.net/aktuell/feuilleton/fotokunst-weder-ein-speicherfund-noch-die-helene-anderson-collection-es-gab-einmal-eine-pionier-sammlung-mit-meisterlicher-fotografie-1277846.html. Huge controversy surrounds this collection.

14. The Root of Evil

1. NPG, 026/006.

2. Gesa Jeuthe, *Kunstwerte im Wandel: Die Preisentwicklung der Deutschen Moderne im Nationalen und Internationalen Kunstmarkt 1925 bis 1955* (Berlin: Akademie Verlag, 2011), 61–62.

3. NPG, 031/009.

4. John Weitz, *Hitler's Banker* (London: Warner Books, 1999), 90–91.

5. Ibid., 91–92; cf. *Literary Digest*, May 28, 1927, 8.

6. Ibid., 100.

7. Ibid., 96.

8. William L. Shirer, *The Rise and Fall of the Third Reich* (London: Mandarin Books, 1991), 134.

9. David R. L. Litchfield, *The Thyssen Art Macabre* (London: Quartet Books, 2006), 79.

10. Ibid., 135.

11. Ibid., 87.

12. Ibid., 136.

13. Hellmut Lehmann-Haupt, *Art under a Dictatorship* (New York: Oxford University Press, 1954), 37–39.

14. Ibid., 40.

15. George Bernard Shaw's witty response to *Entartung*—which means "degeneration" —was published in 1908 under the title *The Sanity of Art*.

16. ODNB, Joseph Duveen and Colnaghi Family.

17. Litchfield, *Thyssen Art Macabre*, 85–86.

18. Ibid., 86.

19. NPG, 026/006.

20. Ibid., 031/032; 121/073 and 031/033.

21. Ibid., 031/034.

22. Ibid., 121/075.

23. Lehmann-Haupt, *Art under a Dictatorship*, 43.

24. Ibid., 62.

25. Jeuthe, *Kunstwerte im Wandel*, 45.

26. Ibid., 43. See end note 48. Verlag Zuschlag, 1995, 35; Winkler 2002, 321.

15. Chameleons and Crickets

1. Gesa Jeuthe, *Kunstwerte im Wandel: Die Preisentwicklung der deutschen Moderne im nationalen und internationalen Kunstmarkt 1925 bis 1955* (Berlin: Akademie Verlag, 2011), 40 (see table).

2. Ibid., 41; cf. letter from Oskar Schlemmer to Will Grohmann, 10 November 1930.

3. According to Marie's letter 121/081, Hildebrand and Helene were not living with them.

4. NPG, 031/036.

5. Sybil Gordon Kantor, *Alfred H. Barr, Jr., and the Intellectual Origins of the Museum of Modern Art* (Cambridge, MA: MIT Press, 2002), 191–94.

6. Peggy Guggenheim was dubbed "Prophetess of the Blue Four" in 1925 in the *San Francisco Examiner*, November 1, 1925.

7. William L. Shirer, *The Rise and Fall of the Third Reich* (London: Mandarin Books, 1991), 138.

8. Albert Speer, *Inside the Third Reich* (London: Phoenix, 1995), 43.

9. Ibid., 45.

10. Ibid., 46.

11. Ibid., 49.

12. NPG, 121/086.

13. Ibid., 121/088.

14. Evidence of this may be in the Gurlitt papers held by the German government.

15. NPG, 026/088.

16. Ibid., 026/022. See Diarmuid Jeffreys, *Hell's Cartel: IG Farben and the Making of Hitler's War Machine* (London: Bloomsbury, 2008), 177. The issue of premium imports versus synthetic materials would become extremely heated in the years ahead, striking at the heart of Göring's Four-Year Plan.

17. NPG 026/099 and 026/007.

18. Shirer, *Rise and Fall of the Third Reich*, 144.

19. Ibid., 144–45.
20. John Weitz, *Hitler's Banker* (London: Warner Books, 1999), 127.
21. Hindenburg stood purely to defeat Hitler. Neither he nor his backers were in any doubt that he could not survive another seven-year term.
22. Toby Thacker, *Joseph Goebbels: Life and Death* (London: Palgrave Macmillan, 2009), 127.
23. Shirer, *Rise and Fall of the Third Reich*, 158–59.
24. Thacker, *Joseph Goebbels*, 129.
25. Shirer, *Rise and Fall of the Third Reich*, 165–66.
26. Ibid., 168–69.
27. Thacker, *Joseph Goebbels*, 135.
28. Weitz, *Hitler's Banker*, 126.
29. Shirer, *Rise and Fall of the Third Reich*, 170.
30. Thacker, *Joseph Goebbels*, 135–36.
31. Shirer, *Rise and Fall of the Third Reich*, 180–81.
32. Ibid., 183.
33. Ibid.
34. NPG, 026/012.
35. Ibid., 026/014.
36. Ibid., 026/016.
37. Ibid., 026/018.

16. The First Stolen Lives

1. Jonathan Petropoulos, *Art as Politics in the Third Reich* (Chapel Hill, NC: University of North Carolina Press, 1996), 19.
2. William L. Shirer, *The Rise and Fall of the Third Reich* (London: Mandarin Books, 1991), 192.
3. Ibid., 192–93. Documented at the Nuremberg War Trials. General Franz Halder claimed he'd heard it at a luncheon in 1942 when Göring boasted about it. For a general overview, see www.historylearningsite.co.uk/reichstag_fire_1933.htm.
4. Ibid.
5. Ibid.
6. Ibid., 194.
7. Ibid., 197.
8. NPG, 026/033.
9. GETTY, Eduardo Westerdahl Papers, ref. 861077, November 14, 1932 letter.
10. Ibid., January 14, 1933, letter.
11. Ibid., June 3, 1933, letter.
12. Ibid.
13. Gesa Jeuthe, *Kunstwerte im Wandel: Die Preisentwicklung der deutschen Moderne im nationalen und internationalen Kunstmarkt 1925 bis 1955* (Berlin: Akademie Verlag, 2011), 52; cf. Fuchs: *Organisation und Ziele des Reichsverbands des Deutschen Kunst*

und Antiquitätenhandels, in *Die Weltkunst*, 7–31, 1933. See also Ottfried Dascher, *Die Ausgrenzung und Ausplünderung von Juden*, Essen, 2003, 129.

14. Petropoulos, *Art as Politics in the Third Reich*, 20.
15. Ibid., 20–21.
16. Hüneke, *Degenerate Art*, 127.
17. Ibid., 24. Ferdinand Möller Stiftung (Foundation), set up by Möller's daughter (now deceased), has refused to respond to my emails and letters asking for an interview or further details about Möller's activities.
18. Toby Thacker, *Joseph Goebbels: Life and Death* (London: Palgrave Macmillan, 2009), 140–41. Petropoulos, *Art as Politics*, 24. Shirer, *The Rise and Fall of the Third Reich*, 200.
19. GETTY, Eduardo Westerdahl Papers, ref. 861077, August 13, 1933, letter.
20. Ibid.
21. Ibid., July 29, 1933.
22. NPG, letter 026/020.
23. Ibid.
24. www.musikmph.de/musical_scores/vorworte/017.html.
25. NPG, 026/021.
26. Ibid., 026/022.
27. Ibid., 026/024.

17. Chambers of Horrors

1. Hellmut Lehmann-Haupt, *Art under a Dictatorship* (New York: Oxford University Press, 1954), 63–64.
2. Victor Klemperer, *I Will Bear Witness 1933–1941* (New York: Modern Library, 1999), 9–10.
3. Ibid., 10–11.
4. Ibid., 14.
5. Avraham Barkai, *From Boycott to Annihilation: The Economic Struggle of German Jews 1933–1943* (Hanover, NH: University of New England Press, 1989), 14.
6. Ibid., 4.
7. William E. Dodd, Jr., and Martha Dodd, *Ambassador Dodd's Diary, 1933–1938* (London: Victor Gollancz Ltd., 1941), 30.
8. Jonathan Petropoulos, *Art as Politics* (Chapel Hill, NC: University of North Carolina, 1996), 21.
9. Victor Klemperer, *I Will Bear Witness 1933–1941*, 9–10.
10. Ibid. These comprised 88.5% of the operating budget.
11. Albert Speer, *Inside the Third Reich* (London: Phoenix, 1995), 60.
12. Ibid., 61.
13. AAA—Valentin, Jane Wade Papers, Lutheran Birth Certificate from Saint Jakobi Church.
14. Gesa Jeuthe, *Kunstwerte im Wandel* (Berlin: Akademie Verlag, 2011), 53. Ottfried

Dascher, *Alfred Flechtheim. Sammler—Kunsthändler* (Verleger Wädenswil, 2012), 537–38. For further reading, see Thea Sternheim's *Tagebücher* 2 (1925–1936) for Flechtheim's state of mind.

15. See the chapter entitled "The Lion Tamer."
16. See www.alfredflechtheim.com. Flechtheim Munich Case memo MS2014-01-28.
17. BP, undated letter prior to March 30, 1933 from Vömel to Bernoulli.
18. Jeuthe, *Kunstwerte*, 53. See also Verlag Beckmann, 1893, 19 and PhD Thesis Tiedemann 2010, 85. There are demonstrable connections between their stock in 1936.
19. Ibid., 53–54.
20. Ibid.
21. Ibid.
22. Petropoulos, *Art as Politics*, 28.
23. Ibid., 29.
24. Stephanie Barron, ed., *Degenerate Art—The Fate of the Avant-Garde in Nazi Germany* (New York: Harry N. Abrams, 1991). Christoph Zuschlag, "An Educational Exhibition," 83.
25. NPG, 214/001.
26. Ibid., 026/024.
27. Zuschlag, "An Educational Exhibition," 84–85. Also Olaf Peters, ed., *Degenerate Art*, Karl Stamm, "'Degenerate Art' on Screen" (New York: Prestel Publishing, 2014), 196.
28. Hüneke, *Degenerate Art*, "On the Trail of Missing Masterpieces," 122.
29. Ibid., 121.
30. John Weitz, *Hitler's Banker* (London: Warner Books, 1999), 204, 208–10.

18. The Four Horsemen

1. NPG, 195/001.
2. The Gurlitt papers in the possession of the German government may give more information.
3. Hüneke, *Degenerate Art*, "On the Trail of Missing Masterpieces" (New York: Harry N. Abrams, 1991), 121.
4. Lynn H. Nicholas, *The Rape of Europa* (London: Macmillan, 1997), 12–13.
5. Ibid., 10–11.
6. Hellmut Lehmann-Haupt, *Art under a Dictatorship* (New York: Oxford University Press, 1954), 74–75.
7. Nicholas, *Rape of Europa*, 12.
8. Hüneke, *Degenerate Art*, 122.
9. Ibid.
10. William E. Dodd, Jr., and Martha Dodd, *Ambassador Dodd's Diary, 1933–1938* (London: Victor Gollancz Ltd., 1941), 236, 397, 428.
11. Nicholas, *Rape of Europa*, 24.
12. Janda, in *Degenerate Art*, 113.
13. Ibid.

14. Ibid., 89; cf. Rave, *Kunstdiktatur*, 145–46.

15. Ibid., 90. Some sixty-five cities responded to Goebbels's telegram on November 23, 1937, inviting them to bid on dates for their own showing of the exhibition.

16. John Weitz, *Hitler's Banker* (London: Warner Books, 1999), 192.

17. Ibid., 193.

18. Ibid.

19. Ibid., 220; cf. Schacht, 457.

20. Nicholas, *Rape of Europa*, 23.

21. Hüneke, *Degenerate Art*, 124. Franz, Roh, *Entartete Kunst—Kunstbarbarei im Dritten Reich* (Hannover, Germany: Fackelträger-Verlag, 1962), 51. Petropoulos, "From Lucerne to Washington, DC" in *Degenerate Art* (New York: Neue Galerie, 2013), 283. The Möller Stiftung (Foundation) has set itself the task of financing this database of *all* purged art.

22. Roh, *Entartete Kunst*, 52.

23. Hüneke, *Degenerate Art*, 124.

24. Ibid.

25. The family correspondence limped on after Cornelius's death for a few months. The Gurlitt papers with the German government may shed more light.

19. Tradecraft

1. Jonathan Petropoulos, *Art as Politics* (Chapel Hill, NC: University of North Carolina, 1996), 92–93. Also Avraham Barkai, *From Boycott to Annihilation* (Hanover, NH: University of New England Press, 1989), 84–87; BAB, R43II/1238c, 17.

2. Esther Tisa Francini, Anna Heuss, and Georg Kreis, *Fluchtgut—Raubgut: Der Transfer von Kulturgütern in und über die Schweiz 1933–1945 und die Frage der Restitution*, Expertkommission Schweiz—Zweiter Weltkrieg, Bd. 1 (Zurich: Chronos, 2001), 67. This is the Swiss Expert Commission's first effort at an historical analysis of the role Switzerland played with regard to both "Escape Goods" and "Looted Goods."

3. Petropoulos, *Art as Politics*, 76; Iselt, *Sonderbeauftragter des Führers* (Cologne: Böhlau Verlag, 2010), 100. Also BAB R55/21015 and R55/21017 for details.

4. Roh, *Entartete Kunst*, 53.

5. Hüneke, *Degenerate Art*, 125.

6. Ibid., 127; cf. letters to Franz Hofmann October 14, 1938 and Rolf Hetsch October 28, 1938 from (ZStA, Best. 50.01-1017, bl. 49).

7. Lynn H. Nicholas, *The Rape of Europa* (London: Macmillan, 1997), 25.

8. Hüneke, *Degenerate Art*, 127.

9. Ibid.; cf. Nachlass Ferdinand Möller, Berlinische Galerie, letter November 9, 1938.

10. Ibid., 128.

11. I suspect Böhmer's inclusion had more to do with his "closeness" to Barlach, with whom even Hitler had voiced a willingness at some sort of reconciliation. Barlach's wife was also Böhmer's mistress.

12. Francini, *Fluchtgut*, 67.

13. Ibid., 72.

14. Ibid., 71.

15. Barkai, *From Boycott to Annihilation*, 174–75; cf. Yad Vashem Archive, JM/2828.

16. Francini, *Fluchtgut*, 137.

17. Halvorsen was introduced by Kirchbach. Gurlitt dealt with him for his Oslo exhibition while still at the museum in Zwickau.

18. Francini, *Fluchtgut*, 137.

19. Ibid., 139.

20. Ibid., 215.

20. The Treasure Houses

1. Helen Fry, *Spymaster: The Secret Life of Thomas Kendrick* (London: Kindle edition, 2014). I had the pleasure of working with Helen on several film scripts where she shared her deep knowledge of the Anschluss and the war.

2. Avraham Barkai, *From Boycott to Annihilation* (Hanover, NH: University of New England Press, 1989), 133. Grynszpan maintained he was avenging the injustice of the deportation of his parents to Poland on October 28.

3. There are still sacred items of Judaica which have yet to find a home some seventy years later.

4. Both headlines are from November 11, 1938.

5. Ibid., 138.

6. Author interview with David Toren (aka Klaus Garnowski) in his Manhattan apartment June 4, 2014.

7. BAB, R2-12920 microfilm.

8. NARA, RG153, roll 0001, 86.

9. Albert Speer, *Inside the Third Reich* (London: Phoenix, 1995), 127–28.

10. Speer, 154.

11. Pevsner's career was launched in Dresden. He had Jewish ancestors, so when the opportunity arose to move his family to London, he did.

12. Francini, *Fluchtgut*, 144.

13. Stephanie Barron, ed., *Degenerate Art* (New York: Harry N. Abrams, 1991), 138; cf. Kreis, *"Entarte" Kunst für Basel*, 12–13.

14. Ibid.; cf. Kreis, 168–69.

15. Ibid., 140.

16. Francini, *Fluchtgut* (Zurich: Chronos, 2001), 216; private correspondence with Jonathan Petropoulos.

17. Ibid., 139.

18. Ibid., 140.

19. Ibid.

20. Ibid. Notwithstanding this reference, the author of this otherwise finely researched article has based the statement that "Germany had invaded the free city of Danzig" that day on the William F. Arntz papers. No such invasion took place that day. The

nearest pre–World War II significant event was on June 17, with the return of the refugee ship *St. Louis*, which had been refused entry to the United States and Cuba, returned to Belgium. Almost all of its refugees were later slaughtered by the Nazis.

21. Ibid., 141.
22. Ibid., 144, 145.
23. Francini, *Fluchtgut*, 215.
24. Alice Goldfarb Marquis, *Alfred H. Barr, Jr.* (Chicago: Contemporary Books, 1989), 177–78.
25. Ibid., 178.
26. AAA, Jane Wade Papers, Nazi Authorization dated November 14, 1936.
27. Ibid.
28. Marquis, *Alfred H. Barr, Jr.*, 178.
29. Ibid., 178–79.
30. BAB, R55/21019; also Francini, *Fluchtgut*, 145.

21. The Posse Years

1. NARA, M1934, RG226, roll 0001, 173–78. Gould, a Nazi hostess, was also reputed to be the mistress of three different Nazis.
2. www.dictionaryofarthistorians.org/posseh.htm.
3. Ibid.
4. Kathrin Iselt, *Sonderbeauftragter des Führers* (Köln: Böhlau Verlag, 2010), 98–99, note 94. BAB, R 55/20.744, fol. 92–114.
5. NARA, CIR no. 4: 57–59.
6. Francini, *Fluchtgut* (Zurich: Chronos, 2001), 220, 239n.
7. Author interview with Elisabeth Novak-Thaller, director Lentos Museum, Linz, May 24, 2013. The original will be on display in 2015 at the Liège *Exhibition about Degenerate Art*; microfilm printout in BAK B323/134.
8. Francini, *Fluchtgut*, 216.
9. Lynn H. Nicholas, *The Rape of Europa* (London: Macmillan, 1997), 69.
10. Ibid., 68.
11. Ibid., 69.
12. BAK, B323/134, f. 70, 10 December 1940.
13. Ibid.
14. Ibid. This is a summarized translation of the letter.
15. Jonathan Petropoulos, *Art as Politics* (Chapel Hill, NC: University of North Carolina, 1996), 264–65.
16. BAK, B323/134, fol. 70, no. 381.
17. Ibid., fols. 68–70.
18. AAA, Curt Valentin Papers, Beckmann file, Buchholz to Beckmann June 14, 1940.
19. Ibid.
20. Ibid., Valentin to Beckmann, June 8, 1940.
21. BAK, B323/134, fol. 40, no. 211; fol. 41, no. 213; fols. 63–65.

22. See AAA, Curt Valentin Papers; SAC, SpK BA Land G251, letter August 6, 1946.

23. SAC, SpK BA Land G251, fol. 79.

24. Ibid., fol. 78.

25. BAK, B323/134 is littered with Gurlitt's *"Heil Hitler!"* salutations, the first one dated September 10, 1941.

26. Ibid.

27. Ibid., 79. Karla Langhoff's statement is here, too.

28. www.lootedart.com. Toren v Bavarian Government and German Federal Government.

29. Ibid., 78.

30. Ibid., 79.

31. Ibid.

32. www.interactive.ancestry.com/30299/rddeu1824b_078875-0227/14903396?backurl =http%3a%2f%2fsearch.ancestry.com%2fcgi-bin%2fsse.dll%3fgst%3d-6&ssrc =&backlabel=ReturnSearchResults&rc=835,2728,1020,2750. A 1935 Hamburg telephone book unlocked the mystery surrounding Theo Hermsen. No expert or archivist with whom I spoke or corresponded, including the director of the Dutch Restitution Services, had any information on Hermsen other than that provided to Gurlitt in his statements to Allied interrogators.

22. Swallowing the Treasure

1. NARA, CIR no. 4.

2. NARA, Vlug report, RG239/roll 0008, 5–6.

3. Charles Williams, *Pétain* (London: Little Brown, 2005), 333.

4. A few online references for initial further information can be found at: www.eye witnesstohistory.com/dunkirk.htm or www.historylearningsite.co.uk/dunkirk.htm.

5. Henri Michel, *Paris Allemand* (Paris: Albin Michel, 1981), 19.

6. Williams, *Pétain*, 332.

7. Churchill urged Reynaud (prime minister of France) to wire Roosevelt for help. See Williams, *Pétain*, 319–22.

8. Ibid., 29.

9. Williams, *Pétain*, 335–36.

10. Lynn H. Nicholas, *The Rape of Europa* (London: Macmillan, 1997), 116; cf. Shirer, *Third Republic*, 914.

11. Emmanuelle Polack and Philippe Dagen, eds., *Les carnets de Rose Valland* (Paris: Fage Editions, 2013), 9–10; cf. Valland, *Le front de l'art* (Paris: Librairie Plon, 1961), 49.

12. Jonathan Petropoulos, *Art as Politics* (Chapel Hill, NC: University of North Carolina, 1996), 129.

13. Nicholas, *Rape of Europa*, 119.

14. Ibid., 120.

15. Ibid., 121.

16. Petropoulos, *Art as Politics*, 125–26.

17. IMT, *Trial of the Major War Criminals*, 8:68.

18. Petropoulos, *Art as Politics*, 128.

19. Valland, *Le front de l'art*, 48.

20. Polack and Dagen, *Les carnets de Rose Valland*, 15.

21. Valland, *Le front de l'art* (Paris: Librairie Plan, 1961), 55–56.

22. Nicholas, *Rape of Europa*, 127–28.

23. Ibid., 128.

24. Ibid., 131–32; Polack and Dagen, *Les carnets de Rose Valland*, 19.

25. Ibid., 142.

26. Anne Sinclair, *21 rue la Boétie* (Paris: Éditions Grasset et Fasquelle, 2012). Also CDJC, XIa-230a.

27. CDJC, XXIX-36, Aryanization of Wildenstein. Wildenstein left for the United States on January 29, 1941.

28. Ibid., 78–79.

29. AAA, Valentin Papers, letter March 31, 1942.

30. CDJC, XXI-14, XXI-15, letter June 23, 1942.

31. CDJC, CX-217, letter November 27, 1942.

32. Ibid.

33. Nicholas, *Rape of Europa*, 157–58.

34. Frederic Spotts, *The Shameful Peace* (London: Yale University Press, 2010), 159.

35. Ibid., 150.

36. Nicholas, *Rape of Europa*, 124.

37. Spotts, *Shameful Peace*, 151.

23. Viau

1. Lynn H. Nicholas, *The Rape of Europa* (London: Macmillan, 1997), 153.

2. BAK, B 323/134, fol. 68, no. 372.

3. webarchive.nationalarchives.gov.uk/20070706011932/www.raf.mod.uk/bomber command/jul42.html.

4. NARA, DIR nos. 12, 37.

5. ANF, AJ40/573, export application 37.875, Gurlitt list December 17, 1942.

6. There are several examples of Gurlitt's poor French in AJ 40. He even provided translations in German for his addressee, fearing he hadn't made himself understood.

7. CDJC, XIf-32, November 17, 1941.

8. ANF, AJ40/573, export applications 37.876, 38.218, 38.263, 38.606. Also the Viau Auction Catalogue in the same file.

9. *Le Nouvel Observateur*, www.rue89.nouvelobs.com/rue89-culture/2013/11/26/tableaux-nazis-gurlitt-a-fait-bonnes-affaires-france-247841.

10. ANF, AJ40/573, press clipping from the *Pariser Zeitung* last page (unnumbered).

11. Ibid.

12. Ibid. Memo stamped February 23, 1943.

13. Ibid. Memo January 26, 1943. The underlining is mine.

14. Ibid.
15. Ibid.
16. Kathrin Iselt, *Sonderbeauftragter des Führers* (Vienna: Böhlau Verlag, Köln, 2010), 181. Scholars repeat the story that Posse named Voss his successor on his deathbed. Yet Voss was one of the most unlikely candidates, not only for his supposed political convictions but also because he hadn't been employed by one of the big museums, only as the director of Wiesbaden, despite his admired scholarship. Given Hitler's convoluted thinking, this might have been an advantage alongside his tremendous credentials in nineteenth-century German and Italian Renaissance art, particularly if Hitler was considering an invasion to "support" (meaning invade) Italy after the defeat of Rommel's Afrikakorps.
17. Nicholas, *Rape of Europa*, 171.
18. Ibid., 130.

24. King Raffke

1. BAK, B323/134, f. 60, no. 322 3.
2. ANF, AJ 40/574, letter July 27, 1944. Other letters are, among others, AJ 40/574, export applications 38650—38658, 38662–38668, letter April 11, 1943, letter January 11, 1944, April 7, 1944, and application no. 26522, letter June 16, 1944.
3. Rose Valland, *Le front de l'art* (Paris: Librairie Plon, 1961), 72–73.
4. Ibid., 90.
5. Ibid., 91, law of April 7, 1942.
6. Ibid., 92, Bunjes report August 18, 1942.
7. Emmanuelle Polack and Philippe Dagen, eds., *Les carnets de Rose Valland* (Paris: Fage Éditions, 2011), 71 (fol. 82).
8. Ibid.
9. Jonathan Petropoulos, *Art as Politics* (Chapel Hill, NC: University of North Carolina, 1996), 159.
10. ANF, AJ40/574. Gurlitt is labeled "the main exporter to the German authorities" through his agent Hermsen. The April 11, 1943 letter is salient detailing the difficulties the authorities had with Gurlitt.
11. Valland, *Le front de l'art*, 93.
12. Ibid., 106–7.
13. Ibid., 107. For Voss's official statement about the Schloss Collection heist, see CIR no. 4, attachment 27.
14. BAB, R 43 II/1653, fol. 89, letter from Gurlitt to Voss, September 4, 1944, and R 43II/1651a, fol. 33, Voss to Lammers September 6, 1944.
15. Ibid., 106–10.
16. Polack and Dagen, *Les carnets de Rose Valland*, 71.
17. Ibid.
18. BAK, B323/45-51, fol. 56 re the Schloss Collection in the "Dresden Catalogue."
19. Valland, *Le front de l'art*, 178–83. Many scholars describe this May event as the one

that took place in mid-July. Valland, however, describes two separate events—the one on May 27, 1943, and the one from July 19 to 23, 1943. Four days after the July "trial," these were driven to the garden of the Jeu de Paume under guard and heaped onto the bonfire. Valland *omits* the May bonfire from her contemporaneous journal. See Polack and Dagen, *Les carnets de Rose Valland*, 71 (fol. 85).

20. Ibid., 182. Valland believed that only those paintings deemed as fakes, poorly restored, or of no intrinsic value were destroyed. In his statement to the ALIU after capture on August 15, 1945, DIR no. 4, page 5, Gustav Rochlitz said, "Scholz talked frequently in almost hysterical terms about the 'degenerate' nature of all modern French painting."

21. BAK B323/109, f. 119, Reimer to Reger, September 29, 1943. Italics are mine.

22. ANF, AJ 40/573 and AJ40/574, Hermsen file, export application 13678 dated March 27, 1944.

23. Ibid., cover letter for invoice.

24. Petropoulos, *Art as Politics*, 159–60.

25. Ibid., April 5, 1944 letter.

26. BAB, R 55/667.

27. ANF, AJ 40/573 and AJ 40/574. Eighteen of the 129 export applications were clearly in the name of Schmidt and the Dorotheum—nos. 13679, 17528, 21495, 22272, 22273, 24065, 24066, 27068, 27069, 27068, 27069, 27238, 27239, 27668, 27861–27863, 28332, 29418, 29419, 29629, 31237, 31701, and 31702.

28. BAB, R8 XIV/12, fol. 2. These are the foreign exchange applications by Hermsen. See also Iselt, *Der Sonderbeauftragter für Linz*, 288–89.

29. ANF, AJ 40/573 and AJ40/574, Hermsen file, export application 33019, October 1943.

30. My analysis takes into consideration *all* the details of the 129 applications made by either Hermsen or Gurlitt in AJ40/574 and AJ40/573 and is based entirely on the statistical evidence.

31. Lynn H. Nicholas, *The Rape of Europa* (London: Macmillan, 1997), 157.

32. Petropoulos, *Art as Politics*, 141–42.

33. ANF, AJ 40/573 and AJ40/574, export applications. I reviewed *all* export applications between 1941 and 1944. These were filed by the exporter name and application number. Each application had its own file. They are kept in two large archival boxes at the ANF. The Gurlitt/Hermsen file alone is too large for a single box.

34. ANF, AJ 40/574, export application no. 18089.

35. ANF, AJ 40/573 and AJ40/574, all 33 rejected applications and a number of accepted ones of the 129 in total.

36. ANF, AJ 40/574, export application nos. 7577, 7578, 8091.

37. BAK, B323/134, fol. 66, no. 356; fol. 64, no. 351; fol. 62, nos. 341, 337 (on Gurlitt French export licenses); fol. 49, no. 262 for example.

25. Quick, the Allies Are Coming!

1. NARA, RG 239, roll 0050, 6. On the following page (7) the valid remark is made that

Buchholz could never have opened up his bookshop/gallery in Lisbon without the prior approval of the German government.

2. Georg Wacha, *Jahrbuch des OÖ Musealvereins 149/1* (Linz: Gesellschaft für Landeskunde, Festschrift Gerhard Winkler, 2005). "Der Kunsthistoriker Dr. Justus Schmidt," 644–45.

3. Lynn H. Nicholas, *The Rape of Europa* (London: Macmillan, 1997), 218; Robert Edsel, *Monuments Men* (London: Preface Publishing, 2009), 52–53.

4. NA, www.nationalarchives.gov.uk/documents/records/looted-art-in-depth-intro.pdf, 3.

5. BAK, B323/134, fol. 53, no. 285.

6. BAK, 323/182 is solely dedicated to this.

7. James Rorimer, *Survival* (New York: Abelard Press, 1950), 153.

8. BAK, B323/134, fol. 49, no. 259.

9. It is possible that more details could be gleaned by proper forensic financial analysis of the Gurlitt papers held by the German government.

10. ANF, AJ 40/574, applications 28558–28564 are good examples.

11. Ibid., application 27864, July 3, 1944.

12. BAK, B323/134, fol. 49, no. 262.

13. Ibid., fol. 47, no. 250.

14. Ibid., fols. 47, 46, 30 for example.

15. Ibid., fol. 42, 43.

26. Surrendered . . . or Captured?

1. Victor Klemperer, *To The Bitter End* (London: Phoenix, Kindle edition, 2013).

2. Joseph W. Angell, *Historical Analysis of the Dresden Bombing February 13–14*, USAF Historical Division Research Studies Institute, HQ, US Military, Air University, 1953, conclusion [pages not numbered]. The Nazis claimed that some 200,000 people were killed. In 2010, a German commission confirmed a figure of up to 25,000.

3. Frederick Taylor, *Dresden: Tuesday, February 13, 1945* (New York: HarperCollins, 2004), 278, 279.

4. Henny Brenner, *The Song Is Over* (Tuscaloosa, AL: University of Alabama Press, 2010), 53. This is a short, simple and heartrending eyewitness account of a Jewish girl surviving in Dresden.

5. Ibid., 59.

6. SKD, Vorakten, Nr. 54/7, 14–15, 67.

7. Ibid., Vorakten, Nr. 52/3, 283–285; Nr 54/11–13.

8. NARA, CIR no. 4: 51. Gurlitt claimed that Hermsen had died in Paris at the end of 1944. Despite extensive searches in Paris, there is no proof that he did. Gurlitt also claimed that he was introduced to Hermsen by Herbert Engel in Paris, which would make the presence of his next-door neighbor being a Dutchman called Hermsen an extraordinary coincidence beyond reason.

9. Brenner, *The Song Is Over*, 62–65.

10. Ibid., 60.
11. NARA, M1944, RG 239, roll 0006, 12.
12. In a foreword written for an unpublished exhibition catalogue in Düsseldorf's archives, Gurlitt claimed in November 1955, "It was only later, after a communist village mayor had confiscated them, that I was able to secure their release with a bit of cunning and, thanks to a good Russian who was delighted with two bottles of schnapps on a rainy night, slip them through the Iron Curtain." Gurlitt withdrew this foreword, stating that it should not be published "for all kinds of reasons." See *Der Spiegel*, November 18, 2013 article.
13. One of the greatest treasures looted was the Amber Chamber from the opulent Czar's Catherine Palace at Tsarskoe Selo. In January 1945, Albert Speer evacuated it from Königsberg along with other highly valuable works. See minute 31 of the documentary *The Amber Room—Lost in Time (Part I)*, Yutaka Shigenobou, producer (2006).
14. BAK, 323/134, fol. 45, no. 237.
15. All twenty-four banks in Dresden were destroyed—along with their bank vaults—in the British firebombing of the city. Gurlitt would later claim that he had more than RM 250,000 in cash in his account there.
16. Telephone conversation with Stephan Holzinger, February 24, 2014.

27. House Arrest

1. Shirer (in 1960) and Bullock (originally published in 1952) wrote that Bormann disappeared in the Battle of Berlin. Antony Beevor, in *Berlin* (London: Penguin, 2003), relates Axmann's story. Axmann, head of the Hitler Youth, claimed that on May 1, 1945, he fled the bunker with Bormann and Hitler's surgeon, Ludwig Stumpfegger, at the helm of the last faithful followers. German tanks led them from the city toward the south. After the lead tank exploded, slightly wounding the trio, Axmann turned west. Bormann and Stumpfegger decided to head east, to follow the rail tracks out of the city. When Axmann found them again, they were lying on their backs where the Invalidenstrasse crosses the railway tracks, presumably shot in the back. Axmann continued on, escaping from Berlin. Six months later he was captured. The rumors about Paraguay began as early as June 1945, when Bormann's longtime chauffeur was certain he'd seen Bormann in Munich shortly after May 1.
2. www.jewishvirtuallibrary.org/jsource/Holocaust/women.html, entry for Gerda Bormann.
3. Others were Wiesbaden (Voss's former collecting point under the Nazis), Schönebeck, Goslar. When Neuschwanstein and Altaussee were discovered, these acted as temporary collecting points, too.
4. McKay died in 1998. After interviewing Gurlitt, he acted as one of the lawyers at Nuremberg. Obituary www.articles.chicagotribune.com/1993-02-08/news/9303176747 _1_associate-judge-house-arrest-single-murder-case.
5. NARA, www.fold3.com, M1946, RG260/roll 0134, "Interrogation of Art Dealers —Hildebrand Gurlitt," 94.

6. Ibid.

7. Ibid. Bauer, as a persecuted Jew, joined the US Army in 1941 and was coopted by the Third Army as a translator. Other examples exist, such as Howard Triest, who translated for the psychiatrists at Nuremberg (see Helen Fry, *Inside Nuremberg Prison*, Kindle edition, 2011).

8. Ibid., Life History, 83.

9. See *Der Spiegel* article, November 18, 2013 containing the foreword to the exhibition catalogue written by Hildebrand Gurlitt in 1955.

10. NARA, www.fold3.com, M1946, RG260/roll 0134, 83.

11. Ibid.

12. www.photo.dresden.de/de/03/nachrichten/2008/c_82.php?lastpage=zur%20Ergebnisliste.

13. NARA, www.fold3.com, M1946, RG260/roll 0134, 84.

14. Ibid., 84. I could find no such book on Käthe Kollwitz published under the name of Hildebrand Gurlitt.

15. NARA, CIR no. 4: 51. It was McKay's initial interview that discovered these facts.

16. Spk BA, Land G251, 48.

17. NARA, www.fold3.com, M1946, RG260/roll 0134, 87.

18. This figure comes from the sum of the export application transactions carried out by Gurlitt as represented in AJ40/573 and AJ40/574.

19. NARA, www.fold3.com, M1946, RG260/roll 0134, 84.

20. Ibid.

21. Ibid., 85.

22. Ibid.

23. Ibid. Italics are mine.

24. Ibid. Organization Todt was a major projects engineering division of the Nazi army, infamous for its slave labor.

25. Ibid., 86.

26. www.dictionaryofarthistorians.org/Voss.

27. NARA, M1946, RG260/roll 0134, 84.

28. Ibid.

29. Ibid., 86–89.

30. Lynn H. Nicholas, *The Rape of Europa* (London: Macmillan, 1997), 121; cf. NA RG 260/411, Keitel to CIC France, September 17, 1940.

31. NARA, M1946, RG260/roll 0134, 86.

32. Ibid.

33. Nicholas, *Rape of Europa*, 122. According to Gurlitt, at the time this was purchased by a "foreign buyer" for $40.

34. In 1950 it was agreed that the Gurlitt collection could return to the owner.

35. Joint Chiefs of Staff JCS 1067 remained secret until October 17, 1945. The Allied Control Council formed from US, British, French, and Russian occupying forces officially ran Germany from the signing of the Potsdam Agreement, on August 2,

1945, until 1955. Directive no. 9, dealing with war criminals, became law on August 30, 1945.

36. AAA, interview with Robert F. Brown, October 27 and December 14, 1981, for the AAA/Smithsonian Institution. A transcript of the interview can be found in the S. Lane Faison Papers at the AAA.

37. www.monumentsmenfoundation.org/the-heroes/the-monuments-men/faison-lt.-cdr.-s.-lane-jr.

38. NARA, M1941, RG 260/roll 0031, 64.

39. Ibid., 59.

40. I thank Jonathan Petropoulos for sharing this information with me, which helped to explain some of the deficits in the reporting which I would have otherwise expected to see.

41. I am deeply indebted to Jonathan Searle for having taken such pains to write his thorough report, dated January 14, 2014. The citation is from page 1.

42. Ibid., 3.

43. Ibid.

44. NARA, CIR no. 4 Supplement, December 15, 1945, 1.

45. Outside Germany, art looters were punished. For example, Hermann Bunjes of the ERR was imprisoned in France, where he committed suicide. Wendland and Stocklin, too, were jailed. Von Behr and his wife also committed suicide when France was liberated. Ambassador Abetz was murdered in 1956.

28. Under the Microscope

1. NARA, Safehaven Papers, M1934, RG 226, Project Safehaven, 1942–1946, WASH-SPDF-INT I, roll 0001, 3.

2. Ibid., 8.

3. NARA, M1944, RG 239, roll 0051, 83.

4. Ibid., 101–2.

5. NARA, Safehaven Papers, M1934, RG 226, roll 0001, 12.

6. GETTY, 86061, Douglas Cooper Papers, Box 39, Report on Looted Art in Switzerland.

7. Ibid., 1–3.

8. Ibid., 3.

9. Ibid., 4–19.

10. Ibid., 14.

11. Ibid.

12. NARA, Safehaven Papers, M1934, RG 226, roll 0001, 19.

13. Ibid., 1–29.

14. Ibid., 29.

15. GETTY, 86061, Douglas Cooper Papers, Box 39, October 24, 1945 letter.

16. NARA, M1944, RG 239, roll 0092, 66.

17. Ibid., 67.

18. Ibid., 60.

19. Ibid., 60–61.

20. There were also several concentration-camp trials before the subsequent Nuremberg Military Tribunals. The twelve trials are: the Doctors Trial (December 1946–August 1947), the Milch Trial (January–April 1947), the Judges Trial (March–December 1947), the Pohl Trial (April–November 1947), the Flick Trial (April–December 1947), the IG Farben Trial (August 1947–July 1948), the Hostages Trial (July 1947–February 1948), the RuSHA Trial (October 1947–March 1948), the Einsatzgruppen Trial (September 1947–April 1948), the Krupp Trial (December 1947–July 1948), the Ministries Trial (January 1948–April 1949), and the High Command Trial (December 1947–October 1948).

21. See Peter Grose's monumental *Allen Dulles, Spymaster*, book 2, "Cold Sunrise" chapter for the first incident of the Cold War.

22. www.law.harvard.edu/library/digital/court-of-restitution-appeals-reports.html.

23. NARA, Vlug Report, M1944, RG 239, roll 0008, 1.

24. Ibid., 6.

25. Ibid.

26. Ibid., 6–8, 30, 33, 56, 59.

27. NARA, M1926, RG 260, roll 0035, 14.

28. NARA, M1944, RG 239, roll 0081, 8.

29. Spk BA, Land G251, 6,7,9,11–15.

30. NARA, DIR no. 12: 18–19.

31. Ibid., 24.

32. ANDE, Carton 195 côte A 169, letter dated February 10, 1946 from Gurlitt to Valland.

33. Ibid.

34. Ibid.

35. NARA, RG 239, roll 0006, report of Lieutenant Col. Manuel, May 5, 1945.

36. Ibid., 86

37. Declaration No 01 345 cover page.

29. Düsseldorf

1. The Steiner/Waldorf schools aim to enhance children's imaginations, and cultivate independent thinking that can be tested scientifically.

2. NARA, M1944, RG 239, roll 0054, 375 to the Roberts Commission in the Vaucher Draft List of Dealers dated 17-3-45 states, "VOEMEL, Galerie Alex, Düsseldorf, Reported Specialist in Dutch Painting." He was then put on the list of "White Dealers" (meaning not "Black Listed"). See M1944, RG 239, roll 0055, 11. Vömel fared less well with the Germans. From a PC made available to me, there are a series of letters leading to legal action from Der Senator für Volksbildung from 1951 to 1952 concerning looted art in the case of Alice Victor against "Galerie Flechtheim." Vömel was found not guilty of any charges, since he had faithfully served Hitler, as did the judge of the trial.

3. Wolfgang Gurlitt always landed on his feet. His deal with the City of Linz Museum

was a delightful way for him to launder his art. Always an impossible man to pin down in a deal, Wolfgang fell out with Linz, however, when they felt he was taking advantage of the museum by insisting on having his art gallery (to sell his additional looted art from) as part of the deal. Wolfgang left them with a questionable heritage—and several paintings of looted art, which have since been returned. Source: Author interview with Linz director Elisabeth Nowak-Thaller, May 24, 2014.

4. NARA, DIR no. 12: 11–12. The Strasbourg trip that Wolfgang undertook was, contrary to what Voss and Wolfgang claimed, aimed at bringing back to Germany significant artworks held in the city by his longtime confidante, business partner, and lover, Lilli Agoston, who was originally from Strasbourg. After the war, Wolfgang claimed that he saved the part-Jewish Lilli by marrying her off to a Dane called Christiansen-Agoston. Lilli was brought to Altaussee to live with Wolfgang, his first wife, Julie Goeb, and his second wife, Käthe, as well as his two daughters in their small chalet.

5. NARA, Outshipment 243 from Wiesbaden Collecting Point, December 15, 1950.

6. AAA, Valentin Papers, letter from Dr. P. Beckmann to M. Beckmann, March 1, 1950.

7. Ibid.

8. Nonmonetary gold means gold rings, gold jewelry, and gold teeth.

9. Telephone conversation with Stephan Holzinger dated February 24, 2014, revealed the extent of Cornelius's talent as an artist.

10. V&A exhibition catalogue *German Watercolors, Drawings and Prints 1905–1955—A Mid-Century Review of German Art 1905–1955*, loan exhibition sponsored by the Republic of Germany and circulated by American Federation of the Arts, introduction, 3.

11. This is my analysis from the catalogue.

12. www.lostart.de/gurlitt.

13. Goepel applied for several positions, and nearly landed a job at the Bavarian State Paintings Collection; however, it was felt that his record during the war would not hold up to close scrutiny. It is possible that since Voss was also living in Munich at the time he had been consulted in the decision. Given that we now know about Goepel working under Gurlitt's direction in France, it is probable that Goepel resented his former associate. From 1948 Goepel worked as an editor at Prestel-Verlag until his death in 1966, and was cofounder of the Max Beckmann Society in 1953.

14. NARA, M1949, RG 260, roll 26, 4.

15. When I discussed this suspicion with art experts, they agreed that the date makes his death more than a mere coincidence and points to some Nazi motivation.

30. Aftermath and Munich

1. Lammers's wife and only daughter committed suicide when Hitler ordered him to be shot. When Lammers died, in 1962, he was buried in the same plot as they were, in Berchtesgaden.

2. This is no longer the case, leaving the Swiss feeling bloodied by the onslaught on their

highly lucrative banking system, and wondering why other countries should have the right to penetrate it to gain access to funds from tax evaders and terrorists.

3. NARA, M1949, RG 260, roll 26, 2.
4. www.lootedart.com newsletter of February 7, 2014; cf. FAZ article.
5. Ibid.
6. LMD, Standesamt München II 1968/539.
7. www.deutsche-biographie.de/sfz41057.html.
8. Any evidence either way may well be in the Gurlitt papers in the German government's possession.
9. LMD, Standesamt München II 1968/539.
10. www.spiegel.de/international/germany/spiegel-interview-with-cornelius-gurlitt -about-munich-art-find-a-933953.html.
11. Author interview with the director of the LMD. I am especially grateful to Anton Löffelmeier for sharing this information with me.

31. The Lion Tamer

1. www.spiegel.de/international/germany/spiegel-interview-with-cornelius-gurlitt -about-munich-art-find-a-933953.html.
2. Ibid.
3. Ibid.
4. www.lootedart.com newsletter, February 7, 2014.
5. Author's telephone conversation with Stephanie Barron, February 18, 2014.
6. NARA, M1949, RG 260, roll 26, 2.
7. Stuart E. Eizenstat, *Imperfect Justice: Looted Assets, Slave Labor, and the Unfinished Business of World War II* (New York: Public Affairs, 2004), 191.
8. www.ft.com/cms/s/0/b6c4c78e-4860-11e3-a3ef-00144feabdc0.html#ixzz3 FN4zaABP.
9. I am grateful to Mel Urbach and Markus Stoetzel for the interviews they granted me in New York and in Marburg.
10. Author interview with Markus Stoetzel, Marburg, July 15, 2014.
11. www.ft.com/cms/s/0/b6c4c78e-4860-11e3-a3ef-00144feabdc0.html#ixzz3 FN4zaABP.
12. Author interview with Markus Stoetzel, Marburg, July 15, 2014.
13. www.ft.com/cms/s/0/b6c4c78e-4860-11e3-a3ef-00144feabdc0.html#ixzz3 FN4zaABP.

32. Feeding Frenzy

1. www.online.wsj.com/news/articles/SB10001424052702304908304579561840264114 668?.
2. www.spiegel.de/international/germany/spiegel-interview-with-cornelius-gurlitt -about-munich-art-find-a-933953.html.
3. Ibid.

4. Ibid.

5. Author interview with Anton Löffelmeier of the LMD.

6. www.online.wsj.com/news/articles/SB100014240527023049083045795618402641 14668?.

7. I thank Stephan Holzinger, former spokesman for Cornelius Gurlitt, for providing me with an English version of this document.

8. Ibid.

9. His brother-in-law would also inherit personal items under a separate will, such as the Munich flat and the house in Salzburg.

10. Reiterated by several Swiss banking contacts who wish to remain anonymous.

11. www.online.wsj.com/news/articles/SB100014240527023049083045795618402641 14668?.

12. www.dailymail.co.uk/wires/ap/article-2655398/Germany-looted-Matisse-belongs -Jewish-family.html#ixzz3FSNEriTH.

13. The reply given stunned me and was later reiterated. My interest in Gurlitt was ignited.

SELECTED BIBLIOGRAPHY

Primary Sources

AAA   Jane Wade Papers, 1903–1971

Max Beckmann Papers, 1904–1974

S. Lane Faison Papers, 1922–1981

Transcript of Oral History with James Plaut, June 29, 1971

James Plaut Papers 1929–1980

James Rorimer Papers 1932–1982

George Leslie Stout Papers 1855–1978

Jacques Seligmann & Co. Records 1904–1978, (bulk 1913–1974)

Catalogues of Exhibitions organized by Curt Valentin, 1929–1948

ANDE—Côte 209SUP1:

1/4515 (Paul Rosenberg)

2/4535 (Alfonse Kann)

4/4541 (G. & J. Seligmann)

2/45392 (Seligmann)

20/4527 (Lindon)

1/1048 (Hermsen)

ANF   AJ/38/321–841 (Jewish Spoliations Series)

AJ/38/1109–140 (Jewish Spoliations Series)

AJ/38/5171–431

AJ/38/15166–77 (identity cards for foreigners)

F37/38—(IEQJ)

F/21/7116–8 (export licenses)

F/48/252–55

F/49/259–63

F/50/265–67
F/50/269
F/50/270
F/51/273–274
F/51/276
F/51/275
F/52/279
AJ/40/01 (German Archive Series)
AJ/40/37
AJ/40/539 (Ambassador Abetz)
AJ/40/573–74 (Gurlitt/Hermsen export license applications)
AJ/40/588–91 (Treuhand/châteaux)
AJ/40/600 (Gould)
AJ/40/611(Claude Bernheim)
AJ/40/817 (Dresdner Bank)
AJ/40/819 (Borchers)
AJ/40/880 (Rothschild)
AJ/40/1006 (Bernheim Galerie)
AJ/40/1042 (Cézanne)
AJ/40/1202
AJ/40/1215
AJ/40/1279
AJ/40/1487 (Guggenheim)
AJ/40/1578
AJ/40/1587

BAB   R55/21015 (Gurlitt Berlin/Hamburg)
           R55/21017 (Buchholz inventory)
           R55/21019 (Böhmer)
           R55/21020 (Haberstock)
           R8034-III/170 (anti-Semitism Ludwig Gurlitt)
           R2-12920 microfilm

BAK   B323/1202 (Wiedemann inventory)
           B 323/54 (Oskar Bondy)
           B323/44 (Dorotheum Purchases)
           B 323/50 and B 323/186 (Schloss)
           B 323/89 (Führerbau)
           B 323/1212 (Linz/Louvre)
           B 323/1213 (Linz)
           B 323/192 (photo album)
           B 323/250 (restitution to Gurlitt)
           B 323/249 (outshipment Gurlitt)

B 323/331, /332, /75, /135, /136, /137, /138, /139, /140, /142, /147, /148, /149, /155, /156 (art dealers)

B 323/134 (Linz)

B 323/124, /153, /156, /369 (Gurlitt)

B323/371 (Haberstock)

B323/363 (Caspari, Cassirer)

B 323/357 (Dietrich)

B 323/379, /380, /381 (Lange, Liebermann, and Lohse, respectively)

B 323/399 (Voss)

B 323/331 (Buemming, Dietrich, Fischer, Franke, Hildebrand and Wolfgang Gurlitt, Haberstock correspondence)

B 323/322 (Neumann)

B 323/153 (Hermsen Paris)

B 323/174 (Lange, Dietrich)

B 323/173 (Gurlitt Dresden invoices/Böhmer)

B 323/331 (list of Hitler's collection)

B 323/583 (Bormann correspondence re Linz)

B 323/235 (list of artworks held at the Neue Residenz Bamberg)

CDJC   XXVa-186 (Loebl and Engel)

XXIX-36 (Aryanization of Wildenstein)

XXVa-327 (Ribbentrop)

XXIII-61a (outlawing Jews at Hôtel Drouot)

XIa-230a (IEQJ at Rosenberg's Gallery)

XIb-614 (letter regarding public auctions)

XIb-615 (letter from Sezille to Ader)

XIb-617 (letter from Ader)

XIb-631 (letter from Sezille to Ader)

XIf-32 (Sezille letter halting sale at Versailles)

CIX-6 (interdiction to Drouot)

CX-127 (letter to Jacques Charpentier)

CXVIII-8 (David-Weill)

XX-13 (general documents 1940–46)

CXVII-38 (Rothschild seizures)

CXVII-143 (Radio-Diffusion Bernheim)

LXXVII-15 (Behr)

CVII-63 (Pellepoix re Schloss)

LXXIX-9 (Feldpolizei rapports)

CCCLXXXIX-15 (*New York Times* article)

LXXXIX-66 (Frank J. Gould)

LXII-15 (letter from Behr to Göring)

IV-213(25–62) (*Annuaire téléphonique allemande*)

V-100 (Schenker & Co.)

V-101 (art at German Embassy)

V-103 (Schenker payments)

CV-39 (interception of correspondence to Zurich)

CL6997222, 953632-Masterfile, Office of Alien Property Custodian, Annual Report; Holocaust Assets, Vesting Order 3711; NARA, RG 131, Office of Alien Property (OAP) Entry 65F-1063.

GETTY   Edouardo Westerdahl Papers, ref. 861077; 86061, Douglas Cooper Papers, Box 39, Report on Looted Art in Switzerland

IMT, *Trial of the Major War Criminals*, 8

LMD, Standesamt München II 1968/539

NARA—College Park, Maryland:

RG 226, Records pertaining to Safehaven Files:

     Box 62, Jews in Belgium

     Boxes 115–70, German Control of Swiss Economy

     Box 93, Swiss attitude to Germans and Jews

     Box 247, Collection of War Crimes Evidence

     Box 255, Enemy Activity in South America

     Box 262, Industrial Diamond Trade

     Box 263, Situation Report in Portugal

     Box 303, Intelligence on Germans in Switzerland

     Box 449, Germany's diamond smuggling methods

RG 226, Project Safehaven, 1942–1946, WASH-SPDF-INT I, roll 0001,

RG239/microfilm rolls 0006; 0008 (Vlug Report); 0050; 0054

RG 260, Records of the U.S. Occupation Headquarters:

     Boxes 118–19, File 000.5, War Crimes

     Box 129, File 00.7, Fine Arts

     Boxes 288–89, File 386.7, Frozen Assets including Funds

     Box 289, File 386.7, Documents to Alien Property Custodian Section

     Boxes 315–17, File 602.3, Restitution

     Boxes 317–18, File 602.3, Reparations

RG 260, Records of the Economics Division, General Correspondence Central Files:

     Boxes 46–47, File 007, Fine Arts, Museums, Archives, Cultural Objects

     Boxes 81–87, File 386, Restitution

     Boxes 88–90, File 386, Reparations

     Box 111, File 0004.1, Historicals, Museums, Antiquities

     Boxes 115–16, File 007.2, Fine Arts and Cultural Objects

     Boxes 143–55, File 386, Restitution

     Boxes 156–57, File 387, Reparations

     Box 172, File 004.2, Banks and Banking & File 007, Fine Arts and Objects

     Box 196–97, File 386, Restitution & File 387, Reparations

     Box 209, File 004.2, Banks and Banking, & File 007, Fine Arts & Objects

RG 260—Records of the Property Division (General Records 1944–50), Boxes 1–18

RG260, microfilm roll 0026; 0031; 0134; CIR no. 4, DIR no. 12

RG 153, microfilm roll 0001

RG 84—Records of the Foreign Service Posts of the Department of State (Embassy Records), File 711.3–8

Angell, Joseph W. *Historical Analysis of the Dresden Bombing February 13–14*. USAF Historical Division Research Studies Institute, HQ, US Military, Air University, 1953.

NPG—All 263 family letters and biographical data.

SAC—Gurlitt File from Northern Bavaria. Spk BA Land G 251.

Internet Primary Sources

www.lostart.de: List of Gurlitt artworks believed to be of questionable origin. Press Release (Pressmitteilung von 9 April 2013) von Press und Informationsamt der Bundesregierung—*Empfehlung der Beratenden Kommission für die Rückgabe NS-verfolgungsbedingt entzogener Kulturgüter.*

www.lootedart.com: Up-to-date information, in English, regarding the ongoing investigations into the Gurlitt find.

www.fold3.com: American original documents from the Ardelia Hall Collection at the National Archives in Washington, DC.

www.faz.net: *Frankfurter Allgemeine Zeitung* online.

www.wsj.com: *Wall Street Journal* online.

Internet Secondary Sources

Boym, Svetlana. "Conspiracy Theories and Literary Ethics: Umberto Eco, Danilo Kis and the Protocols of Zion." *Comparative Literature* 52, no. 2 (1999): 97–122. www.jstor.org/stable/1771244.

Burtsev, Vladimir. "The Elders of Sion: A Proved Forgery." *Slavonic and East European Review* 17, no. 49 (1938): 99–104. www.jstor.org/stable/4203461.

Dinnerstein, Leonard. "Henry Ford and the Jews: A Mass Production of Hate." *Business History Review* 76, no. 2 (2002): 365–67. www.jstor.org/stable/4127850.

Woeste, Victoria Saker. "Insecure Equality: Louis Marshall, Henry Ford and the Problem of Defamatory Antisemitism, 1920–29." *Journal of American History* 91, no. 3 (2004): 877–905. www.jstor.org/stable/3662859.

Bevir, Mark. "The West Turns Eastwards: Madame Blatavsky and the Transformation of the Occult Tradition." *Journal of the American Academy of Religion* 62, no. 3 (1994): 747–67. www.jstor.org/stable/1465212.

Grant, Mark. "Steiner and the Humours: The Survival of Ancient Greek Science." *British Journal of Educational Studies* 47, no. 1 (1999): 56–70. www.jstor.org/stable/3122384.

Mosse, G. L. "The Mystical Origins of National Socialism." *Journal of the History of Ideas* 22, no. 1 (1961): 81–96. www.jstor.org/stable/2707875.

Staudenmaier, Paul. "Race and Redemption: Racial and Ethnic Evolution in Rudolf Steiner's Anthroposophy." *Novo Religio: The Journal for Alternate and Emergent Religions* 1, no. 3 (2008): 4–36. www.jstor.org/stable/10.1525/nr.2008.11.3.4.

Weikart, Richard. "Progress through Racial Extermination: Social Darwinism, Eugenics, and Pacifism in Germany 1860–1918." *German Studies Review* 26, no. 2 (2003): 273–94. www.jstor.org/stable/143326.

Jordan, David Starr. "The Ways of Pangermany." *Scientific Monthly* 4, no. 1 (1917).

Catalogues

Barr, Alfred H., ed. *The Museum of Modern Art New York Painting and Sculpture Collection.* Paris: Les Éditions Braun & Cie, 1950.

Barron, Stephanie. *Degenerate Art—The Fate of the Avant-Garde in Nazi Germany.* New York: Los Angeles County Museum of Art, Harry N. Abrams, 1991.

Bishop, Janet, Cécile Debray, and Rebecca Rabinow, eds. *The Steins Collect: Matisse, Picasso, and the Parisian Avant-Garde.* New Haven: San Francisco Museum of Modern Art, Yale University Press, 2011.

Die Alte und neue spanische Kunst. Kunstverein Hamburg, August–September 1935.

Peters, Olaf, ed. *Degenerate Art—The Attack on Modern Art in Nazi Germany 1937.* Neue Galerie New York, March 13–June 30, 2014. New York: Prestel Publishing, 2014.

Portz, Hubert. *Zimmer frei für Cornelia Gurlitt, Lotte Wahle und Conrad Felixmüller, 26 April–14 June 2014.* Landau: Knecht Verlag, 2014.

Reyger, Leonie, ed. *German Watercolors, Drawings and Prints 1905–1955—A Mid-Century Review of German Art 1905–1955.* Exhibition catalogue. Washington, DC, 1956.

von Halasz, Joachim. *Hitler's Degenerate Art.* London: World Propaganda Classics, 2008.

Wacha, Georg. *Jahrbuch des OÖ Musealvereins 149/1.* Linz: Gesellschaft für Landeskunde, Festschrift Gerhard Winkler, 2005. "Der Kunsthistoriker Dr. Justus Schmidt," 639–54.

Primary Sources (Art)

Polack, Emmanuelle and Philippe Dagen. *Les carnets de Rose Valland.* Paris: Fage Editions, 2011.

Valland, Rose. *Le front de l'art 1939–1945.* Paris: Librairie Plon, 1961.

Secondary Sources (Art)

Feliciano, Hector. *The Lost Museum.* New York: Basic Books, 1997.

Flechner, Uwe, ed. *Das verfemte Meisterwerk: Schicksalswege moderner Kunst im Dritten Reich.* Berlin: Akademie Verlag GmbH, 2009.

Francini, Esther Tisa, Anna Heuss, and Georg Kreis. *Fluchtgut—Raubgut, Der Transfer von Kulturgütern in und über die Schweiz 1933–1945 und die Frage der Restitution.* Expertkommission Schweiz—Zweiter Weltkrieg, Bd. 1. Zurich: Chronos, 2001. 67.

Games, Stephen. *Pevsner—The Early Life: Germany and Art.* London: Continuum Books, 2010.

Iselt, Kathrin. *Sonderbeauftragter des Führers: Der Kunsthistoriker und Museumsmann Hermann Voss.* Köln: Böhlau Verlag, 2010.

Jeuthe, Gesa. *Kunstwerte im Wandel: Die Preisentwicklung der deutschen Moderne im nationalen und internationalen Kunstmarkt 1925 bis 1955.* Düsseldorf: Akademie Verlag, 2011.

Kalkschmidt, Eugen. *Carl Spitzweg und Seine Welt*. Munich: Verlag F. Bruckmann KG, 1945.

Kantor, Sybil Gordon. *Alfred H. Barr, Jr., and the Intellectual Origins of the Museum of Modern Art*. Cambridge, MA: MIT Press, 2002.

Kott, Christina. *Préserver l'art de l'ennemi? Le patrimoine artistique en Belgique et en France occupées, 1914–1918*. Brussels: Peter Lang, 2006.

Lehmann-Haupt, Hellmut. *Art under a Dictatorship*. New York: Oxford University Press, 1954.

Litchfield, David R. L. *The Thyssen Art Macabre*. London: Quartet Books, 2006.

Marquis, Alice Goldfarb. *Alfred H. Barr, Jr.: Missionary for the Modern*. Chicago: Contemporary Books, 1989.

Müller, Melissa and Monika Tatzkow. *Lost Lives, Lost Art: Jewish Collectors, Nazi Art Theft, and the Quest for Justice*. London: Frontline Books, 2010.

Nicholas, Lynn H. *The Rape of Europa*. London: Macmillan, 1994.

Petropoulos, Jonathan. *The Faustian Bargain—The Art World in Nazi Germany*. New York: Oxford University Press USA, 2000. Kindle edition.

———. *Art as Politics in the Third Reich*. Chapel Hill, NC: University of North Carolina Press, 1997.

Roh, Franz. *"Entartete" Kunst: Kunstbarbarei im Dritten Reich*. Hannover, Germany: Fackelträger-Verlag, 1962.

Rorimer, J. J. and Gilbert Rabin. *Survival—The Salvage and Protection of Art in War*. New York: Abelard Press, 1950.

Roxan, David and Ken Wanstall. *The Rape of Art*. New York: Coward-McCann, 1965.

Spotts, Frederic. *The Shameful Peace*. London: Yale University Press, 2010.

Urban, Martin. *Emil Nolde: Catalogue Raisonné of the Oil-Paintings, Volume 2, 1915–1951*. Translated by Gudrun Parsons. London: Philip Wilson Publishers, 2001.

Vergo, Peter. *Art in Vienna 1898–1918: Klimt, Kokoschka, Schiele and Their Contemporaries*. London: Phaidon, 1975.

———, *The Blue Rider*. Oxford: Phaidon, 1977.

Secondary Sources (Finance)

Barkai, Avraham. *From Boycott to Annihilation: The Economic Struggle of German Jews 1933–1943*. Hanover, NH: Brandeis University Press/University of New England, 1989.

Grose, Peter. *Allen Dulles, Spymaster: The Life and Times of the First Civilian Director of the CIA*. London: André Deutsch, 2004.

Taylor, Frederick. *The Downfall of Money*. London: Bloomsbury, 2013.

Weitz, John. *Hitler's Banker: Hjalmar Horace Greeley Schacht*, London: Warner Books, 1999.

Secondary Sources (History)

Apel, Dora. *Cultural Battlegrounds—Visual Imagery and the Tenth Anniversary of the First World War in Weimar Germany*. PhD thesis, University of Pittsburgh, 1995.

Asquith, Margot. *The Autobiography of Margot Asquith*. London: Weidenfeld & Nicolson, 1995.

Balfour, Michael. *Propaganda in War 1939–1945*. London: Routledge & Keegan Paul, 1979.

Becker, Jean-Jacques. *The Great War and the French People*. Leamington Spa, UK: Berg Publishers, 1985.

Bell, P. M. H. *The Origins of The Second World War in Europe*, 2nd ed. London: Longman, 1997.

Benns, F. L. and M. E. Seldon. *Europe 1914–1939*. New York: Meredith Publishing, 1965.

Bond, Brian. *War and Society in Europe 1870–1970*. Stroud: Sutton Publishing, 1998.

Brenner, Henny. *The Song Is Over—Survival of a Jewish Girl in Dresden*. Tuscaloosa, AL: University of Alabama Press, 2010.

Bullock, Alan. *Hitler: A Study in Tyranny*. London: Book Club Associates, 1973 revised edition.

Burckhardt, Jacob. *Die Kultur der Renaissance in Italien—Ein Versuch*. Urheberrechtsfreie Ausbgabe, 2011. Kindle edition.

———. *Judgements on History and Historians*. London: George Allen & Unwin, 1959.

Churchill, W. S. *The World Crisis 1911–14*. London: Thornton Butterworth Ltd., 1923.

———. *The World Crisis 1911–1918*, vols. 1 and 2. London: Odhams Press Ltd., 1939.

Darby, Graham. *Hitler, Appeasement and the Road to War, 1933–41*. London: Hodder & Stoughton, 1999.

Diehl, James M. *Paramilitary Politics in Weimar Germany*. Bloomington, IN: Indiana University Press, 1977.

de Jaeger, Charles. *The Linz File: Hitler's Plunder of Europe's Art*. Exeter, England: Webb & Bower, 1981.

Duffy, Christopher. *Through German Eyes: The British & the Somme 1916*. London: Weidenfeld & Nicolson, 2006.

Eckley, Grace. *Maiden Tribute—A Life of W. T. Stead*. Philadelphia: Xlibris, 2007.

Edsel, Robert M. and Bret Witter. *Monuments Men*. London: Preface Books, 2009.

Eizenstat, Stuart E. *Imperfect Justice: Looted Assets, Slave Labor, and the Unfinished Business of World War II*. New York: Public Affairs, 2004.

Farmborough, Florence. *Nurse at the Russian Front: A Diary 1914–18*. London: Constable & Company, 1974.

Gay, Peter. *Weimar Culture: The Outsider as Insider*. New York: W. W. Norton & Company, 2001.

Gold, Mary Jane. *Marseilles Année 40*. Paris: Phébus, 2001.

Guggenheim, Peggy. *Out of This Century: Confessions of an Art Addict*. London: André Deutsch, 1979.

Harwood, Ronald. *Taking Sides*. London: Faber & Faber, 1995.

Hitler, Adolf. *Mein Kampf*. London: Pimlico, 1997.

Horn, Wolfgang. *Kulturpolitik in Düsseldorf: Situation und Neubeginn nach 1945*. VS Verlag für Sozialwissenschaften, University of Düsseldorf, adaptation of doctoral thesis, 1981.

Jeffreys, Diarmuid. *Hell's Cartel: IG Farben and the Making of Hitler's War Machine.* London: Bloomsbury, 2008.

Kempf, Beatrix. *Suffragette for Peace.* London: Oswald Wolff, 1972.

Kershaw, Alister. *Murder in France.* London: Constable, 1955.

Kimball, Warren. *Forged in War.* London: HarperCollins, 1997.

Klemperer, Victor. *I Will Bear Witness 1933–1941, A Diary of the Nazi Years.* New York: Modern Library, 1998.

———. *To the Bitter End: The Diaries of Victor Klemperer 1942–45.* Phoenix: Kindle edition, 2013.

Koldehoff, Stefan, Ralf Oehmke, and Raimund Stecker. *Der Fall Gurlitt—Ein Gespräch.* Berlin, Nicolai Verlag, 2014.

Kroeger, Brooke. *Nellie Bly: Daredevil. Reporter. Feminist.* New York: Kindle edition, 2013.

Layton, Geoff. *Germany: The Third Reich, 1933–45.* London: Hodder & Stoughton, 1992.

Lee, Stephen J. *The European Dictatorships 1918–1945.* Oxford: Routledge, 1987.

Levi, Erik. *Mozart and the Nazis.* London: Yale University Press, 2010.

Machtan, Lothar. *The Hidden Hitler.* Oxford: Perseus Books, 2001.

Marlow, Joyce, ed. *The Virago Book of Women and the Great War.* London: Virago Press, 1998.

McNichols-Webb, Mary Alice. *Art as Propaganda—A Comparison of the Imagery and Roles of Woman as Depicted in German Expressionist, Italian Futurist and National Socialist Art.* PhD thesis, University of Michigan, 1988.

Michel, Henri. *Paris Allemand.* Paris: Albin Michel, 1981.

Passant, E. J. *A Short History of Germany 1815–1945.* Cambridge: Cambridge University Press, 1966.

Ramsay, David. *'Blinker' Hall Spymaster: The Man Who Brought America into World War I.* Stroud: The History Press, 2009.

Schmeitzner, Mike and Francesca Weil. *Sachsen 1933–1945.* Berlin: Ch.Links Verlag, 2013.

Shirer, William L. *The Rise and Fall of the Third Reich.* London: Mandarin Paperback, 1991.

Sinclair, Anne. *21 rue la Boétie.* Paris: Éditions Grasset & Fasquelle, 2012.

Sluga, Hans. *Heidegger's Crisis: Philosophy and Politics in Nazi Germany.* Cambridge, MA: Harvard University Press, 1993.

Speer, Albert. *Inside the Third Reich.* London: Phoenix, 1995.

Taylor, Frederick. *Dresden: Tuesday, February 13, 1945.* New York: HarperCollins, 2004.

Thacker, Toby. *Joseph Goebbels: Life and Death.* London: Palgrave Macmillan, 2009.

Tuchman, Barbara W. *The Proud Tower: A Portrait of the World Before the War, 1890–1914.* New York: Bantam Books, 1967.

———. *The Guns of August.* New York: Ballantine Books, 1994.

Waite, Robert G. L. *Vanguard of Nazism: The Free Corps Movement in Postwar Germany 1918–1923.* New York: W. W. Norton & Company, 1969.

Weiss, Stuart L. *The President's Man: Leo Crowley and Franklin Roosevelt in Peace and War.* Carbondale, IL: Southern Illinois University Press, 1996.

Williams, Charles. *Pétain,* London: Little Brown, 2005.

Winter, J. M. *The Great War and the British People.* Cambridge, MA: Harvard University Press, 1986.

Winter, J. M. and Jean-Louis Robert, eds. *Capital Cities at War.* Cambridge: Cambridge University Press, 1997.

Zweig, Stefan. *The World of Yesterday.* Plunkett Lake Press e-book, Kindle edition, 2012.

———. *The Society of the Crossed Keys.* London: Pushkin Press, 2013.

INDEX

Abwehr (Military Intelligence), 210, 212, 321

Acheson, Edward C.
  initiatives in conflict with, 275, 284, 285–97
  as unraveling Nazi methods, 280–81, 284

Adolf Hitler im Felde 1914–1918 (Mend), 55

ALIU (Art Looting Investigation Unit)
  Hildebrand deposed by McKay, 266–75
  initiatives conflicting with, 275, 280, 285–87
  Nazi art theft probe by, 258, 267, 271, 279, 353*n*45

Alldeutscher Verband (Pan-German League), 321
  mainstream nature of, 34–35, 36, 37, 38, 39

Alleinschulde (sole war guilt), 80, 321

Almas-Dietrich, Maria, as Hitler dealer, 222–23, 243, 249, 284

Amann, Max, 55, 118

Anschluss (Austrian annexation), 181, 183, 190

anti-Semitism
  of German nationalism, 18, 31, 34, 38
  of Hitler, 30, 32, 111, 129–30, 140, 145, 156
  of Nazi Party, 61–63, 220, 232

Arbeitsgemeinschaften (labor associations), 321

Arbeitskommandos (Units of Black Reichswehr or Black Defense League), 103, 321

arms industry, 40, 41, 173, 179, 197

art and artifacts, 3, 4, 100. *See also* internationally exploitable art
  death camps link to, 159, 192, 221, 258, 275, 276, 298, 354*n*20
  as easier to recover, 310–11
  freedom in exchange for, 203
  Germany rearming funded by, 173, 247
  as gone missing, 201, 228–30, 235, 239–43, 248–51
  as hidden away, 202
  Jeu de Paume Museum with, 218–19
  making opportunistic market in, 143, 209–10

art and artifacts (*continued*)
  market upheaval in, 139, 142
  as Nazi target, 170, 175, 238–39, 247–48,
    251, 280
  as not harmless, 137–38, 175
  as political tool, 39, 62, 140
  racism united with, 137–38
  Swiss simplify trade in, 188–90, 251
art dealer, 20
  Aryanization of Jewish, 168, 170, 209, 221
  Commission Dealers as, 174, 184–89,
    193, 201, 204–5
  Nazis bad for, 168–70
art history, 56, 64–65, 82, 90, 138–39
Art Looting Investigation Unit. *See* ALIU
Art Loss Register, 4, 311
art museum, 59, 112, 322. *See also*
    Kunstverein
  degenerate exhibits in, 171, 172
  directors purged from, 175–76
  divesting modern art, 172
  "health, stable art" exhibit in, 172
Aryan mythology, 110–11
"Aryanization," 168, 170, 209, 221
atonement tax. *See Sühneleistung*
Austria, World War I, 51
  Anschluss of, 181, 183, 190
  Austrian Social Democrats of, 36
  Commission Dealers work in, 203–4
  countries from, xiii
  dissent in, 34
  Dual Alliance of, 36–37
  Great War begins for, 44–46
  Hildebrand base in, 204–5
  Hitler need to save, 32
  Kristallnacht in, 184, 191
  Posse plunders art of, 203
  Triple Alliance of, 36–37

Bacon, Francis, 225
Ballmer, Karl, 295–97

banking privacy, in Switzerland, 1, 2–3,
    198, 280, 284, 303, 326*n*1, 355*n*2
Barlach, Ernst, 10
Barr, Alfred A., 197–200, 337*n*10
Bauch, Bruno, 62–63
Bauer (colonel), 95
Bauhaus, 106, 158
Beckmann, Max, 23, 61
  as Hildebrand reference, 290–91
  The Lion Tamer of, 201, 296
  as Malverbot, 187
  Nazi limit sales of, 170
  OAP seized works of, 10
Beckmann, Peter, 297–98, 300
Behr, Kurt von, 217, 218
Der Belfried, as *Flamenpolitik* (Flemish
    cultural politics), 59
Belgium. *See also Flamenpolitik*
  art plunder of, 218
  German anti-Semitism in, 61, 62
  Monuments Men (German) work in,
    59–63
  Nazi invasion of, 201, 213
  neutrality guaranty for, 36
  as Ruhr occupier, 103
Berenson, Bernard, 138–39
Berlin Königliche National-Galerie, 20
Berlin Secession, 22
Bernhardi, Friedrich von, 36
Bernstein, Carl and Felice, 20
Bismarck, Otto von, 18–19, 35–36
Black Defense League. *See*
    Arbeitskommandos
Der Blaue Reiter (Blue Rider Group,
    Kandinsky's Expressionist art
    movement from Munich), 22–23,
    321
Blomberg, Werner von, 151
Böcklin, Arnold, 20, 22
Böhmer, Bernhard A., 174, 184–89, 201,
    296, 343*n*11
Bolshevism, 14, 170

Bormann, Martin, 222–23, 265, 289–90, 351n1
  as Hildebrand customer, 251, 258, 287–88
Brecht, Bertolt, 107
Bridge Expressionist art movement. *See* Die Brücke
Britain. *See* Great Britain
brownshirts. *See Sturmabteilung*
Die Brücke (the Bridge Expressionist art movement, which originated in Dresden), 22–23, 321
brutality. *See Einzelaktionen*
Buchenwald death camp, 192
Buchholz, Karl, 13, 239, 258
  as Commission Dealer, 174, 180, 184–89
  as Flechtheim assistant, 126, 127
  as Hildebrand partner, 196, 249
  NY gallery of, 10–11, 186, 249
Bülow, Bernhard von, 37
Bunjes, Hermann, 216, 220, 221
Burckhardt, Jakob, 64–65
Bürgermeister (mayor), 31

Carnegie, Andrew, 23, 25–26
Caspari, Anna, 127
Cassirer, Paul, 126
Cavell, Edith, 51–53
Chagall, Marc, 10, 85, 176, 223
  Cornelius III with, 306, 315
  Hildebrand owning, 274, 296–97
Charpentier, Claude, 221–22
Christian Social Party, 37, 38
Christianity, 18–19, 111, 165, 166
Cicero, 306
Circle of Friends of the Economy. *See* Freundeskreis der Wirtschaft
The Cistercian Monasteries in Belgium, 59–60

Clemens, Walter, 290
Combat League for German Culture. *See Kampfbund für deutsche Kultur*
Commission Dealers
  action of, 174, 180, 184–89, 193, 201
  Austrian work of, 203–5
  depot of, 185, 196, 200, 259
  Fluchtgut and *Volksvermögen* for, 187
  Haberstock against, 194–95
  Swiss simplify trade for, 188–90, 251
Commission for Reich Leader Rosenberg. *See* ERR
Commission for the Seizure and Disposal of Degenerate Art. *See* Commission Dealers
communist, 33–34, 75
  fights with, 86, 96, 124
  Germany safe from, 153
  Hitler as, 54
  Luxemburg as, 78, 96
  Papen demise by, 150–51
  Reichstag fire by, 154–55
concentration camps, 159, 221, 258, 276, 354n20
  art theft connected with, 275
  Buchenwald as, 192
  gold from, 298
Cooper, Douglas, 281–84, 285
Cordon Sanitaire, 80, 109, 134
Corinth, Lovis, 22
cultural politics. *See Kulturpolitik*
Currency Control Command Unit. *See* Devisenschutzkommando

Dada art, 105
Darmstäedter, Gertrud, 68
Dawson, Christopher, 133
declaration of imminent war. *See Kriegesgefahr*
Defense League. *See* Wehrverein

Degas, Edgar, 10

Demeures Historiques (Historic Buildings Commission), 216, 321

Denmark, 74, 201

Der Spiegel, 304–5, 306, 307, 309, 314, 351*n*13

Deutsche Kulturwacht (German Culture Watch), 170–71

Deutschen Allgemeinen Zeitung, 62

Deutscher Kunstbericht (German Art Report), 172

Deutschvölkischer Schutz und Trutzbund (German Nationalist Protection and Defiance Federation, more commonly known as the Organization Consul), 321

Devisenschutzkommando (Currency Control Command Unit), 223, 321

Diels, Rudolf, 154

Dietrich, Otto, 146

Dimitrov, Georgi, 155

diversity, 24, 30, 31

Dix, Otto, 10, 107, 170, 296

Dolchstoss ("stab in the back"), 72, 83

Donandt, Rolf, 43, 49–50

Dorotheum, 203–4, 242

Doyle, Arthur Conan, 280

Drang nach Osten (drive to the East), 37, 321

Dresden, Germany
  firebombing of, 253–54, 255, 256, 351*n*15
  Hildebrand home in, 15, 17, 225–26, 252, 257–61
  Kristallnacht in, 254
  New Secession of, 23

Dresdner Anzeiger, 112

Drexler, Anton, 87

Das Dritte Reich (Moeller) (The Third Reich), 124

drive to the East. *See Drang nach Osten*

Dual Alliance, 36–37

Dulles, Allen, 275, 287

Durand-Ruel, Paul, 20

Düsseldorf school, 20

Eastern European immigrants. *See Ostwanderer*

Eckart, Dietrich, 88, 95, 96

Edel, Christoph, 316–17, 318

Ehrenburg, Ilya, 105

Ehrhardt, Hermann, 94, 95

Eichmann, Adolf, 6, 299

Einkreisung (encirclement), 36, 321

Einsatzstab Reichleiters Rosenberg (Special Commission for Reich Leader Rosenberg). *See* ERR

Einzelaktionen (allegedly unrelated individual acts of brutality), 165–66, 321

emergency money. *See Notgeld*

Enabling Act, 156

encirclement. *See Einkreisung*

Enemy Property Control. *See Feindvermögen*

Engel, Herbert, 249

Enlightenment. *See Haskalah*

Entartete Kunst Austellung (Degenerate Art Exhibition), 172, 177–79

Entartung (degeneration) (Nordau), 137–38

Ephrussi, Charles, 20, 203, 327*n*15

Epp, Ritter von, 88

ERR (Einsatzstab Reichleiters Rosenberg)
  as art plunderer, 217, 218, 234–35, 237, 258, 289–90
  as battling Kunstschutz, 234
  as focus of ALIU, 258

Erzberger, Matthias, 93

Exodus 34:7, 263

Expressionist art, 10, 107, 143–44, 172

Faison, S. Lane, 275–76, 279

FBI (Federal Bureau of Investigation), 11–12, 249, 326n4, 326n6

Fechter, Paul, 62, 66, 84

Feder, Gottfried, 87–88

Federal Association of Artists. *See* Reichsverband Bildender Künstler

Federal Bureau of Investigation. *See* FBI

Feindvermögen (Enemy Property Control), 289, 322

Feininger, Lyonel, 106, 170

Felixmüller, Conrad, 43, 84

Ferdinand, Franz (archduke), 44

Feuerbach, Anselm, 20

Fichte Society, 39, 65

Fischer Auction, 195–201

Fischer, Theodor
  German art auction of, 196–201
  in Hildebrand black-market, 249
  sale of Picasso by Böhmer, 201
  as top German art dealer in Switzerland, 195

Flamenpolitik (Flemish cultural politics), 126, 321
  Der Belfried in, 59
  Belgium annexation goal of, 61
  Monuments Men (German) work in, 59–63
  Osthaus reply in, 61
  propaganda of, 59

Flechtheim, Alfred, 60–62, 337n8
  as art dealer, 126–27, 142
  The Lion Tamer of, 310–12
  Nazi targeting, 157–58, 159–60, 169, 310
  Schulte "Aryanized" gallery of, 168
  as wandering in fear, 168–69

Flechtheim heirs, 311–12

Flottenverein (Naval League), 38, 41, 321

Fluchtgut (objects of value sold at a huge discount to flee Nazi persecution), 187, 203, 322

Focus magazine, 310, 315–16, 318

fondation (foundation), 284

France, 135
  aggression of, 34
  Alsace-Lorraine of, 36, 37, 80
  arms spending of, 41
  art of, 219–20, 239, 242, 244, 290, 292
  Cordon Sanitaire by, 80, 109, 134
  ERR as top plunderer in, 234–35, 289
  "Exodus" from, 213–15
  fortified lines of, 36
  Franco-Russian alliance of, 36–37
  German war plans for, 41
  in Great War, 44–46, 48
  Hildebrand struggle in, 207–8
  Monuments Men (German) doubted by, 58
  Nazi invasion of, 201, 213–15

Franco-Russian Alliance, 36–37

Franke, Günther, 126, 300

Frankfurter, Alfred, 197–98, 344n20

Frankfurter Allgemeine Zeitung, 118

Frässle, Nikolaus, 306

freedom. *See Freiheit*

Freemasonry, 31, 111, 169, 223

Frehner, Mathias, 318

Freiheit (freedom), 321

Freikorps (violent paramilitary groups formed from the former Imperial German Army), 77–78, 321, 334n2, 334n20
  Göring control of, 110, 112–14
  as path to SA, 82–83
  Riga campaign of, 91–92

fremdvölkisch (of an alien people), 62–63, 322

Freud, Sigmund, 302

Freundeskreis der Wirtschaft (Circle of Friends of the Economy), 146, 322

Frick, Wilhelm, 158

Friedlander, Max J., 187

Friedmann, David, 191, 272, 318

Fritz Gurlitt Gallery
  Gurlitt, Wolfgang, owner of, 18, 22, 84
  Impressionist exhibit at, 20
  Kirchbach bailout of, 146
Der Führer. See Hitler, Adolf, Third Reich of
Führerbau (Hitler museum in Munich), 319
  as art storage for Linz, 177, 194, 238, 239
Führermuseum, 12

Gaceta del Arte (the Art Gazette), 156
Garnowski, Klaus, (aka David Toren),
  191–93, 255, 319
Gauleiter (regional Nazi Party leader),
  123, 183, 193, 257, 322
Gebt mir vier Jahre Zeit (Give me four
  years' time, Hitler's warning to the
  modern art community), 178–79, 322
Gemäldegalerie (art museum/picture
  gallery), 322
Generallandschaftsdirektor (of a
  governmental region administrative
  director), 94
Gericht (Judgment), 55
German Battle League, 110
German culture
  art in degeneration of, 137–38
  Fichte Society for, 39, 65
  rallying shield of, 39
German Empire, 326n1, 330n23, 330n25.
  See also Weimar Republic
  Alsace-Lorraine of, 36, 37, 80
  annexing Belgium goal, 61
  arms spending of, 41
  Bismarck maker of, 18–19, 35
  Dual Alliance of, 36–37
  Great War of, 44–46, 48, 72–76
  Ottoman Empire ally of, 50
  Triple Alliance of, 36–37
  Wilhelm II of, xiii, 14, 74, 76
German Expressionism, 4–5
German first strike, 36

German Imperial Navy. See Kriegsmarine
German nationalism, 18, 31, 34, 38
German Romantic painters, 20
German Workers' Party, 87–88, 95
Germany. See also Weimar Republic
  art pays for rearming, 173, 180–81, 183,
    184, 187–88
  conquest of France by, 213–15
  Cordon Sanitaire of, 80, 109, 134
  defeats of, 3, 231
  as hated by Soviets, 258–59
  Hindenburg, P., of, 134, 137, 151, 155,
    156
  Hitler chancellor of, 151
"Give me four years' time" (Hitler). See
  Gebt mir vier Jahre Zeit
Goebbels, Joseph, 170
  as Hildebrand customer, 124, 258
  "The Idea and Sacrifice" of, 123
  Kümmel working for, 217
  as RBK, RMVP, and RKK head, 155,
    167
  Reichstag of, 108–9, 144, 146–49, 155
  safety for treasure of, 246
Goepel, Erhard, 104, 237, 289–90, 300,
  355n13
Goethe, Johann Wolfgang von, 54, 174,
  202, 231
Goldschmidt, Jakob, 115
Goltz, Field Marshal, 36
Göring, Hermann, 96, 195
  art pays for rearming, 173, 180–81, 183,
    184, 187–88
  art volume of, 219–20
  as Hildebrand customer, 258
  as Nazi, 109–10, 147, 238
  putsch of November 9 by, 112–14
  Reichstag of, 149, 154
  safety for treasure of, 246
Gotthelf, Maya, 290
Gottlieb (The Master), 142
Goya portrait, 12

Great Britain, 4, 135, 311
    arms spending of, 41
    as for Belgium neutrality, 36
    bombing Hildebrand home, 225
    countries in, xiii
    Dutch and Belgian art sale illegal in, 247
    Edward VII of, 14, 26
    Entente Cordiale of, 36
    fight from France of, 213–14
    in Great War, 44–46, 48–49, 73
    London Declaration in, 288
Great War, 27, 67
    assassination spark for, 44
    Hitler in, 52–53, 54–55
    as setting stage for WWII, 6, 70
    start of, 44–46, 48–49, 66, 72
Gropius, Walter, 106
Grosz, George, 105, 107
Gurlitt, Annarella, 20, 21, 161
Gurlitt, Cornelia ("Eitl") (sister)
    affairs of, 43–44, 47, 66, 84
    Donandt friend of, 43, 49–50
    as fine art student, 15
    as Great War nurse, 50–51
    Paris life of, 42–44, 47
    suicide of, 84–85
Gurlitt, Cornelius (father), 118–22
    Art Since 1800 by, 109
    The Cistercian Monasteries in Belgium,
        59–60
    Der Belfried of, 59
    brothers of, 15, 19, 20
    death of, 181–82
    as Expressionism collector, 4–5
    as first-degree Mischling, 161, 174
    liked Hitler, 156
    as husband of Marie, 15
    as Monument Man, 58
    Pan-Germanism embraced by, 34, 36, 38
    as son of Louis, 18
    as Technical University historian, 16
    Weltanschauung enabling, 5

Gurlitt, Cornelius III (son), 4, 261
    with Chagall, 306, 315
    confiscated collection of, 315–16
    estate donated by, 318, 319
    Hildebrand as hero to, 302–3
    legal issues resolved, 317
    The Lion Tamer sold by, 201, 310, 311–12
    liquidating art, 299, 301, 303, 306–7
    mysteries of, 304–5, 306–7, 309–10, 314
    as recluse art hoarder, 152
    tax evasion investigation of, 314
    Two Riders on the Beach of, 193, 252, 255
    as unaware of illegality, 309–10
Gurlitt, Else Lewald (grandmother), 18, 19,
        327n9
Gurlitt, Friedrich ("Fritz") (uncle). See also
        Fritz Gurlitt Gallery
    death of, 21
    as father of Gurlitt, Wolfgang, 18
    as favorite of Tschudi, 20
    as friend of Bernsteins, 20
    Gurlitt, A., wife of, 20
    insanity of, 17, 18, 20
    Waldecker assistant to, 20
Gurlitt, Heinrich Louis Theodor ("Louis")
        (grandfather), 2–4, 17, 18, 171
Gurlitt, Helene Hanke (wife), 168, 170,
        259, 260, 261, 300
    death of, 306
    as Hildebrand's wife, 105–8, 152, 209
    Kirchbach helping, 305–6
    liquidating art, 301, 303–6
Gurlitt, Hildebrand ("Putz"), as early life,
        33, 34, 96–97, 333n3
    adaptive morality of, 70, 138–39, 144,
        182, 209
    American trip of, 118–22
    as art advisor to Kirchbach, 100, 130–32,
        138, 142–44, 146, 151, 162, 193, 292–93
    art broker success of, 126–32, 139,
        142–44, 151–52, 170, 172
    art history focus of, 56, 82, 90, 125

Gurlitt, Hildebrand (*continued*)
  as Expressionist collector, 4–5, 22, 106,
    107
  Flechtheim targeting of, 62
  Great war experience of, 49–51, 52, 56,
    66
  as Hamburg Kunstverein, 145, 162
  Jewish heritage of, 18, 90, 160, 168, 174
  Kirchbach protecting, 179
  Kurt Kirchbach collection, 132, 138
  mental instability of, 63–64, 65–67
  in Monuments Men (German), 57–62,
    63
  museum director support for, 141
  Mutschmann as obstacle for, 128–29,
    130, 140–41
  siblings of, 15, 42–44, 47, 85
  Weltanschauung enabling, 5
  as Zwickau museum head, 122, 128–29,
    140–41
Gurlitt, Hildebrand ("Putz"), as Hitler's
    art thief, 351*n*12
  Abwehr work of, 210, 212
  art caches of, 256
  Aryanized Kunstkabinett of, 209
  Austrian base of, 204–5
  black market of, 249
  bombed home and gallery of, 225
  Bormann customer of, 251, 258, 287–88
  as Buchholz partner, 196, 249
  as Commission Dealer, 174, 184–89,
    194, 201, 204–5
  Cornelius III son of, 261
  deceitful practices of, 207, 212, 231,
    239–42, 243, 245, 248–49
  as dehumanized, 209–10, 232
  Dresden home of, 225–26, 253–54, 255
  Gurlitt, Wolfgang, as owing, 143, 204–5
  Haberstock struggle with, 207–8
  Helene wife of, 105–8, 152, 209, 259,
    260, 261
  Hermsen as "front" for, 211–13

Hertmann outraged by, 209–11
  Hitler customer of, 2, 4, 14, 251, 258
  Kirchbach protection of, 193
  as Kollwitz dealer, 12, 86, 249
  modern art Kunstkabinett of, 208,
    209–10, 309
  Monuments Men (Allied) avoiding,
    245
  New York business of, 12, 249
  Posse and RMVP work of, 201, 203, 212
  as *Raffke* king, 234
  refuge for, 255, 257–61
  Renaissance art broker cover for, 162,
    170
  as RKK member, 170
  Speer with, 209, 233, 251, 258
  success of, 156–57, 168–72, 184, 201,
    209–10, 225
  syncing alibi with Voss, 259–60
  theft of lives by, 5–6, 193, 201, 210, 261
  Two Riders on the Beach of, 210
  as unfettered, 12, 248–49, 251
  Valentin NY channel of, 12, 249
  Viau Paris auction acts of, 226–30,
    242–43, 274–75
  Voss facilitator for, 230, 251, 291
Gurlitt, Hildebrand ("Putz"), as
    imprisoned, 353*n*45
  art of, 267, 271, 272, 274, 296–97
  as deposed by McKay of ALIU, 266–75
  under house arrest, 266–75, 276–77, 279
  Kirchbach helping, 293
  Kunstkabinett of, 208, 209–10, 309
  Kunstverein job for, 293
  as not linked to Buchholz or Valentin, 13
  references for, 288–89, 290–92
  release of, 294
  sequestered art release for, 290
Gurlitt, Hildebrand ("Putz"), postwar
    years of
  art as hostage, 294, 295
  Beckmann exhibition of, 297–98

collection released to, 296–97
enemies and victims of, 300
Swiss vault of, 2, 320
US exhibit of, 299–300
as unpunished, 5–6
as unsinkable, 297
Gurlitt, Johannes ("Hans"), 15, 20
Gurlitt, Louis. *See* Gurlitt, Heinrich Louis Theodor ("Louis")
Gurlitt, Ludwig, 15
Gurlitt, Manfred, 146, 161, 296
Gurlitt, Marie Gerlach (mother), 15, 91, 326n2
    at Die Brücke exhibition, 22
    as daughter of *Justizrat,* 16
    as Expressionist collector, 4–5, 106, 107
Gurlitt, Otto, 15
Gurlitt, Renate ("Benita") (daughter), 182, 255, 261
    cancer of, 313
    Hildebrand as hero to, 302–3
    liquidating art, 301, 303
    wife of Frässle, 306
Gurlitt, Wilhelm, 15
Gurlitt, Wilibald ("Ebb") (brother), 15, 68, 296
    as Army officer, 49, 52
    as music student, 15
    as second-degree *Mischling,* 174
Gurlitt, Wolfgang, 190, 246, 296, 354n3, 355n4
    as Fritz Gurlitt Gallery owner, 22, 84
    as indebted to Hildebrand, 143, 204–5
    as son of Fritz, 18
    as Zuckmeyer friend, 128
Gurlitt Task Force, 316, 318

Haberstock, Karl, 127, 193, 243, 261
    against Commission Dealers, 194–95
    rivalry with Hildebrand, 207–8
    as deceitful, 207
    working with Posse, 194, 203
Hague Convention, 14, 23, 25, 26, 27
Hanfstaengl, Ernst ("Putzi"), 96
Harrer, Karl, 87
Haskalah (Enlightenment), 18
Heckel, Erich, 22, 170
Heidegger, Martin, 253
Hermsen, Theo, 296, 346n32, 350n8
    as Hildebrand "front," 211–13
    Hildebrand Paris office by, 212–13, 241–42
    Viau auction acts of, 226–27, 242–43
Hertmann, Ingeborg, 209–11, 226, 293–94
Hess, Rudolf, 150
    German Workers' Party member, 87
    List Regiment member, 55
    "peace mission" of, 222
    putsch of November 9 by, 112–14
Hessen, Philipp von, 147
Hetsch, Rolf, 170, 187
Hildebrand. *See* Gurlitt, Hildebrand
Himmler, Heinrich, 150, 287
    Freundeskreis der Wirtschaft of, 146–47
    safety for treasure of, 246, 248
Hindenburg, Oskar von, 150–51
Hindenburg, Paul von, 134, 137, 151, 155, 156
Historic Buildings Commission. *See Demeures Historiques*
History of Art (Pevsner), 104
Hitler, Adolf, early life of, 23, 27, 33, 71, 82
    art as political tool for, 39
    failing Academy of Fine Arts, 31
    Flanders wounding of, 73
    "Give me four years' time," 178–79
    in Great War, 48, 52–53, 54–55
    on ills of Marxism and Jews, 32
    Kubizek friend of, 28
    learning craft in, 31, 37–38

Hitler, Adolf, early life of (*continued*)
  Linz redesigns of, 28–29
  as loathing diversity, 24, 30, 31
  modern art hated by, 10, 31, 133, 159,
    175
  Monuments Men (German) noted
    by, 58
  Pan-Germanism embraced by, 34,
    36, 38
  save Austria goal of, 32
  in Workers' Party, 87–88
Hitler, Adolf, rising to power, 101, 103, 153
  art bolshevism of, 129–30, 167–68
  Aryan mythology of, 110–11
  as called the Führer, 123
  chancellorship of, 150–51
  as communist, 54
  "German Days" of, 110
  magnates target of, 146
  Mein Kampf of, 118
  as Nazi leader, 95–96, 144–45, 173
  putsch of November 9 by, 112–14,
    117–18
  stock market crash opportunity for,
    136–37
Hitler, Adolf, Third Reich of, 237
  as Almas-Dietrich customer, 222–23,
    243, 249, 284
  as anti-Semitic, 30, 32, 111, 129–30, 140,
    145, 156
  death of, 265
  Enabling Act empowering, 156
  Europe dominated by, 201
  as Hildebrand customer, 2, 4, 14, 251,
    258
  many enemies of, 159
  total control of, 173
Hitler, Klara (mother), 32
Hitler, Paula (half sister), 27
Hofer, Walter Andreas, 195
Hoffmann, Adolf, 86
Hoffmann, Heinrich, 222

Holland
  Great Britain forbids sale of art from,
    247
  looting art of, 210, 219, 289–90
  Nazi invasion of, 201, 213
  Wilhelm II flees to, 74, 76
Holz, Richard, 140, 141
Hönig, Eugen, 157–58, 170, 171, 174
Hudson Shipping Company, 10–11

"The Idea and Sacrifice," 123
Institut d'Études des Questions Juives
    (IEQJ) (Institute for the Study of the
    Jewish Question), 71, 215, 322
Institute of Arts, 143–44
internationally exploitable art
  British warn about, 247
  death camps link to, 159, 192, 221, 258,
    275, 276, 298, 354n20
  Entartete Kunst as, 187–88
  rearmament funds sourced from, 179,
    180, 247
  Vienna art seized for, 183, 203–5
  Washington Principles for recovering,
    310–11, 317
  works seized for, 180–81, 184, 187
Iron Cross, 55, 161, 176
"isms," new age of, 33–34, 39
Italia Irredenta (territory of native
    Italian-speaking people in Austria-
    Hungary), 34, 322

Jaujard, Jacques, 216, 218, 220, 238, 241,
    242
Jeu de Paume, 218–19
Jewish Reform movement, 19
Jews, 90. *See also* anti-Semitism
  Aryanizing art dealers from, 168, 170,
    209, 221
  atonement tax on, 184

as Christian converts, 18–19
economic exclusion of, 184
German citizenship for, 19
as German misfortune, 18, 32, 62–63, 111, 130, 140
Iron Cross no help for, 161, 176
Jewish Bolshevism, 170
"Jewish question" about, 71, 215, 322
Kristallnacht against, 184, 191, 254
of mixed race *(Mischling)*, 160, 161, 168, 174
Nazi boycotting, 165–66
Palestine home for, 71
Registration of Property of, 184
as Toleration Regulation exempt, 169–70, 174
as unsafe in Vichy France, 234
Volksvermögen illegal for, 187
Johnson, Samuel, 125
Judenzählung (census of Jews in military), 62
Jugendstil (young style), 30
Jugendstil Viennese Secessionist, 30, 31
justice councillor. *See Justizrat*
Justizrat (justice councillor), 16

Kaesbach, Walter, 157–58
Kahnweiler, Daniel-Henry, 127
Kahr, Gustav von, 110, 112–14
Kampfbund für deutsche Kultur (KDK) (Combat League for German Culture), 140, 170, 322
Kandinsky, Wassily, 22–23, 90, 106
Kantstudien (Bauch), 62–63
Kapp, Wolfgang, 94–95
KDK. *See* Kampfbund für deutsche Kultur
Keppler Kreis (Keppler Circle), 147, 150
Kirchbach, Kurt, 95, 339n16
helping Gurlitts, 146, 179, 193, 293, 305–6

Hildebrand advisor to, 100, 130–32, 138, 142–44, 146, 151, 162, 193, 292–93
Nazi contributions of, 146–47, 162
as saving modern art, 162
Kirchner, Enrst Ludwig, 22–23
Kirdorf, Emil, 146
Klee, Paul, 10, 22–23, 106
Klimt, Gustav, 30, 31, 106
Knauer, Gustav, 213, 229, 271
Kokoscha, Oskar, 10
Kolig, Anton, 43–44, 47, 329n3
Kollwitz, Käthe, 10, 12, 86, 107, 249
Kommission zur Verwertung beschlagnahmter Werke entarteter Kunst (Commission for the Seizure and Disposal of Degenerate Art). *See also* Commission Dealers
Hetsch of, 184
Kriegesgefahr (a declaration of imminent danger of war), 45, 322
Kriegsmarine (German Imperial Navy), 41, 322
Kristallnacht (Night of Broken Glass), 184, 191, 254, 319
Krupp, Gustav, 98, 100, 132
Krupp conglomerate, 116, 305
Kubizek, August, 28
Kulturpolitik (cultural politics), 158–59
Kümmel, Otto, 216–17
Kunstkabinett (art collection), 208, 209–10, 309
Kunstmuseum, Bern, 318, 319
Kunstschutz. See Monuments Men (German)
Kunstschutz im Krieg (Art Preservation During War) (Clemen), 57
Kunstverein (art association, funded by the regions), 125, 322
Hildebrand director of, 145, 162, 210, 232, 269, 291, 293, 294, 296
RKK membership needed, 168

labor associations. See
    Arbeitsgemeinschaften
Lammers, Hans-Heinrich, 193, 300–1, 303
    as Nuremberg witness, 298
    as overruled by Himmler, 287
    payments by, 212, 277
Land (province), 16
Lang, Fritz, 107
Lange, Hans W., 170, 210, 227, 228, 272
Léda au cygne, 235
Lederhosen (leather shorts), 83, 322
Lehmann-Haupt, Hellmut, 165
Lenin, Vladimir, 67
Lewald, Fanny, 15, 19, 327n9
Ley, Robert, 158
Liebermann, Max
    Berlin Secession of, 22
    death of, 210
    of Düsseldorf school, 20
    Martha wife of, 210
    Nazi limit sales of, 170
    as represented by Fritz, 22
    Two Riders on the Beach of, 191–93, 210,
        296
    Wagon on the Dunes of, 296
Liebknecht, Karl, 107
Linz, Austria, 28–29, 194–95, 328n13.
        See also Sonderauftrag Linz
The Lion Tamer
    Cornelius III selling, 201, 310–12
    in Hildebrand post-war collection, 274,
        296, 299–300
    on tour in U. S., 299–300
List Regiment, 54–55
"living space" fears, 36
Lohse, Bruno, 12, 272, 235–39, 241
London Declaration, 288
looted art, 2–5
    death camps link to, 159, 192, 221, 258,
        275, 276, 298, 354n20
    from Paris, 215–17, 223–30, 242–44
    recovery of easier, 310–11

from Vienna, 183, 203–5
Washington Principles for recovering,
    310–11, 317
lord mayor. See Oberbürgermeister
Lossow (major general), 112–14
Lost Art Database, 300
Ludendorff, Erich, 94–95, 112–14
Lueger, Karl, 31, 37, 38
Lüttwitz (general), 95
Luxemburg, Rosa, 78, 96

Machtergreifung (seizure of power by the
    Nazis), 166, 322
"Mahdi's Tomb," 30
Mahler, Gustav, 30
Malverbot (prohibition to paint), 175, 187,
    322
Mann, Heinrich, 128
Marc, Franz, 22–23, 170
Marcks, Gerhard, 10
Markham, James E., 11
Marlborough Gallery, 127
Marlowe, Christopher, 7
Marxism, 32, 33
McKay, Dwight, as Hildebrand deposer,
    266–78
Mein Kampf (Hitler), 71, 101, 118, 123, 129,
    136, 145
Meissner, Otto, 150–51
Memorandum and Lists of Art Looted by
    the French in the Rhineland in 1794
    (Kümmel), 217
Mend, Hans, 54–55
Mendelssohn, Moses, 19
Mend-Protokoll (Mend), 55
Metropolitan Museum of Art, in NY, 10,
    120
Military Intelligence. See Abwehr
Mischling (of mixed race), 160, 168, 174,
    322
of mixed race. See Mischling

modern art, 162. *See also Entartete Kunst Austellung*
  as forbidden to Germans, 209
  Hildebrand room of, 208, 209–10, 309
  Hitler hatred of, 10, 31, 133, 159, 175
  Nazi seizure of, 181, 187
  Paris burning of, 238–39
Möller, Ferdinand, 142, 296
  as Commission Dealer, 174, 184–89
  Ribbentrop protecting, 158–59
Montlong, Ritter Oskar von, 51
Monuments Men (German), 203, 331n11
  opportunistic crimes of, 58
  people in, 57–60, 61, 62–63, 220, 226
  WWII reactivating, 216, 220, 234
Monuments Men/Women (Allied), 245, 247
  initiatives conflicting with, 275, 276, 280, 285–87
  people in, 270, 289–90, 291–92
  as unraveling Nazi methods, 280–85
  unskilled as investigators, 277
moral decline, 38, 105, 209
Morgenthau's Boys, 275, 280, 285–87
Mort-Homme Ridge (Dead Man's), 55
Mühlmann, Kajetan
  as focus of ALIU, 258
  in Holland, 213, 289–90
  in Poland, 205–6
  as Vienna *Gauleiter,* 183, 193
Munich, Germany, 86
Museum of Modern Art, in NY, 143, 185, 197
Mutschmann, Martin
  as *Gauleiter,* 123, 257
  as obstacle for Hildebrand, 128–29, 130, 140–41
Myth of the Twentieth Century (Rosenberg), 140

National Defense Force. *See Reichswehr*
National Socialist German Workers' Party. *See NSDAP*
Nationale Vereinigung, 95
Naval/Navy League. *See Flottenverein*
Nazi Party. *See also* NSDAP
  Allied trials, hangings and sentencing of, 286–87, 288, 298, 354n20
  Americas as art market of, 204, 249, 251, 293
  anti-Semitism of, 62–63, 220, 232
  art focus of, 140, 157, 170, 175, 181, 187, 247–48, 251, 286–87
  Bauch philosopher of, 62–63
  as boycotting Jews, 165–66
  death camps of, 159, 192, 221, 258, 275, 276, 298, 354n20
  election results for, 108–9, 146–49, 155
  Enabling Act empowering, 156
  enemies of, 130
  Expressionism antithesis of, 10, 107
  Flechtheim targeted by, 126, 157–58, 159–60, 168, 169, 221, 310, 311, 312
  foreign influence purge by, 144
  Freemason targeting of, 31, 111, 169, 223
  Goebbels in Zwickau for, 123–24
  Göring member of, 109–10
  Hitler head of, 95–96, 144–45, 173
  invasions by, 191–94, 201, 213–14
  London Declaration against, 288
  putsch of November 9 by, 112–14
  Reichstag control of, 148
  rise of, 4, 97, 109
  struggle over cultural politics in, 158–59
  Swiss art refuge of, 188, 195, 251, 280
  Zwickau center for, 123
Nazi Party leader, regional. *See* Gauleiter
Nazis seizure of power. *See Machtergreifung*
Nehru, Jawaharlal, 24
Neue Künstler-Vereinigung München (New Artists' Association of Munich), 322

Neumann, J. B., 120–21, 126–27, 169

Die Neunte Elfte. See putsch of November 9

Neumann-Nierendorf Gallery, 120–21, 126–27, 169

New Art Circle (NY), 120–21

New Objectivity art, 105

New Secession, 23

Nierendorf, Karl, 120–21, 126–27

Nietzsche, 64–65

Night of the Long Knives, 150

Nolde, Emil, 10, 23, 106, 170, 175

Nordau, Max, 137–38

Notgeld (emergency money), 116, 322

Novembergruppe, 106

NSDAP (German abbreviation for the Nazi Party, National Socialist German Workers' Party), 322. See also Nazi Party

Nuremberg Laws, 160, 187

Nuremberg Trials, 266, 275, 286–87, 288, 298

OAP. See Office of Alien Property, US

Oberbürgermeister (lord mayor), 140–41, 322

objects of value. See Fluchtgut

Oertel, Robert, 242

of an alien people. See fremdvölkisch

Office of Alien Property, US (OAP), 10, 11, 249

Office of Strategic Services. See OSS

OMGUS (Office of the Military Government of the United States), 286, 287, 322

"On the Concept of the Nation" (Bauch), 62–63

Operation Gericht, 55

Organization Consul. See Deutschvölkischer Schutz und Trutzbund

OSS, 275, 280, 285–87. See also ALIU

Osthaus, Karl Ernst, 61

Ostwanderer (Eastern European immigrants), 90, 322

Ottoman Empire, 50

Pabst, Waldemar, 77, 95

Pan-German League. See Alldeutscher Verband

Pan-German nationalism, 16, 34–39

Papen, Franz von, 148–49, 150–51

paramilitary groups. See Freikorps

Paris

    art collections seized in, 215–17, 238–39

    art scene, 43

    art trade booming in, 225, 227

    auctions resume in, 221, 227

    liberation of, 245

    Nazi treat art differently in, 223–30

    Viau auction in, 226–27, 242–44

Pechstein, Max, 23

Penfield, Frederic C., 51

Pétain, Henri, 213–15, 220

Pevsner, Nikolaus, 104, 112

Picasso, Pablo, 223

picture gallery/art museum. See Gemäldegalerie

Pinder, Wilhelm, 104, 112

Plaut, James S., 270, 276, 279

Plutarch, 212

Poincaré, Raymond, 98–100

Poland, 108, 177, 191–94, 201, 205–6

Pölnitz, Gerhard von, 260, 261

Pommer, Erich, 107

Popov, Blagoi, 155

Port of New York Authority, 11

Portrait du père de l'artiste, 235

Posse, Hans, 112

    Austrian art plundering, 203

    death of, 226, 230

    as director Sonderauftrag Linz, 194–95, 201, 289–90

profiteers. *See Raffkes*
prohibition to paint. *See Malverbot*
Project Safehaven, 275, 280, 285–87
propaganda. *See also* RMVP
  art as, 62
  effectiveness of, 157
  Flamenpolitik as, 59
  Monuments Men (German) for, 62
Propagandaministerium. *See* RMVP
Prussians, 36, 38, 39
putsch of November 9, 112–14, 117–18

of racial mixture. *See Mischling*
racism in art, 137–38
Rae, Edwin, 290
Raffkes (profiteers), 99, 105, 117, 234, 322
Rave, Paul Ortwin, 178
RBK (Reichskammer der Bildenden
  Künste), 157–58, 167, 322
rearmament through art, 173, 179, 180–81,
  183, 184, 187–88
Reemtsma, Philipp, 98, 100, 132
regional art association. *See* Kunstverein
regional Nazi Party leader. *See* Gauleiter
Reich Chamber for the Visual Arts. *See* RBK
Reich Ministry for Public Enlightenment
  and Propaganda. *See* RMVP
Reichskammer der Bildenden Künste
  (RBK) (Reich Chamber for the Visual
  Arts). *See* RBK
Reichskulturkammer (Reich Chamber of
  Culture). *See* RKK
Reichsministerium für Volksaufklärung
  und Propaganda (Reich Ministry for
  Public Enlightenment and
  Propaganda). *See* RMVP
Reichstag
  burning of, 154–55
  elections for, 108–9, 144, 146–49, 155
  Nazi control of, 148
  Potsdam reopening of, 155

Reichsverband Bildender Künstler
  (Federal Association of Artists), 141
Reichswehr (National Defense Force), 92,
  94, 322, 335n6
Reimer, Gottfried, 195, 231, 239–42
Remarque, Erich Maria, 42
Rentenmark (anti-inflation currency),
  116–17
Ribbentrop, Joachim von, 151, 158–59, 246
Ring, Grete, 61, 126, 169
RKK *(Reichskulturkammer),* xiv, 168, 170
RMVP (Reichsministerium für
  Volksaufklärung und Propaganda),
  155, 158, 167, 170, 201, 203, 212, 214
Rochlitz, Gustav, 249
Röhm, Ernst, 88, 112–14, 148, 150, 153
Roosevelt, Franklin, 286
Roosevelt, Teddy, 14, 25, 35
Rosenberg, Alfred, 140, 217
Rosenberg, Paul
  collection of, 272, 281, 283, 318
  as Flechtheim associate, 168
Rosterg, August, 146
Rothschild family, 71, 183, 202, 203, 215, 234
Rousseau, Theodore Jr., 276, 279
Ruhr Red Army (Rote Soldatenbund), 95
Ruhr region, 41, 98, 103, 108, 146
Ruins by the Sea (Guardi), 12
Russia. *See also* Soviet Union (USSR)
  aggression of, 34, 135
  arms spending of, 41
  Bolshevism in, 14, 67
  as cause of German woes, 111
  Constantinople quest of, 37
  Czar Nicolas II of, 14, 26, 40–41
  failed revolution of, 35
  Franco-Russian alliance of, 36–37
  in Great War, 44–46, 67
  Japan peace with, 35
  "the curse of God" on, 35
  Wilhelm II hostile to, 35
Rust, Bernhard, 158

SA. *See* Sturmabteilung
Sachlichkeit (fresh objectivity), 4–5
Sachs, Paul, 247
Schacht, Hjalmar, 75, 147
   as currency commissar, 115–17, 134–37
   as Hitler Economic Minister, 173, 179–80
Schardt, Alois, 158
Schiele, Egon, 30
Schiller, Friedrich, 153, 183
Schleicher, Kurt von, 148–51
Schlemmer, Oskar, 170
Schlieffen, Alfred von, 41
Schloss Collection theft, 235–36, 237
Schloss Niederschönhausen, 185, 196, 200, 259
Schmidt, Justus, 246
Schmidt-Rottluff, Karl, 22
Schnitzler, Georg von, 146
Scholz, Robert, 175, 177, 235, 238–39
Schönerer, Georg von, 37–38
Schopenhauer, Arthur, 115
Schulte, Alfred E., 168
Schweizerische Verrechnungsstelle (SVSt). *See* SVSt trust
Searle, Jonathan, 275–78
Second World War. *See* WWII
Seeckt, Hans von, 94, 103
Seisser, Hans Ritter von, 112–14
Shakespeare, William, 163, 246, 295
socialism, 33
Sonderauftrag (Special Commission), 322
Sonderauftrag Linz (Special Project for Linz)
   art market domination of, 174, 194–95, 201, 203–5, 212, 245
   as focus of ALIU, 258, 271, 279, 353*n*45
   Führerbau storing art for, 177, 194, 238, 239
   Haberstock named Posse for, 194
   as Hildebrand customer, 12, 212, 251
   safety for treasures of, 246–47, 248, 251
   war crimes of, 289–90

South America, 251
Soviet Union (USSR, Union of Soviet Socialist Republics), 72
   Germans loathed by, 231, 258–59
   London Declaration with, 288
   Nazi invasion of, 201
   Stalin of, 14, 135
   Weimar treaty with, 98
Special Commission. *See* Sonderauftrag
Special Project for Linz. *See* Sonderauftrag Linz
Speer, Albert, 351*n*13
   with Hildebrand, 209, 233, 251, 258
   as Nazi party member, 144–45, 167–68
"stab in the back." *See* Dolchstoss
Stinnes, Hugo, 95, 98
Stoetzel, Markus, 311–13
storm troopers. *See* Sturmabteilung
Strasser, Gregor, 146, 148, 150–51
Strasser, Otto, 148
Sturmabteilung (SA, storm troopers, brownshirts), 82–83, 110, 323
Sühneleistung (atonement tax), 184
SVSt trust, 188–89, 204
swastika, 94
Switzerland
   as art trade center, 188, 195, 204, 266
   banking privacy in, 1, 2–3, 198, 280, 284, 303, 326*n*1, 355*n*2
   fondation hides identity in, 284
   Gurlitt vault in, 1, 2, 4, 5, 320
   as Nazi art refuge, 251, 280
   SVSt trust eased art trade in, 188–90

Tanev, Vasil, 155
Thoma, Hans, 22
Thoreau, Henry David, 14
Thyssen, August, 98
Thyssen, Fritz, 132, 135–36, 146
Thyssen conglomerate, 116
Tirpitz (admiral), 41

Tittmann, Fritz, 123
Toleration Regulations, 169–70, 174
Torgler, Ernst, 154
Trading with the Enemy Act, 10–11
Treaty of Versailles, 6, 72, 80–81, 83, 108, 177, 179
Triple Alliance, 36–37
Truman, Harry, 275, 286–87, 352n35
Tschudi, Hugo von, 20, 39, 327n16
Two Riders on the Beach, 252, 255, 296, 318
    Friedmann tragedy of, 191–93
    Liebermann tragedy of, 210

United Kingdom (UK). See Great Britain
United States
    FBI of, 11, 12
    Great War entry of, 66, 72
    Hildebrand suspected by, 288–89, 294, 295, 296–97
    interest conflicts in, 275, 280, 285–87
    McKinley, 35
    not linking art theft and genocide, 286–87
    Office of Alien Property, 11
    OMGUS, 286, 287, 322
    targeting Nazi genocide and slave labor, 286–87
    WWII entry of, 231
Urbach, Mel, 311
Utikal, Gerhard, 217–18

Valentin, Curt, 13, 142, 221, 310
    Buchholz NY by, 10–11, 12, 168, 185, 186, 204, 208, 249
    as enemy alien, 11
    as first-degree Mischling, 168
    at Fischer Auction, 197–201
    as Flechtheim associate, 142, 159
    Nazi authorization papers of, 200

Valland, Rose, 216, 245, 349n19, 349n20
    as French Monuments Woman, 291–92
    inventorying stolen French art, 218–19, 235
van den Bruck, Moeller, 124
van der Lubbe, Marinus, 154
Versailles. See Treaty of Versailles
Viau Paris auction, 226–27, 242–44
    mystery of, 228–30, 274–75
Vichy France, 215, 221, 233, 234, 236
Vienna
    art collections seized in, 183, 203–5
    as diverse metropolis, 24
    Hitler learning despotic craft in, 31, 37–38
    as loathed by Hitler, 24, 30, 31
    Lueger as mayor, 31, 38
    "Mahdi's Tomb" in, 30
    Mühlmann rape of, 183, 193
Vlug, Jean, 289–90
Voegler, Albert, 146
Volk; völkisch (people; of the people (folk) or folkloric), 323
Völkischer Beobachter, 123, 170
Volksvermögen (folk wealth), 187
Vömel, Alex, 127, 187, 296
    as Flechtheim manager, 159, 169, 293, 310, 354n2
Voss, Hermann, 62, 276, 291, 305
    as Allies set free, 296
    as Hildebrand facilitator, 230, 251, 291
    refuge intent of, 255
    as replacing Posse at Linz, 230, 271, 272–73, 348n16
    syncing alibi with Hildebrand, 259–60, 266

Waetzold, Wilhelm, 157–58
Waldecker, Willi
    as adulterer with Gurlitt, A., 21, 161
    as assistant to Fritz, 20

Wandervögel (the wandering birds), 83
war guilt, sole. *See Alleinschulde*
Washington Principles, 310–11, 317
Weber, Walter, 12
Wehrverein (Defense League), 38, 323
Weill, Kurt, 106
Weimar Republic, xiii
  as degenerate to Hitler, 129
  elections in, 108–9, 144, 146–49,
    155
  Enabling Act end of, 156
  Expressionist antidote for, 107
  Hitler likes plight of, 110
  moral decline in, 105
  as "November criminals," 88
  Raffkes in, 99, 105, 117
  Reichswehr beyond control of, 92, 94
  Soviet treaty of, 98
  upheaval in, 75–81, 86–87, 91–92, 93,
    97–100, 105, 108–9, 134–37, 148,
    149
Weltanschauung (worldview, but has come
    to mean the Nazi worldview), 5, 106,
    108, 137–38, 232
Wendland, Hans, 249
Westerdahl, Eduardo, 156
Wiene, Robert, 107
Wigman, Mary, 105

Wilhelm II (kaiser), 33
  as anti-French and Russian aggression,
    34, 35
  Bismarck sacked by, 35–36
  empire envy of, 14, 35, 36
  exile of, 74, 76
  expansion plans of, 34, 37, 41
  of German Empire, xiii, 14
  Tschudi exiled by, 39
Wilson, Woodrow, 46–47, 52
Wolff-Metternich, Franz, 234
world view. *See Weltanschauung*
World War I. *See* Great War
World War II (WWII)
  art hidden away in, 202
  German control of Europe, 201
  Hitler death end of, 265
  Nazi invasions in, 191–94, 201, 213–14
  Polish invasion start of, 191–94

Yad Vashem Holocaust museum, 4
young style. *See Jugendstil*

Zuckmeyer, Carl, 127–28
Zurich, Switzerland, 1, 2, 4, 5, 320
Zwickau, 122, 123, 128–29, 140–41